CADOGAN GU

Other titles in the Cadogan Guides series:

AMSTERDAM
AUSTRALIA
BALI
BERLIN
THE CARIBBEAN
ECUADOR,
   THE GALÁPAGOS
   & COLOMBIA
GREEK ISLANDS
INDIA
IRELAND
ITALIAN ISLANDS
ITALY
MEXICO
MOROCCO
NEW YORK
NORTHEAST ITALY
PORTUGAL
PRAGUE
ROME
SCOTLAND

SOUTH ITALY
SOUTHERN SPAIN: GIBRALTAR &
   ANDALUCÍA
SPAIN
THAILAND
TUNISIA
TURKEY
TUSCANY, UMBRIA & THE MARCHES
VENICE

Forthcoming:

CENTRAL AMERICA
CYPRUS
GERMANY
ISRAEL
JAPAN
MADRID & BARCELONA
MOSCOW & LENINGRAD
PARIS
SOUTH OF FRANCE: PROVENCE, CÔTE
   D'AZUR & LANGUEDOC- ROUSSILLON

ABOUT THE AUTHORS

Travel writers Dana Facaros and Michael Pauls and their two children have left their semi-cat Piggy in Umbria, and have taken Michael's musical saw and Dana's indescribable boar mating call and the computer to France. The Facaros/Pauls *Cadogan France* series is launched in early 1992 with their guide to The South of France: Provence, Côte d'Azur and Languedoc-Roussillon.

Dear Readers,
      Please, please help us to keep this book up to date. We would be delighted to receive any additional information or suggestions. Please write to us or fill in the form on the last page of this book. Writers of the best letters will be acknowledged in future editions, and will receive a free copy of the Cadogan Guide of their choice.

The Publisher

CADOGAN GUIDES

NORTHWEST ITALY

DANA FACAROS and MICHAEL PAULS

CADOGAN BOOKS
London, United Kingdom

THE GLOBE PEQUOT PRESS
Chester, Connecticut

Cadogan Books Ltd
Mercury House, 195 Knightsbridge, London SW7 IRE

The Globe Pequot Press
138 West Main Street, Chester, Connecticut 06412, USA

Cover design by Keith Pointing
Cover illustration by Povl Webb
Maps drawn by Thames Cartographic Services Ltd

Series Editor: Rachel Fielding

First published 1990
Updated and revised 1992

A Catalogue record for this book is available from the British Library

ISBN 0–947754–38–5

Library of Congress Cataloging-in-Publication Data
Facaros, Dana
Northwest Italy / Dana Facaros and Michael Pauls: illustrations by Pauline Pears.—2nd ed.
p.   cm.—(Cadogan guides)
'A Voyager book.'
Includes bibliographical references and index.
ISBN 1–56440–031–X
1. Italy, Northern—Description and travel—Guide-books.
I. Pauls, Michael.   II. Title.   III. Series.
DG601.F33   1992   91–36768
914.5'104929—dc20   CIP

Photoset in Ehrhardt on a Linotron 202
Printed and bound in Great Britain by
Redwood Press Limited, Melksham, Wiltshire

CONTENTS

Part V: Lombardy and the Lakes *Pages 163–286*

Architectural, Artistic and Historical Terms *Pages 287–89*

Chronology *Pages 290–94*

Language *Pages 295–307*

Further Reading *Pages 308–309*

General Index *Pages 310–18*

Index of Artists and Craftsmen *Pages 318–20*

LIST OF MAPS

ACKNOWLEDGEMENTS

We would particularly like to thank Michael Davidson and Brian Walsh, whose unfailing good humour helped us through the darkest corners of Italy, and who have contributed substantially to this book by updating all the practical information. We would like to thank the Italian National Tourist Office, and all the local and municipal tourist boards who so kindly answered all our questions that had answers and loaded us down with enough information to write several more volumes about Italy. Special thanks go to Paola Greco, in London, and the Terni tourist office for their kind help to Michael and Brian. Also we would like to extend our warmest gratitude to Mario, Fiorella, Alessandra and Sara who never minded having a couple of extra children in their happy home; to Anna and Tito Illuminati, who guided us through the intricacies of life in Rosciano and always let us use their phone; to Bruce Johnston, for his innumerable suggestions and his Deux Chevaux; to longtime residents Clare Pedrick, Anne, and Santimo, for their invaluable insights into the Italian miosma; to Carolyn Steiner and Chris Malumphy, who crossed the Atlantic to cheer us up; and especially to Rachel Fielding, who like Hercules in the Augean stables, makes us printable.

The updaters, Michael and Brian, would especially like to thank Fechin Maher for his help and hospitality in Milan; also, Pat and George.

The publishers would like to raise a special cheer for the unsung heroes of the typesetting department at Redwood Press—Bob, Jim, Rod, Hans and Andy.

To Michael and Brian

INTRODUCTION

A couple of years ago, when we could hardly tell Lecco from Lecce or Lucca, our publisher said: write a guide to Italy. It nearly killed us. Even worse (after all, travel writers are a dime a dozen these days) the result, all 850 pages of it, nearly killed a few readers who tried to carry it around on their holidays.

The fault wasn't entirely ours, but Italy's. More than a big Boot, it is like the world's Christmas stocking, overflowing with gifts the world probably doesn't even deserve, from art (two, perhaps three notable works per inhabitant) to natural beauty, great cities, atmospheric hilltowns, gardens, superb wine and food, and all the rest. Even when weighed against Italy's most obvious disadvantages—it can be ruinously expensive, polluted, closed for restoration, the post is disgraceful, and the government is as Byzantine as a cow's stomach—it is still a delightful place to be, full stop.

Dividing Italy into more portable portions seems the obvious answer; this book covers the northwest regions of Piedmont and the Aosta Valley, Liguria, and Lombardy, an area perhaps lacking the immediate identity of a Veneto or Tuscany. Much of it was long a major bone of contention between France, Spain, and the Holy Roman Emperor, not to mention a home-grown cast of bully boys and bosses; and yet it was the Piedmontese and a couple of hot-bloods from Liguria named Garibaldi and Mazzini that led the fight to unite Italy 130 years ago. Perhaps because of this, or because this is where warm Mediterranean *italianità* meets the cool pragmatic north head on that this corner is the most dynamic and diverse in Italy, the most open to innovation. Some of the first art in Europe was found in the Palaeolithic caves along the Riviera.

Of course parts of Piedmont, Lombardy, and Liguria have been on the familiar holiday map for years, especially the Italian Lakes, the Riviera, and the Alpine playgrounds of Mont Blanc and the Matterhorn. But the whole of the northwest is one of the best kind of presents that one can find in one's Christmas stocking—a book that seems to have new stories every time you open it.

Guide to the Guide

The northwest is the most prosperous area of the republic, the most industrial, but the most dramatically scenic, the land of Alps and lakes. Beginning in the northwestern corner, there are the regions of **Piedmont and the Aosta Valley**, the birthplace of modern Italy. At the 'mountains' feet', as the name implies, green and hilly Piedmont encompasses both excellent ski slopes in its western Alpine arc and table-flat rice paddies to the east. Car-manufacturing Turin is the region's capital, a fine Baroque city undeservedly left out of most itineraries. Much of southern Piedmont, around Asti and Alba, is given over to the cultivation of Italy's greatest wines. The proximity of France has had an excellent influence on the Piedmontese kitchen; white truffles are the speciality in the autumn.

The northwest's most spectacular scenery, however, is contained in the small, autonomous, bilingual (French and Italian) region of the Valle d'Aosta. The Aosta valleys are one of Italy's great holiday playgrounds, with Courmayeur, Breuil-Cervinia, and other stunning Alpine resorts on the southern slopes of giants like Mont Blanc (Monte Bianco) and the Matterhorn (Cervino), near legendary Alpine passes like the Great St Bernard, and the lovely Gran Paradiso National Park. Aosta, the fine little capital, is nicknamed the 'Rome of the Alps' for its extensive ruins.

Over the lush Maritime Alps lies one of Italy's smallest regions, **Liguria**, a beautiful arc of coast that is better known as the Italian Riviera. In the centre lies Genoa, Italy's biggest seaport, while on either side are famous, overripe resorts like San Remo, Alassio, Rapallo, Portofino, Portovenere, and the magnificent Cinque Terre villages. The climate is especially mild: palms, olives, flowers, and vines grow in profusion. The seafood and the dishes with *pesto* sauce are superb.

East of Piedmont lies the relatively large region of **Lombardy**. First is a section on Italy's second city, **Milan**, adopted home of Leonardo da Vinci, centre of fashion and finance, a city that throbs with life and excitement, a vision of the new Italy; it has the most art, the biggest cathedral, La Scala opera, and a viper for its symbol. The next section covers **Southern Lombardy**, including the three jewels of Lombardy's Po plain: Pavia, capital of Italy in the Dark Ages, violin-making Cremona, and the Renaissance art city of Mantua.

Northern Lombardy, and a piece of eastern Piedmont and western Veneto, all form part of **The Italian Lakes**, that lovely and legendary district beloved of poets since Roman times. Westernmost is little Lake Orta and the famous Simplon Tunnel near Domodossola; nearby Lake Maggiore has its Borromean isles and the world-famous resort of Stresa. Then comes zig-zagging Lake Lugano, which Italy shares with Switzerland, and lovely Lake Como, with resorts deeply engraved on the English traveller's Romantic memory—Bellagio, Cernobbio, Tremezzo, and Menaggio. From the northeast bank of Como extends the Valtellina, surrounded by Lombardy's rugged Alps, stretching all the way to Bormio and the western confines of Stelvio National Park. To the south of the Valtellina are more lakes—Iseo and tiny Idro—and two excellent art cities, Bergamo and Brescia. Easternmost is Lake Garda, nicknamed the 'Riviera of the Dolomites' for its dramatic surroundings. Sirmione, Gardone, Limone, and Riva are its most famous resorts; famous wines grow between its eastern shore and Verona.

The Best of the Northwest

The following highly subjective list, may help you decide where to spend your time.

Art Museums: No lack here. Works by the greatest artists of Italy and beyond are in the Brera, Ambrosiana, and the Galleria Poldi Pezzoli, all in **Milan**; the Galleria Sabauda and the Museo d'Arte Antica in **Turin**; the Galleria Carrara in **Bergamo**; Villa Favorita in **Lugano**; the Pinacoteca Tosio-Martinengo and Museum of Christian Antiquities in **Brescia**; and the National Gallery of Liguria and Palazzo Bianco in **Genoa**.

Casinos: There are only four casinos in all Italy, and three are in the northwest: **San Remo** on the Riviera, **St-Vincent** in Aosta, and **Campione d'Italia** on Lake Lugano.

Castles: fairytale castles of Issogne and Fénis, in **Aosta**; medieval Doria castle at **Dolceacqua**; Castello Sforza at **Soncino**; Rocca di Angera, on **Lake Maggiore**, with frescoes; Malpaga, the Renaissance castle of the great *condottiere* Bartolomeo Colleoni, with more interesting frescoes (near **Bergamo**); romantically beautiful Scaliger castles at **Sirmione** and **Malcésine**, on Lake Garda.

Caves: Grotte di Bossea, with an underground river, and stalactites, near Frabosa **Soprana**. Grotta della Basura and Grotta di S. Lucia, beautiful caves inhabited in the Middle Palaeolithic era, at **Toirano**; Grotta Azzura, at the islet of Palmaria, near **Portovenere**; stalactite Grotta delle Meraviglie, at **Zogno** (Val Brembana).

Cemeteries: For flamboyance in this life as well as the next, **Genoa's** Staglieno Cemetery and **Milan's** Cimiterio Monumentale take the cake.

Cities: **Turin, Milan, Genoa**—all big but a lot of fun; **Cremona, Bergamo** and **Mantua** earn a special mention for their design and architecture; also **Pavia** and **Asti**.

Gardens: The climate of the Riviera and the larger lakes lends towards a remarkable diversity of plant life, ranging from alpine varieties to cacti. Some of Italy's most fabulous gardens are here: Isola Bella, Isola Madre, and the Villa Taranto, on **Lake Maggiore**; Hruska Botanical Gardens and Sigurta Gardens by **Lake Garda**; Villa Carlotta and the villas at Bellagio, on **Lake Como**; Le Torbiere, waterlily garden by **Iseo**; **Mantua's** Valletta Belfiore is famous for its lotus blossoms in July and August. On the Rivieria: Hanbury Gardens near **Ventimiglia**, Villa Luxoro at **Nervi**, and Villa Durazzo-Pallavicini at **Pegli**. In Piedmont, there are the La Burcina hill gardens at Pollone, near **Biella**.

Landscapes: The famous **lakes**, of course, would exhaust any honest writer's stock of adjectives. To these we can add nearly every alpine valley in **Aosta**, and the mighty glacier-bound peaks of **Stelvio National Park**. The northwest has more than its share of enchanting scenery: the upper **Bergamask valleys**, running into the Orobie Alps; **Le Langhe** and **Roero**—Piedmont wine country around Alba and Asti; romantic **Val Vigezzo**, between Domodossola and the Swiss border; the renowned **Riviera di Levante**, especially between Portofino and the Portovenere, on the Gulf of Poets; and utterly quiet and serene nooks like the **Val Taranto** and valleys south of **Morbegno** in the Valtellina, and little valleys around **Cuneo** in Piedmont.

Man-made Wonders: *Cristo degli Abissi*, a bronze, underwater statue at **San Fruttuoso**, east of Genoa; covered bridge at **Pavia**; Colossus of St Charles Borromeo, at **Arona** on Lake Maggiore; **S. Caterina del Sasso**, also on Lake Maggiore, a convent built on a cliff face; Il Vittoriale and tomb of Gabriele D'Annunzio, at **Gardone Riviera**; Sacro Monte of **Varallo**, home of the best 16th-century 3-D art in Italy; the Pertuis de la Traversette, above **Piano del Re** and the source of the Po, a 75 m tunnel dug for mule trains in 1480 by the Marquis of Saluzzo.

Natural Wonders: the coastline around Liguria's **Cinque Terre** and the changing sea colours at **Punta Chiappa**, by Camogli; the fairy pyramids of **Zone**, by Lake Iseo; **Val Malenco**, north of Sondrio, the richest mineralogical valley in the Alps; the **crotti** cellars at **Chiavenna**; *ciciu* chimney rocks at **Villar San Costanzo** in the Valle Maira.

Opera: La Scala, of course, with its opera museum, while **Turin** and **Genoa** both maintain respectable companies. Other things operatic include the Donizetti Museum and Theatre in **Bergamo** and the spurious but appropriately sombre 'Casa di Rigoletto' in **Mantua**.

Parks: Gran Paradiso National Park, home of the ibex and chamois (between Valle d'Aosta and Piedmont); **Palanfre Natural Reserve**, and **Parco Naturale dell'Argentera**, in the Maritime Alps; **Monte di Portofino** has been preserved as a natural seaside park; glacier-frosted **Stelvio National Park**, at Bormio.

Small Towns and Villages: Charming villages are scattered all over the northwest. In Liguria there are the famous **Cinque Terre** and **Portovenere**, Riviera 'hilltowns', but also lesser known medieval villages like **Taggia, Dolceacqua, Albenga, Sarzana**, and **Chiavari**, a fishing village. Among the prettiest villages in Piedmont and Aosta is Romanesque **Avigliana**, in the Valle di Susa; **Moncalvo** and **La Morra** in the wine district; and **Arnaz** and **Avise**, little Alpine villages in the Valle d'Aosta. In Lombardy and the lakes region, look for **Orto S. Giulio**, on Lake Orta and Renaissance **Castiglione Olona**, near Varese; **Sabbioneta**, an ideal Renaissance town near Mantua; **Bellagio** on Lake Como; **Cornello del Tasso** and **Clusone**, north of Bergamo; **Sirmione and Malcésine**, on Lake Garda.

Spas: Boario Terme, in the Val Camonica and **San Pellegrino**, in the Val Brembana are the most famous; also hot sulphur springs in Piedmont at **Acqui Terme, Terme di Valdieri** near Borgo San Dalmazzo and **Lurisia** near Fabrosa Soprana.

Unexpected Museums: A truly pharaonic Egyptian museum and an automobile museum, at **Turin**; the Luigi Marzoli Museum of Arms, in **Brescia**; History of Spaghetti museum, at **Pontedassio**, near Imperia; a Chinese museum (Museo d'Arte Orientale) and two museums of pre-Colombian art (the Museo Americanistico Lunardi and the Museo Etnografico), all in **Genoa**; Museo Stradivariano, in **Cremona**, devoted to violins and violin-making; Simplon Tunnel exhibits at the Museo Civico, in **Domodossola**; Umbrella Museum, at **Gignese**, by Lake Maggiore; Walser Folklore museums at Pedemonte (north of Varallo) and Staffa (in the Valle Anzasca); **Marengo** battle museum; hat museum (Museo del Cappello Borsalino) at Alessandria; Waldensean Museum at **Torre Péllice**; Martini Museum, of the history of wine and vermouth, at **Pessione** (east of Turin).

Waterfalls: the grand 300-m **Cascata della Frua**, north of Domodossola (weekends only); **Acqua Fraggia**, near Borgonuovo (Valchiavenna), topped by a 17th-century Pompeii; lovely **Cascata del Varone**, near Riva del Garda; spurting **Piss di Pesio** near the Certosa di Pesio in southern Piedmont (spring only).

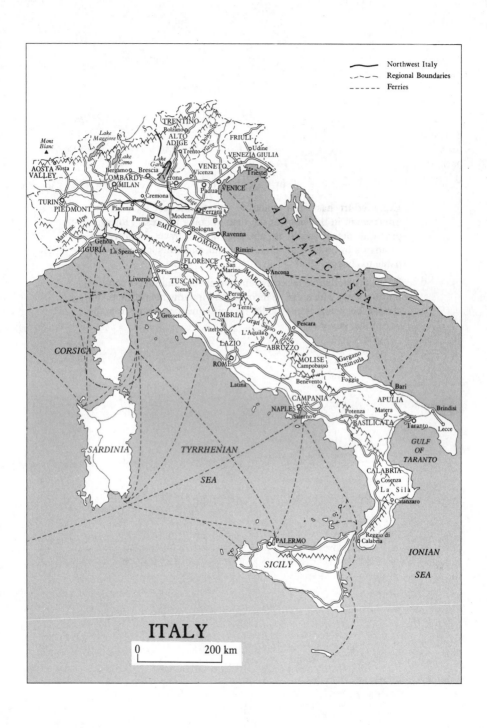

Northwest Italy
Regional Boundaries
Ferries

Mont
Blanc

Lake
Maggiore

TRENTINO-
Bolzano
ALTO
ADIGE

FRIULI-
Udine
VENEZIA GIULIA

Lake
Como

Lake
Garda

Trento

Dolomites

AOSTA
VALLEY

Aosta

Bergamo

Brescia

VENETO
Vicenza

Verona

Trieste

LOMBARDY

MILAN

Padua

VENICE

TURIN

Cremona

Po

Adige

PIEDMONT

Piacenza

Ferrara

A D R I A T I C

Parma

Modena

Maritime Alps

EMILIA

Bologna

Ravenna

Genoa

LIGURIA

La Spezia

ROMAGNA

Rimini

FLORENCE

e

San
Marino

Ancona

S E A

Livorno

Pisa

MARCHES

TUSCANY

Siena

Tiber

Perugia

Grosseto

UMBRIA

Terni

Gran Sasso d'Italia

Pescara

CORSICA

Viterbo

L'Aquila

LAZIO

ABRUZZO

ROME

MOLISE

Gargano
Peninsula

Campobasso

Latina

Benevento

Foggia

Bari

CAMPANIA

APULIA

NAPLES

Potenza

Matera

Brindisi

Salerno

BASILICATA

Taranto

Lecce

SARDINIA

TYRRHENIAN

SEA

GULF
OF
TARANTO

CALABRIA

Cosenza

La Sila

Catanzaro

PALERMO

Reggio di
Calabria

IONIAN

SICILY

SEA

ITALY

0   200 km

PLEASE NOTE

Every effort has been made to ensure the accuracy of the information in this book at the time of going to press. However, practical details such as opening hours, travel information, standards in hotels and restaurants and, in particular, prices are liable to change.

We will be delighted to receive any corrections and suggestions for improvement which can be incorporated into the next edition, but cannot accept any responsibility for consequences arising from the use of this guide.

Part I

GENERAL INFORMATION

Owls of the Valle d'Aosta

Before You Go

A little preparation can make your trip many times more enjoyable (or at least less frustrating). Although this book was designed to be especially useful to frequent visitors who are ready to poke into some of Italy's nooks and crannies, it will also get you around the major sights if this is your first trip; study the Guide to the Guide (pp. ix–x) and the list of Festivals (pp. 22–6) to get some idea of where you want to be and when. There are several tour operators who specialize in holidays to Italy. In the UK Citalia (tel (081) 686 5533 or (071) 408 4120) probably has the widest range. (See also pp. 30–1 for Self-Catering Holidays and pp. 21–2 for Special Interest Holidays.) You can pick up free hints, brochures, maps, and information from the Italian National Tourist Offices, at the following addresses; an especially useful booklet to request is the annually updated *Travellers' Handbook*, which has loads of good information and current prices.

UK: 1 Princes Street, London W1R 8AY (tel (071) 408 1254; telex 22402).
Eire: 47 Merrion Square, Dublin 2, Eire (tel (001) 766397; telex 31682).
USA:
630 Fifth Avenue, Suite 1565, New York, NY 10111 (tel (212) 245 4961; telex 236024).
500 N. Michigan Avenue, Chicago, Ill. 60611 (tel (312) 644 0990/1; telex 0255160).
360 Post Street, Suite 801, San Francisco, California 94108 (tel (415) 392 6206; telex 67623).

Canada: Store 56, Plaza 3, Place Ville Marie, Montreal, Quebec (tel (514) 866 7667; telex 525607).

Once you know where you want to go, you can pick up more detailed information by writing directly to any of the city or provincial tourist offices. These are usually very helpful in sending out lists of flats, villas, or farmhouses to hire, or at least lists of agents who handle the properties.

Getting to Northwest Italy

By Air

Regular Scheduled Flights

Finding a flight to Italy is no problem—Alitalia, British Airways, British Caledonian, Aer Lingus, Pan Am, TWA, Air Canada, and a score of other airlines will whisk you directly to Milan, Turin, or Genoa. For the latest and most accurate information on air fare bargains call Air Travel (071) 636 5000, a free service which provides a list of current deals, allowing you to select the one that suits your pocket and timetable.

There are advantages in paying out for a normal fare, mainly that it does not impose any restrictions on when you go or return; most are valid for a year. To sweeten the deal, Alitalia in particular often has promotional perks like rental cars (Jetdrive), or discounts on domestic flights within Italy, on hotels, or on tours. Ask your travel agent. Children under the age of two travel for 10 per cent of the adult fare on British Airways flights; Alitalia have a nominal charge of £20. Children between 2 and 12 travel for half fare, and bona fide students with proof of age and school attendance between the ages of 12 and 25 receive a 25 per cent discount on British Airways flights, and a 20 per cent discount on Alitalia.

The same carriers listed above have a variety of discounts for those who book in advance or are able to decide their departure and return dates in advance. If you're travelling from Europe, you can save quite a tidy sum by paying for your ticket when you make your reservations (Eurobudget); an extra advantage is that the return date is left open. Travellers from anywhere can save money by downing a little alphabet soup— PEX, APEX, and SUPERPEX, which like Eurobudget require reservations and payment at the same time on return-only flights. PEX (or APEX) fares have fixed arrival and departure dates, and the stay in Italy must include at least one Saturday night; from North America the restrictions are at least a week's stay but not more than 90 days. SUPERPEX, the cheapest normal fares available, have the same requirements as PEX, but must be purchased at least 14 days (or sometimes 21 days in North America) in advance. Disadvantages to PEXing are that there are penalty fees if you change your flight dates. At the time of writing, the lowest SUPERPEX fare between London and Milan in the off-season is £173; from New York around $600.

Other advantages of taking a regular flight over a charter are an increase in reliability in dates and in punctuality, and you're not out of a wad of cash if you miss your flight. Also, if you live in neither London or New York, they will often offer big discounts to get you from your home airport to the international one. If you live in the boondocks, you can dial some '800' numbers to check out prices for yourself: Alitalia's number is 800 223 5730.

From the USA, you almost always have to go through New York, and can fly directly only to Rome and Milan. Fares from Canada are often much higher than they are from the States. Also, it's worthwhile checking on budget fares to London (especially if Virgin Atlantic stays around), Brussels, Paris, Frankfurt, or Amsterdam; these routes are more competitive than the Italian ones, and you may save money by either flying or riding the rails to Italy from there.

Charter Flights

These aren't as much of a bargain to Italy as they are to other Mediterranean destinations, though they're certainly worth looking into—check ads in the travel section of your newspaper (*Sunday Times* and *Time Out* are especially good) and your travel agent. From London, ABC Direct Travel (243 Euston Road, tel (071) 388 7588) has regularly scheduled charters to Milan, Genoa and Turin; from the US, CIEE has regular charters from New York to Rome (tel 800 223 7402). Other charter flights are usually booked by the big holiday companies. To find out about extra seats on these and on commercial flights, visit your local bucket shop (in the USA, call Access (tel 800 333 7280) or Air Hitch for similar services—check listings in the *Sunday New York Times*). Pickings are fairly easy in the off season, and tight in the summer months, but not impossible. You take your chances, but you can save some of your hard-earned dough.

The problem with charters is that they are delayed more often than not, and since the same plane is usually commuting back and forth it can mean arriving at 3 am. Another disadvantage is that you have to accept the given dates, and if you miss your flight (bus and train strikes in Italy do make this a distinct possibility) there's no refund. Most travel agencies, however, offer traveller's insurance that includes at least a partial refund of your charter fare if strikes and illness keep you from the airport.

Students

Besides saving 25 per cent on regular flights, students under 26 have the choice of flying on special discount charters. From the US, CIEE (see above) is a good place to start looking. From Canada, contact Canadian Universities Travel Services, 44 St George St, Toronto, Ontario M55 2E4, tel (416) 979 2406. From London, check out STA Travel, 117 Euston Road, NW1 or 86 Old Brompton Rd, SW7, for telephone enquiries for European destinations ring (071) 937 9921; WST, 6 Wrights Lane W8 (071) 938 4362 or USIT, 52 Grosvenor Gardens, SW1, tel (071) 730 8518.

By Train

This region of Italy is easily accessible by rail from the UK; one night on the train and you are there. At the time of writing, return second-class fares and times of travel from London are to Alassio: £140 (26 hours); Brescia: £140 (24 hours); Como: £140 (22 hours); Desenzano (Lake Garda): £140 (23 hours); Genoa: £138 (23 hours); Milan: £199 (22 hours); San Remo: £135 (22 hours); Stresa (Lake Maggiore): £138 (21 hours); Turin: £127 (19 hours).

These trains require reservations and a couchette, and are a fairly painless way of getting there. Discounts are available for families travelling together, for children—free under age 4 and 40 per cent discount between the ages of 4 and 8. Under 26-ers, students or not, can save up to 40 per cent on second-class seats by purchasing

Eurotrain tickets available in the UK from any student travel office in the UK, many high street travel agents or direct from Eurotrain tel (071) 730 3402. Eurotrain also has a kiosk at Victoria Station which is open from 8 am to 8 pm seven days a week. Eurotrain tickets are also available throughout Europe at student travel offices (CTS in Italy) in main railway stations. Any rail tickets purchased in Britain for Italy are valid for two months and allow any stopovers you care to make on the way.

Rail travel to Italy becomes an even more attractive option if you intend to purchase an Inter-Rail pass (in Europe), or a EurRail pass (from North America). Inter-Rail cards (about £175) are sold by British Rail to people under 26 and offer discounts of over 30 per cent in Britain and 30 or 50 per cent on Channel Ferries, and unlimited passage on the Continent, and are valid for a month. Inter-Rail Senior cards offers similar discounts to people over 60. These passes are a good deal if you plan to do lots and lots of rail travel and can't be bothered to buy tickets, etc. They seem rather less rosy if your travelling is limited to Italy, where domestic rail tickets are one of the few bargains available. Within Italy itself there are several discount tickets available (see below, travelling within Italy), which you can inquire about at CIT Italian State railways offices before you leave home:

UK: Marco Polo House, 3 Lansdowne Road, Croydon CR9 1LL, tel (081) 686 0677 or at any branch of Thomas Cook Ltd.
USA: 666 Fifth Ave, New York NY 10103, tel (212) 223 0230
There's also an 800 number you can call from anywhere: (800) 223 0230
Canada: 2055 Peel St, Suite 102, Montreal, Quebec H3A 1VA, tel (514) 845 9101

By Coach

The least expensive and least comfortable way to get to Italy is by coach. For information, contact National Express and Eurolines who run services to Milan and Turin from Victoria Coach Station, Buckingham Palace Road, London SW1, (tel (071) 730 0202).

By Car

Driving to Italy from London is a rather lengthy and expensive proposition, and if you're only staying for a short period figure your costs against Alitalia's or other airlines' fly-drive scheme. Depending on how you cross the Channel, it is a good two-day trip—about 1600 km from Calais to Rome. Ferry information is available from the Continental Car Ferry Centre, 52 Grosvenor Gardens, London SW1. You can avoid many of the costly motorway tolls by going from Dover to Calais, through France, to Basle, Switzerland, and then through the Gotthard Tunnel over the Alps; in the summer you can save the steep tunnel tolls by taking one of the passes. You can avoid some of the driving by putting your car on the train (although again balance the sizeable expense against the price of hiring a car for the period of your stay): Express Sleeper Cars run to Milan from Paris or Boulogne. Services are drastically cut outside the summer months, however. For more information, contact the CIT offices listed above.

To bring your car into Italy, you need your car registration (log book), valid driving licence, and valid insurance (a Green Card is not necessary, but you'll need one if you go through Switzerland). Make sure everything is in excellent working order or your slightly bald tyre may enrich the coffers of the Swiss or Italian police—it's not uncommon to be stopped for no reason and have your car searched until the police find something to stick a fine on. Also beware that spare parts for non-Italian cars are difficult to come by, almost impossible for pre-1988 Japanese models. If you're coming to live in Italy, remember that cars with foreign plates are supposed to leave the country every six months.

Before leaving, you can save yourself about 10–15 per cent of expensive Italian petrol and motorway tolls by purchasing **Petrol Coupons**, issued to owners of GB-registered vehicles by London's CIT office (see above), at Wasteels Travel, 121 Wilton Rd, London SW1, tel (071) 834 7066, or at your local AA or RAC office (though ring them ahead to make sure they have the coupons in stock) or at the frontier from Italian Auto Club offices. Coupons are sold only in person to the car-owner with his or her passport and car registration, and cannot be paid for in Italian lire—prices are tagged to current exchange rates, and unused coupons may be refunded on your return. Along with the coupons and motorway vouchers, you get a *Carta Carburante* which entitles you to breakdown services provided by the Italian Auto Club (ACI) (offices in Northwest Italy (pp. 12–13). At the time of writing motorway tunnel tolls are:

Mont Blanc Tunnel, from Chamonix (France) to Courmayeur: small car or motorcycle L15 000 single, L19 000 return. Medium-sized car (axle distance 2.31–2.63 m) L23 000 single, L29 000 return. Large cars (axle distance 2.64–3.30) or cars with caravans L31 000 single or L38 000 return.

Fréjus Tunnel, from Modane (France) to Bardonecchia: same as above except for large cars or cars with caravans (trailers) L30 000 single, L39 000 return.

Great St Bernard, from Bourg St Pierre (Switzerland) to Aosta: small car or motor-cycle: L13 500 single, L19 000 return. Medium car L20 000 single, L28 000 return. Large car or car with caravan L27 000 single, L38 000 return.

Traveller's Insurance and Health

You can insure yourself for almost any possible mishap—cancelled flights, stolen or lost baggage, and health. While national health coverage in the UK and Canada takes care of their citizens while travelling, there is no similar scheme in the US. Check your current policies to see if they cover you while abroad, and under what circumstances, and judge whether you need a special traveller's insurance policy. Travel agencies sell them, as well as insurance companies; they are not cheap.

Minor illnesses and problems that crop up in Italy can usually be handled free of charge in a public hospital clinic or *ambulatorio*. If you need minor aid, Italian pharmacists are highly trained and can probably diagnose your problem; look for a *Farmacia* (they all have a list in the window detailing which ones are open during the night and on holidays). Extreme cases should head for the *Pronto Soccorso* (First Aid services). The emergency number from anywhere in Italy is 113.

Few Italian doctors speak even rudimentary English; contact your embassy or consulate for a list of English-speaking doctors.

What to Pack

You simply cannot overdress in Italy; whatever grand strides Italian designers have made on the international fashion merry-go-round, most of their clothes are purchased domestically, prices be damned. Now whether or not you want to try to keep up with the natives is your own affair and your own heavy suitcase—you may do well to compromise and just bring a couple of smart outfits for big nights out. It's not that the Italians are very formal; they simply like to dress up with a gorgeousness that adorns their cities just as much as those old Renaissance churches and palaces. The few places with dress codes are the major churches and basilicas (no shorts or sleeveless shirts), the casinos, and some of the smarter restaurants.

After agonizing over fashion, remember to pack small and light: trans-Atlantic airlines limit baggage by size (two pieces are free, up to 62 inches in height and width; in second-class you're allowed one of 62 inches and another up to 44 inches). Within Europe limits are by weight: 23 kilos (59 lbs) in second-class, 30 kilos (66 lbs) in first. You may well be penalized for anything bigger. If you're travelling mainly by train, you'll especially want to keep bags to a minimum: jamming big suitcases in overhead racks in a crowded compartment isn't much fun for anyone. Never take more than you can carry, but do bring the following: any prescription medicine you need, an extra pair of glasses or contact lenses if you wear them, a pocket knife and corkscrew (for picnics), a flashlight (for dark frescoed churches, caves, and crypts), a travel alarm (for those early trains) and a pocket Italian-English dictionary (for flirting and other emergencies; outside the main tourist centres you may well have trouble finding someone who speaks English). If you're a light sleeper, you may want to invest in ear plugs. Your electric appliances will work in Italy if you adapt and convert them to run on 220 AC with two round prongs on the plug. Of course, what you bring depends on when and where you go . . . .

Climate

As Italian temperature charts go, the northwest has the most thrilling, and in the flesh the weather here is simply much more fun than it is in most places; if you've ever dreamed of doing a slalom in a bikini, or prefer the view of glacier-topped mountains through the fronds of a palm tree, or like your picnics in January by the sea, this is the place to go. In Northwest Italy the Alpine climate meets the Mediterranean head on, and on the whole, the Mediterranean wins. Some belts, like the Maritime Alps that separate Piedmont from Liguria, get rain by the bucket, creating a lush botanical hothouse; Turin's climate, on the other hand, is almost identical to Copenhagen's. The Riviera enjoys such a mild winter that flowers and olives are its cash crops; Mantua and the other cities along the Po are chilly and fog-bound in the winter, and steam baskets in August. The Italian Lakes are large enough to maintain a Mediterranean climate at alpine altitudes, and their shores are decorated with some of Italy's most beautiful and diverse gardens. Europe's largest rice fields, at Vercelli, are only an hour's drive from the rolling vineyards around Asti that produce Italy's noblest wines and its finest truffles.

Each season offers its charms and its chances. **Winter**, unless it's a freak year, is obviously the time for skiing and snow holidays in the Alps, for leisurely 'wintering' on the Riviera, for seeing Milan, Turin, and Genoa, at their cultural liveliest, when you can meet more natives and find the sights blissfully uncrowded (but sometimes closed!). Frequent fogs and mists, especially on the lakes and along the rivers, are the real drawback; sometimes they can last for weeks on end. **Spring**, with its warmer temperatures, blossoming trees, and flowers, is delightful, and outside the Easter holidays rarely crowded, even in June. A few days of intermittent rain is about the worst that can happen. During the **summer** the shores of the lakes and Riviera are very crowded, there are scores of festivals and special events, though the cities are more or less abandoned to the tourists from August to September 15. This is the time to go walking in the mountains, or even take summer ski lessons; it rarely rains, and outside the plains the temperatures are usually remarkably pleasant. **Autumn** is another choice time to go for the magnificent colour, the grape harvests, the relaxed pace, and blue balmy days (though in October and November, the rains can intrude).

Average Temperatures in °C (°F)

	January	*April*	*July*	*October*
Genoa	8.4 (47)	14.5 (58)	24.6 (76)	18.1 (64)
Milan	1.9 (35)	13.2 (55)	24.8 (76)	13.7 (56)
Turin	0.3 (32)	12.0 (53)	23.2 (73)	12.2 (53)
Alps				
Bardonecchia	−1.6 (29)	6.1 (43)	17.7 (63)	8.2 (46)
Great St Bernard	−9.2 (16)	−4.3 (27)	6.9 (44)	−7.9 (18)
Sauze d'Oulx	−1.0 (30)	1.1 (34)	11.5 (52)	−1.3 (30)
Lakes				
Lake Como	6.0 (43)	13.3 (55)	23.7 (74)	9.8 (50)
Lake Maggiore	5.2 (41)	12.9 (54)	23.9 (74)	10.1 (50)
Lake Garda	4.0 (39)	13.2 (55)	24.5 (76)	14.7 (58)
Riviera				
San Remo	9.7 (49)	14.4 (58)	23.4 (73)	17.9 (64)
Alassio	11.9 (53)	15.4 (60)	25.7 (78)	15.8 (61)
Chiavari	9.9 (50)	14.0 (57)	22.9 (72)	12.8 (54)

Average monthly rainfall in millimetres (inches)

	January	*April*	*July*	*October*
Genoa	109 (4)	82 (3)	35 (2)	135 (5)
Milan	62 (3)	82 (3)	47 (2)	75 (3)
Turin	11 (½)	74 (3)	65 (3)	59 (2)
Alps				
Bardonecchia	22 (1)	84 (3)	35 (2)	98 (4)
Great St Bernard	24 (1)	80 (3)	43 (2)	165 (7)
Sauze d'Oulx	22 (1)	61 (3)	06 (0)	310 (12)
Lakes				
Lake Como	74 (3)	47 (2)	12 (½)	20 (1)
Lake Maggiore	90 (4)	61 (3)	20 (1)	22 (1)
Lake Garda	31 (1)	62 (3)	72 (3)	89 (4)
Riviera				
San Remo	67 (3)	56 (2)	14 (½)	88 (4)
Alassio	67 (3)	53 (2)	10 (½)	17 (1)
Chiavari	136 (5)	138 (5)	14 (½)	46 (2)

Passports and Customs Formalities

To get into Italy you need a valid passport or a British Visitor's Card. Nationals of the UK, Ireland, USA, Canada, and Australia do not need visas for stays up to three months. If you mean to stay longer than three months in Italy, get a visa from your Italian consulate or face the prospect of having to get a *Visa di Soggiorno* at the end of three months—possible only if you can prove a source of income and are willing to spend a couple of exasperating days at some provincial Questura office filling out forms.

According to Italian law, you must register with the police within three days of your arrival. If you check into a hotel this is done automatically. If you come to grief in the mesh of rules and forms, you can at least get someone to explain it to you in English by calling the Rome Police Office for visitors, tel (06) 4686, ext. 2858.

Italian Customs are usually benign, though how the frontier police manage to recruit such ugly, mean-looking characters to hold the submachine guns and drug-sniffing dogs from such a good-looking population is a mystery, but they'll let you be if you don't look suspicious and haven't brought along more than 150 cigarettes or 75 cigars, or not more than a litre of hard drink or three bottles of wine, a couple of cameras, a movie camera, 10 rolls of film for each, a tape-recorder, radio, phonograph, one canoe less than 5.5 m, sports equipment for personal use, and one TV (though you'll have to pay for a licence for it at customs). Pets must be accompanied by a bilingual Certificate of Health from your local Veterinary Inspector. You can take the same items listed above home with you without hassle—except of course your British pet. US citizens may return with $400 worth of merchandise—keep your receipts. British subjects are permitted £200 worth of dutiable merchandise.

There are no limits to how much money you bring into Italy, although legally you may not transport more than L400 000 in Italian banknotes, though they rarely check.

On Arrival

Money

It's a good idea to bring some Italian lire with you when you arrive; unforeseen delays and unexpected public holidays may foul up your plans to change at a bank when you arrive. Travellers' cheques or Eurocheques remain the most secure way of financing your holiday in Italy; they are easy to change and insurance against unpleasant surprises. Credit cards (American Express, Diners Club, Mastercard, Access, Eurocard, Barclaycard, Visa) are usually only accepted in hotels, restaurants, and shops (but never at any petrol stations) frequented by foreign tourists—Italians themselves rarely use them—and it is not unknown for establishments to fiddle with the exchange rates and numbers on your bill once you've left. Use them with discretion.

There's been a lot of loose talk about knocking three noughts off the Italian lira, but it never seems to happen; as it is, everybody can be a 'millionaire'. It is also confusing to the visitor unaccustomed to dealing with rows of zeros, and more than once you'll think you're getting a great deal until you realize you've simply miscounted the zeros on the price tag. Some unscrupulous operators may try to take advantage of the confusion when you're changing money, so do be careful. Notes come in denominations of L100 000, L50 000, L10 000, L5000, L2000, and L1000; coins are L500, L200, L100, L50, L20, all the way down to the ridiculous and practically worthless aluminium coinage of L10, L5 and L1. Telephone tokens (*gettoni*) may be used as coins as well and are worth L200.

The easiest way to have money sent to you in Italy is for someone from home to get a bank to telex the amount to an Italian bank, and for you to go and pick it up. Technically—and if you're really lucky—it shouldn't take more than a couple of days to arrive, but make sure the telex includes the number of your passport, ID card, or driver's licence, or the Italians may not give you your money. Save all the receipts of your currency exchanges.

Getting Around

Italy has an excellent network of airports, railways, highways, and byways and you'll find getting around fairly easy—until one union or another takes it into its head to go on strike (to be fair, they rarely do it during the high holiday season). There's plenty of talk about passing a law to regulate strikes, but it won't happen soon, if ever. Instead, learn to recognize the word in Italian: *sciopero* (SHOW-per-o) and be prepared to do as the Romans do when you hear it—quiver with resignation. There's always a day or two's notice, and strikes usually last only 12 or 24 hours—just long enough to throw a spanner in the works if you have to catch a plane. Keep your ears open and watch for notices posted in the stations.

By Train

Italy's national railway, the FS (*Ferrovie dello Stato*) is well run, inexpensive (though prices have recently risen, it is still cheap by British standards) and often a pleasure to ride. There are also several private rail lines around cities and in country districts. We have tried to list them all in this book. Some, you may find, won't accept Inter-Rail or EurRail passes. On the FS, some of the trains are sleek and high-tech, but much of the rolling stock hasn't been changed for fifty years. Possible FS unpleasantnesses you may encounter, besides a strike, are delays, crowding (especially at weekends and in the summer), and crime on overnight trains, where someone rifles your bags while you sleep. The crowding, at least, becomes much less of a problem if you reserve a seat in advance at the *Prenotazione* counter. The fee is small and can save you hours standing in some train corridor. On the upper echelon trains, reservations are mandatory. Do check when you purchase your ticket in advance that the date is correct; unlike in some countries, tickets are only valid the day they're purchased unless you specify otherwise. If you're coming back the same way in three days or less, save money with a *ritorno* (a one-way ticket is an *andata*). A number on your reservation slip will indicate in which car your seat is—find it before you board rather than after. The same goes for sleepers and couchettes on overnight trains, which must also be reserved in advance.

Tickets may be purchased not only in the stations, but at many travel agents in the city centres. Fares are strictly determined by the kilometres travelled. The system is computerized and runs smoothly, at least until you try to get a reimbursement for an unused ticket (usually not worth the trouble). Be sure you ask which platform (*binario*) your train arrives at; the big permanent boards posted in the stations are not always correct. If you get on a train without a ticket you can buy one from the conductor, with an added 20 per cent penalty. You can also pay a conductor to move up to first class or get a couchette, if there are places available.

There is a fairly straightforward hierarchy of trains. At the bottom of the pyramid is the humble *Locale* (euphemistically known sometimes as an *Accelerato*), which often stops even where there's no station in sight; it can be excruciatingly slow. When you're checking the schedules, beware of what may look like the first train to your destination—if it's a *Locale*, it will be the last to arrive. A *Diretto* stops far less, an *Expresso* just at the main towns. *Rapido* trains whoosh between the big cities and rarely deign to stop. On some of these reservations are necessary, and on some there are only first-class coaches. On all of them, however, you'll be asked to pay a supplement—some 30 per cent more than a regular fare.

The FS offers several passes. One which you should ideally arrange at a CIT office before arriving in Italy is the 'Travel-at-Will' ticket (*Biglietto turistico libera circolazione*), available only to foreigners. This is a good deal only if you mean to do some very serious train riding on consecutive days; it does, however, allow you to ride the *Rapidos* without paying the supplement. Tickets are sold for 8, 15, 21, or 30-day periods, first or second class, with 50 per cent reduction for children under 12. At the time of writing an eight-day second-class ticket is around £65, first-class £102. A more flexible option is the 'Flexi Card' which allows unlimited travel for either 4 days within a 9-day period (second class £48, first class £70), 8 days within 21 (second class £66, first class £100) or 12 days within 30 (second class £86, first class £128) and you don't have to pay any supplements. Another ticket, the *Kilometrico*, gives you 3000 kilometres of travel, made on a maximum of 20 journeys and is valid for two months; one advantage is that it can be used by up to five people at the same time. However, supplements are payable on Intercity trains. Second-class tickets are currently £68, first-class £116. Other discounts, available only once you're in Italy, are 15 per cent on same-day return tickets and three-day returns (depending on the distance involved), and discounts for families of at least four travelling together. Senior citizens (men 65 and over, women 60) can also get a *Carta d'Argento* for L10 000 entitling them to a 30 per cent reduction in fares. For young people under 26 a *Carta Verde* entitles one to a 30 per cent discount (20 per cent in peak season—Easter and Christmas holidays and 25 June to 31 August).

Refreshments on routes of any great distance are provided by bar cars or trolleys; you can usually get sandwiches and coffee from vendors along the tracks at intermediary stops. Station bars often have a good variety of take-away travellers' fare; consider at least investing in a plastic bottle of mineral water, since there's no drinking water on the trains.

Besides trains and bars, Italy's stations offer other facilities. All have a *Deposito*, where you can leave your bags for hours or days for a small fee. The larger ones have porters (who charge L800–1000 a piece) and some even have luggage trolleys; major stations have an *Albergo Diurno* ('Day Hotel', where you can take a shower, get a shave and haircut, etc.), information offices, currency exchanges open at weekends (not at the most advantageous rates, however), hotel-finding and reservation services, kiosks with foreign papers, restaurants, etc. You can also arrange to have a rental car awaiting you at your destination—Avis, Hertz, Eurotrans, and Autoservizi Maggiore are the firms that provide this service.

Beyond that, some words need to be said about riding the rails on the most serendipitous national line in Europe. The FS may have its strikes and delays, its petty crime and bureaucratic inconveniences, but when you catch it on its better side it will treat you to a dose of the real Italy before you even reach your destination. If there's a choice, try for one of the older cars, depressingly grey outside but fitted with comfortably upholstered seats, Art Deco lamps, and old pictures of the towns and villages of the country. The bathrooms are invariably clean and pleasant. Best of all, the FS is relatively reliable, and even if there has been some delay, you'll have an amenable station to wait in, full of clocks; some of the station bars have astonishingly good food (some do not), but at any of them you may accept a well-brewed *cappuccino* and look blasé until the train comes in. Try to avoid travel on Friday evenings, when the major lines out of the big cities are packed. The FS is an honest crap shoot; you may have a train uncomfortably full of Italians (in which case stand by the doors, or impose on the salesmen and other parasites in first class, where the conductor will be happy to change your ticket). Now and then, you and your beloved will have a beautiful 1920s compartment all to yourselves for the night.

By Coach and Bus

Intercity bus travel is often quicker than train travel, but also a bit more expensive. The Italians aren't dumb; you will find regular bus connections only where there is no train to offer competition. Buses almost always depart from the vicinity of the train station, and tickets usually need to be purchased before you get on. In many regions they are the only means of public transport and are well used, with frequent schedules. If you can't get a ticket before the bus leaves, get on anyway and pretend you can't speak a word of Italian; the worst that can happen is that someone will make you pay for a ticket. Understand clearly that the base for all country bus lines will be the provincial capitals; we've done our best to explain the connections even for the most out-of-the-way routes.

City buses are the traveller's friend. Most cities label routes well; all charge flat fees for rides within the city limits and immediate suburbs, at the time of writing around L1000. Bus tickets must always be purchased before you get on, either at a tobacconist's, a newspaper kiosk, in many bars, or from ticket machines near the main stops. Once you get on, you must 'obliterate' your ticket in the machines in the front or back of the bus; controllers stage random checks to make sure you've punched your ticket. Fines for cheaters are about L20 000, and the odds are about 12 to 1 against a check, so you may take your chances against how lucky you feel. If you're good-hearted, you'll buy a ticket and help some overburdened municipal transit line meet its annual deficit.

By Taxi

Taxis are about the same price as in London. The average meter starts at L2500, and adds L600 per kilometre. There's an extra charge for luggage and for trips to the airport; and rates go up after 10 pm and on holidays.

By Car

The reasons for bringing your own car to Italy (or renting one) are obvious; often the best places can only be reached on your own. Don't bring your car if you're going to spend most of your time in the large cities—parking is impossible in Milan, improbable in Turin and Genoa, and a headache even in smaller cities like Bergamo or Pavia. You'd do better to take public transport in the big cities, and hire a car for your excursions into the countryside. Purchase the excellent green-cover **maps** issued by the Italian Touring Club (obtainable in good Italian bookshops, or from Stanfords, 12 Long Acre, London WC2; or Rizzoli International Bookstore, 712 Fifth Avenue, New York).

Be prepared, however, to face not only the highest fuel costs in Europe (when everyone else lowered theirs with slumping international prices, Italy raised them) but also the Italians themselves behind the wheel, many of whom, from 21-year-old madcaps to elderly nuns, drive like idiots, taking particular delight in overtaking at blind curves on mountainous roads. No matter how fast you're going on the *autostrade* (Italy's toll motorways, official speed limit 130 km per hour) someone will pass you going twice as fast. Americans in particular should be wary about driving in Italy. If you're accustomed to the generally civilized rules of motoring that obtain in North America, Italy will be a big surprise. Italians, and their northern visitors, do not seem to care if someone kills them or not. Especially in the cities, rules do not exist, and if you expect them to stop riding your tail you'll have a long time to wait. Even the most cultured Italians become aggressive, murderous humanoids behind the wheel, and if you value your peace of mind you'll stick with public transport.

If you've purchased petrol coupons (see 'Getting to Northwest Italy'), you'll find the petrol stations that accept them put out signs. Many stations close for lunch in the afternoon, and few stay open late at night, though you may find a 'self-service' where you feed a machine nice smooth L10 000 notes. Petrol stations in the cities also sell the discs you can put on your windscreen to park in the *Zona Disco* areas of a city. Autostrada tolls are high—to drive on the A1 from Milan to Rome will cost you around L40 000. The rest stops and petrol stations along the motorways are open 24 hours. Other roads—*superstrada* on down through the Italian grading system—are free of charge. The Italians are very good about signposting, and roads are almost all excellently maintained—some highways seem to be built of sheer bravura, suspended on cliffs, crossing valleys on enormous piers—feats of engineering that will remind you, more than almost anything else, that this is the land of the ancient Romans. Beware that you may be fined on the spot for speeding, a burnt-out headlamp, etc.; if you're especially unlucky you may be slapped with a *Super Multa*, a superfine, of L100 000 or more. You may even be fined for not having a portable triangle danger signal (pick one up at the frontier or from an ACI office for L1500).

The ACI (Automobile Club of Italy) is a good friend to the foreign motorist. Assistance number 116; English-speaking operators are on duty 24 hours to answer your questions; if you need a tow, your car will be taken to the nearest ACI office:

Alessandria: Corso F. Cavallotti 19, tel (0131) 60 553
Aosta: Piazza Roncas 7, tel (0165) 362 208
Asti: Piazza Medici 21–22, tel (0141) 53 534/5
Bergamo: Via A. Maj. 16, tel (035) 247 621

Biella: Viale Matteotti 11, tel (015) 351 047
Brescia: Via XXV Aprile 16, tel (030) 3746
Como: Viale Masia 79, tel (031) 573 433
Cremona: Via XX Settembre 19, tel (0372) 29 601
Cuneo: Corso Brunet 19B, tel (0171) 55 961
Domodossola: Via A. de Gasperi 12, tel (0324) 42 008
Genoa: Viale Brig. Partigiane 1, tel (010) 567 001
Imperia: Piazza Unità Nazionale 23, tel (0183) 25 742
Ivrea: Via dei Mulini 3, tel (0125) 423 327
La Spezia: Via Costantini 18, tel (0187) 511 098
Mantua: Piazza 80° Fanteria 13, tel (0376) 325 691
Milan: Corso Venezia 43, tel (02) 7745
Novara: Via Rosmini 36, tel (0321) 30 321
Pavia: Piazza Guicciardi 5, tel (0382) 301 381
San Remo: Corso O. Raimondo 47, tel (0184) 500 295
Savona: Via Guidobono 23, tel (019) 386 671
Sondrio: Via Milano 12, tel (0342) 212 213
Turin: Via Giolitti 15, tel (011) 57 791
Varese: Viale Milano 25, tel (0332) 285 150
Vercelli: Piazza Alciati 11, tel (0161) 65 032
Vigevano: Viale Mazzini 40, tel (0381) 85 120

If driving your own car, your ordinary licence is valid in Italy if it is accompanied by a translation, although an International Driving Licence is more convenient to carry (and necessary for those who hire cars). Insurance is mandatory in Italy. A 'Green Card' will be sufficient for 40 to 45 days (you can also purchase 'Frontier Insurance' when you enter), but for longer stays an Italian insurance policy is required. If you are caught breaking the Italian highway code (note that the size of your car determines your speed limit), it is advisable to pay the fine for your *infrazione* to the policeman writing your ticket.

Hiring a Car
Hiring a car is fairly simple if not particularly cheap. Italian car rental firms are called *Autonoleggi*. There are both large international firms through which you can reserve a car in advance, and local agencies, which often have lower prices. Air or train travellers should check out possible discount packages.

Most companies will require a deposit amounting to the estimated cost of the hire, and there is 18 per cent VAT added to the final cost. At the time of writing, a 5-seat Fiat Panda costs around L80 000 a day. Petrol is much more expensive than in the UK.

Hitch-hiking
It's legal to thumb a ride anywhere in Italy except on the *autostrade*. The problem is that in most rural places there isn't that much traffic, and you may have a long wait. Increase your chances by looking respectable and carrying a small suitcase instead of a huge backpack.

13

By Motorbike or Bicycle

The means of transport of choice for many Italians, motorbikes, mopeds, and Vespas can be a delightful way to see the country. You should only consider it, however, if you've ridden them before—Italy's hills and aggravating traffic make it no place to learn. Italians are keen cyclists as well, racing drivers up the steepest hills; if you're not training for the Tour de France, consider Italy's mountains and hills well before planning a bicycling tour—especially in the hot summer months. Bikes can be transported by train in Italy, either with you or within a couple of days—apply at the baggage office (*ufficio bagagli*). Renting either a motorbike or bicycle is difficult; depending on how long you're staying, you may find it sensible (especially if you're coming from North America) to buy a second-hand bike in Italy when you arrive, either in a bike shop or through the classified ad papers put out in nearly every city and region. Alternatively, if you bring your own bike, you'll have to check the airlines to see what their policies are on transporting them.

By Yacht

The Riviera is lined with facilities for yachts, though they may not be equipped for a long stay. The harbourmaster's office (*capitaneria di porto*) at your first Italian port of call with give you a document called a *costituto*, which you will have to produce for subsequent harbourmasters; this allows the purchase of tax-free fuel. For further information write to either of these organizations: Federazione Italiana Vela (Italian Sailing Federation) Porticciolo Duca degli Abruzzi, Genoa or the Federazione Italiana Motonautica (Italian Motorboat Federation) Via Cappuccio 19, Milan.

Facilities for the Handicapped

Hotel listings sometimes make a note of which establishments are suitable for the physically handicapped. There are also a number of tours that can make a holiday much smoother—a list is available from the National Tourist Office. RADAR publishes an extremely useful book, *Holidays and Travel Abroad—A Guide for Disabled People*, available for £3.00 from their offices at 25 Mortimer St, London W1M 8AB, tel (071) 637 5400. Another useful book, *Access to the World: a Travel Guide for the Handicapped* by Louise Weiss, covers a wide range of topics with listings for individual countries. It's available for $14.95 from Facts on File, 460 Park Ave South, New York, NY 10016.

Embassies and Consulates

UK
Rome (embassy): Via XX Settembre 80a, tel (06) 482 5441
Genoa: Via XII Ottobre 2, 13th floor, tel (010) 564 833 or 564 8345
Milan: Via San Paolo 7, tel (02) 869 3442
Turin: British Consul Trade Office, Corso Massimo D'Azeglio 60, tel (011) 683 921

Eire
Rome: Largo Nazareno 3, tel (06) 678 2541

USA
Rome (embassy): Via Vittorio Veneto 121, tel (06) 4674
Genoa: Banca d'America e d'Italia Building, Piazza Portello 6, tel (010) 282 741
Milan: Via P. Amedeo 2/10, tel (02) 2900 1841

Canada
Rome: Via de Rossi G. Gattista, tel (06) 841 5341

Banking Hours and National Holidays

Banking hours in Italy are Monday to Friday 8:35–1:35 and 3–4, though these vary slightly from place to place. Most banks, shops and museums are closed on the following national holidays:

1 January (New Year's Day)
6 January (Epiphany)
Easter Monday
25 April (Liberation Day)
1 May (Labour Day)
15 August (Assumption, also known as *Ferragosto*, the official start of the Italian holiday season)
1 November (All Saints Day)
8 December (Immaculate Conception)
25 December (Christmas Day)
26 December (*Santo Stefano*, St Stephen's Day)

Time

Italy is one hour ahead of Greenwich Mean Time. From the last weekend of March to the end of September, Italian Summer Time (daylight saving time) puts the country ahead another hour, though moves are afoot to standardize time changes in Europe for 1992.

Post Offices

The postal service in Italy just plain stinks. It's the most expensive in Europe, and disgracefully slow; if you're sending postcards back home you can count on arriving there before they do. If it's important that it arrive in a week or so, send your letter *Expresso* (Swift Air Mail) or *Raccomandata* (registered delivery), for a L2000 supplement fee. Stamps (*francobolli*) may also be purchased at tobacconists (look for a big black T on the sign), but you're bound to get differing opinions on your exact postage. Mail to the UK goes at the same rate as domestic Italian mail, but it's still twice as much to send a letter from Italy to Britain than vice versa. Air-mail letters to and from North America quite often take three or four weeks. This can be a nightmare if you're making hotel reservations and are sending a deposit—telex or telephoning ahead is far more secure if time is short.

Ask for mail to be sent to you in Italy either care of your hotel or addressed *Fermo Posta* (poste restante: general delivery) to a post office, or, if you're a card-holder, to an American Express Office. When you pick up your mail at the *Fermo Posta* window, bring your passport for identification. Make sure, in large cities, that your mail is sent to the proper post office, easiest is to the **Posta Centrale**.

The Italian postal code is most inscrutable in dealing with packages sent overseas. Packages have to be of a certain size, and under a certain weight to be sent in certain ways, and must have a flap open for inspection or be sealed with string and lead. You're best off taking it to a stationer's shop (*cartolibreria*) and paying L500 for them to wrap it—they usually know what the postal people are going to require.

Telegrams (sent from post offices) are expensive but the surest way to get your message out of Italy. You can save money by sending it as a night letter (22 words or less).

Telephones

Like many things in Italy, telephoning can be unduly complicated. In many places you'll still find the old token *gettoni* telephones, in which you must insert a token (or better yet, several) before dialling. *Gettoni* cost L200 and are often available in machines next to the telephones, or from bars, news-stands, or *tabacchi*. If more *gettoni* are required while you are speaking, you'll hear a beep, which means put in more *gettoni* quickly or you'll be cut off. For long-distance calls (anywhere in Italy with a different telephone code), put in as many as the telephone will take (about 10) and be ready to feed in more as you go along. Any unused *gettoni* will be refunded after your call if you push the return button. Other public phones will take either coins, phone cards, or *gettoni*.

For international calls, head either for a telephone office with booths (usually only in the larger cities and major train stations, operated by either SIP or ASST) or a bar with a telephone meter. If you want to reverse the charges (call collect) you must do it from an office (tell them you want to telephone '*a erre*' and fill out the little card). Rates are lower if you call at a weekend (after 2:30 pm on Saturday until 8 am Monday morning—unfortunately just when many provincial telephone offices are closed). Phoning long-distance from your hotel can mean big surcharges.

Direct-dial codes are: USA and Canada 001, UK 0044 (leaving out the '0' before the British area code). If you're calling Italy from abroad, the country code is 39, followed by the area prefix—omitting the first '0'.

Museums

National museums in Italy are generally open 9–1 and closed on Mondays; the more important ones stay open until 5 or 6 in the afternoon, and on Sunday mornings. Most outdoor sites (archaeological excavations, castles, etc.) are open from 9 until sunset. Admission prices have gone up rapidly in recent years; in general the more visited and well known the site, the more you'll pay—usually between L1000 and L6000. Children under 12 are free. Privately-run museums and sites, of which there are few, have different hours and are more expensive on the whole (these will be referred to in the text).

Police Business

There is a fair amount of petty crime in Italy—purse snatchings, pickpocketing, minor thievery of the white-collar kind (always check your change) and car break-ins and

16

theft—but violent crime is rare. Nearly all mishaps can be avoided with adequate precautions. Scooter-borne purse-snatchers can be foiled if you stay on the inside of the pavement and keep a firm hold on your property; pickpockets most often strike in crowded street cars and gatherings; don't carry too much cash or keep some of it in another place. Be extra careful in train stations, don't leave valuables in hotel rooms, and always park your car in garages, supervised car parks, or on well-lit streets, with temptations like radios, cassettes, etc., out of sight. Purchasing small quantities of reefer, hashish, cocaine, and LSD is legal, although what a small quantity might be exactly is unspecified, so if the police don't like you to begin with, it will probably be enough to get you into big trouble.

Once the scourge of Italy, political terrorism has declined drastically in recent years, mainly thanks to special squads of the *Carabinieri*, the black-uniformed national police, technically part of the Italian army. Local matters are usually in the hands of the *Polizia Urbana*; the nattily dressed *Vigili Urbani* concern themselves with directing traffic, and handing out parking fines. If you need to summon any of them, dial 113.

Lavatories

Frequent travellers have noted a steady improvement over the years in the cleanliness of Italy's public conveniences, although as ever you will only find them in places like train and bus stations and bars. Ask for the *bagno*, *toilette*, or *gabinetto*; in stations and the smarter bars and cafés, there are washroom attendants who expect a few hundred lire for keeping the place decent. You'll probably have to ask them for paper (*carta*). Don't confuse the Italian plurals: *Signori* (gents), *Signore* (ladies).

Women and Children

Italian men, with the heritage of Casanova, Don Giovanni, and Rudolph Valentino as their birthright, are very confident in their role as great Latin lovers, but the old horror stories of gangs following the innocent tourist maiden and pinching her behind are out of date. Most Italian men these days are exquisitely polite and flirt on a much more sophisticated level; still, women travelling alone may frequently receive undesired company, 'assistance', or whatever, from local swains (usually of the balding, middle-age-crisis variety): a firm '*no!*' or '*Vai via!*' (Scram!), repeated as often as necessary, will generally solve the problem, which can be greatly reduced if you avoid lonely streets and train stations after dark. Travelling with a companion of either sex will buffer you considerably from such nuisances.

Even though a declining birthrate and the legalization of abortion may hint otherwise, children are still the royalty of Italy, and are pampered, often obscenely spoiled, probably more fashionably dressed than you are, and never allowed to get dirty. Yet with all those strikes against them, most of them somehow manage to be well-mannered little charmers. If you're bringing your own *bambini* to Italy, they'll receive a warm welcome everywhere. Many hotels offer advantageous rates for children and have play areas, and most of the larger cities have permanent **Luna Parks**, or funfairs. If a **circus** visits the town you're in, you're in for a treat; it will either be a sparkling showcase of daredevil skill or a poignant, family-run, modern version of Fellini's *La Strada*.

If you need to bargain with the small fry to obtain their cooperation in all the palaces, churches, and museums that you want to see (but they don't), a day at Lake Garda's **Gardaland**, Italy's closest approximation to Disneyland should be worth at least three museums and eight churches; other activities in this hot corner of family fun are the nearby **Safari and Dinosaur Park**, by Pescantina, or **Parco Minitalia** at Capriate S. Gervasio, or the **Zoo di Preistoria** (more dinosaurs) at Rivolta d'Adda.

The big cities can be fun for kids, too. **Milan**'s Natural History Museum not only has stuffed rhinos but there's a good playground in the gardens nearby; other good bets are the canal tours, a trip to the top of the Duomo, and the Museum of Science and Technology (though there are hardly enough buttons to push and things 'to do' for kids under 10). **Turin** has a small zoo, a large auto museum, a puppet museum (Museo della Marionetta), and lots of mummies in its Egyptian museum. In **Genoa** there's the Giacomo Doria Museum of Natural History, the boat tour of the harbour and incline railways to ride. Other possibilities on the Riviera: **Camogli** with an aquarium in its castle, and a naval museum full of ships' models etc. Even larger naval museums are at **La Spezia** and **Pegli** (west of Genoa). Kids usually like the **San Remo** flower market, and the nearby ghost town of **Bussana Vecchia**.

Sports and Activities

Skiing and Winter Sports
This region, home of the sunny side of Europe's highest peaks is probably best known for its skiing and winter sports—resorts like Courmayeur, Breuil-Cervinia, Sauze d'Oulx, Sestriere, Macugnaga, and Bormio are only some of the best known of a wide array of resorts. Facilities are on a par with other countries and are usually less expensive. There are high and low ski seasons—prices are highest during the Christmas and New Year holidays, in part of February, and at Easter. Most resorts offer *Settimane Biance* (White Weeks) packages, which include room and board and ski passes for surprisingly economical rates; they are easy to purchase at a travel agent once you arrive in Italy, or you can write in advance to a particular resort. We have included the major ones in the text; the National Tourist Office can supply particulars on other special ski holidays. Other winter sports—ice skating and bob-sledging in particular, are available at the larger resorts.

Nearly every resort has a few ski instructors, or, for something different, you can take up the sport in the summer on a number of Alpine glaciers—at Bormio, Stelvio, and Passo Stelvio; there are others at Cervinia-Breuil and Courmayeur at Aosta; in the mountains of Novara province at Formazza and Macugnaga; and Alagna Valsesia in Vercelli province.

Hiking and Mountaineering
These sports become more and more popular among the Italians themselves every year, and the country has a good system of marked trails and Alpine refuges. The Alps offer spectacular, unforgettable scenery that makes even the stiffest climb worth while. Many of the trails and refuges are kept up by local offices of the Italian Alpine Club (CAI), located in every province (even the flat ones, where they organize excursions into the

hills). If you're taking some of the most popular trails in the summer (especially around the Lakes and in Aosta), you would do well to write beforehand to reserve beds in the refuges. The local tourist offices can put you in touch with the right people and organizations. Walking in the Alps is generally practicable between May and October, after most of the snows have melted; all the necessary gear—boots, packs, tents, etc.—are readily available in Italy but for more money than you'd pay at home. The CAI can put you in touch with Alpine guides or climbing groups if you're up to some real adventures, or write to the National Tourist organization for operators offering mountaineering holidays. Some resorts in the Alps have taken to offering *Settimane Verde* (Green Weeks)—accommodation and activity packages for summer visitors similar to the skiers' White Weeks.

Water Sports

The rocky promontories of the Riviera di Levante are a favourite for underwater sports as is the sea around Isola Gallinara near Alassio; the marine life is rich and colourful, and the sea a clear turquoise. Every province has information on fishing from boats and from the shore or with a snorkel, available from the local branch of the Federazione Italiana della Pesca Sportiva. On the whole, though, it's no secret that Italy's coasts are no longer as inviting as they used to be, although the Tyrhennian has fared considerably better than the algae-plagued Adriatic. On the Riviera, try to stay away from big ports like Genoa, La Spezia, and Savona. As for the lakes, the smaller ones like Viverone, Varese, and Mergozzo are much better for swimming than their more famous neighbours, though a quick cool-off dip in Maggiore, Como, or Garda has yet to prove fatal.

Hunting and Fishing

The most controversial sport in Italy is **hunting**, pitting avid enthusiasts against a burgeoning number of environmentalists, who have recently elected the first Greens to parliament; anti-hunting petitions garner thousands of signatures, and the opening day of the season is marked by huge protests. It is, indeed, rather painful to run into some macho Italian hunter returning from the field with a string of tiny birds around his belt; in many places they have been hunted so thoroughly that it's rare to hear a bird sing. Without their natural predators, pesky insects and poisonous snakes have become a problem in many rural areas. Boar hunting is also extremely popular. Fishing is more ecologically sound; many freshwater lakes and streams are stocked, and if you're more interested in fresh fish than the sport of it, there are innumerable trout farms where you can practically pick the fish up out of the water with your hands. Sea fishing, from the shore, from boats, or under water (however, it is illegal to do so with an aqualung) is possible almost everywhere without a permit; to fish in fresh water you need to purchase a year's membership card for L5000 from the Federazione Italiana della Pesca Sportiva, which has an office in every province; they will inform you about local conditions and restrictions.

Yacht Charters

Equinoxe Viaggi: Via dei Mille 18, 10123 Turin, tel (011) 519 903
Eritros: Via Montebello 2, 10124 Turin, tel (011)839 7246
Orizzontiblu: Corso Adriatico 16, 10129 Turin, tel (011) 581 770.

Gamma Yachting: Porto Turistico 17, 16043 Chiavari (GE), tel (0185) 312 603
Golondrina: Via Mimose 12, 17027 Pietra Ligure (SV), tel (019) 647 415
Horca Myseria, Via Pelitti 1, 20126 Milan, tel (02) 255 2585
Noi Blu, Via G. Cavalcanti, Milan, tel (02) 282 6766
Settemari, Via Cherubini 6, Milan, tel (02) 4800 9403
Sailors' Centre Genova: Via Lanfranconi 1, 16121 Genoa, tel (010) 592 089

Golf
This is the best region in Italy for duffers, though you would do well to write or ring beforehand for details and times before planning a big day on the links. Courses that take guests (and hire clubs in case you haven't brought your own) are as follows:

AOSTA VALLEY
Cervino (9 holes), 11021 Cervinia, tel (0166) 949 131
Courmayeur (9 holes), 11013 Courmayeur, tel (0165) 89 103

PIEDMONT
Biella (18 holes), 13050 Magnano, tel (015) 679 151
Claviere (9 holes), 10050 Claviere, tel (0122) 878 917
Le Chiocciole (9 holes) 12062 Cherasco, tel (0172) 48 772
La Fronde (18 holes), 10051 Avigliana (near Turin), tel (011) 938 053
I Roveri (27 holes), 10070 Fiano (near Turin), tel (011) 923 5719
Margara (18 holes), 15043 Fubine, tel (0131) 778 555
Piandisole (9 holes), 28057 Premeno, tel (0323) 47 100
La Serra (9 holes), 15048 Valenza, tel (0131) 977 544
Sestriere (18 holes), 10058 Sestriere, tel (0122) 76 276
Stresa (18 holes), 28040 Vezzo, tel (0323) 20 101
Stupinigi (9 holes), 10135 Torino, tel (011) 343 975
Turin (27 holes), 10070 Fiano Torinese, tel (011) 923 5440

LOMBARDY
Barlassina (18 holes), 22030 Birago di Lentate, tel (0362) 560 621
Bergamo (18 holes), 24030 Almenno S. Bartolomeo, tel (035) 640 028
Bogliaco (9 holes), 25080 Toscolano Madermo, tel (0365) 643 006
Carimate (18 holes), 22060 Carimate, tel (031) 790 226
Lanzo (9 holes), 22024 Lanzo d'Intelvi, tel (031) 840 169
La Pineta (18 holes), 22070 Appiano Gentile, tel (031) 933 202
La Rossera (9 holes), 24060 Chiudono, tel (035) 838 600
Le Rovedine (9 holes), 20090 Noverasco di Opera (Milan), tel (02) 5760 2730
Menaggio e Cadenabbia (18 holes), 22010 Grandola ed Uniti, tel (0344) 32 103
Milan (27 holes), 20052 Parco di Monza, tel (039) 303 081
Molinetto (18 holes), 22063 Cernusco sul Naviglio (Milan), tel (02) 923 8500
Monticello (36 holes) 22070 Cassina Rizzardi, tel (031) 928 055
Royal Sant'Anna (9 holes), 22048 Annone di Brianza, tel (0341) 577 551
Santa Martretta (9 holes), 27029 Vigevano, tel (0381) 76 872
Varese (18 holes) 21020 Luvinate, tel (031) 229 302
Villa d'Este (18 holes), 22030 Montorfano, tel (031) 200 200

LIGURIA
Arenzano (9 holes), 16011 Arenzano (Genoa) tel (010) 912 7296
Garlenda (18 holes), 17030 Garlenda, tel (0182) 580 012
Marigola (6 holes), 19032 Lerici, tel (0187) 970 193
Rapallo (18 holes) 16035 Rapallo, tel (0185) 50 210
San Remo (18 holes), 18038 San Remo, tel (0184) 67 093

Spectator Sports
The Northwest is also a prime area for spectator sports: **football** fans can take in First Division matches at Milan (Milano and Inter) or Turin (Juventus and the less fortunate Torino). For many people Monza is synonymous with **motor racing** and the Italian Grand Prix in early September. There are three **casinos** if you want to dress up and try your luck: St-Vincent in the Valle d'Aosta, San Remo on the Riviera, and Campione d'Italia on Lake Lugano. You have to be over 18 and bring your passport to get in.

Courses for Foreigners and Special Holidays

There are several schools in northwest Italy offering courses for foreigners. The Italian Institute (UK: 39 Belgrave Square, London SW1X 8NX, tel (071) 235 1461; USA: 686 Park Avenue, New York, NY, 10021, tel (212) 397–9300) has information on them; if you're a graduate student, ask about scholarships available from your Italian consulate (apparently many are never used because no one knows about them). There are summer courses for interpreters and translators at Turin, run by the Istituto Superiore per Segretari Europei, Via Bligney 5, Torino; summer courses in Italian language and culture at Gargnano, on Lake Garda, run by Milan University (write to the Università degli Studi, Via del Perdono 7, Milano); summer courses on Italian culture, journalism, and economics, run by Genoa University at Santa Margherita Ligure (Corsi Internazionali Studi Italiani, Via Balbi 5, Genova). Between May and October, there are advanced courses for classical guitar, piano, and singing at Vercelli; in July, a course on the history and technique of frescoes at Arcumeggia (Varese).

Special Interest Holidays and Tours are an increasingly popular way to travel. Tour operators in northwest Italy include:

ALTERNATIVE TRAVEL GROUP (walks in the Cinque Terre) 69–71 Banbury Road, Oxford OX2 6PE, tel (0865) 310 399
CAMPER & NICHOLSON MAYFAIR (yacht charters in Liguria) 31 Berkeley St, London W1, tel (071) 491 2950
C.H.A. (walks and mountaineering at Lakes Iseo and Maggiore) Birch Heys, Cromwell Range, Manchester, tel (061) 225 1000
CHEQUERS (racing at Monza) 3 Market Square, Dover, Kent CT16 1LZ, tel (0304) 204 515
CITALIA (city breaks to Milan and Turin) Marco Polo House, 3–5 Lansdowne Road, Croydon CR9 1LL, tel (081) 686 5533
GARDEN TOURS (of the lake district) Premier Suite, Central Business Exchange, Central Milton Keynes MK9 2EA, tel (0908) 60955

GRAND U.K. (senior citizens at Riva del Garda) Aldwych House, Bethel St, Norwich NR2 1NR, tel (0603) 619 933

JUST MOTORING JUST TICKETS (racing at Monza), Lincoln Oaks, Ranelagh Grove, Broadstairs, tel (0843) 65 160

MAGNUM (senior citizens at Limone del Garda) 7 Westleigh Park, Blaby, Leicester, tel (0533) 777 123

OAK HALL EXPEDITIONS (Christian expeditions; hotels or camping), Otford Manor, Shorehill Lane, Otford, Kent, tel (0732) 63 131

RAMBLERS HOLIDAYS (walks and mountaineering at Macugnaga) 13 Fretherne Road, Welwyn Garden City, Herts, tel (0707) 331 133

SPECIALTOURS (art and architecture, gardens and villas throughout the region) 81a Elizabeth St, London SW1W 9PG, tel (071) 730 2297.

TRAVEL WITH FRIENDS (sightseeing and opera) 117 Regent's Park Rd, London NW1, tel (071) 483 2297

WILLIAM WHITTAM (Two schools in May: Villas, gardens and treasures of Lakes Como and Lombardy; and Painting and Writing at the Villa Cipressi. Summer schools at the University of Sterling, UK) Sundial Studios, Moor End Road, Mellor, SK6 5PS, tel (061)427 5709

Festivals

Although festivals in Italy are often more show than spirit (there are several exceptions to this rule), they can add a note of colour and culture to your holiday. Some are great costume affairs dating back to the Middle Ages or Renaissance; others recall ancient, pre-Christian religious practices; and there are a fair amount of music festivals, antique fairs, and most of all, festivals devoted to the favourite national pastime: food. Note that many dates are liable to slide into the nearest weekend.

January

2	S. Defendente Bean Festival, **Castiglione d'Asti**, in which beans are collected door to door and cooked communally.
Jan–July	Opera and ballet at La Scala, **Milan**; opera (until mid June) at the Teatro Regio, **Turin**.
6	*Carcavegia*, at **Premosello Chiovenda** (Novara) an ancient folk rite culminating in the burning of effigies of an old man and old woman. Three Kings Procession, in **Milan**.
Mid-Jan	*Orchidea*, orchid and bonsai show, **Genoa**.
Mid-Jan–May	Operas at the Teatro Comunale, **Genoa**; chamber music at the Unione Musicale, **Turin**; musical afternoons (*I pomeriggi musicali*) at **Milan**.
20	San Sebastiano, processions in **Dolceacqua**.
22	Dance of the Swordmakers, **Giaglione** (Valle di Susa).
26	Bonfire of the Giubiana, **Cantù** (Como), bonfire and fireworks.

29	Bean festival, **Bellinzago Novarese**, another very old bean pot luck meal, this time in honour of San Giulio.
30–31	*Fiera di Sant'Orso*, a 1000-year old handicrafts fair in **Aosta**.
31	San Giulio, with a boat procession, **Lake Orta**.

February

1–3	San Biagio and the Blessing of the Throats, at the church on Monte Bracco, at **Revello** (Cuneo).
Beginning of Feb	Week-long **San Remo** pop song festival.
Carnival	The most traditional carnival celebrations in the northwest are at **Ivrea** (famous as the only one anywhere that follows a script, with a cast of 1500, ending with a Battle of Oranges); **Schignano** (Como province, with a parade of the *bei*, or elegant figures, and the *brutti*, or ragged ones, all ending with a dummy in the bonfire); **Bagolino** (Brescia, with a similar contest between the sumptuous and grotesque); in **Milan** there are plenty of events for children, floats, etc throughout the week).
Ash Wednesday	Carnival's funeral, at **Borgosesia** (in Vercelli province, a comic funeral for carnival, with plenty to drink); also *Bigolada*, **Mantua**, communal feasting on spaghetti with anchovies in main piazza; polenta and codfish feast at **Ivrea**.
11–12	San Benedetto, **Taggia**, fireworks and bonfires and next day, parade of historical costumes and music. San Bello, at **Berbenno**, (Sondrio), a folk festival celebrated in memory of a very handsome friar, who founded a monastery in the area.
First Sun in Lent	Traditional carnival at **Grosio** (Sondrio), with floats and food; *Pitu festival*, at **Tronco** (Asti) where a turkey becomes the scapegoat for all the troubles of the past year, and although condemned, is allowed to make its last will—all accompanied by lots of Barbera wine.
15	San Faustino, **Brescia**, patron saint fair and festival.

March

All month	Autumn-winter fashion collections, **Milan**.
Mid-March	International Cat show, **Genoa**; carnival of Sant'Ambrogio, **Milan**; snow surfing championships at **Pila**, in the Valle d'Aosta.
12	*Polentonissimo* festival, **Monastero Bormida** (Asti), recalling the generosity of the Marchese della Rovere who fed a group of starving tinkers lost in a snowstorm; parade and events, and lots of polenta and *frittata*.
Good Friday	Procession of the *Macchine*, at **Vercelli**, a procession of floats of wooden statues representing Christ's passion.

Easter	Parade of Easter floats, at **Bormio**; dried stockfish feast at **Melazzo** (Alessandria).
end of March	Antiques fair, at **Turin**.
end of March–first week April	Handicrafts fair, **Genoa**

April

Mid-month	**Turin**'s famous auto show (even-numbered years only); Billiard championships at **St-Vincent**.
9–10	Re-enactment of the Oath of the Lombard League, at **Bergamo**, with historical costumes and pageantry.
30	*Polentone* festival, at **Ponti** (Alessandria) another public feast, this time on a giant codfish omelette and polenta.
End April–first week May	*Ortafiori*, flower festival at **Orta S. Giulio**.

May

All month	Piano competition, **Bergamo** and **Brescia**.
sometime	*Palio del Carroccio*, at **Legnano**, celebrating defeat of Barbarossa by Lombard League.
3	Offering of the *Palio*, at **Asti**, a 700-year-old ceremony in which residents of the city's quarters dress in historical costumes to present a banner of conciliation to the patron saint; other events include flag-tossing display.
2nd Sun	Fishermen's festival, at **Camogli**, great fish feast cooked in giant frying pan.
Corpus Domini	Decorated streets form background for processions in **Premana** (Como) and **Grosio** (Sondrio).

June

All summer	Humour festival, at **Bordighera**.
All June	Festival Cusiano di Musica Antica, **Orta S. Giulio**.
First week	Automotoretrò, market fair of antique cars and motorcycles and parts, **Turin**.
4	Navigli Festival, **Milan**, events in the Navigli district; historical pageant and flag tossing to commemorate imprisonment of François I, at **Pizzighettone** (Cremona).
Pentecost	Festival of the Boat, ancient rituals at **Baiardo** in Liguria.
6	Festa of San Gerardo, **Monza**, feast of patron saint who once rescued the ill during a flood by spreading his mantle on the waters, where it turned into a raft.
Second weekend	*Maseng* festival, **Isola d'Asti**, feast and music marking the first hay harvest; Joust at **Nizza Monferrato**, with food, music and bareback riding.

23–24	San Giovanni, at **Turin**, with fireworks, and **Ossuccio** (Como), a 300-year- old festival with dramatic illuminations in snail shells on the islet of Comacina, boat procession, flag throwing, and folk music; also celebrations at **Genoa**.
29	Festival of the sea, **Alassio**, procession of boats decked with flowers.

July

All month	International Ballet festival at **Nervi**, near Genoa; concerts and dances at the Roman Theatre and organ recitals at the cathedral, in **Aosta**.
2	Festa della Madonna della Foppa, **Gerosa** (Bergamo), marking an apparition of the Virgin.
23	Festa of the Crucifix, **Oggebbio**, (Novara), with folksongs, bonfires, dances, etc. Black Bread festival at **Perloz**, Valle d'Aosta.
3rd Sun	Medieval Festival of the Magdalen, at **Taggia** in Liguria.
29–30	Melon Festival at **Casteldidone** (Cremona).
Last Sun	*Pizzoccheri* festival, woodland feasting on grey noodles at **Teglio** (Sondrio); Lights on the sea, at **Arma di Taggia**; Historical carnival at **Robella** (Asti), with figures representing the court of Monferrato.
31	Handicraft fair, **St-Vincent**.

August

First Sun	Festival of the Sea, at **La Spezia**; summer fair of Sant'Orso, **Aosta**.
6	*Travail di veillà* festival at **Challand-St-Anselm**, Valle d'Aosta.
2nd Sun	Historical regatta of the city quarters, at **Ventimiglia**.
12–20	Handicrafts fair and competition, **Aosta**.
13	*Corsa di Tsarettoun*, traditional race of small carts, at **Étroubles** (Valle d'Aosta).
14	*Torta dei Fieschi*, at **Lavagna** (Genoa), historical re-enactment of a famous medieval wedding.
15	Ferragosto holiday, marked by the exhibition of the *madonnari*, or artists who draw on the pavement, at **Curtatone** (Mantua); also Festival of the *muretto* and *palio* of the sea, at **Alassio**; Hazelnut festival at **Canelli** (Asti); Canine fidelity award, in **Genoa**, for the most faithful and courageous Italian dogs; Sea festival at **Diano Marina**.
Last week	S. Vito, with big fireworks, at **Omegna** (Lake Orta).
End of Aug–Sept	*Settimane Musicale*, musical weeks at **Stresa** on Lake Maggiore.

25

September
Early Sept | Italian Grand Prix, **Monza**.

First 3 weeks | Settembre Musica, in **Turin**; *Douja d'or* wine festival in **Asti**.

2nd Sun | *Palio degli Asini*, donkey race at **Borgomanero** (Novara); a horse *palio*, with Renaissance costumes, at **Isola Dovarese (Cremona)**.

3rd Sun | **Palio at Asti**, one of the biggest and most elaborate in Italy; festival of *Crotti*, at **Chiavenna** (Sondrio), with songs, dances, wine, and food.

3rd Sun | Grape festival, at **Chambave** (Aosta).

25–Oct | International piano competition, **St-Vincent**.

October
All month | Spring-summer fashion collections, **Milan**; battling cows, throughout the Valle d'Aosta.

First Sun | *Palio degli Asini*, at **Alba**, a re-enactment of a *palio* in 1275, when the troops of Asti were outside the walls and there were only donkeys to ride; *Festa della Madonna del Rosario*, **Montodine** (Cremona), with an illuminated procession of boats down the River Serio and fireworks.

2nd Sun | *Vendemmia del Nonno*—old-fashioned grape harvest in **Castagnole Monferrato**.

22 | St Michael's Day finals of the *Bataille des Reines* (Battle of Cows) to find the region's dominant heifer, **Aosta**.

End of month | Chestnut festival, **Perloz** (Aosta).

November
3 | Religious procession at **Stupinigi** in honour of St Hubert, patron of hunters.

First half | Wine and cheese fair at **Cuneo**.

Third week | International dog show, **Genoa**.

December
First week | Snail festival and winter fair, at **Borgo San Dalmazzo** (Cuneo), snails and other good things to eat.

7 | Feast of Sant'Ambrogio, **Milan** and 'O Bei O Bei' antique market by church.

2nd-3rd week | Ligurian handicrafts fair, **Genoa**.

17 | Festa di San Lazzaro, at **Portacomaro** (Asti), with feasting on tripe and chick peas.

Christmas Eve | Torchlight procession of the shepherds, at **Canneto sull'Oglio** (Mantua); torchlight procession and bonfire at **Castelletto d'Orba** (Alessandria); Nativity tableau, at **Chambave** (Aosta); underwater Christmas crib at **Laveno** (Varese) until Epiphany.

26

Shopping

'Made in Italy' of late has become a byword for style and quality, especially in fashion and leather, but also in home design, ceramics, kitchenware, jewellery, lace and linens, glassware and crystal, chocolates, bells, Christmas decorations (especially *presepi*, figures for Christmas cribs), hats, straw work, art books, engravings, handmade stationery, gold and silverware, bicycles, sports cars, a hundred kinds of liqueurs, wine, aperitifs, coffee machines, gastronomic specialities, antique reproductions, as well as the antiques themselves. If you are looking for the latter and are spending a lot of money, be sure to demand a certificate of authenticity—reproductions can be very, very good. To get your antique or modern art purchases home, you will have to apply to the Export Department of the Italian Ministry of Education—a possible hassle. You will have to pay an export tax as well; your seller should know the details.

Italians don't care for department stores, but there are a few chains—the classiest is the oldest, *Rinascente*, while *COIN* stores often have good buys in almost the latest fashions. *Standa* and *UPIM* are more like Woolworth's; they have good clothes selections, housewares, etc., and often supermarkets in their basements. A few stay open throughout the day, but most take the same break as other Italian shops—from 1 pm to 3 or 4 pm. Be sure to save your receipts for Customs on the way home. Shipping goods is a risky business unless you do it through a very reputable shop. Note well that the attraction of shopping in Italy is strictly limited to luxury items; for less expensive clothes and household items you'll always, always do better in Britain or America. Prices for clothes, even in street markets, are often ridiculously high. Bargains of any kind are rare (though in January prices are slashed on everything) and the cheaper goods are often very poor quality.

Milan is Italy's major shopping city for nearly everything (see p. 189) but especially for designer fashions, shoes, furniture, and housewares; big-city competition keeps prices lower than most other cities in Italy, and usually much lower than what you'll find in the boutiques of Portofino or Stresa. San Remo is a popular shopping excursion for the French, and caters for their taste with French fashions and perfumes, etc. at lower prices than Paris. Turin, besides cars, makes costume jewellery and accessories, Como is famous for its silks, Biella for its woollens; lace is made in the fishing towns of the Riviera (most famously Portofino), and at Walser villages like Forbello, north of Varallo; woodworking is the main craft of the mountain valleys, especially the Valle d'Aosta, site of two annual craft fairs. You can have your own violin or cello made to order in Cremona, or buy a bar of its famous nougat *torrone*; pick up a *Borsolino* hat in Alessandria; or gold and silver jewellery at Valenza, near Alessandria; eiderdowns and wrought iron at Sampeyre (Cuneo); olive oil on the Riviera; Chiavari for towels and tablecloths; or Zoagli (near Rapallo) for velvets; Castiglione Olona holds a major antiques market the first Sunday of each month.

Italian clothes are lovely, but if you have a large-boned Anglo-American build, you may find it hard to get a good fit, especially on trousers or skirts (Italians are a long-waisted, slim-hipped bunch). Men's shirts are sold by collar size only, and shoes are often narrower than the sizes at home.

Sizes

Women's Shirts/Dresses					Sweaters				Women's Shoes					
UK	10	12	14	16	18	10	12	14	16	3	4	5	6	7	8
US	8	10	12	14	16	8	10	12	14	4	5	6	7	8	9
Italy	40	42	44	46	48	46	48	50	52	36	37	38	39	40	41

Men's Shirts

UK/US	14	14½	15	15½	16	16½	17	17½
Italy	36	37	38	39	40	41	42	43

Men's Suits

UK/US	36	38	40	42	44	46
Italy	46	48	50	52	54	56

Men's Shoes

UK	2	3	4	5	6	7	8	9	10	11	12
US	5	6	7	7½	8	9	10	10½	11	12	13
Italy	34	36	37	38	39	40	41	42	43	44	45

Weights and Measures

1 kilogramme (1000 g)—2.2 lb
1 etto (100 g)—¼ lb (approx)
1 litre—1.76 pints

1 lb—0.45 kg
1 pint—0.568 litres
1 quart—1.136 litres
1 Imperial gallon—4.546 litres
1 US gallon—3.785 litres

1 metre—39.37 inches
1 kilometre—0.621 miles

1 foot—0.3048 metres
1 mile—1.161 kilometres

Where to Stay

Like everywhere else in Europe, the hotels and pensions in Italy are classified and their prices accordingly regulated by the Provincial Tourist Boards. Price lists are posted on the door of every room, along with the prices of extras like continental breakfast or full or half board, and air conditioning if it is considered an 'extra'. Heating, if called for, is free of charge, although in modest establishments you may have to pay extra for a bath.

In Italy the hotel rates are annually adjusted (always upward) in March, although some places retain the right to boost prices during the tourist season and lower them after September. Reservations are essential in summer. The Italian Tourist Office annually publishes lists of hotels and pensions with their most recent rates and amenities, which are very helpful (although note that the Tourist Boards do not make reservations). **Throughout this book, prices listed are for a double room; it will be mentioned if this does not include a private bath.** As a general guide, expect to pay on average (in lire) in 1992.

28

Category	Double with Bath
Luxury (*****)	L300–700 000
Class I (****)	L200–400 000
Class II (***)	L100–200 000
Class III (**)	L60–100 000
Class IV (*)	L40–75 000
Pension	L30–50 000

Single travellers should be aware that, if a hotel has only double rooms left, the charge is legally supposed to be no more than two-thirds the price of a double. Many hoteliers will nevertheless try to charge you a double, and if the bed is a double, you'll probably have to pay it. Having another bed brought into a room adds another third to the price.

Note that many pensions and hotels in resort areas expect you to eat at least half your meals there (when they have restaurants, that is; some do not) and to stay a minimum of three days, especially in summer. Italian pensions are usually family-run establishments, so they are more relaxed (and noisier) than their hotel equivalents. Beware, also, of assuming anything at all about a hotel by its government stars, although 'Luxury' is luxury is luxury. The hotel owners are given enough discretion in rating their hotels to make guidelines somewhat unreliable. Some hotels are purposely classed lower to attract the bargain-minded traveller, although they may charge as much as a Class I hotel.

One of the biggest chains in Italy is the Jolly Hotels, always reliable if not all up to the same standard; these can generally be found near the centre of larger towns. Motels are operated by the ACI (the Italian Automobile Club) or by AGIP (the big oil company, and usually located along major routes outside cities). These cater for motorists and are adequate, if nothing special. For AGIP motel reservations contact (in London) Quo Vadis Ltd, 243 Euston Road, London NW1 (tel (071) 388 7512).

Note that for all overnight accommodation you will be asked for your passport for registration purposes. Contact the local Provincial Tourist Board (EPT or APT) if you feel you have any genuine grievance about your hotel.

Inexpensive Accommodation

Bargains are few and far between in Italy. The cheapest kind of hotel is called an inn, or *locanda*; some provinces treat these as one-star hotels or list them separately (or not at all). The majority of inexpensive places will always be around the railway station, though in the large cities you'll often find it worth your while to seek out a more pleasant location in the historic centre. You're likely to find anything in a one-star Italian hotel. Often they will be practically perfect, sometimes almost luxurious; memorably bad experiences will be few, and largely limited to the major cities (around the train stations!).

Besides the youth hostels (see below), there are several city-run hostels, with dormitory-style rooms open to all. In cities like Rome, Venice, Assisi, Florence, and many others, religious institutions often rent out extra rooms. Monasteries in the country sometimes take guests as well; if you seek that kind of quiet experience, bring a letter of introduction from your local priest, pastor, etc. Women can make arrangements through the *Protezione della Giovane*, an organization dedicated to finding inexpensive and virtuous lodgings in convents, hostels, etc. They have desks in major railway stations, or you can contact them at their headquarters at Via Urbana 158, Rome, tel 460 056.

Youth and Student Hostels

Youth Hostels (*Alberghi per la Gioventù*) may be found in Milan (Piero Rotta), Turin (two, at Via Gatti and Via Albany); Bergamo; Mantua (Sparafucile); on Lake Como (Villa Olmo) also at Menaggio (La Primula) and Domaso, and Lecco-Germanedo (del Resegone); the Wuillermin hostel at Finale Marina (Savona); Savona (Villa Cesare de Franceschini; Genoa (Quarto del Mare); Riva del Garda (Benacus). Those at Milan, Turin, Bergamo, and Genoa are open throughout the year, while most of the others are open only from March–October. If you're coming during Easter holidays or in the high summer season, write ahead (at least a month in advance) with the date of arrival and departure, and the number and sex of your party. You can get more information by writing to the head organization in Italy, the Associazione Alberghi per la Gioventù, Palazzo del Civiltà del Lavoro, Quadrato della Concordia 00144 Rome, tel (06) 593 1702.

Self-Catering Holidays: Villas, Flats, and Farmhouses

Self-catering holiday accommodation is *the* way to beat the high costs of Italy, especially if you're travelling with the family or with a group of friends. Most of the possibilities in the northwest are flats on the Riviera or cottages on the Lakes, but every province has a certain number of farmhouses and rural accommodation available through its local Agriturist office (see addresses below). These are often very reasonably priced, and often include extras like chickens, rabbits, horses, and cheap homegrown produce and wine.

One place to look for holiday villas is in the Sunday paper; or, if you have your heart set on a particular area, write to its tourist offices which can supply a list of local rental agencies. These ought to provide photos of the accommodation to give you an idea of what to expect, and make sure all pertinent details are written down in your rental agreement to avoid misunderstandings later. In general minimum lets are for two weeks; rental prices usually include insurance, water, and electricity, and sometimes linen and maid service. Don't be surprised if upon arrival the owner 'denounces' (*denunziare*) you to the police; according to Italian law, all visitors must be registered upon arrival. Common problems are water shortages, unruly insects (mosquitoes and scorpions), and low kilowatts (often you can't have your hot water heater and oven on at the same time). Many of the companies listed below offer, in addition to homes, savings on charter flights, ferry crossings or fly-drive schemes to sweeten the deal. Try to book as far in advance as possible for the summer season.

UK Villa and Flat Agencies
CITALIA **(Pietra Ligure, Diano Marina)** Marco Polo House 3–5, Lansdowne Road, Croydon CR9 1LL, tel (081) 686 5533
COSMOS **(Pietra Ligure, Loano, Diano Marina)**, Tourama House, 17 Homesdale Rd, Bromley, Kent, tel (081) 480–5799
EUROVILLAS **(Gargnano, Prabione, Tignale,** all on Lake Garda) 36 East St, Coggeshall, Essex, tel (0376) 561156
INTERHOME **(Ceriale, Cipressa, La Mortola, Pietra Ligure, Ventimiglia, Lake**

Ledro, Lake Lugano, Lake Como, Limone di Garda, Riva di Garda, Sirmione, Luino) 383 Richmond Rd, Twickenham, tel (071) 891 1294
ITALIAN ESCAPADES (villas and palazzi on the **Lakes**), 227 Shepherd's Bush Road, London W6 7AS, tel (081) 748 4999
MAGIC OF ITALY (**Lake Garda**), 227 Shepherd's Bush Road, London W6 7AS, tel (081) 748 4999
TRAVEL CLUB (**Lake Orta**), 54 Station Road, Upminster, Essex, tel (04022) 25 000
VILLAS ITALIA (**Tellaro, Riva del Garda, Limone di Garda, Torbole**) Hillgate House, 13 Hillgate Street, London W8 7SP

Provincial Agriturist Offices (for rural and farmhouse accommodation)
VALLE D'AOSTA
Corso Battaglione Aosta 24 11100 **Aosta**, tel (0165) 44 506

PIEDMONT
Via Trotti 118, 15100 **Alessandria**, tel (0131) 43 151
Via Cesare Battisti 31m 14100 **Asti**, tel (0141) 53 855
Via Oberdan 17/A, 13051 **Biella** (VC), tel (015) 22 179
Corso IV Novembre 8, 12100 **Cuneo**, tel (0171) 2143
Via Ravizza 4, 28100 **Novara**, tel (0321) 20 787
Corso Vittorio Emanuele 58 (3° piano) 10121 **Torino**, tel (011) 513 297
Piazza Zumaglini 14, 13100 **Vercelli**, tel (0161) 53 831

LIGURIA
Via degli Orefici 7/30, 16123 **Genova**, tel (010) 206 563
Corso Mombello 16, 18038 **San Remo**, tel (0184) 85 486
Via Cadorna 4, 19100 **La Spezia**, tel (0187) 26 564
Via Patrioti 69/1, 17031 **Savona**, tel (0182) 540 940

LOMBARDY
Via Borgo Palazzo 133, 24100 **Bergamo**, tel (035) 244 480
Via Creta 50, 25125 **Brescia**, tel (030) 222 861
Via Leoni 13, 22100 **Como**, tel (031) 261 090
Piazza Comune 9, 26100 **Cremona**, tel (0372) 26 201
Piazza Martiri Belfiore 7, 46100 **Mantova**, tel (0376) 369 121
Via Ripamonti 35, **Milano**, tel (02) 5830 2670
Corso Mazzini 1/B, 27100 **Pavia**, tel (0382) 21 715
Via Trento 56, 23100 **Sondrio**, tel (0342) 214 197
Via Magenta 52, 21100 **Varese**, tel (0332) 283 425

Alpine Refuges

In the mountains, the Italian Alpine Club operates refuges on the main mountain trails. These offer simple accommodation, often with restaurants (listed along with the hotels in the sections on individual provinces). For up-to-date information on the refuges, write to the Club Alpino Italiano, Via Ugo Foscolo 3, Milano (tel (02) 805 5824). Charges average L10 000 a night, with a 20 per cent increase from December to April.

Camping

Most of the official camp sites are near the sea, but there are also quite a few in the mountains and near the lakes, and usually one within commuting distance of major tourist centres. A complete list with full details for all of Italy is published annually in the Italian Touring Club's *Campeggi e Villaggi Turistici*, available in Italian bookshops for L28 000, or you can obtain an abbreviated list free from the Centro Internazionale Prenotazioni Federcampeggio, Casella Postale 23, 50042, Calenzano (Firenze); request their booking forms as well to reserve a place—essential in the summer months, when the tents and caravans (campers) are packed cheek to cheek. Camping fees vary according to the camp ground's facilities, roughly L5000 per person (less for children); L5000–15 000 per tent or caravan; and L4000 per car. Camping outside official sites is kosher if you ask the landowner's permission first.

Camper and Caravan Hire

Autocaravan Bergamo, Via Borgo Palazzo 107/a, **Bergamo**, tel (035) 243 827
Centro Caravan, Via Esperanto 4, **Aosta**
Centro Ligure Caravan, Corso Europa 315, **Genoa**, tel (010) 399 1298
Galbiati Caravan, Località Grand Chemin 87, St Christophe (near **Aosta**), tel (0165) 34 552
Giramondo, Viale Industria 315, **Vigevano** (Pavia), tel (0381) 40 976
Grillo Sport, Via Pra' 23/R, **Genoa**, tel (010) 666 288
Holiday Rent-a-Camper, Via Carmagnola, Casalgrasso (**Turin**), tel (011) 975 842
Intercaravan, Via Galvani 24, **Legnano** (Milan), tel (0331) 592 368
L'Oasi Camper, Via Crea 49, **Turin**, tel (011) 700 876
Lubam, Via Novara 558, 20153 **Milan**, tel (02) 358 0544
Paolini C & G, Via Privata Ciele 52, **La Spezia**, tel (0187) 503 466
Setratour, Piazza Tirana 24/6, 20147 **Milan**, tel (02) 415 8508
Skimar, Via S. Mansueto 5, 20136 **Milan**, tel (02) 5518 3121
Valsesia Centro Caravans, SS. 142, 19 Bielle Laghi, **Brusnengo** (Biella), tel (015) 95 225

Buying a House

There are only so many villas on the Riviera and by the lakes, and when one comes up on the market, only a nabob could afford it. But rural real estate is one of Italy's great buys, and the recommended way to do it is to buy a run-down property and restore it to your own needs and taste. But beware the pitfalls.

One estate agent is constantly amazed that his English clients invariably express two major concerns about a property: drainage and the presence of a bidet in the bathroom, as if it were a tool of the devil! What they should be asking are questions about water supply, electricity, and road access—often big problems for that isolated, romantic farmhouse that has caught your eye. Another thing to remember before purchasing a home or land is that you need permission from the local *comune* to make any changes or improvements, and it's no good buying anything unless you're pretty sure the *comune* will consent (for a sizeable fee, of course) to let you convert the old cellar or stable into a spare bedroom. Another thing to remember is that though there are no annual rates (property tax) to pay, there's a 10 per cent IVA (VAT) to be paid on the purchase price for a house and 17 per cent on land, as well as a hefty Capital Gains Tax on selling price and profit to be paid by the seller. Italians tend to get round this by selling at one price and writing down another on the contract. But remember if you sell you'll be in the same bind.

Once you've agreed to buy, you pay a deposit (usually 25–30 per cent) and sign a *compromesso*, a document that states that if you back out, you lose your deposit, and if the seller changes his mind, he forfeits double the deposit to you (be sure your *compromesso* includes this feature, called *caparra confirmatoria*). Always transfer payment from home through a bank, taking care to get and save a certificate of the transaction so you can take the sum back out of Italy when you sell. After the *compromesso*, your affairs will be handled by a *notaio*, the public servant in charge of registering documents and taxes who works for both buyer and seller. If you want to make sure your interests are not overlooked, you can hire a *commercialista* (lawyer-accountant) who will handle your affairs with the *notaio*, including the final transfer deed (*rogito*), which completes the purchase at the local Land Registry. Upon signing, the balance of the purchase price generally becomes payable within a year. The next stage for most buyers, restoration, can be a nightmare if you aren't careful. Make sure the crew you hire is experienced and that you're pleased with their work elsewhere—don't hesitate to ask as many other people in your area as possible for advice. One book that offers some clues on the ins and outs of taxes, inheritance law, residency, gardening etc, is *Living in Italy*, published by Robert Hale, London 1987.

Eating Out

In Italy, the three Ms (the Madonna, Mamma, and Mangiare) are still a force to be reckoned with, and in a country where millions of otherwise sane people spend much of their waking hours worrying about their digestion, standards both at home and in the restaurants are understandably high. Best of all for the travelling trencherman or woman, the Italians are equally manic when it comes to preserving regional traditions in the kitchen; if you are ever bored poring over a menu in northwest Italy, you've been nipped in the tastebuds.

Of the four regions in this book, Piedmont and its cousin, the Valle d'Aosta, with their mixture of Italian and French influences, are the most culinarily ambitious. Part of the challenge comes in matching the fluid rubies from Piedmont's wine cellars, beginning with the brilliant Bs *Barolo*, *Barbaresco* and *Barbera*. Both regions cook with butter instead of olive oil, and spare the spices and tomatoes, in favour of cheeses, mushrooms, and aromatic (and expensive) white truffles; these figure in Piedmont's favourite *bagna cauda*, a rich, savoury dip for cardoons (edible thistles), Savoy cabbage, or other raw vegetables. The regional pasta dish is *agnolotti*, similar to ravioli and usually filled with lean beef and spinach. Throughout the northwest, rib-sticking polenta (a thick maize pudding) is frequently served; the Piedmontese like it topped with Fontina or other mountain cheeses. Popular second courses are game dishes like chamois, pheasant, or hare simmered in wine sauces, or mountain trout, veal and chicken (including the celebrated Chicken Marengo, cooked in white wine and served with croutons, fried eggs, and crayfish).

Just over the Maritime Alps in Liguria, it's a completely different kettle of fish (and lots of other seafood besides). The cuisine is Mediterranean—no melted cheese or butter but some of Italy's most fragrant olive oil, fresh basil and pine nuts—the main ingredients of Liguria's addictive *pesto* sauce. Another speciality is *focaccia*, a soft pizza that can be simply sprinkled with rosemary or elaborately filled with olives, spinach, cheese, and ham. And when you're tired of seafood, try a *torta* or *cima*—vegetables and eggs, or meat rolled in a pastry. Liguria's vineyards produce strong young wines; a few glasses of *Dolceacqua DOC* on a sunny afternoon and you'll join the natives' siesta in no time.

As Europe's major producer of rice, Lombardy is the land of rice and nonpareil *risottos*, ranging from the traditional saffron-tinted *risotto alla milanese* to seasonal concoctions with *porcini* mushrooms or asparagus, or even fruit in some *cucina nuova* restaurants; also try homemade pasta with gorgonzola. A wide variety of fish, fresh or sun dried, comes from the lakes; and admirers of slippery dishes like eels, frogs, or snails will find happiness in the lowlands of the Po. Donkey meat appears with alarming frequency on menus from Lake Orta to Mantua; even King Kong would balk before *stu'a' d'asnin cünt la pulenta* (stewed donkey with polenta). But don't despair—more common main courses include *osso buco*, *cotoletta alla milanese* (Lombard wiener schnitzel), duckling, and the hearty regional pork and cabbage stew, *cazzoela* or *cassuoela* (two of 25 different spellings). Lombardy's best wines come from the sunny hillsides of the Valtellina (*Grumello*, *Sassella* or *Inferno*).

Restaurants open from noon to 3 or 4 pm and from 7 or 8 until 11 pm, and later in the summer. In the hierarchy of eating establishments, the *ristorante* is the most elaborate, though in practice it has become somewhat arbitrary whether a place is called *ristorante*, *trattoria* or *osteria* (inn). Service is generally 12 per cent, and there is also a *coperto e pane* (cover and bread) charge of L2000 or so. Tipping is discretionary, but customary. Tax law in Italy orders restaurants and bars to give patrons a receipt (*scontrino*), which you are supposed to take out of the restaurant with you and carry for 300 metres in case the receipt police stage one of their rare ambushes.

At a *rosticceria*, *gastronomia*, or *tavola calda* you can choose from a buffet of prepared dishes. Some of these establishments are quite elaborate while the modest ones don't even have chairs (or extra charges). If you're used to eating a light lunch instead of a major Italian midday feast, they're the answer. *Pizzerie* are often combined with *trattorie*, but you can order just a pizza for Italy's most filling bargain meal (though often evenings only, and with a 20 per cent service charge for ordering just pizza and beer).

Many places offer *prezzo fisso* (set price) or *menu turistico* meals—often a real bargain, if rarely a gastronomic epiphany. Posh joints with gourmet pretensions sometimes offer a *menu degustazione*, a (relatively) inexpensive fixed-price array of the chef's specialities. Of course you can always order *alla carta* from the menu, which is divided into the following categories (a fuller list of items on the menu can be found at the end of this book).

Antipasti (hors d'oeuvres). These are often sumptuously displayed to tempt you the minute you walk in; common starters are seafoods, vegetables, salami, ham, olives, etc.
Minestre. Broth or ministrone soups, or pasta dishes. The latter come under the sub-heading of *Pasta Asciutta*. Many Italians skip the antipasti, which are often as dear as they are good, and go straight for the spaghetti, before tackling the second course, or

secondo. Note that you will be expected to have both a pasta and a main dish to follow, which can be a sharp surprise to one's digestive system if not used to it.

Pesce. Fish, often according to availability, since it is always fresh.

Carne. Meat, which includes chicken, beef, lamb, veal and pork. With meat or fish, you eat a *contorno* (side dish) of your choice—often salad, vegetables or potatoes.

Dolce o Frutta. Sweet or fruit, the latter being more popular after a big meal. Common sweets are the famous Italian ice cream, exotic cakes or pastries.

Wine of course is the most popular accompaniment to dinner. *Vino locale* (house wine) is the cheapest and usually quite good. Mineral water (*acqua minerale*) comes with or without added or natural carbonization (or *gas*, as the Italians call those little bubbles). Italian beer, always served cold, is average. A small, black coffee puts the final touch to an Italian meal.

Bars have little in common with American bars or English pubs, and can be anything from luxurious open-air cafés to dingy back-alley meeting rooms for the boys to bright stainless steel places you could easily mistake for a pharmacy. All serve primarily coffee in the form of *espresso* (small, stormy and black, possibly *corretto*, 'laced' with brandy or grappa), or a *cappuccino* (with foaming milk, drunk by Italians only before noon). Many people eat a quick breakfast at a bar, where you can help yourself to hot *cornetti* (croissants) or other pastries, with a refill or two as the morning wears on.

Of course you can also get wine, beer, mineral water, juices, etc. at a bar, at any time of the day from 7 am to midnight. Most booze is much less expensive than at home, as long as it's not imported. Standing at the bar is about a third cheaper than sitting at a table to be served. Chances are you'll be asked to collect a receipt from the *cassa* (cash desk) before being served, especially in the cities.

Note: The **prices** quoted for restaurants in this book are **averages for a meal of three courses and wine, per person**. In most you can eat for less, depending on what you order, but beware of the extra charges—service, *coperto*, and tax—that can add up to 20 per cent to the bill.

Part II
HISTORY AND ART

Frescoes in Manta (Piedmont)

History

Some 50,000 years ago, when the Alps were covered by an ice cap and the low level of the Mediterranean made Italy a much wider peninsula than it is now, Neanderthal man was gracing the Ligurian Riviera with his low-browed presence. Like his cousins elsewhere in Europe, he lived in caves, hunted, made friends with bears (see the Grotta della Basura in Toirano), and beautifully adorned his dead.

Northwest Italy's jumbly geography isolated Neanderthal man's successors. Among the more intriguing pocket-sized cultures they left behind are the Neolithic–Iron Age graffiti artists of the Val Camonica; the Bronze and Iron Age statue-stele people of La Spezia; and the quiet folks who lived in Bronze Age resort villages over the water at Lakes Orta, Varese, and Ledro.

From 900 BC to Julius Caesar

By 900 BC, when most of the peninsula was inhabited by the 'Italics'—a collection of distinct tribes with similar languages—northwest Italy (all known as Liguria in antiquity) stood apart. In the northeast (antiquity's Cisalpine Gaul) native Celtic populations were absorbed by the Italics and colonized by the sophisticated Etruscans, but in the north-west the Ligures were content to carve a few menhirs and blip each other on the head. Especially fierce groups inhabited the eastern Riviera and Valle d'Aosta; Phoenician and Greek merchant ships paid fleeting calls, finding little incentive to return.

The same 390 BC invasion of 'Gaulish' Celts that made the geese cackle on Rome's Capitol brought the first hints of civilization to northwest Italy. Merging with the locals to become the Celto-Ligurians, they at least made whacking good swords, and gave the Romans their word *carro* for chariot. But even their chariots couldn't keep out the legions a hundred years later, in a general Italian conflagration that pitted the Romans against the Samnites, Northern Etruscans, and Celts. The Romans beat everyone once and for all and annexed most of Italy by 283 BC. Important Roman colonies in the northwest grew up at Mediolanum (Milan), Brixia (Brescia), Augusta Taurinorum (Turin), Como, Cremona, and Genoa; Luni and Aosta were founded specifically to chill local Ligurian and Gaulish hotheads.

Being a less developed area, the northwest suffered less from Roman misrule than other parts of Italy. There was little wealth to tax, and little for rapacious Roman governors to steal. Liguria and Cisalpine Gaul had little to do with the endless civil wars, famines and oppression that accompanied the death throes of the Roman Republic elsewhere. They did endure a last surprise raid by two Celtic tribes, the Cimbri and Teutones, who crossed over the Riviera and the Alps in a two-pronged attack in 102 BC. Gaius Marius, a capable though illiterate Roman general, defeated them decisively, using his popularity to seize power in Rome soon after.

Marius sided with the popular party, those opposed to the greed and tyranny of the Senatorial elite, and the vast class of *nouveaux riches* created by the centuries of conquest and booty. His rule, though followed by a bloody reactionary dictatorship under another general, Sulla, prefigured the rise to power of another populist statesman, **Julius Caesar**.

After forming the First Triumvirate with Pompey and Crassus (59 BC), Caesar got what he really wanted: a military command, and he marched on Transalpine Gaul with well-known results. When Pompey grew jealous and turned against him, he turned back, 'crossed the Rubicon' and became master of Rome until his career ended four years later in 44 BC, on the daggers of a clique of senatorial bitter-enders.

44 BC–AD 475: The Empire

In the Pax Romana of Caesar's heir Augustus, the northern regions evolved from wild border territories to settled, prosperous provinces full of thriving new towns. Of these, the most important was Mediolanum—Milan. The lakes became a favourite holiday destination for Rome's elite. Trade flourished along new roads like the Via Aemilia to Genoa and the Via Postumia to Cremona; and Mantua gave birth to Virgil just in time to put into words Rome's faith in its divine destiny.

But after over two centuries at the glorious noonday of its history, in the 3rd century the Roman empire began to have troubles from without as well as within. For all it cost to maintain them, the legions were no longer a formidable military machine. Bureaucratic and a little tired, their tactics and equipment were falling behind those of the Persians and even some of the cleverer German tribes. By 268 the empire on both its eastern and western fronts had begun to fall to the 'barbarians', only to be salvaged once again under dour soldier-emperors like **Diocletian** (284–305) who completely revamped the structure of the state. His fiscal reforms, for example fixing prices and decreeing that every son must follow the trade of his father, ossified the economy and made the creeping

37

decline of the empire harder to arrest. A gigantic bureaucracy was created, and taxes soared as people's ability to pay them declined. The biggest change was the division of the empire into halves, each ruled by a co-emperor called 'Augustus'. The western emperors after Diocletian usually kept their court at army headquarters in Milan, the de facto capital while Rome itself became a marble-veneered backwater.

The empire had become an outright military dictatorship, in a society whose waning energies were entirely devoted to supporting an all-devouring army and bureaucracy. Medieval feudalism had its origins in this period, as the remaining freehold farmers sold their lands and liberty to the local gentry—for protection's sake, but also to get off the tax rolls. In the cities, the high taxes and uncertain times ruined trade; towns both large and small began their fatal declines.

The confused politics of the 4th century are dominated by **Constantine** (306–337), who ruled both halves of the empire, defeated various other contenders in 312, and adroitly moved to increase his political support by the Edict of Milan (313), declaring Christianity the religion of the empire. It had already become the majority religion in the East, but until then largely identified with the ruling classes and urban populations in Italy and the West.

The disasters began in 406, when the Visigoths, Franks, Vandals, Alans, and Suevi overran Gaul and Spain. Italy's turn came in 408, when Western Emperor Honorius had his brilliant general Stilicho (who himself happened to be a Vandal) murdered. A Visigothic invasion followed; Alaric sacked Rome in 410; in Milan St Augustine, probably echoing the thoughts of most Romans, wrote that it seemed the end of the world must be near. Rome should have been so lucky; judgement was postponed long enough for **Attila the Hun** to pass through Italy in 451.

So completely had things changed, it was scarcely possible to tell the Romans from the barbarians. By the 470s, the real ruler in Italy was a Gothic general named **Odoacer**, who led a half-Romanized Germanic army and probably thought of himself as the genuine heir of the Caesars. In 476, he decided to dispense with the lingering charade of the Western Empire. The last emperor, Romulus Augustulus, was retired to Naples, and Odoacer had himself crowned king at Italy's Gothic capital, Pavia.

Fairly Good Goths and Really Nasty Lombards

At the beginning, the new Gothic-Latin state showed some promise; certainly the average man was no worse off than he had been under the last emperors. In 493, Odoacer was replaced (and murdered) by a rival Ostrogoth, **Theodoric**, nominally working on behalf of the Eastern Emperor at Constantinople. Theodoric proved a strong and able, though somewhat paranoid ruler; his court at Ravenna witnessed a minor rebirth of Latin letters, most famously in the great Christian philosopher Boethius. Nevertheless, stability was compromised by religious quarrels between the Arian Christian Goths and the Orthodox Catholic populations in the cities.

A disaster as serious as those of the 5th century began in 536, with the invasion of Italy by the Eastern Empire, part of the relentlessly expansionist policy of the great **Justinian**. The historical irony was profound; in the birthplace of the Roman Empire, Roman troops now came not as liberators, but foreign, largely Greek-speaking conquerors. Justinian's brilliant generals, Belisarius and Narses, ultimately prevailed over the Goths in a series of terrible wars that lasted until 563, but the damage to an already stricken society was incalculable.

Italy's total exhaustion was exposed only five years later, with the invasion of the **Lombards**, a Germanic people who worked hard to maintain the title of Barbarian; while other, more courageous tribes moved in to take what they could of the empire, the Lombards had ranged on the frontiers like mean stray curs. Most writers, ancient and modern, mistakenly attribute the Lombards' name to their long beards; in fact, these redoubtable nomads scared the daylights out of the Italians not with beards but with their long *bardi*, or poleaxes.

Narses himself first invited the Lombards in, as mercenaries to help him overcome the Goths. Quickly understanding their opportunity, they returned with the entire horde in 568. By 571 they were across the Apennines; Pavia, one of the old Gothic capitals and the key to northern Italy, fell after a long siege in 572. The horde's progress provided history with unedifying spectacles from the very start: King Alboin, who unified the Lombard tribes and made the invasion possible, met his bloody end at the hands of his queen, Rosamunda—whom he drove to murder by forcing her to drink from her father's skull.

They hadn't come to do the Italians any favours. The Lombards considered the entire population their slaves; in practice, they were usually content to sit back and collect exorbitant tributes. Themselves Arian Christians, they enjoyed oppressing both the orthodox and pagan, for nothing warmed a Lombard heart like gratuitous violence—they apparently had all the bad habits Italian historians like to attribute to the Goths. Throughout the 6th century their conquest continued apace. The popes, occasionally allied with the Lombards against Byzantium, became a force during this period, especially after the papacy of the clever, determined **Gregory the Great** (590–604), who in 603 managed to convert the Lombard Queen Theodolinda and her people to orthodox Christianity. By then things had stabilized. Northern Italy was the Lombard kingdom proper, centered at Pavia and Monza, while semi-independent Lombard duchies controlled much of the peninsula.

In Pavia, a long succession of Lombard kings left little impression. However, under the doughty warrior King Liutprand (712–744), Byzantine weakness made the Lombards exert themselves to try to unify Italy. Liutprand won most of his battles, but gained few territorial additions. A greater threat was his ruthless successor, Aistulf, who conquered almost all of the Byzantine Exarchate; in 753, even Ravenna fell into his hands. If the Lombards' final solution were to be averted, the popes would have to find help from outside. The logical people to ask were the Franks.

Enter Charlemagne

At the time, the popes had something to offer in return. For years, the powerful Mayors of the Palace of the Frankish Kingdom had longed to supplant the Merovingian dynasty and assume the throne for themselves, but needed the appearance of legitimacy that only the mystic pageantry of the papacy could provide. At the beginning of Aistulf's campaigns, Pope Zacharias had foreseen the danger, and gave his blessing to the change of dynasties in 750. To complete the deal, the new king Pepin sent his army over the Alps in 753 and 756 to foil Aistulf's designs.

By 773 the conflict remained the same, though with a different cast of characters. The Lombard king was Desiderius, the Frankish, his cordially hostile son-in-law, Charlemagne, who also invaded Italy twice, in 775 and 776. Unlike his father, though, Charlemagne meant to settle Italy once and for all. His army captured Pavia, and after deposing his father-in-law he took the Iron Crown of Italy for himself.

The new partnership between pope and king failed to bring the stability both parties had hoped for. With Charlemagne busy elsewhere, local lordlings across the peninsula scrapped continually for slight advantage. Charlemagne returned in 799 to sort them out, and in return got what must be the most momentous Christmas present in history. On Christmas Eve, while praying in St Peter's, Pope Leo III crept up behind him and deftly set an imperial crown on the surprised king's head. The chroniclers understandably do not record his reaction, but as the Roman throng cheered the rebirth of empire, Charlemagne undoubtedly realized that he had been royally done.

Surely the strangest, most fascinating theme of Italian history is the single-minded obsession of the papacy to recreate Rome's ancient *Imperium* all for itself. On that Christmas Eve of 799, Pope Leo meant to sustain not only the idea of empire, but of an empire that belonged to St Peter's successors to dispose of as they wished. It was a brilliant stroke, one that neither Charlemagne nor his descendants could undo, indeed one that offered them many advantages in an Italy they wished to rule as absentee landlords. It changed the political face of Italy for ever, beginning the contorted *pas de deux* of pope and emperor that was to be the mainspring of Italian history throughout the Middle Ages.

The Roots of the Middle Ages

With the disintegration of Charlemagne's empire, Italy reverted to a finely balanced anarchy. Altogether the 9th century was a rotten time, with Italy caught between Arab raiders, who penetrated even into the valleys of Piedmont, and the endless wars of petty nobles and battling bishops. To the Italians, the post-Carolingian era is the age of the *reucci*, the 'little kings', a profusion of puny rulers angling to advance their own interests. After 888, when the Carolingian line became extinct, ten little Frankish Kings of Italy succeeded to the throne at Pavia, each with less power than the last. Their most frequent antagonists were the Lombard Dukes of Spoleto, though occasionally foreign interlopers like Arnolf of Carinthia (893) or Hugh of Provence (932) brought armies over the Alps to try their luck. Worse trouble for everyone came with the arrival of the barbarian Magyars, who overran the north and sacked Pavia in 924.

The 10th century proved somewhat better. Even in the worst times, Italy's cities never entirely disappeared. Sailing, and trading over the sea, always lead to better technologies, new ideas, and economic growth, and in these respects the maritime cities of Italy had become the most advanced in Europe; even inland cities like Milan were developing a new economic importance. In the 900s many were already looking to their own resources, defending their interests against the Church and nobles alike.

A big break for the cities came in 961 when Adelheid, the beautiful widow of one of the *reucci*, Lothar, refused to wed his successor, Berenguer II, Marquis of Ivrea. Berenguer had hoped to bring some discipline to Italy, and began by imprisoning the recalcitrant Adelheid in a tower by Lake Como. With the aid of a monk she made a daring escape to

Canossa and the protection of the Count of Tuscany, who called for reinforcements from the king of Germany, **Otto the Great**. Otto came over the Alps, got the girl, deposed Berenguer, and was crowned Holy Roman Emperor in Rome the following year. Not that any of the Italians were happy to see him, but the strong government of Otto and his successors beat down the great nobles, divided their lands, and allowed the growing cities to expand their power and influence. A new pattern was established; the Germanic Emperors would meddle in Italian affairs for centuries, not powerful enough to establish total control, but usually able to keep out any rivals.

1000–1154: the Rise of the Comuni

At the eve of the new millennium, most Christians were convinced that the turn of the calendar was bringing with it the end of the world. On the contrary, if there had been any social scientists around, they could have reassured everyone that things were looking up. Business was very good in the towns, and the political prospects even brighter. The first mention of a truly independent *comune* (a free city state; the best translation might be 'commonwealth') was in Milan, where in 1024 the first popular assembly (*parlamento*) was deciding which side the city would take in the Imperial Wars. And when that was done, Milan's mighty archbishop Heribert invited the German Frankish king Conrad to be crowned in Milan, founding a new line of Italian kings.

Throughout this period the papacy had declined greatly, a political football kicked between the emperors and the Roman nobles. In the 1050s a monk named Hildebrand (later **Gregory VII**) worked hard to reassert Church power, beginning a conflict with the emperors over investiture—whether the church or secular powers would name church officials. Fifty years of intermittent war followed, including the famous penance in the snow of Emperor Henry IV in Canossa (1077). The result was a big revival for the papacy, but more importantly the cities of Lombardy and the rest of the north used the opportunity to increase their influence, and in some cases achieve outright independence, razing the nobles' castles and forcing them to move inside the towns.

1154–1300: the Lombard League, Guelphs and Ghibellines

While all this was happening, of course, the First Crusade (1097–1130) occupied the headlines, partially a result of the new militancy of the papacy begun by Gregory VII. For Italy the affair meant nothing but pure profit. Trade was booming everywhere, and the accumulation of money helped the Italians to create modern Europe's first banking system. It also financed the continued independence of the *comuni*, who began to discover there simply wasn't enough Italy to hold them all. Cremona had its dust-ups with Crema, Asti with Alba, Monferrato with Chieri, and Milan, the biggest bully of them all, took on Pavia, Cremona, Como, and Lodi with one hand tied behind its back.

By the 12th century, far in advance of most of Europe, Italy had attained a prosperity unknown since Roman times. The classical past had never been forgotten—witness the attempt of Arnold of Brescia (1154) to recreate the Roman Republic. Free *comuni* in the north called their elected leaders 'consuls', and artists and architects turned ancient Roman styles into the Romanesque. Even Italian names were changing, an interesting sign of the beginnings of national consciousness; suddenly the public records show a marked shift from Germanic to classical and Biblical surnames: fewer Ugos, Othos, and Astolfos, more Giuseppes, Giovannis, Giulios, and Flavios.

Emperors and popes were still embroiled in the north. **Frederick I Barbarossa** of the Hohenstaufen, or Swabian dynasty, was strong enough back home in Germany, and he made it his special policy to reassert imperial power in Italy. In 1154, he crossed the Alps for the first of five times, settling local disputes against Milan and Tortona in favour of his allies Pavia, Como, and Lodi; then he continued to Rome, where he traded Arnold of Brescia to Pope Adrian IV (who immediately burned him at the stake) in exchange for an imperial coronation. As soon as he was back over the Alps, Milan set about undoing all his work, punishing the cities that had supported him. Back came Frederick in 1158 to starve Milan into submission and set up imperial governors (*podestàs*) in each *comune*; and when Milan still proved defiant, he destroyed it utterly in 1161. And back over the Alps he went once more, confident that he had taught Lombardy a lesson.

What he had taught northern Italians was that the liberties of their *comuni* were in grave danger. A united front, called the **Lombard League** formed against him, which by 1167 included every major city between Venice and Asti and Bologna (except Pavia and the marquisate of Monferrato), with spiritual backing in the person of Pope Alexander III, whom Frederick had exiled from Rome in favour of his antipope. Twice the Lombard League beat the furious emperor back over the mountains, and in the meantime founded the city-fortress of Alessandria (named after the Pope) to keep tabs on Pavia and Monferrato. When Frederick crossed the Alps for the fifth time in 1174, he was checked by Alessandria's 'walls of straw' and forced by the League to raise his siege; then in 1176, while his forces were in Legnano preparing to attack Milan, the Milanese militia surprised and decimated his army, forcing Frederick to flee alone to Venice to make terms with Pope Alexander. The truce he signed with the League became the Peace of Constance, which might as well have been called the Peace of Pigheads: all that the *comuni* asked was the right to look after their own interests and fight whomever they pleased.

Frederick's greatest triumph in Italy came when he left his grandson **Frederick II** not only emperor but King of Sicily. The second Frederick's career dominated Italian politics for thirty years (1220–50); the popes excommunicated him at least twice, as all Italy divided into factions: the **Guelphs**, under the leadership of the popes, supported religious orthodoxy, the liberty of the *comuni*, and the interests of their emerging wealthy merchant class. The **Ghibellines** stood for the emperor, state economic control, rural nobles, and (sometimes) religious and intellectual tolerance. Frederick's campaigns and diplomacy in the north met with very limited success, and his death in 1250 left the outcome very much in doubt.

His son **Manfred**, not emperor but merely King of Sicily, took up the battle with better luck. In 1261, however, Pope Urban IV set an ultimately disastrous precedent by inviting in **Charles of Anjou**, the ambitious brother of the King of France. As champion of the Guelphs, Charles defeated Manfred (1266), murdered the last of the Hohenstaufens, Conradin (1268), and held unchallenged sway over Italy until 1282, when the famous revolt of the Sicilian Vespers started the party wars up again. By now, however, the terms Guelph and Ghibelline had ceased to have much meaning; men and cities changed sides as they found expedient, and the old parties began to seem like the black and white squares on a chessboard.

Some real changes did come out of all this sound and fury. In 1208 Venice hit its all-time biggest jackpot when it diverted the Fourth Crusade to the sack of Constantinople, winning for itself a small empire of islands. Genoa emerged as its greatest rival in 1284, when its fleet put an end to Pisa's prominence at the Battle of Meloria. And elsewhere around the peninsula, some cities were falling under the rule of military *signori* whose descendants would be styling themselves dukes, like the Visconti of Milan. Everywhere the freedom of the *comuni* was in jeopardy; after so much useless strife the temptation to submit to a strong leader often proved overwhelming. And yet at the same time money flowed as never before; cities built new cathedrals and created incredible skylines of tower-fortresses, dotting the country with medieval Manhattans.

1300–1550: the Renaissance

This paradoxical Italy continued into the 14th century, with a golden age of culture and an opulent economy side by side with continuous war and turmoil. With no threats over the border, the myriad Italian states menaced each other joyfully without outside interference. War became a sort of game, conducted on behalf of cities by paid mercenaries, led by a *condottiere*, who were never allowed to enter the cities themelves. The arrangement suited everyone well. The soldiers had lovely horses and armour, and no real desire to do each other serious harm. The cities were making too much money really to want to wreck the system anyway. Best of all, the worst schemers and troublemakers on the Italian stage were fortuitously removed from the scene. With the election of the French Pope Clement V in 1303, the papacy moved to Avignon.

By far the biggest event of the 14th century was the **Black Death** of 1347–48, in which Italy lost one-third of its population. The shock brought a rude halt to what had been 400 years of almost continuous growth and prosperity, though its effects did not prove a permanent setback. In fact, the plague's grim joke was that it actually made life better for most of the Italians who survived; working people in the cities, no longer overcrowded, found their rents lower and their labour worth more, while in the country farmers were able to increase their profits by tilling only the best land.

In the north, the great power was the signorial state of **Milan**. Under the Visconti, Milan had become rich and powerful, basing its success on the manufactures of the city (arms and textiles) and the bountiful, progressively managed agriculture of southern Lombardy. Its greatest glory came under **Gian Galeazzo Visconti** (1385–1402), who bought a ducal title from the Emperor and conquered nearly all of north Italy before his untimely death, leaving Venice to snatch up tasty titbits on the fringe like Brescia and Bergamo.

Other players on the northwest Italian board included Genoa, a nasty little oligarchy of bankers that made money but contributed nothing to the cultural life of the times; the Duchy of Savoy-Piedmont, a quiet backwater still more closely tied to France than Italy; and semi-independent courts in Saluzzo, Monferrato, and most importantly, Mantua, that survived the rough seas of Italian politics.

And what of the Renaissance? No word has ever caused more mischief for the understanding of history and culture—as if Italy had been Sleeping Beauty, waiting for some Prince Charming to come and awaken it from a 1000-year nap. On the contrary, Italy even in the 1200s was richer, more technologically advanced, and far more artistically creative than it had ever been in the days of the Caesars. The new art and scholarship that began in Florence in the 1400s and spread across the nation grew from a solid foundation of medieval accomplishment. The gilded Italy of the 15th century felt complacently secure in its long-established cultural and economic pre-eminence. The long spell of freedom from outside interference lulled the nation into believing that its political disunity could continue safely for ever; except perhaps for the sanguinely realistic Florentine Niccolò Macchiavelli, no one realized that Italy in fact was a plum waiting to be picked.

1494–1529: the Wars of Italy

The Italians brought the trouble down on themselves, when Duke Lodovico of Milan invited the French King Charles VIII to cross the Alps and assert his claim to the throne of Milan's enemy, Naples. Charles did just that, and the failure of the combined Italian states to stop him (at the inconclusive Battle of Fornovo, 1494) showed just how helpless Italy was at the hands of new nation-states like France or Spain. When the Spaniards saw how easy it was, they, too, marched in, and restored Naples to its Spanish king the following year. Before long the German emperor and even the Swiss entered this new market for Italian real estate. The popes did as much as anyone to keep the pot boiling. Alexander VI and his son Cesare Borgia carried the war across central Italy in an attempt to found a new state for the Borgia family, and Julius II's madcap policy led him to egg on the Swiss, French and Spaniards in turn, before finally crying 'Out with the barbarians!' when it was already too late.

By 1516, with the French ruling Milan and the Spanish in control of the south, it seemed as if a settlement would be possible. The worst possible luck for Italy, however, came with the accession of the insatiable megalomaniac **Charles V** to the throne of Spain; in 1519 he emptied the Spanish treasury to buy himself the crown of the Holy Roman Empire, which made him the most powerful ruler in Europe since Charlemagne. Charles needed Milan as a base for communications between his Spanish, German and Flemish possessions, and as soon as he had bankrupted all of Spain, driven her to revolt, and plunged Germany into civil war, he turned his attentions to Italy. The wars began anew, bloodier than anything Italy had seen for centuries, climaxing with the defeat of the French at Pavia in 1525, and the sack of Rome by an out-of-control imperial army in 1527. The French invaded once more, in 1529, and were defeated this time at Naples by the treachery of their Genoese allies. All Italy, save only Venice, was now at the mercy of Charles and the Spaniards.

1559–1600: Italy in Chains

The final peace negotiated at Château-Cambrésis left Spanish viceroys in Milan and Naples, and pliant dukes and counts toeing the Spanish line almost everywhere else. Yet even as the Italians settled for three long gloomy decades of foreign rule, a new player quietly entered the scene: Piedmont and the House of Savoy. Since the 11th century, the Savoys had ruled their feudal estates on either side of the Alps from their capital at Chambéry; for the great powers of the day, Piedmont was a buffer state and a convenient battleground. But in the late 16th century its resourceful Duke Emanuele Filiberto succeeded not only in ridding his lands of the French, but even avoiding the voracious

Spanish while strengthening Piedmont's institutions—and auspiciously relocating his capital to the Italian side of the Alps, in Turin.

The broader context of the times, of course, was the bitter struggles of the Reformation and Counter-Reformation. In Italy, the Spaniards found a perfect ally in the papacy. One had the difficult job of breaking the spirit of a nation that, though conquered, was still wealthy, culturally sophisticated and ready to resist; the other saw an opportunity to recapture by force the hearts and minds it had lost long before. With the majority of the peninsula still prosperous and nominally controlled by local rulers, both the Spanish and the popes realized that the only real threat would come not from men, but from ideas.

Under the banner of combatting Protestantism, the popes and Spaniards commenced a reign of terror across Italy. In the 1550s, the revived Inquisition was accompanied by public book-burnings, while a long line of Italian intellectuals trudged to the stake— many others buried their convictions or left for exile in Germany or England. The persecutors even went after ancient 'heretics' like the **Waldensians**, who refused to join the new Protestants. (The Waldensians are followers of the 12th-century Peter Waldo and his Poor Men of Lyons, who like St Francis imitated Christ's poverty; condemned by the Church, they took shelter in Piedmont's alpine valleys, where their churches survive to this day.)

In Lombardy, that incorruptible Galahad of the Counter-Reformation, Milan's Archbishop **Charles Borromeo** (1538–84) came out of the Council of Trent determined to make his diocese a working model of Tridentine reforms. One of the most influential characters in Italian religious history, he relentlessly went about creating an actively pastoral, zealous clergy, giving the most prominent teaching jobs to Jesuits and cleansing Lombardy of heresy and corrupt clergy. By re-establishing the cult of Milan's patron, St Ambrose, he developed a sense of Lombard national feeling; with his nephew and successor, Federico Borromeo, he promoted cultural and sorely needed welfare institutions, instilling in the Lombard elite an industrious Catholic paternalism still noted in the region today.

Despite the oppression, the average Italian at first had little to complain about. Spanish rule brought peace to a country that had long been a madhouse of conflicting ambitions. Renaissance artists attained a brilliance and virtuosity never seen before, just in time to embellish the scores of new churches, palaces, and villas of the mid-16th-century building boom. Italy also benefited greatly from Spanish imperialism in the New World—especially the Genoese, who rented ships, floated loans, and snatched up a surprising amount of the gold and silver arriving from America.

1600–1796: the Age of Baroque

Yet the first signs of decay were already apparent. The old mercantile economies were failing, and the wealthy began to invest their money in land instead of risking it in business or finance. After 1600 nearly everything started to go wrong for the Italians. The textiles and banking of the north, long the engines of the economy, both withered in the face of foreign competition, and the old port towns (with the exceptions of Genoa and the new city of Livorno) began to look half-empty as the English and Dutch muscled them out of the Mediterranean.

The Thirty Years War made northwest Italy, especially Monferrato, Piedmont, and the Valtellina once again the battlefield of others. The Valtellina, like many valleys with Protestant majorities, had joined Switzerland when Spain captured Milan; and the Spaniards got their revenge in 1620, when they encouraged the local Catholics to butcher their Calvinist neighbours (antics that inspired other regions, like Ticino, to remain Swiss to this day).

Bullied, humiliated and increasingly impoverished, 17th-century Italy at least tried to keep up its prominence in the arts and sciences. Galileo looked through telescopes, Monteverdi wrote the first operas, and hundreds of talented though uninspired artists cranked out the goods to meet the continuing high demand. This was the age of Baroque—the florid, expensive coloratura style that serves as a perfect symbol for the age itself, an age of repression and thought control where even art became a political tool. Baroque's heavenly grandeur impressed everyone with the majesty of Church and State; its showiness echoed in manners and clothing that became decorously berserk; a race for easily-bought noble titles occurred that would have made a medieval Italian laugh out loud. Italy was being rocked to sleep in a Baroque cradle.

By the 18th century, there were very few painters or scholars or scientists. There were no more heroic revolts either. Italy in this period has hardly any history at all; with Spain's increasing decadence, the great powers decided the future of Italy's major states, and used the minor ones as a kind of overflow tank to hold surplus princes (Napoleon on Elba was the last and most famous of these.). In 1713, after the War of the Spanish Succession, the Habsburgs of **Austria** gained control of Milan and Lombardy, Mantua and the Kingdom of Naples.

The Austrians improved conditions somewhat. Especially during the reigns of Maria Theresa (1740–80) and her son Joseph II (1780–92), two of the most likeable Enlightenment despots, Lombardy and the other Austrian possessions underwent serious, intelligent economic reforms—the head start over the rest of Italy that helped Milan to its industrial prominence today. **Piedmont**, during the War of the Austrian Succession, shook itself loose from the tutelage of France and astutely joined the winning side, earning a royal title ('King of Sardinia') in 1720 for **Vittorio Amedeo II**. The infant kingdom, with its effervescent Baroque capital of Turin, was a little backward in many ways, but as the only strong and free state in Italy it would be able to play the leading role in the events of the next century, and in Italian unification.

1796–1830: Napoleonic Wars and Reaction

Napoleon (that greatest of Italian generals) arrived in 1796 on behalf of the French revolutionary Directorate, sweeping away the Piedmontese and Austrians and setting up republics in Lombardy (the 'Cisalpine Republic'), Liguria, and Naples (the 'Parthenopean Republic'). Italy woke up with a start from its Baroque slumbers, and local patriots gaily joined the French cause. In 1799, however, while Napoleon was off in Egypt, the advance through Italy by an Austro-Russian army, aided by Nelson's fleet, restored the status quo.

In 1800 Napoleon returned in a campaign that saw the great victory at Marengo, which gave him the opportunity to reorganize Italian affairs once more, and to crown himself King of Italy in Milan cathedral. Napoleonic rule lasted only until 1814, but in that time important public works were begun and laws, education and everything else reformed on the French model; immense Church properties were expropriated, and medieval relics put to rest. The French, however, soon outstayed their welcome. Besides hauling much of Italy's artistic heritage off to the Louvre, implementing high war taxes and conscription (some 25,000 Italians died on the Russian front), and brutally repressing a number of local revolts, they systematically exploited Italy for the benefit of the Napoleonic elite and the crowds of speculators who came flocking over the Alps. When the Austrians and English came to chase all the little Napoleons out, no one was sad to see them go.

But the experience had given Italians a taste of the opportunities offered by the modern world, as well as a sense of national feeling that had been suppressed for centuries. The 1815 Congress of Vienna put the clock back to 1796; indeed the Habsburgs and Bourbons seemed to think they could pretend that the Napoleonic upheavals had never happened.

Almost immediately, revolutionary agitators and secret societies sprang up all over Italy. The leading conspirator was Genoa's legendary **Giuseppe Mazzini**, a sincere patriot and democrat. Mazzini agitated frenetically all through 1830–70, beginning with the founding of the *Young Italy* movement. Followed by a small cloud of cops and spies, Mazzini started parties, issued manifestos, plotted doomed revolts, checked in and out of exile, and chaired meetings, all with little practical effect. It was typical of the times, and the disarray and futility among republicans, radicals, and those who simply wanted a united Italy, set the stage for the stumbling, divisive process of the Risorgimento.

The Revolutions of 1848

In March 1848, revolution in Vienna gave Italians under Austrian rule their chance to act. In Milan, it began with a boycott of the Austrian tobacco monopoly. Some troops, conspicuously smoking cigars in public, caused fighting to break out in the streets. In five incredible days, the populace of Milan rose up and chased out the Austrian garrison (led by Marshal Radetzky, he of the famous march tune). Events began to move rapidly. On 22 March, revolution spread to Venice, and soon after Piedmont's **King Carlo Alberto** declared war on Austria, and his army crossed the Ticino into Lombardy.

The King, indecisive as ever, had been pressured into action by his ministers, concerned about the very likely possibility of Piedmont's losing its leadership of the Italian struggle to the liberals and republicans. At first, the odds seemed to favour Italy. Radetzky's army was outnumbered, and could expect little help from Vienna. The Piedmontese won early victories, including one important one at Goito, on 30 May, but under the timid leadership of the King they failed to follow them up. Radetzky fell back to the firm base of Austria's defences in Italy in the western Veneto, where he won a resounding victory, at Custozza, on 25 July, that knocked Piedmont ingloriously out of the war. As a postscript to the disappointments of 1848 in the north, Carlo Alberto unwisely reopened hostilities with Austria the following spring, hoping vainly for aid from the French. His army was vanquished by Radetzky in a single battle, at Novara on 23 April; the woebegone King abdicated in favour of his son Vittorio Emanuele II, and departed for a monastery in Portugal.

47

The Republic of Rome, led by Mazzini, survived a bit longer, thanks to **Giuseppe Garibaldi**. Born in 1807 in Nice (then part of Liguria), Garibaldi had first joined up with Mazzini's *Giovane Italia* in an abortive uprising in 1834; he fled Italy just a step ahead of the death sentence pronounced against him by the Piedmont authorities. In 1836, he served in the Brazilian and Uruguayan wars of independence, but the events of 1848 brought Garibaldi back, and in Rome his experience and his commanding presence soon brought him the leadership of the Republic's forces. These, though still meagre, were growing, their ranks swelled by patriots from across Italy and republican adventurers from across Europe.

Although the Italians resisted heroically, Rome was lost to the superior forces of the French, fighting for the Pope. With his Brazilian wife Anita and a small band of diehards Garibaldi set off, hoping to reach Venice, where Manin's republic still held out against an Austrian siege. Their epic flight saw the dwindling band straggle across Italy, staying a step ahead of the Austrians before finally finding safety in the tiny republic of San Marino.

The Risorgimento

Despite failure on a grand scale, the Italians knew they would get another chance. Unification was inevitable, but two irreconcilable parties contended for the honour of accomplishing it. On one side, the democrats and radicals dreamed of a truly reborn Italy, and looked to the popular hero Garibaldi to deliver it; on the other, moderates wanted the Piedmontese to do the job, ensuring a stable future by making **Vittorio Emanuele II** King of Italy. Vittorio Emanuele's minister, the polished, clever **Count Camillo Cavour** spent the 1850s getting Piedmont in shape for the struggle, building its economy and army, participating in the Crimean War to earn diplomatic support, and plotting with the French for an alliance against Austria.

In the delicate European balance of power, the slightest shift of policy could mean the gravest of consequences. In Paris, Napoleon III—the republican president turned emperor—had come to believe that the 'Italian question' was overdue for a solution. In 1858, Napoleon and Cavour held secret meetings, striking a deal where France would help drive the Austrians out of Italy, in exchange for ceding Nice and Savoy. To cement the new alliance, Napoleon's nephew was to marry the daughter of Vittorio Emanuele, Princess Clotilde.

By the first months of 1859, the Austrians had realized what was happening. They mobilized their Italian armies, and delivered an ultimatum to Piedmont on 19 April. Ten days later, the war began. The French and Piedmontese defeated Austria in two extremely bloody battles, at Magenta and Solferino. Both sides were shocked by the carnage, but it was Napoleon, worried by the threat of Prussian intervention, who blinked first; he signed an armistice with Austria in July 1859, without consulting the Italians. Plebiscites were arranged that gave Nice and Savoy to France, and Tuscany and Emilia to Piedmont.

The settlement left one angry member of the Piedmontese Parliament—a certain Giuseppe Garibaldi, who had held the seat for his home town of Nice, just now given to France in a plebiscite. Nationalists across Italy, along with Garibaldi, felt that the golden opportunity for unification had been derailed by the great powers. They got their chance to act when revolution broke out in Sicily in April 1860. Some Sicilian friends persuaded the depressed Garibaldi to filibuster against the Bourbon kingdom. Nearly a thousand volunteers were gathered, half of them from Lombardy, some from as far as England and Brazil. Garibaldi found them antique weapons, and some red shirts for a uniform, a tradition since the wars in Uruguay, where his troops had chanced upon a consignment on its way to workers in a slaughterhouse.

On 6 May, 1860, the Thousand sailed from Quarto, near Genoa (Cavour tried to stop them at the last minute) and the genuine adventure of Italy's unification began. Garibaldi electrified Europe by beating the Bourbon forces in a quick march across Sicily. The Thousand had become 20,000, and when they crossed the straits bound for Naples it was clear that the affair was reaching its climax. On 7 September, Garibaldi entered Naples, and proclaimed himself temporary dictator on Vittorio Emanuele's behalf.

The March of the Thousand, brilliantly successful though it was, brought more dismay than delight to the Piedmontese. Faced with a genuine democratic challenge to their leadership of the unification, they were presented with a *fait accompli* that could not be undone. Cavour had intrigued madly throughout Garibaldi's campaign, attempting unsuccessfully to foment pro-Vittorio Emanuele revolts in the south. Four days after Garibaldi entered Naples, Cavour made a desperate gamble to stay in the game. The Piedmontese army invaded the Papal States, still protected by the French—blatantly unjustifiable, though Vittorio Emanuele's troops easily conquered Umbria and the Marches.

Pressing southwards to meet Garibaldi, the Piedmontese steered clear of Rome, where a French garrison had remained since 1849. Napoleon III chose not to retaliate; Cavour's gamble had worked. On 3 October, Vittorio Emanuele's army reached Garibaldi's. All courtesies were exchanged, though behind the scenes the King's men were doing everything to discredit the 'irregulars', and belittle their accomplishments. What could have been the making of a nation turned out to be an embarrassingly squalid episode. Garibaldi's volunteers were sent home without even the formalities of gratitude. To Garibaldi himself, the King offered a dukedom and a pension; tactless as ever, the old warrior replied that he had desired 'to make Italy, not a career.' The most selfless and dedicated leader modern Italy has known departed for his home on Caprera, near Sardinia, taking with him no thanks, but a few crates of salt cod, macaroni, coffee and sugar, and seeds for the spring planting.

1861–1915: the Kingdom of Italy

Throughout his reign, the first King of Italy preferred to be known as Vittorio Emanuele II—tacitly implying that all his new conquests were merely additions to his Kingdom of Sardinia. A trivial point, but a symbol of the contradictions that would plague united Italy. With its shameful treatment of Garibaldi and the democrats, the new nation laboured under a curse. Most of its troubles came from the south; for its poor farmers, the new arrangement brought no reform, but instead higher taxes and military conscription—for many the only options were brigandry or emigration. The wealthier Piedmontese had scant sympathy for their plight, and sent in the army to crush all signs of popular discontent.

Camillo Cavour died in June 1861. The governments that followed his had little of the creativity the master statesman had been able to bring to both domestic and foreign affairs. To their critics, it seemed as though rather than uniting Italy, the Piedmontese had swallowed it. Their statist conceptions of government bequeathed Italy the heritage of bureaucracy and endless paper-stamping that plagues it today. Italy was also the most highly taxed nation in Europe, nevertheless finding little money available for education and public works, investments crucial to Italy's chances of catching up with northern Europe.

In 1864, Parliament decided to move the capital from Turin to Florence, a pro-visionary measure until Rome could be captured. The people of Turin responded by rioting, but the necessities of history could offer them no consolation. Later, some unexpected help from outside allowed the new Italy to add two missing pieces. When the Prussians defeated Austria in the war of 1866, Italy picked up the Veneto. Only Rome was left with its French garrison, and when the Prussians beat France at Sedan in 1870, the Italian army marched into Rome almost without opposition.

After 1900, with the rise of a strong socialist movement, strikes, riots, and police repression often occupied centre stage in Italian politics. Even so, signs of progress, such as the big new industries in Turin and Milan, showed that at least the northern half of Italy was becoming an integral part of the European economy. The fifteen years before the war, prosperous and contented ones for many Italians, came to be known by the slightly derogatory term *Italietta*, the 'little Italy' of bourgeois happiness, an age of sweet Puccini operas, the first motor cars, blooming Liberty-style architecture, and Sunday afternoons at the beach.

1915–1945: War, Fascism, and War

Italy could have stayed out of World War I, but let the chance go for the usual reasons—a hope of gaining some new territory, especially Austrian Trieste. Also, a certain segment of the intelligentsia found Italietta boring and disgraceful, and cheered when Italy leapt blindly into the conflict in 1915. After the utter catastrophe at Caporetto (October 1917), the poorly armed and equipped Italians somehow held firm for another year, until the total exhaustion of Austria allowed them to prevail (the *Vittorio Veneto* you see so many streets named after); they captured some 600,000 prisoners in November 1918.

In return for 650,000 dead, a million casualties, severe privation, and a war debt higher than anyone could count, Italy received Trieste, Gorizia, the South Tyrol, and a few other scraps. Italians felt they had been cheated, and nationalist sentiment increased, especially when D'Annunzio led a band of freebooters to seize the half-Italian city of Fiume in September 1919, after the peace conferences had promised it to Yugoslavia. The economy was a shambles, and revolution was in the air; workers in Turin raised the Red Flag over the Fiat plants and organized themselves into soviets. The troubles encouraged extremists of both right and left, and many Italians became convinced that the liberal state was finished.

Enter **Benito Mussolini**, an intriguer in the Mazzini tradition with bad manners and no fixed principles. Before the War he had found his real talent as editor of the Socialist Party paper *Avanti!*—the best it ever had, tripling the circulation in a year. When he decided that what Italy really needed was war, he founded a new paper and contributed mightily to the jingoist agitation of 1915. In the post-War confusion, he found his opportunity. Bit by bit, he developed the idea of **fascism**, at first less a philosophy than an astute use of mass propaganda and a sense of design. With a little discreet money supplied by frightened industrialists, Mussolini had no trouble in finding recruits for his black-shirted gangs, who found their first success bashing Slavs in Trieste and working as a sort of private police for landowners in socialist Emilia-Romagna.

The basic principle, combining left- and right-wing extremism into something the ruling classes could live with, proved attractive to many Italians, and a series of weak governments chose to stand by while the fascist *squadre* cast their shadow over more and more of Italy. Mussolini's accession to power came on an improbable gamble. In the particularly anarchic month of October 1922, he announced that his followers would march on Rome. King Vittorio Emanuele III refused to sign a decree of martial law to disperse them, and there was nothing to do but offer Mussolini the post of prime minister.

Compared to the governments that preceded him, Mussolini looked quite impressive. Industry advanced, great public works were undertaken, with special care towards the backward south. The regime evolved a new economic philosophy, the 'corporate state', where labour and capital were supposed to live in harmony under syndicalist government control. But the longer fascism lasted, the more unreal it seemed, a patchwork government of Mussolini and his ageing cronies, rendered heroic by cinematic technique— stirring rhetoric before oceanic crowds, colourful pageantry, magnificent, larger-than-life post offices and railway stations built of travertine and marble, dashing aviators and winsome gymnasts from the fascist youth groups on parade. In a way it was the Baroque all over again, and Italians tried not to think about the consequences. In the words of one of Mussolini's favourite slogans, painted on walls all over Italy, 'Whoever stops is lost'.

Mussolini couldn't stop, and the only possibility of new diversions lay with the chance of conquest and empire. His invasion of Ethiopia and his meddling in the Spanish Civil War, both in 1936, compromised Italy into a close alliance with Nazi Germany. Mussolini's confidence and rhetoric never faltered as he led an entirely unprepared nation into the biggest war ever. Once more, Italian ineptitude at warfare produced embarrassing defeats on all fronts, and only German intervention in Greece and North Africa saved Italy from being knocked out of the War as early as 1941. The Allies invaded Sicily in July 1943, and the Italians began to look for a clever way out. They seized Mussolini during a meeting of the Grand Council, exiling him to a ski hotel up in the Apennines. The new government under Marshal Badoglio didn't know what to do, and confusion reigned supreme.

While the Allies slogged northwards, in this ghetto of the European theatre, the Germans poured in divisions to defend the peninsula. They rescued Mussolini, in a spectacular exploit with a small plane, and made him set up at Salò, on Lake Garda, governing a puppet state called the Italian Social Republic. In September, the Badoglio government finally signed an armistice with the Allies, too late to keep the War from dragging on another year and a half, as the Germans made good use of Italy's difficult terrain to slow the Allied advance. Meanwhile Italy finally gave itself something to be proud of, a determined, resourceful Resistance that established free zones in many areas, and harassed the Germans with sabotage and strikes. The *partigiani* caught Mussolini in April 1945, while he was trying to escape to Switzerland; after shooting him and his mistress, they hung him by the toes from the roof of a petrol station in Milan.

1945–the Present

Post-War Italy *cinema-verità*—Rossellini's *Open City*, or de Sica's *Bicycle Thieves*—captures the atmosphere better than words ever could. In a period of serious hardships that older Italians still remember, the nation slowly picked itself up and returned things to normal. A referendum in June 1946 made Italy a Republic, but only by a narrow margin. The first governments fell to the new Christian Democrat Party under Alcide di Gasperi, which has run the show ever since in coalitions with a preposterous band of smaller parties. The main opposition has been provided by the Communists, surely one of the most remarkable parties of modern European history. With the heritage of the only important socialist philosopher since Marx, Antonio Gramsci, and the democratic and broad-minded leaders Palmiere Togliatti and Enrico Berlinguer, Italian communism is something unique in the world.

Italians, like everyone else, complain endlessly about their creaky, bureaucratic, monolithic governmental system, but at least it seems to be one perfectly adapted to the Italian psyche. No one knows how it works, though Italians often pretend to, but the general principle seems to be that everyone, even the Communists, has a certain share of the decision-making. The constant parade of collapsing and reforming governments, always led by a Christian Democrat (with the recent exception of Socialist Bettino Craxi) does not mean much, except as an echo of the real decisions which are being made in the back rooms. So far, it has worked well enough. The economic miracle that began in the 1950s continues today, and it has propelled the Italians into sixth place among the world's national economies, despite the continued poverty of the south.

The Italian economy has shown an unexpected capability for innovation; many Italians already talk about it as a new model for development—small firms, usually family-run, with a devoted work-force making something that is unique or at least better than foreign competition. Already luxury goods (fashion, cars, and everything else related to the cleverly promoted mystique of Italian design) are a mainstay, just as they were during the Renaissance and Middle Ages. Big firms like Fiat and Olivetti are success stories in their own right. There are no optimists in Italy, but an outsider might be excused for thinking that this nation may be fully recovered from the political and economic ills that began about 1600.

Art and Architecture, and Where to Find it

Like the rest of Italy, the northwest is packed to the gills with notable works of art and architecture, and it is hard to find even the smallest village without a robust Romanesque chapel, or curlicued Baroque *palazzina*, or a mysterious time-darkened painting by a follower of Leonardo or Caravaggio. Because the 'art cities' of this region (principally Genoa, Milan, Turin, Mantua, Bergamo, Pavia, Brescia, and to a lesser extent, Cremona and the smaller cities of Piedmont) flourished at different periods, there is no one dominant 'golden age' in northwest Italy comparable to the Renaissance in Tuscany or Venice, or the Baroque in Rome. On the other hand, you'll find examples of art of all periods, and of nearly every school. For what the Lombards, Piedmontese, and Ligurians didn't make, they had the money and nous to buy, so their churches, galleries, and palaces are endowed with masterpieces from all over Italy and abroad.

Prehistoric

Some of the first works of art produced in Europe were the stubby little fertility Venuses of the Palaeolithic inhabitants of the Italian Riviera, around the year 40,000 BC. These Neanderthal goddesses and other curios from the misty past are on display at the museums at **Balzi Rossi, Pegli, Toirano,** and **Finalborgo.** The most remarkable works from the Neolithic period up to the Iron Age are the thousands of graffiti rock incisions in several isolated Alpine valleys north of Lake Iseo, especially in the **Val Camonica,** where these ancient masterpieces are protected in a national park (others are in the Upper Valtellina at **Teglio** and **Grósio**). The Bronze- and Iron-Age peoples of the Luini culture made the statue steles now in the civic museum of **La Spezia;** at an islet in **Lake Varese** and by **Lake Ledro** you can visit the site of Neolithic and Bronze-Age lake communities. The civic museum at **Chiavari,** east of Genoa, contains finds from a necropolis proving trade links with the ancient Mediterranean in the 8th and 7th centuries BC.

Roman (3rd century BC–5th century AD)

Apart from the odd menhir and pot, the Ligurians and Celts have left few traces, and even the arches and amphitheatres dutifully put up by their Roman conquerors in their colonies and towns have almost disappeared as these grew to become the region's modern capitals. An exception is **Luni,** the port for Luni (Carrara) marble and garrison to control the fierce Ligurians, and **Pollenzo** near Brà, both of which were abandoned in the Dark Ages and have been excavated. Otherwise, look for Roman walls, street plans, and monuments in **Aosta, Brescia, Susa, Turin,** and **Albenga** as well the 'Villa of Catullus' at **Sirmione** on Lake Garda. **Milan,** once Mediolanum, the capital of the Western Empire, has little to show for its former status apart from the objects in its archaeology museum.

Early Middle Ages (5th–10th century)

Although the brilliant mosaics, such as those in Ravenna, Venice, and Rome—the delight of this period in Italy—are rare here (the only survivors are in chapels in **Milan's** S. Ambrogio and S. Lorenzo Maggiore), the work of the native population under its Lombard rulers was certainly not without talent. There was a marked proclivity in the Italian Dark Ages towards unusual geometric baptistries and churches, many of which may be seen here (**Milan** cathedral, **Albenga, Lomello, Asti, Novara,** the Duomo Vecchio in **Brescia**). Surviving 10th-century churches with frescoes are **Cantù** and **Aosta** (Collegiata dei SS. Pietro ed Orso); during World War II remarkable murals from the 8th century were discovered at **Castelséprio.** The Cappella della Pietà in Milan's S. Satiro is another rare survivor from the 9th century.

Some of the most beautiful works from this period may be seen in the Museum of Christian Art and Abbey of San Salvatore, in **Brescia;** at **Monza,** the treasury of 6th-century Lombard Queen Theodolinda in the cathedral; and the Civic Museum in **Pavia.** Rounding out the period, from the year 1000, are S. Pietro al Monte, near **Civate,** and the haunting **Sacra di San Michele** near Avigliana.

Romanesque and Late Medieval (11th–14th centuries)

In many ways this was the most exciting and vigorous phase in Italian art history, when the power of the artist was almost like that of a magician. Some of Europe's best Romanesque churches were built by Lombard architects and masons, especially the master builders and sculptors hailing from the shores of Lake Lugano (the **Campionese Masters**) and Lake Como (the **Comaschi Masters**). The church of Sant'Ambrogio in **Milan**, last rebuilt in the 1080s, was the great prototype of the Lombard Romanesque, characterized by its decorative rows of blind rounded arches (Lombard arcading); a broad, trianglar façade, sometimes decorated with sculpture or carved friezes; gabled porches supported by crusty old lions (usually having a human for lunch) or hunch-backed telamones; and passages under exterior porticoes or an atrium and a rib-vaulted interior with aisles separated by arches (in some churches supporting internal galleries). Especially impressive are the cathedrals of **Cremona** and **Monza**, Sant'Abbondio in **Como**, S. Michele and S. Pietro in Ciel d'Oro in **Pavia**, and the **Abbazia di Vezzolano**, the finest Romanesque building in Piedmont.

Although the architects of northwest Italy had an ideal opportunity to study the Northern Gothic in **Sant'Andrea**, in **Vercelli** (1219), it only caught on briefly— but long enough to reach a singular climax, and vastness, in the spire-forested cathedral in **Milan**. The transition from pointed, vertical Gothic to the more rounded, classically proportioned Renaissance is wonderfully evident in the Duomo in **Como**, built half in one style, and half in the other; while the abbey of **San Benedetto Po** near Mantua offers a fine mix of Romanesque, Gothic, and Renaissance art and architecture.

Renaissance (15th–16th centuries)

The fresh perspectives, technical advances, and discovery of the individual which epitomize the Renaissance were born in quattrocento Florence and spread to the rest of Italy at varying speeds. In Piedmont, however, the new age scarcely penetrated, and at best occupied an obstructed mezzanine seat: the one major painter born there, Giovanni Antonio Bazzi, better known by the nickname he mockingly gave himself **Sodoma** (1477–1549), moved to Tuscany as soon as he could. The most charming artist who stayed behind was **Giacomo Jaquerio** of Turin (early 15th century), whose springtime fairytale frescoes survive in the castle of the Marchese di Saluzzo at **Manta** and the abbey of Sant'Antonio di Ranverso, at **Buttigliera Alta** (near Rivoli). The colourful, rather naive 'Piedmont school' of painting was centred in **Vercelli** and led by **Gaudenzio Ferrari** (1480–1556), disciple of Leonardo and father of the unique painting-sculptures at Sacro Monte in **Varallo** (other works at **Arona** and **Saronno**).

Liguria, too, had only small dealings with the Renaissance (although in the 15th century it produced a well-known school of sculptors inspired by the Tuscan masters) until Andrea Doria hired Mannerist Perin del Vaga to fresco his palazzo in 1527. Mannerism made the Renaissance end with a bang instead of a whimper by taking many of its most precious tenets and turning them upside down. It, too, began in Florence, which had the background to understand it; transplanting it to Liguria was like exporting bowler hats to Bolivia—out of context, it became pure fashion. Perin was a major influence on the founder of the Genoese school, **Luca Cambiaso** (1527–88), best known for his innovative draughtsmanship and monumental decorative frescoes (Genoa's Palazzo Bianco and S. Matteo). In the 1550s, **Galeazzo Alessi** invented what was to become the Genoese palazzo along Via Garibaldi.

Lombardy, for its part, played a major role in the Renaissance, not so much in giving birth to talent as having the capacity to patronize and appreciate it. Outdoor frescoes— one of the most charming features of the region, especially in the valleys north of Bergamo (see **Clusone**)—were within the realm not only of the nobility but of merchants and bankers. Celebrated patrons of indoor art include Cardinal Branda Castiglioni, who hired the Florentine Masolino (d. 1447) to paint the charming frescoes in **Castiglione Olona**. Lodovico il Moro sponsored the Milanese sojourns of **Leonardo da Vinci** (in the 1480s and in 1506) when he painted not only *The Last Supper* (in S. Maria delle Grazie) but also the haunting *Virgin of the Rocks*, now in the Louvre. Leonardo's smoky shading (*sfumato*) so dazzled the local talent that the next generation or two lay heavily under his spell. Most talented of his followers (Boltraffio, Giampietrino, Cesare da Sesto, Andrea Solario, Salaino, and Marco d'Oggiono) was **Bernardino Luini** (d. 1532), whose masterpiece is the fresco cycle in Santa Maria degli Angioli in **Lugano** (also S. Maurizio and Brera Gallery in **Milan** and in **Saronno**). Among the sculptors inspired by Leonardo was **Cristoforo Solari** (1439–1525), whose tombs of Lodovico il Moro and Beatrice d'Este are among the treasures at the **Certosa di Pavia**.

The perfect symmetry and geometrical proportions of Renaissance architecture were introduced into **Milan** and the north in the 1450s by Francesco Sforza, who hired **Filarete** to design the city's revolutionary Ospedale Maggiore after Brunelleschi's famous Ospedale degli Innocenti in Florence. Lodovico il Moro brought architect **Donato Bramante** of Urbino (d. 1514) to Milan, where he designed the amazing 97-metre long apse of S. Maria presso S. Satiro, the great tribune of S. Maria delle Grazie, and the cloisters of S. Ambrogio before going on to Rome. Most Tuscan of all, however, is the Cappella Portinari in S. Eustorgio, built for an agent of the Medici bank, perhaps by the Florentine Michelozzo.

Elsewhere in Lombardy, **Mantua** became one of Italy's most influential art cities of the Renaissance, thanks to the sophisticated, free-spending Gonzaga dukes. The Gonzaga's court painter was **Andrea Mantegna** (d. 1506), the leading artist in northern Italy along with his brother-in-law Giovanni Bellini; for the dukes Mantegna produced the famous frescoes of the *Camera degli Sposi* (1474), one of the most delightful works of the entire Italian Renaissance. Mantegna was perhaps the most antiquarian of painters, studying the ancients with an intensity only rivalled by the great Florentine theorist and architect **Leon Battista Alberti** (d. 1472), who designed two churches in Mantua, most notably *Sant'Andrea*, in an imaginative re-use of the forms of Vitruvius. Ideal cities, designed from scratch according to Renaissance theories of symmetry and urban planning, were a popular concept in the Renaissance, but Vespasiano Gonzaga was one of few who ever actually built one, **Sabbioneta** (near Mantua).

Uncomfortable next to such refined idealism in Mantua is the Mannerist masterpiece of Raphael's star pupil, **Giulio Romano** (d. 1546): Federico Gonzaga II's pleasure palace, the Palazzo del Tè (1527–34). The 1527 Sack of Rome, an event that shook every Italian to the core, brought madness to some artists who witnessed it (like Rosso

Fiorentino). Giulio Romano fled to Mantua, but in the Palazzo del Tè, one can sense reverberations of the event: art and architecture become ambiguous, their limits confused; Titans shatter painted columns that seem to support the real ceiling. Delight and illusion mingle with oppression; violent contrasts between light and dark echo the starkly defined good and evil of the Counter-Reformation.

Elsewhere in Lombardy, the region's traditional art of sculpture reached its florid epitome in the Renaissance in the person of **Giovanni Antonio Amadeo** of Pavia (d. 1522), best known for the extraordinary ornate façade of the **Certosa di Pavia** and for the design and decoration of the Colleoni Chapel in **Bergamo**. Even more prolific than Amadeo was his follower **Bergognone**, sculptor and painter, whose work turns up everywhere.

Bergamo was the hometown of Lorenzo Lotto (1480–1556) and Palma Vecchio, more closely associated with Venice, though Lotto left some works behind for the folks at home (Accademia Carrara, and at S. Bernardino and S. Spirito). **Brescia** became a minor centre of Renaissance painting, beginning with **Vincenzio Foppa** (d. 1515), one of the leaders of the Lombard Renaissance, a school marked by a sombre tonality and atmosphere; Foppa was especially known for his monumental style (works in **Bergamo** (Accademia Carrara) and **Milan** (S. Eustorgio). Later, when Brescia came under Venetian rule, its artists also turned east: Alessandro Bonvicino, better known as **Moretto da Brescia** (d. 1554), was more influenced by Titian, and painted the first known full-length Italian portrait (1526; works in **Brescia**—Duomo Vecchio and the Galleria Tosio-Martinengo); his Bergamasque pupil, **Giovanni Battista Moroni** (d. 1578), painted many run-of-the-mill religious works, but penetrating portraits of the first calibre (in **Bergamo**'s Accademia Carrara). A third painter of this period was **Girolamo Romanino** (d. 1561), whose works combine the richness of Titian with the flatter Lombard style (S. Maria delle Neve in **Pisogne** and **Cremona** cathedral). The rather naive works of the prolific **Giovanni Pietro da Cemmo**, a quattrocento painter from Brescia's Val Camonica, turn up in many a country parish; in the Valtellina you'll see many works by **Cipriano Valorsa** (c. 1510–1570) of Grósio, nicknamed the 'Raphael of the Valtellina' for the sweet idealism of his work.

Besides the followers of Leonardo da Vinci and the Brescians, Lombardy did produce two extraordinary native geniuses: Arcimboldi and Caravaggio. **Giuseppe Arcimboldi** (d. 1593) of Milan painted portraits made up entirely of seafood, vegetables, or flowers which anticipate the Surrealists and the collages of *objets trouvés*. Unfortunately Arcimboldi became the court painter to the Habsburgs in Prague, and has left works only in **Milan** (Castello Sforzesco) and **Cremona** (Museo Civico). More immediately influential, not only in Italy but throughout 17th-century Europe, was **Michelangelo Merisi da Caravaggio** (1573–1610), who, despite a headlong trajectory through life (perhaps the first true bohemian—anarchic, rebellious, wild, and homosexual, he murdered a man over a tennis game, was thrown out of Malta by the Knights, and was almost killed in Naples before dying on a Tuscan beach) managed to leave behind paintings of a dramatic power that few have ever equalled. He was revolutionary in his use of light, foreshortening, and of simple, country people as models in major religious subjects. Although most of his paintings are in Rome to which he moved in 1590, there are works in **Milan** (Pinacoteca Ambrosiana and Brera Gallery).

Baroque (17th–18th centuries)

If Piedmont contributed little to the Renaissance, it more than made up for it after Duke Emanuele Filiberto transferred his capital to Turin in 1563, beginning the city's transformation into one of Italy's premier Baroque showcases. Architects of rare imagination served the House of Savoy; the Theatine priest **Guarino Guarini** (d. 1683) who previously built churches in Messina, Lisbon, and Paris (all destroyed by earthquakes or Parisians) and spent his last seventeen years creating more fortunate works in **Turin** (the extraordinary geometric diaphanous domes of the Cappella della S. Sindone and S. Lorenzo, the Collegio dei Nobili and Palazzo Carignano); the Sicilian **Filippo Juvarra** (1678–1736), master of historical Italian styles as well as the Baroque avant-garde, who became First Architect to King Vittorio Amedeo II in 1714, endowing Turin with five churches and eight royal residences and *palazzi* (Chiesa del Carmine, Basilica di Superga, Stupinigi hunting lodge, Palazzo Madama, etc.). Lesser-known because most of his works are in small provincial towns is **Bernardo Vittone** (1702–1770), a Piedmont native who edited Guarini and studied Juvarra, and created a unique synthesis of their styles (see the churches in **Vallinotto** near Carignano, **Villanova Mondovì**, and S. Chiara in **Brà**).

In **Milan** these two centuries were far more austere, in part thanks to S. Carlo Borromeo, who wrote a guidebook for Counter-Reformation architects. **Fabio Mangone** (d. 1629) epitomized this new austerity (the façade of the Ambrosiana, S. Maria Podone); the more interesting **Lorenzo Binago** (d. 1629), designed S. Alessandro, with its innovative combination of two domed areas. Most important of all Baroque architects in Milan was **Francesco Maria Ricchino** (d. 1658), whose San Giuseppe follows Binago's S. Alessandro with its two Greek crosses; he created a style of crossings and domes which enjoyed tremendous success (other works include the Palazzo di Brera and the Collegio Elvetico, now the Archivo di Stato, the first concave palace façade of the Baroque).

Milan's best painters of the age all worked in the early 1600s—the mystic and somewhat cloying Giovanni Battista Crespi (called **Cerano**, d. 1632) and the decorative fresco master of Lombardy's sanctuaries, Pier Francesco Mazzucchelli, called **Morazzone** (d. 1626; works at **Varallo** and **Varese**). These two, along with the less interesting Giulio Cesare Procaccini, teamed up to paint the Brera Gallery's unusual 'three master' painting of *SS. Rufina and Seconda*. A fourth painter, Antonio d'Enrico, **Il Tanzio** (d. 1635), was inspired by Caravaggio, with results that range from the bland to the uncannily meticulous (S. Gaudenzio, **Novara**).

After 1630, when Milan and its artists were devastated by plague, **Bergamo** was left holding the paintbrush of Lombard art, in the portraits of **Carlo Ceresa** (d. 1679) and **Evaristo Baschenis** (1617–77), whose meticulous still-life paintings of musical instruments are among the finest of a rather non-Italian genre. From **Brescia** came **Giacomo Ceruti** (active in the 1730s–50s), nicknamed 'il Pitocchetto', whose sombre pictures of idiots, beggars, and other social outcasts are as meticulously obsessive. In sculpture, **Antonio Fantoni** (1659–1734) from Rovetta stands out with his scrolly, elegantly decorative altarpieces and pulpits, perhaps the closest any Italian came to Rococo (works in the Valle Seriana, especially **Alzano Lombardo**).

The early 17th century was a golden age in **Genoa**. The chief Baroque architect was **Bartolomeo Bianco**, who designed Via Balbi and its great University palace (1630). In painting, the Capuchin monk **Bernardo Strozzi** (1581–1644), characterized by quick brushstrokes and light-filled colours, was far and away the leader of the pack, even though he was imprisoned by his Order and on his release moved to Venice in 1630. Other Genoese artists worth looking out for are **Domenico Piola** (d. 1703) and **Gregorio de Ferrari** (d. 1726), masters of decorative frescoes and **Giovanni Benedetto Castiglione** (d. 1665), who could paint in a variety of styles, but is most likeable for his magnificent etchings, many done in a monotype technique of his own invention. Among sculptors, the leader of the Genoese was **Filippo Parodi** (1630–1702), a student of Bernini who added a certain French/Rococo grace to the High Roman Baroque of his master (*Virgin and Child*, in S. Carlo, and *Ecstasy of St Martha*, in S. Marta, both in Genoa).

Two Late Baroque painters marched to a different drummer: **Alessandro Magnasco** (1667–1749) of Genoa, who worked mainly in Milan, and produced with quick, nervous brushstrokes weird, almost surreal canvases haunted by wraiths of light, and **Giuseppe Bazzani** (1690–1769), of Mantua, who used similar quick brushstrokes to create the unreal and strange.

Neoclassicism and Romanticism (late 18th–19th century)

Baroque proved to be a hard act to follow, and in these centuries Italian art and architecture almost ceased to exist. Two centuries of stifling oppression had taken their toll on the national imagination, and for the first time Italy not only ceased to be a leader in art, but failed even to a make a significant contribution.

In Piedmont, at least, Guarini and Juvarra had an eccentric heir in architect **Alessandro Antonelli** (1798–1888), whose towers are landmarks in **Turin** and **Novara**. The vast Galleria Vittorio Emanuele in **Milan** is a 19th-century triumph of engineering, while the **Villa Carlotta**, on the banks of Lake Como, is a triumph of neoclassicism, with works by the master of the age, **Antonio Canova** and his meticulous follower, **Thorvaldsen**. Works by romantic Lombard artists, the *Scapigliati* ('Wild-haired ones') are in **Milan**'s Civic Gallery of Modern Art. Many paintings by their Ligurian contemporaries are in **Nervi**'s Gallery d'Arte Moderna.

20th Century

Italian art nouveau, or Liberty style, left its mark in the cafés of Turin, in the grand hotels of the Riviera and the Lakes, in the residential area around Corso Venezia in **Milan**, and reached an apotheosis in the spa palaces of **San Pellegrino Terme**. But Liberty's pretty, bourgeois charm and the whole patrimony of Italian art only infuriated the young **Futurists**, who produced a number of manifestos and paintings that attempted to speed into modern times (**Milan**'s Civic Gallery of Modern Art, the Brera Gallery, and the Civico Museo d'Arte Contemporanea).

This same urge to race out of the past ('Never look back' was Mussolini's motto after the day he ran over and killed a child) also created modern Italy's most coherent and consistent sense of design. Fascist architecture may be charmingly naive in its totali-tarianism, or warped and disconcerting (**Brescia**'s Piazza Vittoriale or its domestic variety, D'Annunzio's bizarre villa in **Gardone Riviera** on the shores of Lake Garda) but modern Italian architects have yet to match it, or rise above saleable but incredibly boring post-modernism (Milan's 1960 **Pirelli Building** by Gio Ponti and Pier Luigi Nervi's flamboyant 1961 **Palazzo del Lavoro** in Turin are the pick of the bunch). Turin also has a good modern art museum, with a collection of big names if you're lucky enough to find it open (also see the aforementioned museums in Milan). But most of the artistic talent these days is sublimated into cinema, or the shibboleths of Italian design—clothes, sport cars, furniture, kitchen utensils, etc.—and even these consumer beauties tend to be more packaging than content (though in these troubled times, it's hard to think of any that aren't).

Part III

PIEDMONT AND THE AOSTA VALLEY

Mole Antonelliana, Turin

Piedmont

Piedmont (Piemonte), 'the foot of the mountains', is not only the birthplace of the modern Italian state, the source of its greatest river, the cradle of its industry, and the originator of such indispensable Italian staples as vermouth, Fiats, and breadsticks, but also a beautiful region full of surprises. To the north and west tower some of the most important peaks of the Alps, beginning with Gran Paradiso and Monviso, while the small autonomous region of Valle d'Aosta is dominated by world-class heavyweights like Mont Blanc, the Matterhorn, and Monte Rosa. The south is walled off from Liguria and the Mediterranean by the lush green Maritime Alps, which, like the rest of Piedmont, are unspoiled, ill-equipped with the amenities of international tourism, and utterly delightful. Between the Maritime Alps and the Po are miles of rolling hills clad in the noble pinstripe patterns of some of the world's most prestigious vineyards. North of the Po the scenery changes again, going as flat as a railway station *pizza*, criss-crossed by a complicated web of small canals that feed Europe's most important rice fields. And in the centre of the hills, plains, and mountains lies the regional capital Turin, not an industrial by-product as one might suppose, but a charming Baroque city.

Historically, Piedmont is one of Italy's newer regions, its name not even in existence until the 13th century, when it gradually came to encompass the former Marquisates of

Monferrato, Ivrea, Saluzzo, and the County of Turin. The French dynasty of Savoy first got a foothold in Piedmont by marriage in the 11th century, and from the very beginning kept a much tighter rein on their realm than other Italian princes. The rise of independent *comuni*, the republics, and heady ideas of the Renaissance failed to penetrate their feudal fastness. For centuries the population didn't even consider itself Italian, and instead spoke Southern French, or Provençal, which still survives in many a remote valley. Yet, as unprogressive and as uninspired as Piedmont remained throughout Italy's Golden Age, it was the first region to re-surface when the peninsula went under in the tidal wave of invasions and looting of the 16th century; Piedmont's French occupation, begun in 1502, ended 60 years later when Duke Emanuele Filiberto won back his lands with a series of gritty battles. From that point on, the Savoys linked Piedmont's destiny with Italy, treading the troubled political waters of the day with an astute choice of alliances and cautious diplomatic manoeuvring that earned them the title of King of Sardinia in 1713, then in the Risorgimento, the crown of Italy herself.

There were violent riots in Turin when the first king of Italy, Vittorio Emanuele II, moved his capital to Florence, en route to Rome; the Piedmontese rightly sensed that they had been relegated to the knicknack shelf of history. But rather than collect dust, they began Italy's industrial revolution, building the first wool and cotton mills in the torrent-sliced valleys of Biella, the first cars in Turin, the first typewriters in Ivrea, and created a felt hat empire in Alessandria. Piedmont's economy has always been one of the strongest in Italy, with tourism playing only an insignificant supporting role.

But if the Italy you seek includes sensational Alpine scenery, snowy peaks and emerald valleys, and mountain resorts, either ultra-sophisticated or rustic, or somewhere in between; if it includes un-hyped medieval hill villages and castles standing like islands above rolling seas of vines; if it includes fantastic regional cuisine, with a French touch; or if you have a special interest in white truffles, caves, St Bernards, trout fishing, Egyptology, Romanesque architecture, rare flowers, wildlife, or kayaking, you will love Piedmont and Aosta. On the other hand, if your Italy consists of Renaissance art, lemon groves, and endless sunshine, you'd better do as Hannibal did and just pass right on through.

Piedmont and the Aosta Valley Itineraries

Crossing the Alps: most people driving to Italy from Britain take the convenient Mont Blanc Tunnel between Chamonix and Courmayeur. Alternative routes include the Great St Bernard Tunnel, or in the summer, the Little St Bernard Pass, all wonderfully scenic and not far from the A5 to Turin, Milan, or Genoa—though unless you're in a rush, the parallel N. 26 is prettier. The Valle d'Aosta is worth lingering in, with more facilities for tourism than Piedmont: **Courmayeur** and **Breuil-Cervinia** are world-class ski resorts, and there are a score of others in the region's dozen valleys. One of Europe's largest casinos is at **St-Vincent** in the main valley, as are the storybook castles of **Issogne** and **Fénis**. **Ayas** and **Cogne** are perhaps the most beautiful valleys in Aosta, the latter leading to spectacular **Gran Paradiso National Park**, for many people the star attraction of the region with its population of ibex, chamois, and golden eagles.

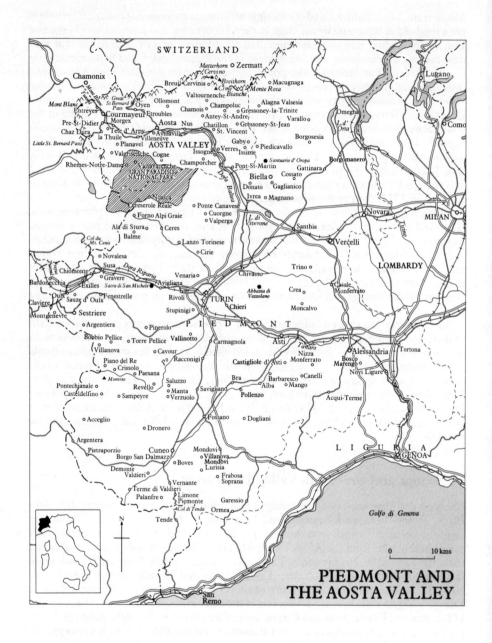

PIEDMONT AND THE AOSTA VALLEY

0   10 kms

Golfo di Genova

62

From Courmayeur you can take what must be the most thrilling ride in all Europe, the cablecar over Mont Blanc to Chamonix. **Aosta**, the capital of the autonomous region, is adorned with Roman and medieval monuments lent a special enchantment by a magnificent backdrop of mountains.

There are several alternative passes to get you over the mountains. Further south, a fine approach is via Val d'Isère and the Col du Mt Cenis to **Susa**, or in winter through the Fréjus Tunnel from St-Jean-de-Maurienne, or through the Col de Montgenèvre, between Briançon and Sestriere. All three routes leave you west of Turin, in the **Valle di Susa** or **Valle del Chisone**, among the most rewarding in Piedmont and easily visited in a circular tour, with stops at the medieval village of **Avigliana** and its provocative Romanesque abbey, the **Sacra di San Michele**, then at the fine old town of **Susa**, and beyond at the well-equipped resorts of **Sauze d'Oulx**, **Bardonécchia**, **Claviere** or fashionable **Sestriere**. In the Valle del Chisone, there's the interesting Waldenses' capital of **Pinerolo**, and the magnificent hunting 'lodge' of the Savoys at **Stupinigi**.

Turin is the cultural centre of Piedmont, having inherited the Savoys' art collections, now housed in the splendid Egyptian Museum, the Galleria Sabauda, and the Museum of Ancient Art, while Turin cathedral inherited the dynasty's most sacred relic, the Shroud of Turin. It is connected by the A6 with Savona, the A4 with Milan, and by the A21 with Parma.

For an out-of-the-ordinary experience in the summer, take in the miles of flooded rice paddies around **Vercelli**, the interesting but scarcely visited capital of rice. **Biella** is full of the bourgeois mansions of Italy's 19th-century textile tycoons; in the surrounding mesh of little valleys is **Oropa**, the holy shrine of Piedmont. Another route takes in the panoramic S232 from Piedicavallo, while yet another leads into the beautiful wooded region of **La Serra**. You could spend a day or two concentrating on the quaint Piedmontese custom of building symbolic New Jerusalems, or Holy Mounts (*Sacro Monte*), a series of chapels containing terracotta statues and frescoes, representing scenes from scripture or a saint's life. The Sacro Monte in **Varallo** is the most splendid and bizarre with its 45 chapels, and there are others almost as good in **Varese** and **Orta**. The region around **Asti** and **Alba** is the land of wine and castles; Asti itself is a fine old town in its own right, and isn't far from the lovely Romanesque abbey in **Albugnano**.

Cuneo is the centre for exploring the Maritime Alps and lovely valleys such as the **Valle Stura**, **Valle Gesso**, and **Valle Vermenagna**. There are small but very pretty resorts at **Frabosa Soprana** and **Garéssio**, and a magnificent set of caves at **Bossea**. The most scenic routes into the mountains are the S20 from Cuneo and the S29 from Alba.

Wines and a Wine Itinerary

Piedmont is one of Italy's finest wine regions, and one of the few where its more celebrated vintages age well (most Italian wines are best drunk very young). Many Piedmontese wines are powerhouses in the alcohol department as well, which may limit how far you get on the local 'wine routes'. The aristocrats of the cellar are grown in the rolling riverside hills around Alba, beginning with the garnet, velvety *Barolo*, one of

Italy's noblest reds with a distinctive wild rose bouquet, produced from Piedmont's exceptional Nebbiolo grapes, given in 1980 the much coveted D.O.C.G. status (guaranteed denomination of controlled origin; in other words it has to pass muster in a wine exam). *Barolo* is aged three years in oak or chestnut barrels before hitting the market; its slightly more delicate Nebbiolo D.O.C.G. cousin *Barbaresco* makes its début in two ('82 and '85 were exceptional years for both).

Other DOC reds from the region are marketed sooner, though most are better with some ageing, like *Nebbiolo d'Alba*, a fine wine that is best after three or four years; the ruby red *Barbera d'Alba*—full-bodied, tart, and 'more palatable' as the Albese primly say, than its rival *Barbera d'Asti*. Dark ruby *Roero*, from the steep left bank of the Tanaro, is a lively, younger, fruity wine. Then there's a confusing bevy of DOC *Dolcetto* reds, all strong, dry, fruity and festive, best drunk a year or so after their *vendemmia* (harvest); among them, perhaps *Dolcetto di Diano d'Alba* stands out for its strength.

Among the paler wines, the most famous is Italy's best known sparkling white, *Asti Spumante*, with its production centre in Mango. Slightly sweet and fruity, Spumante is made through the processing of *moscato* musts in pressurized vats (the Charmat system). *Mocato d'Asti*, sweet and golden and rose-scented, is the most ancient wine of Piedmont, quaffed by the ancient Romans, and still a sentimental favourite, one that evokes for Italians 'dry flowers put in frames...and imitation marble fruit protected by glass bells'.

Other vintages to seek out on wine lists or in the local *enoteca* include *Arneis Roero*, a delightful, delicate, mellow white, the perfect aperitif, or *Gavi*, made from Cortese grapes, both among Italy's finest whites; also the popular ruby-red, raspberry-scented *Freisa*, from the lower Langhe region, which comes either dry, garnet, and slightly acidic, or sparkling and slightly sweet. Tannic *Gattinara* and *Carema* or a well-aged *Lessona* go down pretty easily, too.

Piedmont, with its native wines and access to Alpine herbs, was the birthplace of vermouth, and Turin is still Italy's chief producer. Carpano, the oldest vermouth house (since 1786) bottles the popular bittersweet *Punt e Mes*, while the competition, Martini & Rossi and Cinzano are better known for the classic dry *bianco* and the popular sweet reddish elixir of many an Italian's Happy Hour.

To savour Piedmont's wines properly, the region has developed eight regional cellars (*enotece regionale*) in historic castles and buildings along the 'wine roads' in the provinces of Asti and Cuneo. These cellars are located in **Mango**, in Asti Spumante country; **Barolo**, in the 18th-century castle where the wine was born; **Grinzane**, in the former castle of Camillo Cavour, operated by the 'Knights of the truffle and of the wines of Alba'; **Barbaresco**, in the former church of San Donato; **Roppolo**, in a medieval castle; **Vignale Monferrato**, in the 17th-century Palazzo Callori; **Acqui Terme**, in the ancient cellars of the Palazzo Robellini; and **Castigliole d'Asti**, in the 18th-century castle of the Contessa di Castigliole. Near Turin in **Pessione**, the Martini company operates an interesting wine museum; or, if you're very lucky, you'll be asked to visit one of the *infernotti*—small cellars carved in the tufa to store and enshrine the finest wines; they are especially common around Fubine and Mirabello Monferrato. For more information on Piedmont's wine roads, contact the Regional Tourist Board in Turin at Via Magenta 12, tel (011) 57 171.

TURIN

Detroit without the degradation, the aristocratic capital of the Savoys, an elegantly planned Baroque city of arcades and harmonious squares, frequent venue of international bridge tournaments, the hometown of the famous Shroud, of Juventus, the Red Brigade and vermouth, and reputed centre of black magic in the Mediterranean, Turin (*Torino* in Italian) is the traditional but rather unexpected 'Gateway to Italy'. It stands on the Po, so close to its Alpine sources that this longest and most benighted of Italy's rivers is almost clean. Its cuisine is influenced by France; its winters are colder than Copenhagen's; its most renowned museum is Egyptian. It is also impressively up-to-date: 'Turin stick-in-the-mud?' asks a local brochure. 'Its cars race by; its planes fly over it; it penetrates interstellar space....'

As important Italian cities go, Turin is a relative newcomer. In 1574, a time when the king of Spain held the rest of the peninsula by the bootstrap, feisty 'iron-headed' Emanuele Filiberto of Savoy, descendant of Europe's most ancient ruling house, drove the French and Spanish troops from his territory and moved his capital from Chambéry to Turin, previously little more than a fortified Roman outpost (*Augusta Taurinorum*) and medieval university town. It was a move symbolizing the dynasty's new identity with the Italian portion of Savoy, or Piedmont, a move that was to have the greatest impact on the future. No one at the time suspected that the highly centralized duchy, population 40,000, in the hitherto neglected corner of the peninsula, would one day unite the land, and that Turin would be the first capital of the Kingdom of Italy.

Organization and a deep conservatism were the Savoy secrets—despite the attempts of more liberal leaders, feudalism continued in Piedmont until 1798. The mountain valleys were kept in a tight rein, so that though Turin was the centre of action, the whole region was regarded as one extended city. French remained the chief language until the 19th century, when Count Cavour's peninsular ambitions required that Italian become one of the official languages. Fortunately, Savoy conservatism failed to express itself in the architecture of Turin—even the Baroque wizards of Rome had a hard time matching the city's startling churches and palaces by the audacious 17th–18th century triumvirate of Guarini, Juvarra, and Vittone.

It's a common cliché that the Agnelli family's Fiat Corporation is Turin's new dynasty; founded in 1899, it is not only Europe's largest car manufacturer, but the sixth largest corporation in the entire world. While the historic centre of Turin retains its refined air of a courtly drawing room (no other city in Italy looks anything like it), the glitter and sleekness of the shops are thanks mostly to Fiat money, which is also responsible for the vast suburb of Mirafiori south of Turin, built by the company to house the thousands of workers who have come up from Calabria. Paradoxically, while Turin takes credit for Italy's unification, it has suffered the consequences of that union more acutely, plagued by perhaps the worst relations and bigotry between northern and southern Italians. The latter became Italy's first and most organized proletariat; during World War I, Gramsci, the great philosopher of the Italian Communist party, led the workers' factory councils in occupying the Fiat works in what he hoped would become an Italian Petrograd; the failure taught him that Italians required a different solution, and made him rightly fear that extremism in one form or another would be the end result. Gramsci died in a fascist prison; fifty years after his factory councils experiment the Red Brigade was born in the

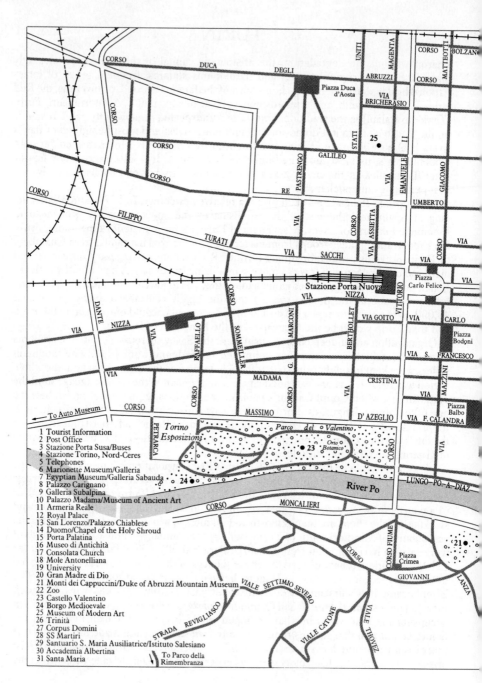

1 Tourist Information
2 Post Office
3 Stazione Porta Susa/Buses
4 Stazione Torino, Nord-Ceres
5 Telephones
6 Marionette Museum/Galleria
7 Egyptian Museum/Galleria Sabauda
8 Palazzo Carignano
9 Galleria Subalpina
10 Palazzo Madama/Museum of Ancient Art
11 Armeria Reale
12 Royal Palace
13 San Lorenzo/Palazzo Chiablese
14 Duomo/Chapel of the Holy Shroud
15 Porta Palatina
16 Museo di Antichità
17 Consolata Church
18 Mole Antonelliana
19 University
20 Gran Madre di Dio
21 Monti dei Cappuccini/Duke of Abruzzi Mountain Museum
22 Zoo
23 Castello Valentino
24 Borgo Medioevale
25 Museum of Modern Art
26 Trinità
27 Corpus Domini
28 SS Martiri
29 Santuario S. Maria Ausiliatrice/Istituto Salesiano
30 Accademia Albertina
31 Santa Maria

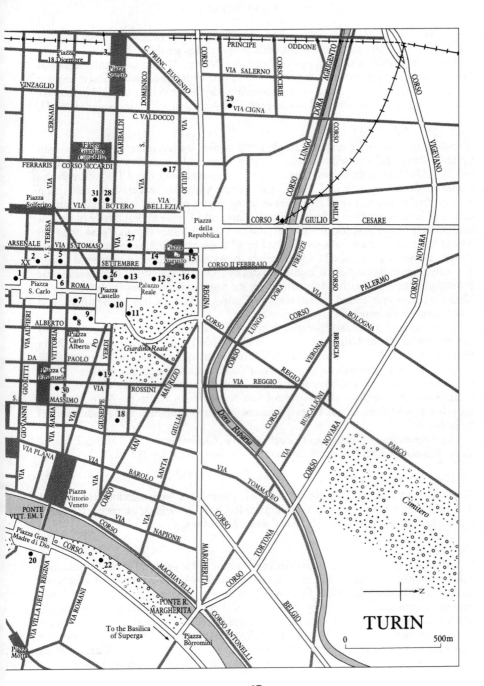

urban anonymity of Mirafiori; their militant sympathizers and radical unionism crippled Fiat in the '70s. Since then prosperity, perhaps more than anything, has exorcized most of Turin's extremist, and even most of its racist, bogeys. With a far-sightedness that American car companies must envy, Fiat made a pact with Japan, mutually agreeing not to export to one another's home markets, which is why 90 per cent of the cars in Italy are made by Fiat, or by Fiat-owned Lancia, or by Fiat-owned Alfa Romeo, bought in 1987.

GETTING AROUND
Turin's massive **Caselle airport**, 15 km north of the city, has direct connections with London, Paris, and Frankfurt as well as flights to major Italian cities. For information call 577 8361. **Airport buses** depart every 45 minutes from the ATIV office at the corner of Corso Siccardi and Via Cernaia. Turin's massive, neoclassical main train station, **Porta Nuova** (tel 517 551), is near the centre of Turin, with connections to Genoa (2 hrs), Milan (1½–2 hrs), Aosta (2½ hrs), and Venice (5 hrs); arrive in time or take in Porta Nuova's nightmarish bar at your own risk. Another station, **Porta Susa** (tel 538 513), at the west end of town, is used by all trains coming into town, while a third station, **Torino Céres** (tel 521 1484), serves the local line to Ciriè, Lanzo, and Céres. The **bus terminal** is on Corso Inghilterra (tel 446 431); though there's also a stop near Porta Susa station; buses head out from here for Aosta's ski resorts as far as Chamonix. There are also year-round connections to Cuneo, Saluzzo, Claviere, Sestriere, and other towns in the province.

Getting around Turin itself is easier than most Italian cities, thanks to a regular grid of streets, served by old-fashioned trams and buses. No 1 links Porta Nuova with Porta Susa; No 4, Porta Nuova station (Via XX Settembre) to the Duomo; No 15 departs from Via XX Settembre, through the centre, down Via Po to the Superga cog tramway. No 16 goes from the Piazza Repubblica down Corso Regina Margherita, Piazza Vittorio Veneto to the Parco di Valentino. Bus 34 from Porta Nuovo heads out to the Auto Museum; suburban bus 41 from Corso Vittorio Emanuele goes to Stupinigi. For a radio taxi, tel 5730 or 5748.

The three major **car hire** firms in Turin are Avis, Corso Turati 15, tel 500 852; Hertz, Corso Marconi 19, tel 650 4504; Maggiore, Via Saorgio 67, tel 212 017.

TOURIST INFORMATION
Main office at Via Roma 222, tel (011) 535 181; also in Porta Nuova station, tel (011) 531 317. Both offices have a free room-finding service. For film listings, concerts, etc., check out the listings in Turin's local/national daily, *La Stampa*.

Via Roma
Central Turin is laid out in a stately rhythm of porticoed streets and jewel-like squares. Like many Roman cities it began as a *castrum*, a chessboard pattern that continued through the Middle Ages. When Emanuele Filiberto made Turin his capital in 1563, this plan was continued and refined by three successive architects; one of their masterpieces was **Via Roma** (1638), lined with the first unified street fronts in Italy. Closing the west end of Via Roma is Porta Nuova; few railway stations deposit the weary traveller anywhere as inviting as Via Roma's first square, the manicured **Piazza Carlo Felice**, where even the traffic intersections are covered with arcades and pots of flowers.

From here, Via Roma leads into the heart of the city, passing through an impressive 'gateway' of twin churches, **Santa Cristina** and **San Carlo**, designed by the Sicilian Baroque genius Filippo Juvarra, court architect to King Vittorio Amedeo II. Behind the churches lies Turin's finest square, **Piazza San Carlo**, a 1638 confection with a flamboyant centrepiece in its bronze **equestrian statue of Duke Emanuele Filiberto** 'the Iron Head,' sheathing his sword after battle, the masterpiece of local sculptor Carlo Marochetti (1838). Turin is a city of ornate elegant cafés, and in Piazza San Carlo you can sip your vermouth in the most celebrated of them all, the 19th-century **Caffè Torino**, a veritable palace of coffee with chandeliers and frescoed ceilings. Just west of the piazza, the **Museo della Marionetta** has fine examples of the peculiarly Italian art of puppet making, from various periods and places (Via S. Teresa 5, open 9–1, weekends 9–1 and 3–6, closed Mon and Aug; adm). The glass-roofed shopping arcade, or **Galleria**, between Santa Teresa and Via Bertola, contains an outstanding Art Deco movie palace, well-named the Lux.

The Egyptian Museum and Galleria Sabauda

These, Turin's most outstanding treasure trove, are just off Piazza San Carlo, sharing the former **Palazzo dell'Accademia delle Scienze**. This monumental bulk, originally designed as a Jesuit college, is the most ponderous and solemn of Turin's landmarks designed by the remarkable Guarino Guarini (1624–83), the Theatine priest and architect who came to work for Carlo Emanuele in 1668 and changed the face of the city.

The **Egyptian Museum** (open 9–2, closed Mon; adm expensive) is rated the second most important in the world, after the museum in Cairo. Begun as a collection of curios in 1628 by Carlo Emanuele I, later Savoys took their pharaohs and mummies rather more seriously, especially Carlo Felice, who acquired the collection of the French Consul General of Egypt and confidant of Mohammed Ali, Bernardo Drovetti (who happened to be from Piedmont), and founded the museum itself in 1824—the first Egyptian museum in the world. Two major Italian expeditions in this century added considerably to the collections, and the museum played a major role in the Aswan Dam rescue digs. It was rewarded with one of the temples it had preserved—the 15th-century BC rock-cut Temple of Ellessya, with a relief of Thothmes III, now reconstructed in the museum.

Other rooms display portions of an immense papyrus library, including several copies of the *Book of the Dead* and the *Royal Papyrus*, listing all the kings of Egypt, from the Sun itself down to the 17th dynasty; Turin's papyrus collection is so extensive that after Jean François Champollion cracked the Rosetta Stone, he came to complete his study of hieroglyphics here. The ground floor houses an excellent collection of monumental public sculpture, notably the black granite Rameses II (13th century BC), the 15th-century BC Thothmes III, and the sarcophagus of a vizier of the 26th Dynasty, Ghemenef-Har-Bak.

Upstairs you can spend hours wandering through the essentials and the trivialities of ancient Egypt: here are artefacts from the Egyptians' daily lives, a reconstruction of the 14th-century BC **Tomb of the architect Khaiè and his wife Meriè** (18th Dynasty) that somehow managed to escape the grave robbers—even the bread and beans prepared for their afterlife remain intact; other rooms contain mummies in various stages of *déshabille*, wooden models of boats and funerary processions, paintings, statuettes, Canopic vases, jewellery, clothing and textiles.

On the top floor, the **Galleria Sabauda** houses the principal collections of the House of Savoy (open 9–2, closed Mon; adm). The Savoys liked Flemish and Dutch art just as much as Italian, giving the Sabauda a variety most Italian galleries lack. Among the Italians are two fine Florentine works, *Tobias and the Archangel Raphael* by Antonio and Piero Pollaiuolo and a fine study of Botticelli's newborn *Venus*, thought to be by one of his students; other works are by Mantegna, Taddeo Gaddi, Sodoma, Tintoretto, Titian, Veronese, and Bergognone. Among the Northerners are Jan van Eyck's *St Francis*, Memling's drama-filled *Scenes from the Passion*, Van Dyck's beautiful *Children of Charles I*, popular scenes and landscapes by Jan Brueghel, *Portrait of a Doctor* by Jacobs Dirk, and Rembrandt's *Old Man Sleeping*. The French have a room to themselves, with works by Poussin, Claude, and Clouet.

Opposite the museum, the undulating brick façade and ornate rotunda of the **Palazzo Carignano** is much more representative of Guarini's work, begun in 1679 for the Savoy-Carignano branch of the royal family—the branch that was to produce Italy's first king, Vittorio Emanuele II, who, as the inscription on top states, was born here. The palace served as the Piedmontese Subalpine Parliament, and later as the first Italian Parliament, which met here on 14 March 1861 to proclaim Vittorio Emanuele King of Italy. The Chamber now forms part of the **Museo Nazionale del Risorgimento**, one of the most interesting of Italy's scores of Risorgimento museums (open 9 am–7 pm, Sun 9–1, closed Mon and holidays; adm, free Sun).

Just south of Palazzo Carignano, on Via Accademia delle Scienze, is an early work by Juvarra, the 1715 **San Filippo Neri**, an ample, spacious church that can trace the origins of its form back to the monumental baths of Rome; Juvarra, altogether an Italian architect's architect, was a master at adapting the designs of the past to the needs of the present.

Palazzo Madama

Parallel to the Via Accademia, the **Galleria Subalpina** (just right, off Via Battisti) is Turin's other shopping arcade, inspired by the Galleria Vittorio Emanuele in Milan. The Galleria Subalpina leads to an elegant coffeehouse, the Caffè Baratti & Milano, and the huge expanse of the **Piazza Castello**, the principal square of Turin, with the **Palazzo Madama** in the middle. Named after the two royal widows ('Madama Reale') who lived here, the palace dates back to the 15th century, though it incorporates in its structure fragments from the eastern Roman gate, the Porta Decumana, as well as the original 13th-century castle. In 1718 one of the Madamas had Juvarra give the old place a facelift—a task Juvarra responded to with an elegant, articulated façade that departed from the typical Baroque of his period with its whispers of Versailles. Juvarra accented the main floor, or *piano nobile*, with a bold array of columns, enormous windows, and a grand staircase that occupies the entire width of the palace. The interior now houses the **Museo Civico di Arte Antica** (at the time of writing closed for restoration, but scheduled to re-open late 1992, with a notable collection of medieval and Renaissance sculpture, stained glass, the illuminated 14th-century law codes of the city of Turin, copies of the famous *Book of Hours* of the Duc de Berry illustrated by Jan van Eyck (you may have to ask the guard to see them); in the Grand Hall pride of place goes to Antonello da Messina's *Portrait of an Unknown Man* (1476), one of his last works. Although scholars now pooh-pooh the legend of Antonello introducing the Flemish technique of oil painting to the Italians, no artist ever combined Northern light with Italian form and volume as well as he—exemplified in this self-possessed gentleman with a very Italian expression on his face. There are books of drawings by Antonello's fellow Sicilian Juvarra, a *St Michael* by the bizarre Florentine Mannerist Pontormo, works by Defendente Ferrari, an anonymous *Holy Trinity*, and more; the second floor has a unique collection of *verre églomisé* (painted glass), dating back to the 15th century.

Under the arcade lining the north side of Piazza Castello, the **Armeria Reale** (open Tues & Thurs, 2:30–7:30, Wed, Fri & Sat 9–2, closed Sun & Mon; adm) contains one of the finest medieval and Renaissance collections of arms, suits of armour, and guns in the world: collections owned and worn by the Savoys, an extraordinary pig-face mask from the 14th century, a sword signed by Donatello, but believed to be a clever forgery, and a magnificent shield from the court of Henri II. The library upstairs contains a famous self-portrait in red ink by Leonardo da Vinci, who looks for all the world like an old magician weary of his own magic.

The Royal Palace and San Lorenzo

The dark apricot **Palazzo Reale** lies just off the Piazza Castello, behind a gate of mounted 'Dioscuri' and Turin's largest parking lot, which doesn't do much for its already bureaucratic façade. This, however, was the main residence of the princes of Savoy from 1646 until 1865, and you can take the tour to learn that they lavished a considerable amount of their subjects' taxes on a tired architectural lullaby with chandeliers and fluffy frescoes. The cases of Chinese porcelain are one of the few highlights (open 9–2 and 3–6 in summer, closed Mon; adm). The Palace's **Giardino Reale** is a far more pleasant place to while away an afternoon, with the Mole Antonelliana (see below) rising above the trees like the headquarters of Ming the Merciless.

The former royal chapel, **San Lorenzo**, stands on the corner of the Piazza Castello. Although bland from the outside, with an unusual octagonal dome as its only distinguishing feature, the interior by Guarini (1668–80) is an idiosyncratic Baroque fantasia, whose geometric complexity and two star-crossed diaphanous domes require some serious contemplation to unravel. Between the Palazzo Reale and San Lorenzo, the **Museo Nazionale del Cinema** is housed in the Palazzo Chiablese, commemorating Turin's role in the early days of Italian cinema, with early projectors, posters, and much more, and screenings in the winter and spring in a replica of an early theatre (but closed indefinitely for 'works').

The Cathedral and the Holy Shroud

Around the corner is Turin's plain **Cathedral of San Giovanni** built by three dry 15th-century Tuscan architects. What it lacks in presence it compensates for with one of the most controversial artefacts of Christendom: the *Shroud of Turin*, brought to the city from the old Savoy capital of Chambéry in the 16th century by Emanuele Filiberto. Although the duke originally intended to build a new church for the relic, his successors settled for a chapel as large as a church, the **Cappella della Sacra Sindone**, built by Guarini 1667–90 (closed until further notice for restoration). This is Guarini's masterpiece, though the lower half—up to the lower tiers of the entablature, were begun by another architect, Amedeo di Castellamonte. On this uneventful base Guarini wove a bold diaphanous cone, where a series of dissonant patterns and forms reaches its climax, zigzagging ever upwards in a basket-weave of arches that suggest the infinite in geometry; above Castellamonte's entablature the normal is purposefully contorted and full of restless energy, jarring the beholder with the unexpected in a burst of wild Baroque Mannerism.

The Shroud, shown only on special occasions, is kept in a silver casket in an iron box in a marble coffer in the urn on the chapel altar; an exact replica, however, is displayed along with a multilingual explanation of the results of several scientific investigations, which tried to determine whether it was possible that the Shroud was used at Christ's burial. Although forensic scientists and their computers concluded that it would have been impossible to forge the unique front and back impressions of a crucified man with a wound in his side and bruises from a crown of thorns, the Shroud failed a carbon-dating test in 1989, and is now believed to date from the 12th century.

The cathedral also contains a fine polyptych of *SS. Crispin and Crispinian* by Defendente Ferrari (in the second chapel), and a copy of Leonardo da Vinci's *Last Supper*, painted when the original began to crumble. Near the cathedral's campanile are the remains of a Roman theatre, while across the piazza stands the impressive Roman gate, the **Porta Palatina**, with its two unusual 16-sided towers. On Saturdays the circular **Piazza della Repubblica** is the site of the 'Balôn' antique and flea market.

Via Giuseppe Garibaldi

The main street heading west from Piazza Castello, Via Giuseppe Garibaldi, passes into another 17th–18th-century neighbourhood. A left turn on Via Botero will lead you shortly to Bernardo Vittone's **S. Maria di Piazza** (1751), one of this architect's few works in the capital, notable for his revival of the medieval squinch to support the dome, creating, like Guarini, an unorthodox geometric play between the circle, square, and octagon. Heading west again on Via Giuseppe Garibaldi, the fifth street on the right, Via Bligny, will take you to Via del Carmine and the **Carmine** church (1732), both street and church designed by Juvarra. The Carmine is one of Juvarra's most innovative churches, its majestic interior of arches, galleries, and windows a unique meld of Northern European architecture with Italian. The chapels along the nave are dramatically illuminated with light pouring in from the gallery windows—a variation on Bernini's famous altars in Rome.

Take Via Bligny down to Via S. Chiara, and turn right for Via della Consolata and the **Consolata Church**. The Consolata is a regular ecclesiastical hotchpotch, with a Roman tower adjacent to its apse, an 11th-century campanile inherited from the demolished church of Sant' Andrea, and two churches, a hexagon and an oval, knitted together by Guarini. Via della Consolata ends in Corso Regina Margherita, where you can see more of ancient Augusta Taurinorum in a fine museum of artefacts, the **Museo di Antichità** at No. 105 (reopening soon after restoration).

The Mole Antonelliana

Turin's towering, idiosyncratic landmark, the **Mole Antonelliana** (or 'Antonelli's massive bulk') is on Via Montebello but can be seen from most corners of the city. Begun in 1863 by the idiosyncratic Piedmontese architect-engineer Alessandro Antonelli, the Mole was intended originally as a synagogue. The project ran out of steam until 1897, when the city completed it, and declared it a monument to Italian Unity; nowadays it serves mainly as an exhibition hall.

Standing some 167 m high, the Mole is a considerable engineering feat. Stylistically, it is harmoniously bizarre—a vaguely Greek temple façade, stacked with a colonnade, a row of windows, a majestic, sloping glass pyramid, a double-decker Greek temple, and a pinnacle crowned with a star, which the city illuminates at night. The Mole has been a lightning rod of madness—Nietzsche thought it was marvellous then permanently went over the edge. If it's open, you can take the lift up to the observation terrace (86 m up) for a fine view of Turin and the Alps beyond.

The lively, arcaded **Via Po**, two blocks from the Mole, is the main funnel from the centre down to the river; it is also the main artery of the city's student life. Although founded in the 14th century, Turin University never gained the prestige of the schools in Padua, Bologna, Naples, Salerno, or Pavia. Its headquarters since 1720, the **Palazzo Università**, lies a block down from Piazza Castello on Via Po; in its courtyard there's a plaque to Erasmus, the most renowned of its alumni. Further down Via Po, turn right on Via Albertina for the **Accademia Albertina**, with a small but interesting collection of drawings by Gaudenzio Ferrari and other members of the Piedmontese school (open weekday mornings).

Via Po widens out to form the long and bewildering **Piazza Vittorio Veneto**, half street and half parking lot, giving onto a bridge over the Po. Across the river, in a commanding setting, stands an imitation Pantheon, the **Gran Madre di Dio** church, while on the wooded hill to the right, on the **Monte dei Cappuccini**, stands the Capuchin church and the **Museo Nazionale della Montagna Duca degli Abruzzi** (Sat–Mon 9–12:30 and 2:45–7:15, Tues–Fri 8:30–7:15; adm), dedicated to Italy's mountains, and their geography and folk customs. If you've brought the children, they may prefer the small zoo in the Parco Ignazio Michelotti (open 8:30–5:30; adm).

Parco del Valentino

On the other bank of the Po stretches Turin's largest park, the Parco del Valentino, named after the 1660 **Castello del Valentino**, built by Madama Reale Maria Cristina, who felt her royal dignity required a French château. This lost château now does time as the university's School of Architecture, with the city's **Botanical Garden** laid out behind, but it isn't the only castle on the block; Turin built another one, along with a mock medieval hamlet, **Castello e Borgo Medievale**, as part of the 1884 Exhibition. The houses are modelled on various types found in Piedmont, while the castle is furnished with baronial fittings (castle open 9–6, Sun 10:30–6, closed Mon and holidays; adm, free Fri; village open 8–8 daily, adm free). A place near the castle hires out bicycles by the day, while along the riverbank you can rent a rowing boat for a fish-eye view of Turin. At the end of Parco del Valentino are the massive buildings of the Turin Exhibition (Torino Exposizioni), where it holds its famous springtime Auto Show in even-numbered years.

Motor Museum

Three km south of the Parco Valentino, at Corso Unità d'Italia 40, is the modern **Museo dell'Automobile Carlo Biscaretti di Ruffia** (bus 34 from Porta Nuova; open 10–6:30, closed Mon; adm). Founded in 1933, its present quarters are a vintage 1960s elephantine exhibition hall; highlights of the collection include the classics of the grand age of Italian car design—Lancias, Bugattis, Maseratis, Alfa Romeos, Italicas, and of course Fiats—as well as some oddities like the asymmetrical 1948 Tarf 1. Further along the Corso d'Italia is another huge exhibition hall, the **Palazzo del Lavoro**, built in 1961 by Pier Luigi Nervi.

Another museum, the **Galleria d'Arte Moderna**, is in a different corner of the city, off Corso Vittorio Emanuele west of the Porta Nuova Station, on Via Magenta. It has one of Italy's best collections of modern art, with works by Klee, Chagall, Modigliani, Renoir, Picasso and more, but like so many of Turin's museums, it's closed for indefinite restoration.

Basilica di Superga

East along the Po, on the metropolitan fringe, a rack railway will take you up to the grand Baroque **Basilica di Superga** (first train at 6 am, last at 8:10 pm). Built on top of a commanding 672 m hill, the delightful trip through the greenwood culminates in Juvarra's acknowledged masterpiece, built to fulfil a vow made by Vittorio Amedeo II during the French siege of Superga. Although there is little particularly innovative in its design, it is one of the most striking Baroque churches in Italy, not only for its simple proportions, but for its location, overlooking Turin and the snow-clad Alps. Juvarra began with the traditional central plan of a mountaintop sanctuary, and added a drum and dome the same size as the body of the church, a design that owes much to (and improves on) Michelangelo's St Peter's in Rome. The blue and yellow interior looks ahead to the 18th century; the crypt contains the tombs of Vittorio Amedeo II and subsequent Kings of Sardinia. Behind the church stretch the long monastic buildings, an effective part of the composition.

Another fine viewpoint, above the elegant, villa-clad hills east of Turin, the **Colle della Maddalena** (770 m) is also the site of the mile-and-a-half-long **Parco della Rimembranza**, a memorial to Turin's World War I dead, planted with some 10 000 trees and crowned by a **Victory** with her torch (1928), the largest cast-bronze statue in the world, nearly 18 m tall.

Pessione, 19 km east of Turin, has Italy's best wine museum, the **Museo Martini di Storia dell'Enologia**, where the history of wine-making is vividly recounted and some of the end products are available for sale (open Tue–Fri 2–5, Sat and Sun 9–12 and 2–5).

Stupinigi

Nine kilometres southeast of Turin, past the dreary suburbs of Mirafiori and the Fiat works, there is a little church holding the relics of St Hubert, patron of the hunt. The trigger-happy king of Savoy, Vittorio Amedeo II, saw his chance to get some good juju for his favourite sport and had the unstoppable Juvarra build a suitable hunting lodge nearby in Stupinigi, on land belonging to the royal Mauritian Order. The stupendous result was the 1730 **Palazzina Mauriziana di Caccia**, a unique star-shaped Rococo palace, surely the most beautiful hunting lodge ever built—a statue of a stag perched on the top, statues and frescoes of the hunt by Carle Van Loo, and *trompe l'oeil* scenes of hanging game try hard to remind you that this is not Cinderella's fairy palace, even though the main oval salon, hung with glittering chandeliers, perfectly fits the bill, and in fact was used for royal wedding receptions. Ownership of the palace and its park has reverted to the Mauritians, who run Stupinigi as a furniture museum (open 9:30–5, holidays 10–1 and 2–5; closed Mon; adm).

ACTIVITIES

There's always something to do in Turin. In season you can take in a match played by one of Italy's premier first-division football clubs, Juventus or Torino, both of whom play in Turin Stadium. Turin's opera house, **Teatro Regio**, in Piazza Castello, was rebuilt after a fire in the '70s and is one of the few modern ones in Italy. From late autumn to late spring it stages ballet and symphony concerts as well as opera; call 839 7956 to see what's coming up. The grand old **Teatro Carignano**, Piazza Carignano, is used for dramatic performances. Tours of the Fiat works are possible; inquire at the company's office on Corso G. Marconi 10. In the summer the city's finest outdoor swimming hole is the Lido di Torino, in pools overlooking the Po at Via Villa Gloria 21 (on the right bank, between Parco del Valentino and the Auto Museum). In July and August the city sponsors **I Punti Verdi**, a festival of plays, ballets, and concerts, performed in the parks by international companies. In September, the **Settembre Musica** is entirely devoted to classical music, featuring two concerts a day in the city's theatres and churches. Look for posters or check the listings in *La Stampa*. St John's Day (24 June) is Turin's big folklore festival. If you'd like to know the future, Turin's sedate fortune-tellers and sorcerers run their operations around Porta Pila.

Turin is a good shopping city, with the smartest shops around Via Roma and Piazza Castello. There are a number of local designers of note who have resisted the move to Milan, perhaps most prominently Borbonese, who does stylish costume jewellery and 'partridge eye' leather. Another good buy in Turin are fine chocolates, *Gianduiotti*, named for Gianduia, a comic figure associated with St John's Day. Art books and books in English are available at the **Libreria Luxemburg**, Via Cesare Battisti 7, near Piazza Carignano. For bargains, don't miss the Saturday morning 'Balôn' flea market in Piazza della Repubblica.

WHERE TO STAY   (tel prefix 011)

Turin's hotels tend to be modern, expensive, and designed for business clients, with little in the way of atmosphere. Nearly all are within easy walking distance of Porta Nuova Station.

For comfort and convenience, Turin's top choice is the old traditional grand hotel, the *******Turin Palace Hotel**, across from the Porta Nuova station at Via Sacchi 8, tel 515 511, it has spacious, soundproof rooms that sit guests gently in the lap of luxury, as well as opulent lobbies, sitting rooms, and an excellent restaurant (L310 000). The ******Jolly Hotel Principi di Piemonte**, Via P. Gobetti 15, tel 532 153, is one of the most elegant hotels in the Jolly chain, with beautiful antique public rooms and luxurious bedrooms fitted out with every convenience an auto magnate could wish for, from a well-stocked frigo bar, cable TV, and direct dial phone; L300 000. If you have a car, the ******Villa Sassi**, located in the hills east of the Po, in a lovely park (Via Traforo del Pino 47, tel 890 556) is the most evocative hotel in the city, with 12 rooms converted into a hotel from a 17th-century patrician villa. In its conversion it has maintained most of its original features—marble floors, fireplaces, and portraits. Baroque and other antique fittings adorn each individually designed room. The Villa has one of Turin's finest restaurants, El Toulà, featuring garden fresh ingredients from the estate, and a renowned wine cellar containing over 90,000 bottles. Minimum stay is three days, and the hotel and restaurant are closed Aug (L310 000, meals around L85 000).

Among the more moderate offerings, the ***Victoria, Via Nino Costa 4, tel 553 710 is one of Turin's most pleasant downtown hotels, with tranquil and simply decorated rooms, all with private bath. It has a little garden, but no restaurant; L110 000 with breakfast. Another good choice near Porta Nuova Station, the stylish ***Stazione & Genova, Via Sacchi 14, tel 545 323, has excellent, recently renovated rooms, all furnished with TVs, and private baths, L115 000. Nearby, the old **Hotel Piemontese, Via Berthollet 21, tel 669 8101 is another good, moderate choice, refurbished and comfortable. **Campo di Marte, a block from Porta Nuova Station at Via XX Settembre 7, tel 530 650, is a fairly large hotel, convenient and respectable if not especially charming (L95 000 with bath, L65 000 without). Among the cheap (and cheap places—mostly seedy dives—are plentiful in Turin, in the streets flanking Porta Nuova) the Scoiattolo is a reasonably priced spot on Viale XXV Aprile, no. 166, and has clean rooms for L50 000, tel 670 472. There's also a youth hostel, on the other side of the river: the Ostello Torino, Via Alby 1, tel 660 2939 has very pleasant, renovated rooms near the Piazza Crimea (bus 52 from the station). L15 000 a head, bed and breakfast, closed between 9 am and 6 pm.

EATING OUT (tel prefix 011)

The kitchens of Piedmont are famous for their flavoursome and sophisticated specialities, combining the best of Northern Italian cuisine with the traditions of Provence. *Grissini* (breadsticks) were invented in Turin and so charmed Napoleon that he introduced them over the border. White truffles are a local obsession, and are often served grated in a *fonduta* (with melted *fontina* cheese from the Valle d'Aosta). The wintertime speciality, *bagna cauda*, a rich hot dip made with butter, olive oil, a white truffle, garlic, anchovies, and cream, is often served with *cardi*, raw artichoke-like thistle, or roasted meats. *Bolliti misti* (mixed boiled meats) and *fricando* (Piedmontese stew) are other popular *secondi*, while the classic first course is *agnolotti*, pasta squares similar to ravioli, stuffed with meat or cheese. The pastries are among the best in Italy—the *Bocca di Leone* is a sinfully rich calorific heavyweight, *torta di nocciole*, a divine hazelnut torte.

Turin's temple of fine cuisine,the Vecchia Lanterna, Corso Re Umberto 21, tel 537 047, is a subdued and classy turn-of-the-century restaurant. The food is an artistic achievement—gourmet delights like quail pâté, ravioli filled with duck, covered with truffle sauce, shellfish salad, a wide variety of stuffed trout, sea bass in the old Venetian style, and much more, accompanied by a perfect wine list. Be sure to reserve (L80–100 000, *menu degustazione* L60 000; closed Sat afternoon, Sun, and often in mid-Aug).

Turin's oldest restaurant, Del Cambio (since 1757), at Piazza Carignano 2, tel 546 690, offers a rare nostalgic trip back to the old capital of Italy, where the menu invites you every Friday 'to eat like a king', with dishes that were served by the Savoys to their guests. The décor, the chandeliers, gilt mirrors, frescoes and cream-coloured walls, red upholstery, and even the costume of the waiters, have all been carefully preserved—Prime Minister Cavour's favourite corner, where he could keep an eye on the Palazza

Carignano (if he were urgently needed a handkerchief would be waved from the window) is immortalized by a medallion. The old recipes have been lightened to appeal to modern tastes. Antipasto choices include *cardi in bagna cauda*; other specialities are *agnolotti*, trout with almonds, boar, beef braised in Barolo, and *finanziera*, Cavour's favourite dish (made of veal, sweetbreads, cocks' combs, *porcini* mushrooms, cooked in butter and wine). Top it off with a slice of homemade *tarte Tatin*, all for a kingly bill—L90–110 000; closed Sun and Aug. Less regal, but charming, the **Due Lampioni**, Via Carlo Alberto 45, tel 839 7409, serves a delightful array of antipasti, many featuring salmon, scampi, and lobster. In the spring try the *gnocchi all'asparagi*, and in autumn the *porcini* mushrooms, followed by rack of lamb or tournedos with *foie gras*. Closed Sun and Aug, L65–75 000.

Yet another excellent restaurant in the same considerable price range is '**L Caval 'd Brons** (The Bronze Horse), Piazza San Carlo 157, tel 553 491, in Turin's finest square, one of its finest restaurants, located up the wrought iron stair. Try the pasta with seafood, followed by duck's breast with sesame seeds, and wild strawberry soufflé (daily *menu degustazione* for L90 000; this is also one of the few restaurants in Italy to offer a gourmet vegetarian menu (L65 000). **Montecarlo**, in central Turin at Via San Francesco da Paola 37, tel 830 815, is one of Turin's most romantic restaurants, located in the atrium of the *palazzo* of the notoriously well-loved Contessa di Castiglione. Under the stone arches a delectable variety of antipasti (marinated swordfish, a flan of peas and scampi, and great pâté) may be followed by carrot soup with barley or homemade gnocchi and well prepared *secondi* like baked liver, lamb, or duck. The desserts are excellent, as is the wine list; closed Sat afternoon, Sun and Aug; L45–55 000.

There are many less expensive choices. **Alberoni**, Corso Mancalieri 288, tel 69 63 255, is on the periphery of Turin, but compensates by having a pretty terrace over the Po, where you can dine out in the summer on Turin's most die-hard traditional dishes from *bagna cauda* for starters to *panna cotta* for dessert, accompanied by garden-fresh vegetables; closed Tues; L40 000. **Arcadia**, Galleria Subalpina 16, tel 53 20 29, is a popular lunchtime spot right in the centre, with excellent antipasti, pasta and country style meat dishes; L35 000, closed Mon.

Big Cheeses, little cheeses, and their admirers in Turin meet at the **Trattoria della Posta**, Strada Mongreno 16, tel 890 193, near the foot of Superga hill. An array of hot antipasti made with cheese paves the way for cheese soufflé, followed by a vast choice of Piedmontese cheeses, both well known and obscure (L45 000). **Da Giuseppe**, Via San Massimo 34, tel 812 2090 or 889 617 offers a wide array of Piedmontese antipasti and specialities very popular with local diners; you'd do well to reserve (closed Mon and Aug, L45 000 with wine). **La Capannina**, Via Donati 1, tel 545 405, is a pleasant, old Piedmontese style trattoria, with slightly more elaborate specialities, many with truffles or mushrooms, a delicious *risotto al Barolo*, and game dishes (chamois one of the more exotic choices). Closed Sun and Aug, L35 000 with wine. **Il Blu**, Corso Siccardi 15b (a few blocks from La Consolata church) tel 545 550, stars enormous, delicious salads and excellent pasta dishes, followed by good grilled meats if you still have room (closed Sun and Aug; L20–30 000). A popular choice in the centre, **Trattoria Toscana**, Via Varazze 5, tel 696 4396 offers good food and plenty of it for L20–30 000 (closed Fri night and Sat). For a light meal under the arcades of Piazza Carlo Felice, across from the Porta Nuova Station, join the crowd at the **Ristorante Brek** (No. 18), tel 534 556, a trendy self-service with islands of salads, soups, fresh breads, etc.; L10 000 should fill you up.

West of Turin: the Susa Valleys

Some of the most spectacular and accessible scenery in Piedmont lies in the Upper Valleys of Susa. Trains from Turin go through the Valle di Susa to the French border at the Mont Cenis Tunnel, while coaches from Turin serve Pinerolo, Sestriere, and Claviere. Skiing is the main attraction in the winter, and the resorts are especially popular among the French, who find the prices considerably more congenial than those on the other side of the Alps. If you come in the summer, be sure to pick up the map of mountain excursions and list of alpine refuges distributed by the tourist offices. Old villages and churches are a constant reminder that this corner of Italy sat out the Renaissance; whereas Baroque dominates in Turin, Romanesque monuments grace the Valle di Susa.

TOURIST INFORMATION
Avigliana: Corso Laghi 240, int A, tel (011) 938 650
Bardonécchia: Viale della Vittoria 44, tel (0122) 99 032
Claviere: Via Nazionale 30, tel (0122) 878 856
Sauze d'Oulx: Piazza Assietta, tel (0122) 85 009
Oulx: Piazza Garambois 5, tel (0122) 831 596 or 831 786
Sestriere: Piazza G. Agnelli 11, tel (0122) 76 045

Turin to Susa

Rivoli, the first large town west of Turin (take bus 36 from Turin's Corso Francia 6) was once the favoured residence of the Savoys, and preserves their **Castello di Rivoli**, built in the 12th century and half remodelled by Juvarra in 1718. In 1984 the castle was restored and converted into a **Museum of Contemporary Art** (open Tues–Sun 10–7; adm expensive), where three floors of art from the '60s to the present—some works created specially for the setting—compete for your attention with the original Baroque frills or the bare bricks that the Savoys never got around to dolling up.

Five kilometres further west in **Buttigliera Alta** is the 12th-century **Abbey of Sant'Antonio di Ranverso**. The unique façade of the church, dominated by three high pitched gables over the three doors, is from the quattrocento; inside (open 9–12 and 3–6, closed Fri and Mon) charming frescoes from the same period by Giacomo Jaquerio adorn the walls, and the altar has a polyptych by Defendente Ferrari (1531). Outside are the remains of a medieval pilgrims' hostel.

Avigliana, the next town, is a Romanesque gem, poised on a low hill near two little lakes, Grande and Piccolo, which from the air look like a giant pair of Italian reflecting sun-glasses. Back on the ground, though, Avigliana has a fine collection of medieval buildings clustered around its two picturesque squares, **Piazza Conde Rosso** and **Piazza Santa Maria**, including the Romanesque churches of **San Giovanni** (with paintings by Defendente Ferrari) and **San Pietro** (with 16th-century French frescoes). Overlooking Avigliana is a ruined **Savoy castle**, erected in 942 by the Count of Turin against the Saracen threat over the Alps, and you can explore the town's own walls from the fine 14th-century **Casa della Porta Ferrata**. Economic decline in later centuries came to a sudden end thanks to dynamite—Alfred Nobel built one of his first factories in town.

From Avigliana it's 14 km up to the most provocative abbey in Piedmont, the **Sacra di San Michele**, a massive block of stone which seems to grow right out of a 960 m ridge of wild and rugged Monte Pirchiriano, overlooking the Dora Riparia valley and the Alps beyond. You can drive up to the parking lot, or pretend you're a monk or pilgrim and make the stout but beautifully scenic, 2-hour trek up by mule path (from Sant'Ambrogio di Torino on the main valley road).

If Cinecittà ever gets around to filming the Son of *The Name of the Rose*, Sacra di S. Michele would make a perfect setting. Founded around the year 1000, the abbey, like all mountaintop shrines dedicated to the Archangel Michael, is a strange place, full of mysterious, half-pagan nuances, a temple dedicated to God's celestial aide-de-camp, built like a seal over an ancient dragon lair. Similar churches are thought to have had roles in medieval initiation rites, and it's significant that the Sacra di San Michele is located just off one of the main pilgrimage routes to Rome—the pilgrimage itself being an important rite of passage of the faith. The Sacra di San Michele, piled on a complicated mass of 27-m substructures, is reached by the covered *Scalone dei Morti*, the 154-step 'Stair of the Dead' hewn out of the rock, and under the *Porta dello Zodiaco*, the Romanesque carvings of the zodiac. The ceiling of the mostly 12th-century church (open daily 9–12 and 2–5, 3–7 in the summer) is supported by a massive, 18-metre stone pillar; in the crypt are buried the early dukes and princes of the House of Savoy-Carignano. The abbey was suppressed in 1622, though since then a few brothers have returned to keep the place up and enjoy the fantastic views over the valley and mountains from its terraces.

Between Avigliana and Susa the main attractions were wrought by Mother Nature: the **Chiusa San Michele**, the narrowest point in the valley; and two narrow gorges, the **Orrido di Chianocco**, near Condove, and the **Orrido di Foresto**, just west of Bussoleno.

Susa

Further up the valley, under the mighty mass of Rocciamelone (3538 m) lies the fine old town of Susa (Roman *Segusio*). Susa may sound Persian, but actually was the seat of the Gaulish chieftain Cottius. He was the kind of fraternizing Gaul that Asterix and Obelix would have liked to slap around with a menhir, one who so admired the Romans and Augustus that he erected the fine 14-metre high **Arco d'Augusto** in the emperor's honour. Augustus returned the compliment by making Cottius a prefect, and naming the Cottian Alps for him. Other remains of ancient Segusio lie above the Arco d'Augusto, including baths, an amphitheatre, and part of an aqueduct. The 11th-century **castle of Countess Adelaide** (the one who gave her hand to Otho of Savoy in 1045) dominates the medieval Piazza della Torre; within you can visit the little **Museo Civico's** small archaeological collection (open April–Sept 3:30–5:30, closed Mon; in the winter Thurs and Sun only, 2:30–4:30).

The centre of medieval Susa is overlooked by the massive tower of the **Cathedral of San Giusto** (1029) and the many-windowed **Porta Romana**, built in the 5th century but often known as the Porta di Savoia. The cathedral contains the prized *Triptych of Rocciamelone*, a Flemish brass portraying the Virgin, saints, and donor, made in 1358; another chapel houses a polyptych by Bergognone. The cathedral's rare 10th-century

Baptismal font, carved in serpentine, was brought here from **S. Maria Maggiore**, a sturdy Romanesque structure with a good campanile, off Via Palazzo del Città. Just to the south of the city walls, stands the 1244 Italian Gothic **Convento di S. Francesco**, founded by Bianca di Savoy, with a romantic miniscule cloister. From here, Via S. Francesco leads round to **Borgo dei Nobili**, a little quarter of 12th- and 13th-century houses used by the Savoyard court when in town.

From Susa the Mont Cenis road (N. 25) leads north to **Giaglione**, a tranquil hamlet spread out under the mountains; its **Chapel of Santo Stefano** has unusual 15th-century exterior frescoes of the Virtues and Seven Deadly Sins. On 22 January the village celebrates its patron's feast day with a 'Dance of the Swordmakers.' Another ancient village visited from Susa, **Novalesa**, has a Romanesque Benedictine abbey founded in the 8th century, still inhabited by monks devoted to the restoration of ancient texts; of the abbey's chapels, one, **Sant'Eldrado**, is still in use and contains good 13th-century frescoes, while others show a definite Byzantine influence. South from Susa, a magnificent by-road loops like spaghetti through mountainous **Orsiera-Rocciavrè Natural Park** on its way to Fenestrelle in the Valle del Chisone.

The Upper Valley

From Susa the road ascends steeply, past the ancient villages of **Gravere** and **Chiomonte**, the latter also the first of the valley's important ski resorts, a wine town, and site of the **Pinacoteca G.A. Levis and Museo Archeologico**, housed in a stately palace of 1619; inside are 450 canvases by (who else?) G.A. Levis (1873–1926), a favourite of Czar Nicholas, while the archaeological section is devoted to finds from a single site called La Maddalena, a backwater of history inhabited without interruption for the past 6000 years. The nearby hamlet **Ramats** produces a good local wine. **Exilles**, further on, lies under the tremendous 12th-century **Forte di Exilles**, that long dominated the valley; illuminated at night it seems to spill over the hill like molten gold. Exilles also has a fine 11th-century parish church.

Oulx, Sauze d'Oulx, and Bardonécchia, at the crossroads of several valleys, near the Mont Cenis Tunnel, are fashionable winter sport centres in what the Italians like to call the Via Lattea, or 'Milky Way.' **Oulx**, ancient capital of the Upper Valley, has taken some hard knocks in the past—a Saracen raid in the 900s, and a series of plagues that continued to devastate the city in spite of the 'perfumers' who burnt juniper wood in the streets night and day against the evil; among its 16th-century buildings and fountains, the impressively medieval stone and wood **Palazzo Galli**, in the old centre, stands out as one of the last examples of the valley's traditional architecture. **Sauze d'Oulx**, the 'Balcony of the Alps' and its plateau **Sportinia**, surrounded by a fine natural amphitheatre, are especially popular with Italian and foreign package tours—though in its *frazione* (hamlet) **Jouvenceaux** you can see some fine examples of the old stone and wood architecture of the region. Just north of Sauze d'Oulx, the **Gran Bosco di Salbertrand**, a large fir and rhododendron forest, has been set up as a natural park, where any kind of motorized vehicle is strictly prohibited.

Bardonécchia, a pretty village of old stone houses known as *grangia*, is an even more developed resort, with summer skiing on the Sommeiller glaciers (3000 m), skating, indoor tennis, riding, hiking and boating in addition to downhill and cross-country skiing.

Bardonécchia has four separate ski areas with their own lifts; one area, Fregiusia-Jafferau is for experts only. The best views in the neighbourhood are from **Monte Colomion** (2026 m), reached by a chair lift; for rock climbers, the biggest thrills await in the remarkable **Valle Stretta**, partly closed in by vertical rock walls. The local wood-carving craft prospers, especially in the form of painted panels of fruit and flower cornucopias called *grappoli*; in Bardonécchia's parish church the choir is by the modern woodcarvers' 15th-century predecessors.

The **Mont Cenis Pass** was a favoured French route into Italy, used by conquerors from Hannibal and his elephants (one of several possible routes proposed by scholars) to Charlemagne and Napoleon, who began the carriage road in 1808. The **Mont Cenis tunnel**, or Traforo del Fréjus, at 12.8 km, is the second longest road tunnel in Europe, opened in 1980, though the rail tunnel was finished back in 1871, just after the completion of the Suez Canal. Both were a tremendous boon to the port of Brindisi and the rest of Europe in the increased speed in communications from that part of the world. Progess continues apace; if in Bardonécchia you feel the urge to bite into an authentic Left Bank *croque-monsieur*, a TGV train can whisk you to Paris in only five hours.

The Valle del Chisone

The 'Milky Way' of winter resorts sweeps around the Upper Susa Valley to **Cesana** and its ultramodern satellite **Sansicario**, lying at the junction of the road to Oulx. Besides a ski resort, Cesana is also a good base for summer walks, as is **Claviere**, lying just below the **Monginevro Pass** (the Roman *Mons Janus*). This was the favoured pass of the Roman emperors and Napoleon (again) in his frequent comings and goings. The Roman god Janus had two faces, and his mountain does, too; Italian Claviere on one face and French Montgenèvre on the other, which nevertheless share lifts and ski passes. The road is equally busy with Italians on cheese and *foie gras* runs to Briançon and French heading the other way to stock up on shoes and Vermouth in Susa.

Fashionable **Sestriere**, the leading resort in Piedmont, was never a real village, but was built up as a summer and winter resort, with tall cylindrical hotels and modern flats, as charming as a state university's dormitories. But the mountains are the main attraction, and Sestriere boasts exceptional slopes and lifts, cross-country trails, ice tracks for winter races, skating rink, snow surfing, and more; in summer you can try to shoot par at Europe's highest golf course, learn to parachute, or play tennis or ride. Of all the resorts, Sestriere has the most nightlife with its lively bars and discotheques. Above Sestriere are the nearly primordial villages of **Bousson, Sauze di Cesana** and **Grangesises**, with traditional wooden Alpine houses, and the remote village and lovely wooded valley of **Argentiera** is a popular destination for cross-country skiers and hikers. A smaller resort, the old town of **Fenestrelle** lies further down the valley.

WHERE TO STAY AND EATING OUT   (tel prefix 0122)
Traditional Valle di Susa cuisine features such delicacies as a fava bean and dried chestnut torte called *fava francha*; *supe grasse*, an oven dish made of bread, cheese, broth, and tomato sauce; and *supe 'dij marghé*, a potato, cabbage, and cheese casserole. Cheeses include *tôme*, cured in the straw of alpine huts, and the weird *tûpinà*, a mix of cheeses pickled in grappa.

In Susa, hotel ***Napoleon, 44 Via Mazzini, tel 62 28 55, is the top place to stay, with a garage and fairly good restaurant in addition to its comfortable rooms (L90–110 000, all with bath). For an excellent meal, **Del Pesce**, Via Monte Grappa 25, tel 62 22 17, offers good solid Piedmontese cooking with a French touch, like gnocchi Paris style and stuffed rabbit. The wine list is good as well (closed Thurs and mid–Sept—mid Oct; L45 000). Between Chiomonte and Frais, there's a youth hostel, **Ostello Lo Yoti**, tel 54 492, with rooms for L12 000 a night.

In Bardonécchia, the ****Riky Grand Hotel, in the middle of town, tel 9353, is the resort's smartest lodgings, ultramodern and very comfortable. Open Dec–5 April and July–Aug, rooms without bath are L88 000, with, L138 000. ***Des Geneys-Splendid**, Viale Einaudi 21, tel 99 001, enjoys a more tranquil setting in the trees, and has a little more character than many resort hotels. Open mid Dec–mid April and July–Aug, all rooms with bath L125 000. Little *Villa Myosotis, open all year, tel 9883, also has a small garden and rooms for L45 000 without bath, L60 000 with. The restaurants are fairly simple; ***Tabor, a hotel-restaurant at Via della Stazione 6, tel 9857, is one place that doesn't just slap out plates of mediocre pasta for the crowds, with specialities like goulash and polenta, trout and almonds, and a Chinese fondu for more than one, if ordered ahead (rooms L110 000, all with bath; meals L50 000, with wine; closed Tues).

In Sauze d'Oulx: you'll have to reserve well in advance to get a room at the ****Capricorno, in Le Clotes, tel 85 273, a very pleasant 8-room lodge reached by chair lift; very intimate and quiet, it's open from Nov–mid April and 13 June–13 Sept, doubles only, all with bath, L150 000.

In Sestriere: the ****Grand Hotel Sestriere, Via Assietta 1, tel 76 476, is the most luxurious and elegant on the slopes, with an indoor pool, spacious rooms, and a fairly good restaurant. Open 3 Dec–5 April, L220 000. ***Miramonti, Via Cesana 3, tel 77 048, is a good little hotel, new like everything else in Sestriere. Open 1 Dec-May and July–10 Sept, L60 000 without bath, L90 000 with. The twin towers that dominate the town belong to the Club Méditerranée: the glamorous one, the **Duchi d'Aosta, tel 77 123, has comfortable rooms, all with private bath for L80 000, while **La Torre**, tel 77 123, is the budgeting single's special, with simple, bathless rooms for L40 000. Both are open mid Dec–15 April; reserve at the club's offices at Largo Corsica dei Servi 11, Milan, tel (02) 704 445. Among the restaurants, **La Baita**, Via Louset 4/a, tel 77 496, is famous for its polenta, served with hare, boar, or tamer dishes, but be discreet, as the owner is very wary of his clientele. Closed Tues and the month of May, L40 000. Another good bet, **Last Tango**, Via La Glesia 1/A, tel 76 337, is run by a chef who worked for years in the London restaurant of the same name. Among the stars here are excellent lamb and game dishes, Piedmontese crêpes (*crespelle*), pâté with ginger, and desserts of ricotta and chestnut cream (L50 000).

Waldensean Valleys: Valle di Chisone and Pinerolo

TOURIST INFORMATION
Pinerolo: Via S. Giuseppe 39, tel (0121) 77 361
Before there were Savoys there were the Princes of Acaia, and Pinerolo was their capital.

Splendidly situated at the junction of two valleys, it preserves several memories of its day as a capital, including the 14th-century **Palazzo dei Principi d'Acaia**, the Romanesque church of **San Maurizio**, with the princes' tombs, the Gothic **Cathedral**, and several streets of medieval houses. In the 17th century the **Fortress of Pinerolo** belonged to the French (who called it *Pignerol*), and here, between 1668 and 1678, they imprisoned the Man in the Iron Mask, the supposed identical twin of Louis XIV.

The Valle del Chisone and the Val Péllice, south of Pinerolo, are commonly known as the **Valli Valdesi**, or Waldensean valleys. The Waldenses were followers of Peter Waldo of Lyon, who, like St Francis of Assisi, was the son of a wealthy merchant who came to renounce all his possessions to preach the gospel; unlike Francis, however, Peter Waldo deeply criticized the corruption of the Church, and was branded a heretic instead of a saint. Condemned by a Lateran Council in 1184, his followers, many from the south of France, took refuge in Piedmont's secluded valleys. The Waldenses became Protestants with the Swiss Reformation, and were frequently persecuted, especially under Carlo Emanuele and Louis XIV in 1655. They briefly took refuge in Switzerland, but returned in 1698 to reconquer their mountain valleys. Vittorio Amedeo agreed to tolerate them as his subjects, although they had to wait until 1848 to gain complete freedom of religion. Today nearly every town in northern Italy has a small Waldensean community; **Torre Péllice** is their centre, with a Waldensean college and small museum. It is also a base for scenic excursions up the valley to **Bobbio Péllice** and **Villanova**, which still has a flood embankment built with money sent by the Waldenses' great supporter, Oliver Cromwell. Between Pinerolo and Saluzzo, lies **Cavour**, birthplace of the great Prime Minister and 'architect of Italian unity'.

North of Turin: the Valli di Lanzo and the Canavese

GETTING AROUND
Trains from the Torino Céres station head north into the Valli di Lanzo; Ivrea is on the busy main route from Turin to Aosta; by train you should get there in less than an hour. A separate rail line links Turin and Cuorgné, at the foot of the Val di Locana and Gran Paradiso National Park. Cuorgné, Lanzo Torinese and Ivrea have buses to the surrounding villages.

TOURIST INFORMATION
Lanzo: Via Umberto I, 9, tel (0123) 28 080
Ivrea: Corso Vercelli 1, tel (0125) 49 687

Valli di Lanzo

Much less visted than the Valle di Susa and Valle del Chisone, the Valli di Lanzo begins to come into its own around Ciriè, beyond the long arm of Turin's industry. Acting as a kind of buffer, on the outskirts of Italo-Motown, is the beautiful park **La Mandria**, originally yet another hunting ground for the trigger-happy Savoys. A toy palace on the grounds served as the royal hunting lodge until grander digs were required, built in 1600 at nearby **Venaria**, with Baroque flourishes added later by Juvarra. Although now used as a barracks, part of it may be visited.

Lanzo Torinese is a pretty town, and a base for excursions into the branching valleys; its most famous monument is the 1378 **Ponte del Diavolo** spanning the River Stura. Impressive even today with its soaring single arch, it has long been attributed to the devil himself. **Usseglio**, in the Val di Viù (bus from Lanzo) is a fine little ski resort.

The railway from Turin peters out at **Céres**, a summer excursion centre at the fork of two pretty valleys. Buses from Céres continue up the Val Grande to scenic **Forno Alpi Graie**, the base for several good walks; another bus winds up the Valle d'Ala to the small ski resort of **Balme**, passing by way of **Ala di Stura** with a chair lift, and **Mondrone** with a lovely waterfall.

Turin to the Valle d'Aosta: the Canavese

A rocky, rolling natural amphitheatre sculpted a million years ago by the Dora Baltea glacier, the Canavese is a peaceful woodsy region of small lakes, vineyards, small towns, and country trattorias.Its main town is **Ivrea**, renowned for its carnivals and typewriters. A Roman colony called *Eporedia*, Ivrea reached its peak of influence in 1002, when its Marquis Arduin was crowned King of Italy. Up in the narrow lanes of the old town stands the 11th-century **Cathedral**, which, despite an unfortunate neoclassical façade, preserves the original towers by the apse and dome. Here and there you can pick out pieces from older buildings, including Roman columns and a sarcophagus. Art includes 12th-century frescoes and paintings in the sacristy by Defendente Ferrari. The mighty **Castle of Ivrea**, built in 1358, guards the River Dora with four lofty towers. In 1908 the Olivetti office machine company was founded in Ivrea and continues to dominate the town's economy.

South of Ivrea is pretty **Lake Candia**, dominated by a 14th-century castle and rows of vineyards that produce a pair of DOC wines, *Erbaluce* and sweet, strong *Passito di Caluso*. Lake Candia is a popular venue for canoe races, and there are boats to hire if you want to give it a go.

Just north of Ivrea, where Serra wines are grown, there are five little lakes; **Lake Sirio** is the largest, site of an 18th-century hermitage, the **Romitorio di San Giuseppe**; **Lake Pistono**'s landmark is the hilltop **Castello Montalto**.

West of Ivrea, the N. 565 is the main route towards the southern confines of Gran Paradiso National Park (see pp. 97–8). Two towns on the way make tempting stops, especially if you've got space in the boot of your car. **Castellamonte** is a ceramics town, one that specializes in decorative ceramic stoves, while the ancient town of **Cuorgné**, and its neighbour to the south, **Valperga**, are known for their cottage industries of beaten copper. Cuorgné has a fine cluster of medieval buildings, especially along Via Arduino, where the Lombard King Arduin once resided. Valperga has a 15th-century castle and church.

North of Cuorgné, at Ponte Canavese, the N. 460 veers west up the Val di Locana, lining the river Orco. The scenery becomes increasingly splendid as it approaches the waterfalls of **Noasca**.The snowbound peaks of Gran Paradiso rise up majestically around the meadows and larch forests of **Ceresole Reale** at the entrance to the National Park; its 'royal' name derives from a battle in 1544, when the French armies of Francis I defeated those of Emperor Charles V. It stands on the shores of **Lake Ceresole Reale**, a quiet oasis of deep blue among the rough and tumble snowy giants that frown down from above.

WHERE TO STAY AND EATING OUT

Near Ivrea on the shores of pretty Lake Sirio, *****Sirio** (tel (0125) 424 247) is a fine medium-sized hotel in a garden setting (L105 000). Ten km west of Ivrea at Loranzè the *****Panoramica** (Via S. Rocco 7, tel (0125) 76 321) has not only 10 very modern rooms (L95 000) but also the best restaurant in the region, usually full of Olivetti executives, chatting over exotic ravioli, seafood terrine, or a delicate breast of duck with olives (*menu degustazione* L60 000, working lunch L35 000; closed Fri, Sat lunch, Sun eve). Up at Ceresole Reale, by Gran Paradiso park, the cosy ****Chalet del Lago** makes a great base for exploring (tel (0124) 95 128; open June–Sept, L50 000).

Valle d'Aosta

At French-speaking Pont-St-Martin, the road enters the autonomous Valle d'Aosta— one of the most spectacularly beautiful regions in Italy. Rimmed by the highest mountains in Europe—Mont Blanc (4807 m/15,780 ft), the Matterhorn ('Cervino' in Italian, 4478 m/14,690 ft), Monte Rosa (4554 m/15,200 ft) and Gran Paradiso (4061 m/13,402 ft), the Aosta valleys are one of Europe's most popular summer and winter playgrounds, dotted with lakes and serenaded by rushing streams. Emerald meadows lie beneath great swathes of woodland, hills and gorges are defended by fairytale castles. With Piedmont, Aosta shares one of Italy's most beautiful and largest national parks, **Gran Paradiso**. The opening of the Mont Blanc tunnel (1968) and Great St Bernard tunnel (1964) have

A Turret House, Valle d'Aosta

85

created an international boom in winter sports in the region, while autostrade link the resorts with Turin and Milan.

The Valle d'Aosta has been compared to a leaf, transversed by a main vein (the Dora Baltea valley) with a dozen smaller veins, or valleys, branching off on either side. Each valley has its own character; in most of them French or Provençal, is the dominant language, although Italian is understood everywhere. English comes in a poor third, outside of the major resorts. Although the Valle d'Aosta has traditionally owed allegiance to the House of Savoy, from the 11th to the 18th centuries it governed itself by an Assembly of the three estates, a Council, and its own body of law, the *Coutumier*. Union with Italy aggravated linguistic differences, a wound which Mussolini proceeded to rub salt in with his policy of cultural imperialism that insisted on the use of Italian. In defiance, the Aostans played a leading role in the Resistance, and in 1945 the region was granted cultural and a certain amount of administrative autonomy. Most towns are officially bilingual.

Walking the High Roads of the Valle d'Aosta, and Other Summer Sports

Although Mont Blanc and the Matterhorn steal all the headlines with their daredevil sports, anyone with a good pair of legs can walk the two *Alte Vie* (High Roads) of the Valley. The 282 km of well-marked paths, and their innumerable sidetracks, are designed to take in the region's loveliest scenery and to keep you far above the traffic in the centre, at altitudes ranging from 1200 to 3296 m. *Alta Via 1*, from Gressoney to Courmayeur, takes in the northern valleys and pastures under Monte Rosa and the Matterhorn; *Alta Via 2*, from Courmayeur to Château-Champorcher, takes in Gran Paradiso National Park and a chance to watch the ibex and chamois. The walking season runs from the end of June to October; the flowers are usually at their best in July. Before setting out, pick up the Regional Tourist office's free multilingual brochure on the High Road, complete with detailed maps and accommodation information.

The tourist office can also give you a list of the numerous **riding stables** in the valleys. You can play **golf** at the valleys' two 9-hole courses, at Breuil-Cervinia, tel (0166) 949 131, and Courmayeur, tel (0165) 89 103. At the little airport at St-Christophe, near Aosta, you can arrange to go **gliding** or **parachuting**, (tel (0165) 362 442, or brush up your **ski** techniques at one of two summer ski schools at Breuil-Cervinia, tel (0166) 949 076, or Courmayeur, tel (0165) 842 477. The Scuola di Canoa di Courmayeur, at Morgex, tel (0165) 809 051, offers **canoe** lessons and excursions, while **raft excursions** from April to October are run by Rafting Adventure at Villeneuve, tel (0165) 95 082. **Rock climbing courses** and excursions are organized by the Cooperative Interguide, Via M. Emilius 13, tel (0165) 34 983.

Skiing, and Other Winter Sports

The major resorts in the Valle d'Aosta are Courmayeur, Breuil-Cervinia, St-Vincent, Brusson, Pila, and Cogne, but there are many smaller, quieter, and less expensive bases; write ahead for the region's ski handbook with maps of the slopes, lifts, and facilities in each of Aosta's valleys. Prices on the sunny side of the Alps are, like the weather, milder than in France or Switzerland, but can be very high by Italian standards. High season at the resorts, when prices go up about 15 per cent, are in force during the following periods: Christmas–first week of Jan; second week of Feb–mid March; Easter holidays; and July–Aug. If you come during the peak periods, reserve at least three months in advance. Although picking up a week's ski package (*Settimana Bianca*), including hotel and ski pass, from a travel agent is the easiest and least expensive way to go, families and groups of more than two may save money by writing in advance to the Aosta Tourist office for their list of privately owned, self-catering flats in the region (*Elenco di Appartamenti da Affittare*); but again, be sure to do so several months in advance.

If skiing palls, you can always take mush lessons and drive a sledge-dog team, as well as take **sledge-dog excursions** (contact Signore M. Perri, c/o Hotel La Grange, Entrèves, 11013 Courmayeur, tel (0165) 89 274.) At Fenis/Combasse there is **sledging** (*slittino*) in the winter (tel (0165) 768 887, and **bob sledging** at Breuil-Cervinia (tel (0166) 948 745), or **riding** in the snow at Aosta (Scuderia Jolly, tel (0165) 551 580), Cogne (Cooperativa Pegaso, tel (0165) 74 484), Pollein (tel (0165) 53 201) and Introd (Trekking Club Introd, tel (0165) 95 527). **Ice skating rinks** are to be found in Aosta, at Reg. Tzambarlet (tel (0165) 361 472), Cogne (tel (0165) 74 679) and Courmayeur (tel (0165) 842 890). There are **covered public swimming pools** at Aosta (tel (0165) 40 275), Pré-St-Didier (tel (0165) 87 827); Verrès (tel (0125) 920 420), and St-Vincent (tel (0166) 36 90).

Valdaostan Wines

The mountain men of the Aosta Valleys have been producing wine at least since the days of the Roman conquest, if not sooner. The encircling Alps provide not only shelter from extreme temperatures, but take most of the rain, so that the Valleys of Aosta are among the driest regions of Italy; the glare from the glaciers and the stony soil, and the fact that the average vineyard is only about two acres, all contribute to the special quality of the local wine. There's not much of it and it's hard to find outside of the region, but during your stay, look for *Torrette*, a bright, strong red wine with a wild rose bouquet, good with salted meats; *Gamay*, a cousin of Beaujolais, strong, but smooth, and slightly bitter, good with meat dishes; *Arnad-Montjovet*, a wine made mostly from Nebbiolo grapes, ruby red and also good with meats and mountain cheeses; *Chambave Rouge*, deep ruby red and good with sausages; *Pinot Noir*, said to have been first cultivated by the Burgundians in the Dark Ages, full bodied, dry, and a friend of game dishes; *Donnaz DOC*, one of the best, made from special small Nebbiolo grapes, aged in oak casks, where it takes on a slight almond bouquet, good with meat dishes, game, and cheeses; *Enfer D'Arvier DOC*, a red wine from the hottest slopes, full bodied and mellow, good for salted meats, cheeses, sweet and sour dishes, or served as *vin brûlé*, hot with cloves. White wines from the region include *Blanc de Morgex* and *Blanc de la Salle*, made from a native vine grown at the highest altitudes—dry, sharp, and strong, good with antipasti, fish, and dishes with cheese sauce. *Riesling X Sylvaner* is a wine variety imported from Switerland after the last war, designed to take hot and cold growing spells; a fresh, strong wine often served with trout.

GETTING AROUND
Trains from Turin or Milan (a 5-hour trip, changing at Civasso) go through the main valley as far as Pré-St-Didier. The valleys are well served by bus; other frequent coach

connections include Turin or Milan (a 4–5 hr trip) to Courmayeur/Chamonix; Turin–Chamonix–Geneva (2 a day); Aosta–Val d'Isère–Col Iseran (1 a day); Aosta–Martigny (2 a day); Genoa–Alessandria–Courmayeur (summer only). During the summer, there are regularly scheduled excursion buses (SAVDA) from Aosta to Mont Blanc, Lake Geneva, and the Two Savoys/Annecy.

The most breathtaking way to enter Aosta is by cable car from Chamonix over the glaciers of Mont Blanc to Courmayeur. It's expensive (L35 000 round trip) but unforgettable, especially if you're lucky enough to catch the mountain without its frequent veil of mist. The cable car runs during the ski season and in July and August, leaving roughly every hour.

TOURIST INFORMATION
Ayas-Champoluc: Via Varese 16, tel (0125) 307 113
Brusson: Piazzale Municipio 1, tel (0125) 300 240
Gressoney-St-Jean: Villa Margherita, tel (0125) 355 185
Gressoney-La-Trinité, tel (0125) 366 133
St-Vincent: Via Roma 50, tel (0166) 2239
Valtournenche: Via Roma, tel (0166) 92 029
Breuil-Cervinia: Via J.A. Carrel 29, tel (0166) 949 136

Pont-St-Martin and the Val di Gressoney

Besides its stunning Alpine splendour, the Valle d'Aosta is known for its picturesque castles and Roman remains that seem to mark every narrow defile and bend in the valleys. One of Italy's most remarkable Roman bridges, dating from the 1st century BC lies just within the region, at **Pont-St-Martin**; this is one of many spans later attributed to the devil, who is said to have made a deal with the village: the bridge for the first soul that wandered across, only to be cheated when St Martin sent a dog over at dawn. Pont-St-Martin itself is a fine old town, encompassed by vineyards that produce one of Aosta's finest wines.

At Pont-St-Martin two valleys meet: the main Valle d'Aosta along the River Dora, and the wide and pleasant **Val di Gressoney** (or Valle del Lys), gracefully meandering up to the crystal glaciers spilling off mighty Monte Rosa. Unlike the rest of the Aosta region, the people of the Val di Gressoney, the Walser, speak neither French nor Italian, but an obscure dialect of German, having migrated here from the Swiss Valais in the 12th century. Their valley is utterly wholesome, with a solid family feel to it; their traditional Alpine chalets, with wooden balconies bursting with pots of geraniums, are a vision as fresh as childhood and Heidi. The main resorts of the valley are **Gressoney-St-Jean** and the loftier, trendier **Gressoney-la-Trinité**, both good bases for laid-back skiing and walking holidays, the latter with chair lifts up Monte Rosa and ski facilities shared with the Val d'Ayas, the next valley to the west. **Issime**, on the way up from Pont-St-Martin, merits a stop for its gabled parish church, with a façade frescoed with a large 16th-century scene of sinners taking their licks in the Last Judgement as a warning to all passers-by. Issime is a small climbing centre and, like most of the valley, prefers to speak German; oddly the next village, **Gaby**, only 4 km away, is an island of French Provençal.

The Bassa Valle: Pont-St-Martin to Issogne

From Pont-St-Martin, the main valley road continues past the **Donnaz** station, with the impressive remains of the Roman highway hewn 200 yards in the living rock, and then through the narrow **Gorge de Bard**. At the other end, the gloomy **Fortress of Bard** (1034) rises dark and menacing over the village of the same name; in 1800 Napoleon slipped his cannons past in the dead of night, spreading the road with sacking and straw to muffle their wheels.

Picturesque old **Arnaz**, the next village up the valley, has a number of medieval houses and an intriguing Romanesque church built around the year 1000, adorned with frescoes from its restoration in the 15th century. Another ancient town, **Verrès**, lies at the junction of the Val d'Ayas, a crossroads defended by the massive, almost cubic **Fortress of Verrès**, looming up on its promontory. Built in the 14th century on the ruins of an older fort, by Ibelto di Callant, Lord of Verrès, it's a stiff climb up from the town (or a quick drive), and is open for tours 9:30–12 and 2–5:30; closed Wed; adm). Although a treat for true castle fiends, most people will find the nearby residence of the Challant lords, the **Castle of Issogne** (1480), far more enchanting, with a frescoed courtyard that lacks only knights and fair ladies dallying by the fountain, in the shade of the mysterious iron pomegranate tree; the upper apartments, with their period furnishings and tapestries, are equally evocative (same hours as Verrès, but closed on Mon instead of Wed; only 25 people admitted at a time). During Carnival, masked balls are held here in a revival of the old lordly celebrations.

Val d'Ayas

Thickly forested with pines and chestnut groves, the Val d'Ayas winds northwards, with Monte Rosa on the right and the Matterhorn on the left, a walker's paradise and a good place to see traditional, massive Alpine chalets. The first *comune* of hamlets from Verrès, **Challant-St-Victor**, was the cradle of the noble Challant family who ran Aosta before the Savoys and their duke; their ruined castle still hangs over Villa, the main settlement. An even more impressive derelict castle stands further up the Val d'Ayas in **Graines**—an intriguing, 13th-century ruin with a Romanesque chapel. You can reach it from the little resort of **Arcesaz**.

Brusson lies at the crossroads of the Val d'Ayas and the scenic road through the pine forests of the **Colle di Joux** from St-Vincent (see below). Brusson has good holiday facilities amidst its scattered hamlets; one of the best excursions is to walk up to the miniature mountain lakes under Punta Valfredda. From Brusson the road climbs steeply to the picturesque villages of **Lignod** and **Antagnod**, both enjoying fine views of Monte Rosa, then to the most important resort in the Val d'Ayas, **Champoluc**. Here, the single most spectacular excursion is to take the cableway and chair lift to the slopes just below **Testa Grigia** (3315 m), one of the grandest belvederes of the Western Alps. A guide is recommended if you want to continue up all the way to the summit, an ascent rewarded with a breathtaking panorama of Mont Blanc, the Matterhorn, Gran Paradiso, and Monte Rosa, with a sea of peaks paying court around these mighty kings. New lift installations have linked the ski slopes of Champoluc with those of Gressoney-La-Trinité in the next valley. Beyond Champoluc the road ends at quiet Saint-Jacques, an excellent base for walks in the lovely, uninhabited valleys on either side of the village.

St-Vincent and Châtillon

The valley widens at St-Vincent, the 'Riviera of the Alps', an elite spa for the rich and dissipated since the 18th century, boasting more than a mild climate and waters these days, with one of Europe's largest casinos. Besides blackjack, other St-Vincent activities include excursions through the shady chestnut groves and mountains to **St Germain Castle** in **Montjovet**, or up the funicular to the source of the mineral spring, the **Fons Salutis**, or a cultural call at St-Vincent's frescoed Romanesque church, built over the baths of a Roman villa (open June–Sept, Mon, Wed and Fri 4–6).

The main road continues to the Valle d'Aosta's second city, **Châtillon**, which has been given over to industry with little to detain the visitor, besides another **Challant castle**, completely renovated in the 18th century (no admittance), another **Roman Bridge**, and the possibility of a cheese tour at the **Cooperative Latte e Fontina** (daily 9–1 and 4–7, closed Thurs pm, Fri am and Sun). Châtillon is also where you leave the train to catch a bus up Valtournenche.

WHERE TO STAY AND EATING OUT

Valdaostan cuisine is rich fare to insulate you against the cold, and includes dollops of *fontina* cheese in every dish—full of the good natural enzymes that keep the inhabitants blithe and limber into their nineties. Traditional first courses are *zuppa alla valpellinentze*, a bread, *fontina* and cabbage dish baked in the oven, *zuppa freida*, a cold soup made with rye bread, wine, and sugar; various fondues, and the local ham, *prosciutto di Bosses*; then there's the inevitable rib-sticking polenta, *boudins*, or sausages, and veal cutlets in melted *fontina*. Finish up with a *caffè valdaostana*—strong, piping hot coffee with the local grappa, orange peel, and sugar.

Pont-St-Martin (tel prefix 0125): Although few travellers stay overnight, not a few call in for lunch at **Dora**, Pl. Stazione Ferroviaria, tel 82 035. Ring ahead if you want to order the chef's celebrated *fritto misto*, but you won't do too badly, either, by simply showing up and ordering from the menu of Valdaostan and Piedmontese specialities (L35 000).

Gressoney: Hotels in Gressoney-St-Jean are small and homey. ****Stadel**, in Beilciuken, 3 km from St-Jean, tel (0125) 355 264, is one of the more atmospheric places, with 12 very cosy rooms, all with private bath. Open Dec–April and June–mid-Sept, L60–75 000. In Gressoney-La-Trinité, the *****Residence**, tel (0125) 366 148, is a modern hotel in a garden with good views. All rooms have bath, and there's a garage on the premises (open Dec–April and July–mid Sept, L70–100 000).

Ayas-Champoluc (tel prefix 0125): In Champoluc, *****Anna Maria**, Via Croves 5, tel 307 128, is a lovely old mountain chalet, brimful of charm and simple, rustic bonhomie in a magnificent setting, with a garden; the food is delicious. Open 20 June–Aug, L85–105 000 with private bath. At Periasc, near Antagnod, *****Monte Rosa**, Rue Periax La Val 7, tel 305 735, is a delightful, get-away-from-it-all mountain hotel, open year-round. There are tennis courts in its garden (L75–90 000 with bath). At the mouth of the valley, in Verrès, there's elegant dining and cosy lodging at **Chez Pierre**, Via Martorey 43, tel 929 376. The menu varies according to season, as does the favoured spot to dine—in winter by the blazing hearth, in summer in the pleasant little garden.

Try the *agnolotti di carne tartufati*, filled with truffled meat, and venison in bayberry sauce, and finish your meal with a warm slice of apple pie smothered in cream (closed Tues; L45–55 000).
St-Vincent (tel prefix 0166): The *****Grand Hotel Billia, Via Stef. Billia 3, tel 3446, is one of those elegant, terribly grand turn-of-the-century hotels, originally built to take advantage of St-Vincent's curative mineral springs—which it still does, although it is also a magnet for those who come to get soaked at its roulette tables as well. The rooms are superb, many enjoying excellent views. Amenities include an indoor pool, sauna, tennis, and a large, lovely park, and better than average restaurant. Open year-round, the luxurious rooms go for L280–320 000. The ***Posta, near the centre at Piazza XXVIII Aprile, tel 2250, has comfortable if not very glamorous rooms and a nice little park. Open all year, L60–67 000 without bath, L75–80 000 with. The place to celebrate after a lucky streak is the elegant Nuovo Batezar da Renato, Via Marconi 1, tel 3164, within easy walking distance of the casino, with such delicacies as salmon mousse flavoured with wild fennel, duck with peaches, or pigeon stuffed with mushrooms, accompanied by a classy wine list. Closed Wed and Thurs eve; in May, and from the end of June until mid-July, expect a bill around L110 000—or maybe more.

Valtournenche and Breuil-Cervinia

Valtournenche is Italy's picture window on the fabled Matterhorn (in Italian, Cervino), its unique profile rising up majestically at the top of the valley, and visible from nearly every point. The first small resort in the Valtournenche, Antey-St-André, is known for its healthy, mild climate. Roads from here branch off to the west for Torgnon, a very quiet base for walks in the woods, and to the east for La Magdeleine, a small settlement with ski facilities. For complete tranquillity, take the cable car from Buisson to the otherwise inaccessible hamlet of Chamois; from Chamois a chair lift continues up to the lovely green banks of Lake Lod and the ski slopes in the winter.

Valtournenche, the valley capital, is a popular ski resort, and hometown of the renowned Matterhorn guides—memorial plaques posted around the church are a grim reminder of the dangers they face. From Valtournenche you can get a cable car up the Cime Bianche, or take a dramatic walk along the specially constructed galleries through the Gouffre des Buserailles, a narrow gorge carved out by the river Marmore above Crépin.

The valley road ends at sparkling new and smart Breuil-Cervinia, one of Italy's most renowned ski resorts. It enjoys a uniquely grand setting—the Matterhorn to the north, the sweep of the Grandes Murailles to the west, and the Fruggen massif to the east. The resort dates from the construction of the road up in the late 1930s, and although Breuil-Cervinia may look more like a frontier boom town rather than anything vaguely quaint or even Italian, the mountains are everything, with 190 km of ski run, and summer skiing on the glacier at Plateau Rosà (3500 m; L27 000 return); a cable car and lift from here can take you to the top of Piccolo Cervino, from where fantastic ski trails continue down to Zermatt in Switzerland, or along the valley to Valtournenche. The descents are so lengthy that the KL time trials for the world speed record are held here. Other winter sports at Breuil-Cervinia include ice skating, bob sledging, hockey, an indoor swimming-pool and bowling alley. In the summer months, it is the base for ascents of the Matterhorn for the experienced climbers, a feat first achieved from this side in 1867; the route's most precipitous passages are now fitted out with ropes. Other, far less demanding, excursions include the easy hike from Plateau Rosà over the **Colle Superiore delle Cime Bianche**, either to emerald Lake Goillet and its view encompassing the Val d'Ayas, or to the summit of the **Breithorn** (4171 m); the tourist office has maps and information on the trails and ascents.

The Mian Valley: Chambave and Nus

West of Châtillon, **Chambave** is a village swathed in vineyards, under a promontory draped with the ruins of the **Castle of Cly**. Chambave produces a rare and prized golden dessert wine called *Passito di Chambave*. Wine and a modest amount of tourism are the main industries of **Nus**, the next town, a base for visiting two of the region's most remote valleys, the **Val Clavalité**, with the striking **Tersiva Pyramid** at its head, or the **Val St-Barthélemy**, with its scattered villages lost in the trees.

The main attraction of Nus, however, is the **Castle of Fénis**, another built by the Challants, the Viscounts of Aosta throughout the Middle Ages. At Fénis, they outdid themselves in creating a genuine fairytale castle, all asymmetrical towers, turrets and swallowtail crenellations. Within, the castle's court, chapels, and loggias are covered with fine 14th-century frescoes (open same hours as Verrès castle, closed Tues). From here it's 13 km to Aosta: a couple of towns in between offer distillery tours if you ring ahead: in St-Marcel, 'La Val dôtaine', tel (0165) 768 919 and in Quart, 'St-Roch' at Villair, tel (0165) 765 203.

WHERE TO STAY AND EATING OUT   tel prefix 0166
The top hotel in Breuil-Cervinia, ******Cristallo**, Via del Piolet 6, tel 948 121 has no qualms about its recent origins, but stands above the town in all its smart, modern glory. Bold colours and styling, with very comfortable rooms all equipped with TVs and private bath; an indoor swimming pool, tennis, and sauna. Open Dec–April and July–Aug; L190–380 000, depending on the season. The ******Hermitage**, Via Cristallo, tel 948 998, is another excellent hotel, nearer the lifts, with a pool and garden and well-furnished rooms. Open all year, L160–250 000, all rooms with bath. The *****President**, Via Breuil-Cervinia, tel 949 476, offers some of the finest views of the Matterhorn from its windows. Rooms are large and very comfortable; all have private bath. Open Nov–April and July–Aug, L100 000. ****Les Neiges d'Antan**, 4 km from the centre of Breuil at Frazione Cret Perrères, tel 948 775, is a pretty Alpine chalet in tranquil surroundings, where the resort's skyscrapers are hidden from view. The rooms are small but pleasant, and the restaurant is the best in the area, so even if you don't stay you may want to drop by for a traditional mountain meal of salt beef, polenta, cheeses, Valdaostana wines, and homemade desserts. Rooms L90 000, all with bath, meals L35–50 000. Closed July, Oct and Nov. Also a bit out of the way, in Avouil, ***Leonardo Carrel**, at Frazione Avouil, tel 949 077, is a fine, basic Alpine chalet operated by a ski instructor. There are 10 pine-panelled rooms, all with bath and good food in the restaurant. Open all year, the minimum stay is a week—L55–65 000 a day.

Aosta

The 'Rome of the Alps', Aosta enjoys one of the most splendid positions of any Italian city, encircled by regal mountains, divine emanations that appear to hold up the very sky overhead; on clear mornings they envelop the city in a total, shimmering blueness, while their brilliant snowy peaks merge with the clouds to form a magic circle around the city. Aosta owes its historical importance to its position at the crossing of roads from the Mont Blanc and St Bernard passes—a piece of sunny Italy at the crossroads of France and Switzerland. Although looped in by industry, army installations, and dull, modern suburbs, the city's ancient core, with its grand Roman and medieval monuments, retains its unique charm. The street plan has changed little since the days when Aosta was *Augusta Praetoria*, built in 23 BC, after the conquest of the Salassian Gauls, the terror of the Alps. In the Middle Ages Aosta (a corruption of 'Augusta'), was ruled by the Challant Viscounts, and then by the Dukes of Aosta, who owed allegiance to the Savoys. But here the French influence remained stronger than in Piedmont, and you are more likely to hear French or a French dialect in the streets than Italian. Aosta is touristy, but in a relaxed way, part resort and part everyday workplace.

As the centre of transport to all sections of the Valle d'Aosta, the city makes a good base; its also has its 'own' ski resort at nearby Pila, and hosts a full calendar of cultural activities. On 31 January it holds the famous Sant'Orso Fair, a market dating back to the year 1000, where Aosta's talented woodworkers display and sell everything from ladders and chairs to toys and fine sculpture. In July there's a series of organ concerts, and in October the finals of a peculiar 1000-year old Valdaostana sport, the *Bataille des Reines*, the 'Battle of Queens': not some kind of feminist chess game, but a cow butting contest, in which the region's toughest heifers vie for the title of 'Queen of the Horns of the Valle d'Aosta'. Because the cows are sent to pasture without bulls to take on their natural protective role, the heifers have to establish a hierarchy amongst themselves to determine which, in the case of attack, will guard the calves, and which will actively defend the herd. Local contests are run throughout the year (the Aosta tourist office has listings); in the passion of victory, the winning cow, crowned with garlands, may be *carried* about in triumph, the most amazing sight of all.

TOURIST INFORMATION
Piazza Chanoux 3, tel (0165) 33 352

Place Emile Chanoux

Aosta is a hard town to get lost in, with its straight Roman streets branching out from the central **Place Emile Chanoux**. Here are Aosta's French-style town hall, and the IVAT (the local handicrafts association), where local arts and crafts are displayed year round. This is the place to pick up the most traditional souvenir of the Valle d'Aosta: the *coupe d'amitié*, or cup of friendship—a covered cup with 6 to 8 spouts, to be filled on cold evenings with **caffè valdaostana** and passed around. A complete set would include a *grolla* to mix properly the coffee, grappa, and orange peel; the word in local dialect is the same as 'grail', for its similarity to the usual medieval depictions of that holy vessel.

A block from the square tower are the mighty double arches of the **Porta Pretoria**, the original Roman gate, its impressive strength a compliment to the ferocity of the local

Gauls. The central arch was used for cart traffic, while the other two were for pedestrians. To the left of the gate stands the lofty façade of the **Roman Theatre**, one of the best-preserved in Italy, with its *cavea* and *scena* (open summer 9:30–12 and 2:30–6:30, winter 9:30–12 and 2–4:30).

Through the Porta Pretoria, Via Sant'Anselmo is Aosta's main drag, named for St Anselm (1033–1109), Archbishop of Canterbury, the founder of Scholasticism, and a Doctor of the Church, who was born in the street now awash with stuffed St Bernards and garishly labelled bottles of mysterious Alpine elixirs.

Via Sant'Orso to the left leads shortly to the curious Romanesque-Gothic hybrid **Collegiata dei Santi Pietro ed Orso**, founded in the late 10th century. The church is famous for the rare Ottonian frescoes dating from its construction and for its charming little cloister, begun in 1133, its short columns topped by wonderfully carved capitals of white marble, darkened with an artificial patina. The scenes vary from the Bible through mythology; traditionally cloister capitals were one of the few places where monkish sculptors could let their imaginations run wild. The 11th-century crypt contains the remains of Aosta's patron Sant'Orso. Across the lane from the collegiata are the excavations of the Palaeo-Christians' **Basilica di San Lorenzo**, built in the 6th century and destroyed in the 9th; its unusual foundation may be viewed via special walkways (both S. Orso and S. Lorenzo open 8:30–12 noon and 2–7:30 pm, closed Mon).

Via Sant'Anselmo ends at the the triumphal **Arch of Augustus**, built at the founding of the city, to celebrate the victory over the Salassi; the rather incongruous roof was added in the 18th century. On the other side of the arch and over the river Buthier, a fine, single-span **Roman bridge** has outlasted the channel it once crossed, but is still used by Aostans to pass over the dried-up bed.

The Cathedral and Forum

From Place Emile Chanoux, Via Xavier e Maistre leads, on the right, to the scanty remains of the **Roman Amphitheatre** and the 12th-century **Torre del Balivi**. To the left is the **Cathedral**, off Via Monseigneur de Sales, an ancient church rebuilt several times, with a neoclassical façade hiding a Gothic interior. The stained-glass windows are 15th–16th-century Swiss workmanship, while the choir contains finely inlaid 15th-century stalls, and two excellent mosaics, one a 12th-century *Labours of the Months*, the other a 14th-century scene of Mesopotamia. Next to the choir, behind the glass doors, is the newly arranged **Cathedral Museum** (open 10–12 and 3–6, Sun 3–5:45; closed Mon; adm). Although small, the museum contains outstanding treasures like an ivory diptych from the year 406, portraying the Emperor Honorius, tombs (especially the 13th-century effigy of Tommaso II of Savoy, visible in the choir), and Romanesque reliquaries and statues, all well described in a free audio guide in English, accompanied by Pachelbel's Suite.

In front of the cathedral, in Piazza Giovanni XXIII, are the remains of the **Roman Forum** (open 10–12 and 2:30–6, winter 2–4:30). Most intriguing here is the huge 92 m x 87 m **Cryptoporticus** that extended under most of the forum, but whatever purpose it might have served is a mystery. You can also make out the foundation of a Roman temple under the **Casa Arcidiacnale**.

Beyond the forum stands a nearly intact portion of the **Roman Wall**, with **La Torreneuve**, formerly belonging to the House of Challant. Other intact sections of the walls remain in the south, near the station, where three towers survive: **Il Pailleron**, in a garden nearest the station, most maintains its Roman character; the impressive, round **Torre Bramafam** was a Challant defensive work; and the third, the **Torre de Lebbroso**, earned its sad name from a family of lepers who were incarcerated here from 1733 until the last survivor died in 1803.

Around Aosta

Pila, 20 km south of Aosta, is the closest winter/summer resort to the city, with chair lifts up Mt Chamolé (2300 m) that operate in the summer as well as winter. There are trails up the slopes of **Mont Emilius** (3559 m), via Chamolé, that offer stupendous views over the ranges to the north.

More castles loom over the valley west of Aosta, on the Courmayeur road, beginning with the solemn, 13th-century **Castle of Sarre**, rebuilt in the 18th century. After the Risorgimento the kings of Italy, who seemed to spend most of their lives hunting, used it as one of their lodges, and the interior is still full of trophies bagged in the surrounding valleys (closed for restoration, due to reopen 1994). Two, now restored, medieval castles guard the pretty village of St-Pierre, a bit further on; one, the 14th-century **Sarriod-de-la-Tour**, is used for art and archaeology exhibitions, (open 9–6; closed Mon; adm), and the other, the **Castello di St-Pierre**, houses the Natural Sciences Museum (open every day 9–12 and 3–7).

WHERE TO STAY   (tel prefix 0165)
Aosta is not only the central transport node for the region, but it's more likely than most of the resorts to have rooms available if you haven't booked in advance. The best hotel, the ****Valle d'Aosta, Corso Ivrea 146, tel 41 845, is a kilometre from the centre and used mainly as a stopover by travellers on the autostrada. Behind its rippled, modern façade, the furnishings are modern and very comfortable, and all rooms have private baths and frigo bars (L100–165 000). In the centre, the ****Europe, Piazza Narbonne 8, tel 23 63 63, is a cosy, older hotel, with a private parking garage, TVs in each room, and baths in most (L65–100 000 without bath, L95–150 000 with). ***Norden, Corso Battaglione Aosta 30, is a pleasant hotel where you'll be made to feel at home, tel 41 947, L60–90 000, depending on the season. The best choice near the station, the *Monte Emilius, Via G. Carrel 9, tel 35 692, offers clean, bathless rooms for L42–50 000.

EATING OUT
The gourmets agree: the best restaurant in the entire region is the **Cavallo Bianco**, near the centre on Via Aubert 15, tel 362 214. It is beautiful even before the arrival of the antipasti. Located in a 16th-century postal relay station, with a courtyard, baronial fireplace, and beamed ceilings, it has an air of rarefied elegance. The menu changes daily, according to market availability, and wines are extra (à la carte around L120 000, but also a fixed price menu for L80 000; closed Sun eve and Mon, and Oct).

Ba-i-bor (Vecchia Aosta), Via Porte Pretoriane 4, tel 361 186, built right into the Roman walls, has the most striking dining room in Aosta. The food is good, too, featuring homemade pasta, cured venison '*prosciutto*' and trout with almonds, and lots of wines to choose from to help it down (L35–40 000). Just 4 km outside of Aosta, in Saint Christophe, **Casale** (Regione Condemine 1, tel 541 203) is well known throughout the area, not only for its quality but also the quantity of the servings; only an ogre could leave Casale hungry—try the sweet and sour artichoke mould for starters (closed Mon and Dec, L55 000). **Vecchio Ristoro**, Via Tourneuve 4, tel 33 238, is housed in a windmill that functioned until only a few years ago. The food is excellent—hot antipasti, smoked trout and salmon, and an especially good selection of local cheeses (L50 000, closed Sun, Mon lunch and Aug). There are several places along the Via Porte Pretoriane that offer pizza by the slice or *tavola calda* service for lighter, less expensive food.

The Western Valle d'Aosta

Land of slopes and lorries, heady jigsaw-puzzle beauty, smiling Euro-ski bunnies in tight pants, household names like the Great St Bernard and Mont Blanc, lodges with exposed beams, frolicking mountain goats, and a jolly cuckoo-clock sense of fun: if those are a few of your favourite things, you'll love the Western valleys of Aosta.

TOURIST INFORMATION
Cogne: Via Bourgeois 34, tel (0165) 74 040
La Thuile: Via Colomb 4, tel (0165) 884 179
Courmayeur: Piazzale Monte Bianco, tel (0165) 842 060

The Great St Bernard Pass

From Aosta at least two buses a day make the 34 km trip to the Swiss frontier at perhaps the most famous of Alpine passes, the **Col di San Bernardo** (closed Nov–May), its importance now somewhat diminished by the new tunnel, open year round. The road up (N. 27) is uncommonly pretty, affording splendid Alpine vistas through the various valleys and back towards Aosta itself. **Étroubles** is the main resort in the valley, and **Sant' Oyen**, in the midst of emerald meadows, is a quieter holiday centre, with skiing at Flassin.

The legendary **Hospice of St Bernard** lies just on the other side of the Swiss border (passports required). According to legend, the great stone monastery was founded in the 11th century by St Bernard, archdeacon of Aosta, and operated by canons from Marigny, who made it their business to minister to weary and snowbound travellers, many of them pilgrims or churchmen en route to Rome. The hospice is located at the exposed summit of the pass (2469 m), and to aid them in finding people lost in the heavy snows, the canons developed a uniquely hardy breed of dog to assist them in their labours. Magnificent specimens abound near the hospice, and when not engaged in saving the lives of intrepid skiers, they are to be found mugging for the cameras of the intrepid tourist.

Before St Bernard, the pass was known as *Mont Jovis*, after an ancient temple of Jupiter Poeninus, and was frequently crossed by Celts and Romans, and later by the

Emperors; Napoleon moved 40,000 troops through in 1800 to defeat the Austrians at Marengo.

The Valpelline, branching off from the N. 27 at **Variney**, is a handful of unfrequented valleys of unspoiled scenery. Head for **Ollomont**, the base for visiting the lovely Alpine basin known as the Conca di By. There is more fine scenery around the scattered hamlets of **Oyace**, above the river Buthier.

Val di Cogne and Gran Paradiso National Park

From Aosta and St-Pierre, the Val di Cogne stretches south towards the blunt peak of the Gran Paradiso massif (4061 m). The valley's rich magnetite and iron mines were exploited long before its tourism potential; the latter began in earnest with the opening of the national park in the 1920s.

The mouth of the valley is defended by the Challant **Castle of Amayavilles**, its four round-turreted towers dating from the 18th century. Further up, at **Pondel**, the stunning, torrential gorge of the Grand'Eyvia is spanned by a steep **Roman bridge** of 3 BC, still in use today. Beyond lies the *comune* of **Cogne**, a pleasant, busy town that commemorates the traditional source of its livelihood with a fine cast-iron fountain, erected in 1819.

Now a popular resort, Cogne is the main gateway to **Gran Paradiso National Park**, which encompasses the entire massif in its protected boundaries. Set aside as a Savoy hunting reserve in the 19th century, the park was donated to the state by Vittorio Emanuele III in 1919. It played an instrumental role in preserving the ibex (or stambecco, or steinbock), a pretty deerlike creature with long, ridged horns, which numbered only 420 in 1945, all of them in the confines of the park. Since then their numbers have increased tenfold (there are an estimated 3500 in the park), and animals from the park have been reintroduced into many of their old Alpine haunts. Although ibex prefer high altitude, rugged crags, they may be seen around the valleys in the winter and early spring. They share their paradise with the more numerous, shorter-horned chamois, which have a wider range and are more easily spotted—if not here, on a number of local dinner menus. In November and December the males of both species may be seen furiously butting heads for the ladies.

Among the birds you may be lucky enough to see a wall creeper, chough, golden eagle, ptarmigan, nutcracker, or black grouse. The flowers are at their most spectacular in early June; even if you're not up to a long trek over hill and dale to see them, visit the **Paradiso Alpine Botanical Garden**, laid out in 1955 in the lovely **Valnontey** near Cogne (open 15 June–15 Sept, 9–12:30 and 2:30–6; adm).

Cogne has seven camp sites as well as its hotels; within the park there are eight Alpine refuges, many used as hostels during the ski season. If you only have a limited amount of time, the best one to aim for is **Vittorio Sella** (2584 m), a gorgeous walk away through Cogne's vast meadow of Sant'Orso, up into the deep, flower-spangled vale of **Loson**, a favourite rendezvous of ibex and chamois, now that the refuge is no longer a royal hunting lodge. You can return the next day to Cogne through Valnontey. Alternatively, take the *cabinovia* to **Montzeuc** (2100 m) and its belvedere, with fantastic panoramic views of Cogne and the Gran Paradiso massif (open all year except May, Oct, and Nov).

The western reaches of the park, the lush, unspoiled **Valsavarenche** and the **Val de**

Rhêmes may be reached from Villeneuve on the Courmayeur road. In the Valsava-renche, the ideal base is **Dégioz**; from here a track leads up to the Vittorio Sella Refuge, while another, a former royal hunting road, goes to the **Nivolè Pass**, site of another former hunting lodge, now the **Rifugio Albergo Savoia**; an alternative route diverges from this at Lake Djuan for the Entrelor pass and the prettily situated village of **Rhêmes-Notre-Dame** in the Val de Rhêmes. The Valsavarenche summer bus termi-nus, **Pont**, is the base for ascents of Gran Paradiso.

The Main Valley: Villeneuve to Pré-St-Didier

Medieval castles abound in this region. **Villeneuve** is sprawled under the massive, ruined, 12th-century **Châtel-Argent**, while the next town, **Arvier**, is dominated by the slightly later **Château de la Mothe**. Arvier is even more renowned for its wine, *Vin de l'Enfer*. Here, a road forks for the wild and rocky **Valgrisenche**, dominated by the melancholy **Castle of Montmayeur** high on its rock. The Valgrisenche's main villages, **Planaval** and **Valgrisenche**, have the shimmering Rutor glacier for a backdrop; just beyond the latter towers the massive Beauregard dam and its artificial lake.

Back in the main valley, **Avise** is a charming village with two medieval castles on the hillside. It lies at the foot of a romantic gorge, where the **Pierre Taillée** has remains of the Roman road cut into the rock. On the far side you get your first memorable glimpse of Mont Blanc; above the road to the left, **Derby** has a fine collection of fortified medieval houses, a little Gothic church, and a waterfall, the **Cascata di Linteney**. To the right of the road the landmark is the 13th-century **Châtelard tower** in La Salle, a tiny hamlet that boasts the highest vineyards in Europe.

The medieval tower of **Morgex**, headquarters of the upper main valley, or Valdigne, was the administrative seat of the Savoys in the region. The little resort of **Pré-St-Didier**, just beyond, lies at the confluence of the Dora de la Thuile and Dora Baltea rivers. Its warm chalybeate springs are used for skin complaints; its station is the last rail link in the Valle d'Aosta. From here you can pick up buses to La Thuile or Courmayeur.

Little St Bernard Valley

At Pré-St-Didier the scenic road up to the Little St Bernard Pass begins threading forests and dizzily skirting the ravine of the Dora de la Thuile. The town of **La Thuile** is a growing winter resort, with excellent skiing on the slopes of Chaz Dura. In summer the most striking excursion is up to the **Col San Carlo** and the **Tête d'Arpy**, with an azure lake and remarkable view of Mont Blanc.

Above La Thuile, Mont Blanc also forms a stunning backdrop to pretty **Lac Verney**, a mirror in a setting of emerald meadows. A bit beyond, the **Little St Bernard Pass** (2188 m, open June–Oct) is marked by a statue of St Bernard on a column and a relic of the Iron Age: a **Cromlech**, or burial circle marked by stones, with the ruins of two structures on the side. Just on the other side of the French frontier the ancient **Hospice du Petit-St-Bernard** was founded even before St Bernard, with the purpose of sheltering destitute travellers. Formerly run by the same order as the Great St Bernard monastery, this hospice was bombed during World War II, then ceded to France, and has been left abandoned. A former abbot, Pierre Canous, planted an **Alpine Botanical**

garden here in 1897, which, after years of neglect, has been re-established and reopened. From the pass it's 31 km to the first French town, Bourg-St-Maurice.

Courmayeur

In more ways than one Valle d'Aosta reaches its climax in Courmayeur, one of the most stunning, best equipped and most congenial resorts in the Alps. Lying at the foot of Mont Blanc, it is perhaps Italy's most fashionable winter and summer resort, rivalling Chamonix in chic but warmer both in its climate and atmosphere. The skiing is matchless, the scenery mythic in its grandeur, and the accommodation and facilities among the best in the western Alps.

Besides the 100 km of downhill ski runs at **Chécrouit-Val Veny**, served by nine cableways, six chair lifts, 17 ski lifts and helicopters for jet-set thrills, Courmayeur offers magnificent cross-country runs, ice skating, and an indoor swimming-pool: in summer there is skiing on the glacier of Colle del Gigante, a rock-climbing school, golf, tennis, riding, hang gliding, fishing, and spectacular walks, with some 20 alpine refuges in the area. And if the weather turns foul, you can beat a retreat to the **Duca degli Abruzzi Mountain Museum**, open daily 9–6; adm.

One thing Courmayeur isn't is a bargain. A one-way trip through the Mont Blanc tunnel will set you back L20 000, a trip on the thrilling, unforgettable cableway to Chamonix over Mont Blanc and back is L35 000 (passports required), though for considerably less you can go only part of the way to **Punta Helbronner**, with fantastic views of the mountain. The tunnel itself is entered above Courmayeur, beyond the medieval fortress-village of **Entrèves** and **La Palud**, the loftiest of the scattered hamlets of the Courmayeur *comune*; La Palud is also the base for the cableway to France. Another scenic summer excursion is to take the Funavia Courmayeur, departing from the centre of town, to the **Plan Chécrouit**, and from there up to Col de Chécruit. This pass is the base for climbing (1½ hours) **Mont Chétif**, the peak just before Mont Blanc, offering tremendous views into the mighty abyss of the **Aiguille Noire**. An alternative is to take another cable car from the Col de Chécruit to **Creta d'Arp** (2755 m), with more fantastic views and a ski run descending all the way to **Dolonne**.

Two gorgeous valleys run in opposite directions from Entrèves. The **Val Veny** may be ascended by bus as far as Lac Combal, the base for a fairly easy hike to the Rifugio Elisabetta and from there, a three-hour walk up to the **Col de la Seigne** on the French border, with fabulous views in either direction. The most common ascent of Mont Blanc begins at Lac Combal.

The **Val Ferret** beginning at La Palud is enchanting and serene, the site of a golf course, trout streams, and the finest cross-country runs; ther⌐ is accommodation in **Planpincieux**, a quiet resort in the pine trees.

WHERE TO STAY AND EATING OUT (tel prefix 0165)
Étroubles: **La Croix Blanche**, on the main Via Nazionale, tel 78 238, once a post-house, and now a well run inn, with good solid Piedmontese specialities and a massive grill, where simmer all kinds of meats and sausages galore; try the homemade chestnut ice cream for dessert (L45 000).

Cogne: Cogne's poshest hotel, the ******Bellevue**, rue Grand Paradis 20, tel 74 825, is a very comfortable family-run inn, cosy and well-furnished in one of the village's prettiest areas. All rooms have private bath, telephones, and most have balconies; there is a garden, a friendly pub, sauna, and private TVs in the newer annexe. Open Christmas holidays, Feb–March, Easter, 6 June–Sept, L150–160 000. The ****Petit Hotel**, Viale Cavagnet, tel 74 010, is good value for money, open all year, with a garden and tennis court and a friendly atmosphere. All rooms have private baths (L70 000). ***Vallée de Cogne**, Via Cavagnet 7, tel 74 079, is a pleasant little hotel, open all year as well (L44 000 without bath, L46–50 000 with). The best restaurant in Cogne, **Lou Ressignon**, Via Bourgeois 23, tel 74 034, is an attractive chalet serving good, honest Valdaostan specialities—try chamois (*camoscio*) with *polenta* for something out of the ordinary, topped off with a good homemade dessert (closed Mon eve and Tues, L35 000). At Cretaz, just outside of Cogne, the hotel-restaurant **Notre Maison**, tel 74 104 is an all wood chalet, with a big fireplace, cosy chairs, pretty garden, and a good restaurant, where you can feast for L40 000.

Courmayeur: Christmas, Easter, July, Aug, and the second week of Feb through most of March are high season here, when reservations are a must. At other times, if the hotel stays open, you'll find lower prices and more room.

Courmayeur has the best hotels in the region, among them, the ******Pavillon**, Strada Regionale 62, tel 842 420, a Relais & Château member. It has 40 very cosy, commodious rooms with balconies enjoying priceless views, all furnished with colour TVs as well as anything else you might need. A welcoming large stone fireplace, a mellow bar, a heated indoor pool and sauna, and a good restaurant are the Pavillon's other attractions; perhaps best of all, however, it's a mere 100 m to the funavia to Plan Chécrouit (open 23 June–30 Sept and 5 Dec–30 April; L210–290 000). Another de luxe choice, the relaxing ******Palace Bron**, a white chalet at Via Plan Gorret 41, tel 842 545, is a little more than a kilometre above Courmayeur on a pine-forested hill, with beautiful views over the Mont Blanc massif from nearly every room. It's close enough to Courmayeur to be convenient to the slopes, but far enough away to enjoy a rarefied tranquillity. Next to the hotel is an outdoor, lake-like pool; the restaurant and piano bar are elegant (open 20 Dec–30 April and 28 June–6 Sept; all with bath, L160–230 000).

Within easy walking distance of the centre, the *****Hotel Lo Bouton d'Or**, Strada Statale 26, No 10, tel 842 380, is the yellow 'buttercup' of Courmayeur's hotels, offering fine, modern bedrooms and sparkling bathrooms, many with balconies looking up to Mont Blanc as well as a garden, solarium and sauna. Owned by the same family that runs the restaurant **Le Vieux Pommier**, half-board is an option. Closed May and Nov, bed and breakfast L85–95 000. For old-fashioned Alpine charm open year round, *****Hotel del Viale**, Viale Monte Bianco, tel 842 256, will win your heart with its woodsy, cosy atmosphere in an attractive old chalet. Private baths, phones and radios are concessions to modernity (L90 000). ****Petit**, Via Margherita 25, tel 842 426, is also open all year, with pleasant, tranquil rooms near the river, a short walk from the centre (L60 000, all rooms with bath, but no restaurant). A delightful bargain, the ***Bel Soggiorno**, Viale Monte Bianco 63, tel 843 259, has 10 simple, but lovely rooms, showers down the hall, and an attractive garden. Open year round, L38–45 000.

Up in Entrèves, the charmer is *****La Brenva**, tel 89 285. Once a simple royal hunting lodge, it has been a hotel since 1897. The décor has changed little since, though

TVs, air conditioning, and private baths have all since been added. Open year-round; L90 000. Courmayeur, international and trendy though it may be, doesn't usually measure up in the kitchen. Hotel meals are usually watered-down Italo-French cuisine, while decent non-affiliated restaurants are few and far between. In Entrèves, however, the **Maison de Philippe**, tel 89 968, is an institution not only for Italians but the local French and Switzers, and there are those who don't mind paying the tunnel fares just to come over to feast at this jovial temple of Alpine cuisine. And feast is no exaggeration, for if Philippe's doesn't bust your buttons, no place will. The decor is charming, rustic without fussiness, and the tables are laid out on three different levels; in the summer you can dine out in the garden. The calorie-laden food, from the antipasti of salami and ham, to the delicious ravioli filled with *porcini* mushrooms, to the tasty fondue, trout, or game, and the grand dessert finale, will cheer up even the biggest grouch. Closed Tues, May and Nov (L40 000). **Le Vieux Pommier**, Piazzale Monte Bianco 25, tel 842 281, is a tourist favourite with a rustic hyper-Alpine interior and a good solid, Valdaostan cuisine; closed Mon and Oct; L35–50 000.

East from Turin: Vercelli and Novara

East of Turin and north of the Po is a landscape that runs the gauntlet from flood plain to Alpine splendour. This section includes the province of Vercelli and part of Novara; the northern part of Novara, from Lake Orta and Lake Maggiore to Domodossola and the Simplon Pass, have been diverted into the section on the Italian Lakes (p. 216).

GETTING AROUND
This area is especially well served by rail. Frequent trains travel to Vercelli and Novara from Turin and Milan; both cities are also linked with Biella (1 hour). From Novara trains go as far as Varallo in the Valsesia (1¹/₂ hours), where you can catch a bus up to Alagna (another 1¹/₂ hours). Other rail links from Vercelli continue south to Casale Monferrato, Asti, and Alessandria, while Novara has trains to Lakes Orta and Maggiore and beyond.

TOURIST INFORMATION
Vercelli: Viale Garibaldi 90, tel (0161) 64 631
Novara: Via Dominioni 4, tel (0321) 23 398

Vercelli

Several million plates of risotto are born every year on the plain between Turin and Milan, a region that is no less than Europe's greatest producer of rice. Its capital, **Vercelli**, is surrounded by a seemingly endless patchwork of paddies divided by hundreds of irrigation canals that criss-cross the plain, dating back to the 15th century. In summer, when they're newly flooded, they become magical, reflecting the clouds and sunset in an irregular checkerboard of mirrors, a landscape bordering on the abstract, uncanny and desolate, melancholy and beautiful.

Of all the cities in Piedmont, only Vercelli stirred from its feudal hibernation in the Renaissance, producing in the 16th century a school of painters, even though the most brilliant of them, Il Sodoma (born in 1477), soon escaped to more promising territory in Tuscany. Even so, as a minor 'city of art' Vercelli is an old, atmospheric place. Even if you have only an hour between trains, you can take in its chief marvel, the **Basilica di Sant'Andrea**, which looms up just across from the station. The basilica was begun in 1219, funded by Cardinal Guala Bicchieri, papal legate and guardian and 'saviour' of England's Henry III. To thank Cardinal Bicchieri for his aid in obtaining the throne, Henry gave him the the revenues from the Abbey of St Andrew in Chesterton, near Cambridge, and the cardinal used the money to finance the basilica and monastery in Vercelli. Completed nine years later—a lightning clip in those days, thanks to the cardinal's unstinting resources—the basilica, though basically Romanesque, is famous in Italian architectural history as one of the first to display signs of the great new Gothic style from the Ile de France, first adopted by the Cistercian Order; the Gothic whispers in Sant'Andrea's twin bell towers, the flying buttresses, the vaulting in the nave and the plan of the church and cloister.

The change of materials halfway up the façade at first gives the same incongruous impression as a 1960s demi-wood station wagon. The three arched portals are Romanesque, with lunettes over the door attributed to the great 12th-century sculptor Antelami. The lofty interior is majestic and striking in its simple red and white decoration. The cloister, with its cluster columns and sculptural details is quite lovely, and offers the best view of the unusual cupola and the basilica's Romanesque and Gothic features. The massive detached campanile, in the style of the towers, was added in 1407.

Vercelli's grand 16th-century **Cathedral** is a block to the left, in Piazza San Eusebio; of the original Romanesque construction only the bell tower remains. It has an especially valuable library of codices, including some 11th-century Anglo-Saxon poems perhaps brought to Vercelli by Cardinal Bicchieri. The one saintly member of the House of Savoy, the Blessed Amadeo IX, who died in Vercelli castle in 1472, is buried in an octagonal chapel. From the cathedral, the Via Duomo leads past the **Castello d'Amadeo** (to the left, behind Santa Maria Maggiore), then to Via Gioberti and Via Borgogna, site of the **Pinacoteca Borgogna** (open Tues and Thurs 2:30–4:30, and Sun 10:30–12:30), with paintings by Vercelli natives—most famously Sodoma, Gaudenzio and Defendente Ferrari, as well as works from the rest of Italy.

Via Borgogna gives into old Vercelli's main street, **Corso Libertà**; at No 204, be sure to look in at the lovely courtyard of the 15th-century **Palazzo Centori**. The Corso continues to the main square, Piazza Cavour, where markets are held under the Piazza Municipio, and down Via Lucca, the **Church of San Cristoforo**, its interior adorned with a famous series of frescoes (1529–33) by Gaudenzio Ferrari, including his masterpiece, the *Madonna of the Oranges*. Vercelli has an interesting archaeological and historical museum, the **Museo Leone** on Via Verdi, off Piazza Cavour, located in a 15th-century house and Baroque palace (open April–Nov, same hours as the Pinacoteca). From Piazza Cavour, Corso Libertà continues into the newer part of town; in Piazza Zumaglini rice prices are decided in the Rice Exchange, or **Borsa Risi**; here, too, is the national rice board's headquarters.

Novara

Novara is an ancient city, its named derived from *Nubliaria* ('wrapped in mists') but one that has preserved only a few traces of its past; its modern affairs primarily concern cheese, and particularly Gorgonzola, of which Novara is the major producer and distributor. In the central Piazza della Repubblica there's the restored 15th-century **Broletto**, housing Novara's **Museo Civico**, with Renaissance armour, and paintings by Gaudenzio Ferrari and others from Piedmont, as well as one attributed to Antonello da Messina (open 9–12 and 3–7, summer 9–1 and 4–7, closed Mon). Across the piazza stands the **Duomo**, built over the former Romanesque temple in the 1860s by the flamboyant Antonelli (who designed the Mole in Turin); this time, instead of building tall, he built a neoclassical building with one of the largest doorways in Europe: 12.8 × 6 m. Parts of the original cathedral survive, including the campanile, the 12th-century chapel of **San Siro**, with contemporary frescoes, a red brick cloister, and some mosaics in the chancel; in the main body there are fine frescoes, and paintings by Gaudenzio Ferrari and others of the Vercelli school, and a collection of 16th-century Flemish tapestries. The adjoining **Baptistry** dates back to the 5th century, and contains very unusual frescoes of the Apocalypse, painted in the 12th century.

From the piazza, Via San Gaudenzio leads to a startling landmark, the church of **San Gaudenzio**, designed in the 16th century by Pellegrino Tibaldi and topped in the 19th by the inimitable Antonelli with Italy's most phallic dome, one that wouldn't look too out of place in India. A slender spire of several tiers crowns the tower, itself topped by a shining figure of the saint who seems to poke the very sky, all together measuring some 145 m high. San Gaudenzio's pointy 18th-century campanile makes an interesting companion piece. Inside, don't miss the unforgettable *Battle of Sennacherib* by Il Tanzio (1627), where the painter's obsession with realism leads headlong to the bizarre and nightmarish.

Novara has two other museums of interest (all same hours as the Museo Civico). The **Museo Ferrandi** contains a collection garnered in Eritrea and Somalia between 1886 and 1920 by explorer Ugo Ferrandi, while the **Galleria Giannoni** is devoted to 19th-century painting, including important works of the *Macchiaioli* school (Tuscan impressionists) and the *Scapigliatura* movement of Milan.

WHERE TO STAY AND EATING OUT

Vercelli isn't exactly a popular stopover, and its hotels are indifferent. Two convenient establishments in the centre are ****Brusasca da Cinzia**, Corso Magenta 71, not far from the river, tel (0161) 66 010, where rooms have private baths (L60 000), and on the Corso Marcello Prestinari, the ***Croce di Malta** has clean rooms for L40 000, tel 53 712. Nor is the province known for its cuisine, in spite of its rice, though at **Il Paiolo**, Via Garibaldi 72 (the street between the station and the Corso Libertà), tel (0161) 53 577, you can dine well on good hearty risotto, stuffed vegetables, *agnolotti di carne*, and the occasional frog (full meals with wine, L40 000; closed Thurs and July–20 Aug).

Novara does rather better in the hospitality field, and offers some robust DOC red wines like *Sizzano, Ghemme* and *Boca*; of the latter the story is told that it was served to the Patriarch of Venice and an important bishop on a visit to Novara. 'This is wine fit for a bishop!' declared the bishop, but the Patriarch corrected him: 'No, your excellency; this is a wine for a pope!' And sure enough, not long afterwards, the Patriarch was elected to the papacy as Pius X. The most elegant hotel in Novara, ******Italia**, is centrally located on Via Solaroli 10, tel (0321) 399 316, and very modern, well furnished and comfortable, with a garage and one of the best restaurants in the city, with good rice dishes and surprises like chicken curry and chateaubriand. (Rooms, all with bath, L140–175 000, meals L45 000.) *****Europa**, Corso Cavallotti 38A, tel (0321) 30 240, is large and comfortable, convenient to both the centre and station. It has a garage, and all rooms have bath (L90 000). The nicest hotel near the station, ****Moderno**, Corso Garibaldi 25, tel (0321) 25 094, is set back in a bit of greenery and not too noisy (L60 000 with bath). **Caglieri**, Via Tadini 12, tel 45 63 73, is a family-run trattoria specialising in good home cooking: *lingua in salsa verote*, *risotto alle verdure*, *gnocchi*, followed by a hearty *bollito misto*, or roast meat dishes with polenta; L35 000, closed Fri.

North of Novara: Wool and 3-D Chapels

TOURIST INFORMATION
Biella: Piazza Vittorio Veneto 3, tel (015) 35 11 28
Varallo Sesia: Corso Roma 41, tel (0163) 51 280 or 52 299

Biella

Easily reached from either Vercelli or Novara, the wool and textile town of Biella is divided into two—the lower half, **Biella Piano** and the upper, **Biella Piazzo**, linked since 1885 by an incline railway. Biella Piano's chief monuments are clustered in the Piazza Duomo: the lovely little **Baptistry**, dating back to the late 10th century, the mighty nine-storey Romanesque **Campanile** of a now-demolished church, and the town's white elephant, the Gothic **Cathedral**, unfortunately prettified in the last century. Biella Piano also has a fine Renaissance church—one of the few in Piedmont—**San Sebastiano**, begun in 1504 and housing a number of works by the Vercelli school, especially Bernardino Lanino's *Assumption*, and some beautifully carved choir stalls. The city's **Museo Civico** (open afternoons except Sun) is on Via P. Micca 36, with archaeological finds, ceramics, and paintings.

During the Renaissance, wealthy textile merchants built their showy mansions up in Biella Piazzo, which retains much of its patrician air and offers fine views over the city and surrounding mountains. A three-storey **cotton mill** from 1859 stands near the centre, a reminder of what is still the region's lifeblood. Across the river Cervo, in San Gerolamo Park, the former villa of the great Alpine explorer and photographer Vittorio Sella is now the **International Museum of Alpine Photography**, founded in 1948, with his old equipment and photographs of the world's greatest peaks. To visit, ring or write first (tel (015) 23 778).

On the map the environs of Biella look like a plate of spaghetti, a confusing network of squiggly yellow valley roads winding between the mountains. The main attractions, all connected by bus with Biella, include the stately, 16th-century castle in **Gagliànico**, 5 km from Biella; and 12 km to the north, the **Santuario d'Oropa**, the most venerated shrine in Piedmont, founded by St Eusebius in the 4th century, when he returned from the Holy Land with the image of the Black Madonna and Child, reputedly carved by St Luke. The sanctuary consists of three vast quadrangles, a new Baroque basilica, and a remnant of the original frescoed church, sheltering the icon, perhaps the most exotic and pagan image in Christian Italy, jet-black and embellished with a towering golden crown, a starry halo, and costly jewels. A cableway near the sanctuary ascends **Monte Mucrone** (2335 m), with its lake, offering hiking in the summer and skiing in the winter. Further north, **Piedicavallo**, the highest town, is a base for hikes into the Val di Gressoney in Valle d'Aosta, or into the Val Sesia (see below). A few kilometres south of Piedicavallo begins the **Strada Panoramica Zegna** (N. 232) noted for its spectacular views of Monte Rosa.

In late spring thick clusters of rhododendrons and azaleas on Burcina Hill, in the village of **Pollone** (just west of Biella) burst into a dazzling pageant of colour. From here the road twists around to another popular sanctuary, **Graglia**, dedicated to Our Lady of Loreto and prettily located high on a hill. To the southwest of Graglia, at Donata, begins a district known as **'La Serra'** for its steep green morainic ridge. Oaks, chestnuts, birches, and vineyards grow here in arcadian harmony, dotted with unspoiled villages. At the end of the ridge lies the clear, spring-fed **Lago di Viverone**, an unglamorous but soothing place to camp, swim, fish, or mess about in a boat. There's an 18-hole golf course nearby at **Magnano**.

A further 10 km to the south, on the N. 593, is **Borgo d'Ale**, a town of peach orchards and two worthy churches, the Romanesque **San Michele di Clivolo** and the **Chiesa Parrocchiale**, by Bernardo Vittone (1770), one of several that this Rococo wizard built on a hexagonal plan.

Varallo and the Val Sesia

The main rail and road approach to this lovely Alpine valley is from Novara; from Turin, you can change trains at Romagnano. The industrial, lower part of the valley is dotted with textile and cotton mills, but at Varallo the scene begins to change. Varallo is a fine, friendly town embraced by wooded slopes; the river Sesia froths and tumbles here for exciting white-water kayaking or rafting. Varallo has a good **Pinacoteca**, with works by the Vercelli school, and a 1620 *David* by Il Tanzio, a follower of Caravaggio, who portrays the young hero holding up for the viewer the massive, grotesquely realistic head of Goliath. In the same building, the Palace of Museums, there's a **Natural History Museum** (hours change by season—inquire at the tourist office), as well as a fine church, **San Gaudenzio**, artistically piled on top of a stair, best known for its polyptych by Gaudenzio Ferrari. An entire wall of his work, depicting the Life of Christ, is in the **Madonna delle Grazie church**, located at the bottom of the stair up to Sacro Monte.

Located high above the town (608 m; a cable car also makes the trip up), **Sacro Monte** is the five-star attraction of Varallo. It was founded as the Sanctuary of New Jerusalem in 1491 by the Blessed Bernardo Caimi, who wanted to recreate in Piedmont the Holy Shrines of Palestine. The idea caught the fancy of St Charles Borromeo, the Archbishop of Milan, and when the two holy men were done, the result was nothing tub-thumping less than the Disneyland of the Counter-Reformation. The high altar is gilded, exploding Baroque, but what makes the 'Bible really come alive' are the 45 chapels containing

Madonna delle Grazie, Varallo

what must be the world's first dioramas—16th-century 3-D scenes of statuary with fresco backgrounds—some 1000 statues and 4000 painted figures, depicting scenes from the scriptures. The best ones are by Gaudenzio Ferrari and Morazzone (*Ascent to Calvary, Ecce Homo*, and the *Condemnation to Death*). When you can pull yourself away from this sincere but nutty extravaganza, step outside to appreciate the fine **Piazzale della Basilica**, a little gem of porticoes, palm trees, and a little fountain under a pavilion.

North of Varallo extends the **Val di Mastellone**, a scenic valley of deep ravines and Alpine scenery; **Fobello**, famous for its Walser lace-making and embroidery traditions, with a lace museum and school, and **Rimella** are two small resorts. The upper extension of the Val Sesia, the **Val Grande**, is more touristy with main resorts at **Riva Valdobbia**, with Monte Rosa as a background and a parish church with curious exterior frescoes. There are a number of walks beginning here, with the hike over the Colle Valdobbia to the Val di Gressoney in Aosta the most popular. **Alagna**, the last town in the valley, is a popular summer and winter resort under Monte Rosa, with funiculars up into the massif. The Walser population (immigrated from the Swiss Valais in the 12th century), has converted one of their wooden 17th-century homes in the charming hamlet of Pedemonte (3 km up the road from Alagna) into the **Walser Museum**, furnished in the traditional manner.

WHERE TO STAY AND EATING OUT
Biella (tel prefix 015): Business and pilgrimage trade has endowed the city with a far more plush selection of hotels than Vercelli, the provincial capital. The medium-sized ******Augustus**, Via Italia 54 (in the centre), tel 27 554, offers very comfortable lodgings, with bath, TV, and frigo bar in every well furnished room (L160 000). *****Principe** is also centrally located at Via Gramsci 4, tel 28 631, with a friendly bar, and a TV in every room (L90 000 with bath). Cheaper choices include ***La Grande Muraglia**, Via

B. Bona 15, tel 22 669, with simple rooms for L50 000. At dinner time seek out **Grilli**, Via S. Giuseppe Cottolengo 26, tel 849 1623, for unusual seafood dishes, fresh pasta, and homemade desserts (L30 000), or, on the road to the Sanctuary from Biella, **Il Baracca**, Via Santuario d'Oropa 6, tel 21 941, is the oldest and best place to eat in the area, with Piedmontese treats like *bagna cauda, salami della duja,* rice dishes, mixed roast or boiled meats. Closed Wed, L40 000. Up at Oropa itself, **Fornace**, tel 55 122, has a long-established trade in filling up pilgrims with polenta, risotto, and game dishes at affordable prices (L25–30 000).

The ***Castello di Roppolo**, in Roppolo near Lake Viverone, tel (0161) 98 528, has 11 elegant rooms in a former medieval castle, in a lovely setting, each room furnished with private bath (L90 000). Also on the premises, the **Enoteca della Serra**, tel (0161) 98 501, offers a wide selection of Piedmont's finest wines, and an adjacent restaurant featuring local specialities. The Enoteca is open Wed–Sun from March–Oct, weekends only the rest of the year.

Varallo has a few modest inns, the best of which is the ***Monte Rosa**, tel (0163) 51 100, with 18 rooms in a tranquil garden, along with one of Varallo's few restaurants, though this shuts down between Oct and May as well as on Wed (L55 000 with bath; meals L20–30 000). Alternatively, go for a big gourmet spread at the **Hostaria il Castello**, Via Caccia 2, in Varallo Pombia, tel (0321) 95 240 for superb anti-pasta, salads, stuffed veggies or game in season, and classic desserts (L50 000; closed Tues in mid-Aug and Jan). In Alagna, the small ****Cristallo**, tel (0163) 91 285, has the best accommodation in the resort, with luxurious rooms and lots of mountain atmosphere; open Christmas–April and July–Aug, L100 000 with bath. Smaller and simpler, the ****Indren**, a few kilometres from the centre at Reale Inferiore, tel (0163) 91 151, is serene and quiet in a pretty setting. All rooms have bath, L55 000.

Southeast Piedmont

When the Turinese or Milanese come to this region at weekends, their thoughts are more on victuals and drink than on sights. **Alba** and **Asti** are the main wine-growing centres of Piedmont, producing its most famous wines in a supremely civilized land-scape, characterized by lovely, rolling hills, winding roads, dotted with small villages and fortifications. The region's other speciality, white truffles, *tartufi,* the pungent ambrosia of the Italians, are harvested in the autumn with a barrage of ecstatic festivals devoted to gluttony. In October in Asti, daily truffle auctions take place in the wee hours of the morning, when the secretive truffle hunters with their truffle hounds arrive to sell the night's harvest (it's essential to hunt the tasty tubers at night because the best ones are always on someone else's property). A walnut-sized *tartufo* may easily go for L100 000.

GETTING AROUND
Alessandria, Casale Monferrato, Acqui Terme, Asti, and Alba are all linked to one another by rail, and are easily accessible from Turin, Milan, and Genoa. But to really explore the district's scenic 'wine roads' (*strade dei vini*) you need a car. Bus schedules are rarely convenient to many of the outlying villages.

TOURIST INFORMATION
Casale Monferrato: Viale Marchino 2, (0142) 70 243
Alessandria: Via Savona 26, tel (0131) 51 021
Acqui Terme: Corso Bagni 8, tel (0144) 52 142

Casale Monferrato

Between Vercelli and Alessandria, **Casale Monferrato**, Italy's biggest producer of cement, once held, from the 15th century to 1703, the more glamorous position as capital of the Byzantine Paleologo duchy of Monferrato. As Ruritanias go, it had the misfortune to be squarely on one of Europe's main warpaths, and suffered an unfair number of vicissitudes—and perhaps more than its share of glory. Founded before the year 1000 by Aleramo, the duchy blossomed when its duke Conrad was elected King of Jerusalem, as his reward for helping in the Crusades. With the subsequent cultural exchanges with the east, Monferrato became 'the Parnassus of Italy'. When the Alerami dynasty died out in 1305, the duchy came into the hands of the Paleologhi family of Byzantine fame. After a brilliant beginning in the person of William VII, the Paleologhi only lasted until 1530, after which the Gonzaga of Mantua managed to win the hand of the heiress and the dukedom. The Italian wars never permitted them to enjoy it, and by 1630 the duchy was ruled by the Savoys.

The main sight in Casale is the Lombard Romanesque **Cathedral of S. Evasio** (11th- and 12th-century), with an asymmetrical façade, a spacious atrium, and a prize silver crucifix, made in the 12th century by Rhineland craftsmen. Just east of the cathedral, **San Domenico** was founded by the Paleologhi in 1470 and has a striking Renaissance portal. On the north side of Casale are the squat towers of the ducal **castle**, and on Via Alessandria, the more charming **Palazzo of Anne d'Alençon**, with a delightful frescoed 15th-century courtyard. The Duchy was one of the safe havens for Jews in the Renaissance and Counter-Reformation, and Casale's ornate **Synagogue**, built in 1595, now doubles as a Jewish museum, open Sun and holidays, 10–12 and 3:30–6:30.

Alessandria

Alessandria, the provincial capital, was founded in the 12th century by disgruntled nobility from Monferrato who opposed Emperor Frederick Barbarossa and named their new town after Frederick's arch enemy, Pope Alexander III. The city these days is best known as the city of *Borsalino* hats, the world's finest (inquire at the tourist office if you'd like to visit the hat museum **Museo del Cappello Borsalino**). There's little else to see; most impressive is the 12-pointed **Cittadella**, built in 1728 by the Savoys and one of the best-preserved fortresses from the period, with most of its outer works still intact. North of Alessandria, **Valenza** is a major producer of gold and silver jewellery; the goldsmiths' association, the Associazione Orafa Valenzana, holds a permanent exhibition of their craft in the centre of town.

Just 8 km south of Alessandria on the Genoa road, Napoleon defeated the Austrians in 14 June 1800 at what he considered the greatest battle of his career, **Marengo**. The battlefield is marked by a column, and in the village there are monuments to Napoleon and General Desaix, who perished on the field, as well as a museum of the battle in the **Villa di Marengo** (open winter 2:30–5:30, summer 4–7, Sun also in the morning 10–12, closed Mon). Another 6 km south lies **Bosco Marengo**, birthplace of Pope Pius V (1504–72), whose reign was particularly notable for the victory over the Turks at Lepanto. Pius built the magnificent church of **Santa Croce** in the village to serve as his tomb, a masterpiece of green marble and porphyry. The Romans, however, interred him in Santa Maria Maggiore.

Tortona and Acqui Terme

Tortona, east of Alessandria, was the Roman *Dertona*, and still has a sprinkling of Roman remains—most importantly, two monumental tombs at the corner of Viale De Gaspari and Via Emilia. The **Museo Civico**, in the Piazza Marconi, is housed in a 15th-century palace and contains some interesting finds, a good sarcophagus and medieval art. From Tortona the railway continues to Voghera, Pavia, and Milan.

More vestiges of antiquity's biggest bully boys may be seen at the spa, **Acqui Terme** (Roman *Acquae Statiellae*), most notably the four arches of the Roman **Aqueduct** in the park near the hotel and bathhouse Antiche Terme. An **archaeological museum**, in the half-ruined Castello dei Paleologhi, contains mosaics and remains from the ancient baths (9:30–12, 3–6, closed Sun morning). Next to the castle stands the fine Romanesque **Cathedral**, with a good doorway and campanile. The most intriguing site in Acqui, however, is the octagonal pavilion and fountain in the centre of town, called the **Bollente** after the hot sulphuric spring that bubbles up here, leaving the earth in a diabolical cloud of steam.

WHERE TO STAY AND EATING OUT

In Casale Monferrato, the posh place to sleep is the *****Garden**, Viale Montebello 1, tel (0142) 71 701, with as many comforts as any provincial hotel (L90 000, all with bath); alternatively, stay in the historic centre at the old-fashioned ***Botte d'Oro**, Via Paleologhi 19, tel (0142) 2310, with simple rooms for L35 000 without bath, or L45 000 with. **La Torre**, Via Garoglio 3, tel (0142) 70 295, is a restaurant that the Turinese and Milanese drive out of their way to patronize. The offerings are based almost entirely on ingredients procured in the immediate environs, such as risotto with crayfish, spinach-filled tortelli, crêpes with artichoke cream, or breast of duck (closed Wed and most of Aug; a *menu degustazione* will set you back L55 000 and up).

Alessandria's most comfortable hotel, ******Alli Due Buoi Rossi**, Via Cavour 32, tel (0131) 445 252, also has the city's best restaurant. Located in the heart of the city, the rooms are luxurious (L240 000) and the meals feature Piedmontese specialities like *agnolotti* and lasagne (L45 000; closed Fri eve and Sat). ****Londra**, next to the station at Corso Cavalotti 51, tel 51 721, has adequate nondescript rooms (L84 000). In Acqui Terme, you can take the water or mud cure in the pampered environment of the ******Antiche Terme**, Viale Donati, tel (0144) 52 101, set in a pretty park (open June–2 Oct; L85 000, all with bath). *****Nuove Terme**, another thermal establishment, at Piazza Italia 1, tel (0144) 52 106, has comfortable rooms, also in a quiet garden setting, open mid-March–10 Dec (L55 000 without bath, L72 000 with). The best place to dine, **Carlo Parisio**, is at Via Mazzini 14, tel (0144) 56 650, in the centre of town, with a menu of Piedmontese specialities—*bagna cauda*, stuffed vegetables, *agnolotti*, and good roast meats. (Closed Mon and half of July; L50 000.)

Wine, Wine Everywhere: Asti, Le Langhe, and Alba

TOURIST INFORMATION
Asti: Piazza Alfieri 34, tel (0141) 50 357
Alba: Piazza Medford, tel (0173) 35 833

Asti

Former rival of Milan, Asti is an old and noble city that well repays a visit. Although nowadays synonymous with fizzy wine, Asti is proudest of its poet and dramatist, Vittorio Alfieri (1749–1803), perhaps most noted in British history as the fellow who put the horns on the not-so-bonny Prince Charlie, when he ran off with the dissolute pretender's young wife, the Countess of Albany. The high street of Asti is naturally called Corso Alfieri, and all of the city's monuments are within a block of its length. On the Corso's easternmost end stands the church and cloister of **San Pietro in Consavia**, built in the 15th century and housing a small archaeological collection; most intriguing, however, is its round baptistry, perhaps dating as far back as the 10th century, supported by eight thick columns with cubic capitals. Six blocks further west, the Corso passes by the large **Piazza Alfieri** with the tourist office and the Public Gardens. Though sharply triangular, this piazza is the site of Asti's annual horse race, the *Palio*, a tradition of neighbourhood rivalry dating back to 1275 and revived in 1967. As in Siena, the *Palio* combines medieval pageantry and daredevil riding: it takes place on the third Sunday of September, coinciding with Asti's great wine fair.

A block from the Piazza Alfieri is the attractive Romanesque-Gothic **Collegiata di San Secondo**, housing the relics of Asti's patron saint, the Astigiano *Palio* (the banner awarded at the horse race) and a polyptych by Asti's greatest Renaissance artist, Gandolfino d'Asti. There are several old palaces in the neighbourhood, and medieval towers loom over the rooftops—the tall, elegant **Torre Troyana**, across the Corso, and further down the Corso, the **Torre Comentina**, with the swallowtail merlins of the Ghibelline party; the octagonal **Torre De Regibus**; and finally the unusual cylindrical **Torre Rossa**, built on a Roman foundation. Here, detour to the right (north), for the tall **Cathedral**, a 14th-century Gothic monument gaily decorated with checked patterns of red and white stone, the city's colours. It has Baroque frescoes, paintings by Gandolfino d'Asti, and Holy Water stoups constructed from Roman and Romanesque capitals and columns.

Back on the Corso, there's a museum and wild-eyed bust devoted to Vittorio Alfieri. In the basement of the neighbouring Liceo, you can visit the 8th-century **Crypt of Sant'Anastasio** (9–12 and 3:30–5:30, closed Sun and Mon), with notable carved capitals. On Via Mazzini, opposite the Alfieri museum, the **Palazzo Malabayla** is the finest Renaissance palace in Asti. At the eastern end of the Corso, **San Pietro** church has an octagonal Romanesque baptistry. Some 3 km north of town, **Chiesetta di Viatosto** is a pretty-plain Romanesque chapel on a hill, with quattrocento frescoes inside and enchanting views over the hilly and fertile countryside to the Alps.

North of Asti: Monferrato

The province of Asti divides itself into two sections, Monferrato in the north and the Langhe in the south. The gastronomic capital of Monferrato is **Moncalvo** (bus from Asti), with famous wine and truffle festivals. The towers and moats of its castle remain, there's a good Gothic church, **San Francesco**, and many old houses, and most spectacularly, a view of the countryside from the large Piazza Carlo Alberto. Just northeast of Moncalvo, another ancient Black Madonna, similar to the icon at Oropa, is venerated at the **Santuario di Crea**. Its 23 chapels contain late 15th–17th-century frescoes and statues, usually merged together in the fondly kitsch Piedmontese manner; the highest chapel, del Paradiso, has more fine views over the vineyards. Another town just northeast of Asti, **Castagnole Monferrato**, holds a special festival on the second Sunday in October, called **La Vendemmia del Nonno** (Grandpa's Grape Harvest), with old-fashioned grape picking, barefoot wine-crushing, dancing and music. More sophisticated features include a truffle auction, and stalls serving glasses of Barbera and Grignolina, as well as Ruch 130, a new red dessert wine from the region—accompanied by a huge buffet.

In the northwest, in the middle of the countryside near **Albugnano** (22 km from Asti, off the road to Chivasso) the **Abbazia di Vezzolano** is the finest Romanesque building in Piedmont, according to legend founded in 773 by Charlemagne, who had a vision on the site while out hunting. It has a remarkable façade from the early 12th century, adorned with blind arcades and sculpture, and an even more remarkable rood screen that divides the nave in two and is carved with two strips, the upper one depicting the Four Evangelists and the Deposition, the Assumption, and Incarnation of the Virgin, while the lower one has a cast of solid medieval characters sitting in a row, with their names draped over their chests like beauty contestants. On the high altar are 15th-century terracotta figures of the Virgin and Child, worshipped by kneeling figures of St Augustine and Charlemagne, all under a florid Gothic *baldacchino*. Part of the **cloister** is even older than the church, with sculpted capitals, while the newer section is adorned with frescoes of biblical scenes and Charlemagne. The abbey is open daily 9–12 and afternoons 3–6 in the summer, and 2–4 in the winter, except Mon and Fri. Between the abbey and Turin, **Chieri** is a fine old town with an especially interesting **Gothic Cathedral**, finished in 1436, built over Roman and early medieval foundations; its frescoed baptistry dates back to the 13th century.

Alba and Le Langhe

South of Asti, lie the beautiful, fertile hills of Le Langhe, swathed with the intricate woven patterns of the vines that produce Italy's finest red wines—Barolo, Barbera, Barbaresco, Dolcetto, and Nebbiolo. Little villages are clustered on the tallest hills, crowned by their castles, like **Montegrosso**, the main producer of Barbera wine; gastronomic **Costigliole d'Asti**, where the picturesque castle is now used as an Enoteca of regional wines, and **Canelli**, surrounded by vineyards producing muscat grapes, the centre of Asti Spumante production. **Nizza Monferrato** is the site of the **Bersano Museum**, with artefacts related to the history of wine. Further south the hills become higher, and vineyards give way to hazelnuts and maize. If you ever make it as far as **Roccaverano**, on the way from Asti to Savona, stop to see the village's exquisite little

Renaissance church, perhaps a work of the great Bramante himself, or of one of his followers.

Alba, the capital of Le Langhe on the banks of the Tanaro, is an austere medieval city of narrow winding alleys and brick towers, famous for its cuisine and truffles as well as its noble wines. The towers, like those of so many other Italian cities, are a reminder of Alba's days as a free trading city full of battling barons, each contending with each other and with the town council itself, and each prepared to defend its patch of turf against all comers. At the beginning of the 16th century, Alba produced its greatest painter, Macrino, whose *Vergine Incoronata* (1501) hangs in the council chamber of the **Palazzo Comunale**, along with the *Piccolo Concerto* by Mattia Preti, a follower of Caravaggio. The highlight of the 14th-century **Duomo** is the choir stalls, inlaid in 1500 by Cidonio. Most of the towers are within a block of the Duomo. Walk down Via Vittorio Emanuele, through the centre of the medieval town, and you will see the prettiest thing in Alba, the terracotta reliefs of minor Renaissance deities on the 15th-century **Casa Do**.

As plain and tranquil as Alba seems, the town takes a stand when it needs to. Asti was a bitter enemy throughout the Middle Ages; when the Astigiani captured Alba once, they ran their *Palio* around the fallen town's walls. In more recent times Asti once again slighted its neighbour, this time by not formally inviting the people of Alba to the *Palio*—to make fun of the haughty Astigiani, Alba invented its famous 'Donkey *Palio*', just what its name implies, and still run each year on the first Sunday of October. Alba staged a revolt in 1789, following the example of the French. And most recently, during World War II its partisans were among the most daring Resistance fighters in Italy—in 1944 they managed to declare Alba a free republic, and defended it against the Germans for 23 days.

The countryside around Alba, with its hilltop villages, ruined castles and vineyards is quite lovely. Some of the most interesting destinations are the closest: east of Alba, **Barbaresco** and south, **Barolo**, have respectively given their names to renowned red wines; in Barolo the 11th-16th-century Castello Falletti is used as a vintage cellar, wine museum, and *enoteca*. (Almost every important town in the region has such a 'wine museum'. They're rather antiseptic and not much fun, but Castello Falletti in particular is full of surprises for anyone who wants to get to know the region better.)

The village of **La Morra**, the belvedere of Le Langhe, is another base for walks through the vineyards, and for visiting the former Abbey of the Annunciation (now the **Ratti Wine Museum**). **Monforte d'Alba**, south of Barolo, has one of the best-preserved medieval centres of all the Langhe villages.

One of Piedmont's finest castles, dating from 1340, dominates the beautiful concentric village of **Serralunga d'Alba** to the east. The castle may look suspiciously well-preserved; it was completely restored in the 1870s. King Vittorio Emanuele II dallied here with his favourite actress while Cavour and Garibaldi were out unifying Italy. North of Serralunga, Count Cavour had his own castle, at **Grinzano Cavour**. This gifted statesman was a scientific farmer by hobby, and he made his lands here into a model farm, a showcase for the latest machines and techniques from Britain and America. Today the castle is restored, and contains another wine museum.

Brà—a town that's heard all the possible jokes about its name and would thank you not to invent new ones—has some odds and ends from nearby Roman *Pollentia* in the Gothic **Palazzo Traversa** on Via Serra, and one of Bernardo Vittone's masterpieces, the church of **Santa Chiara** (1742). It is fairly simple on the outside; the architect as usual concentrated on the dome, this one built of two shells, the outer one taking the role of Rococo heaven, glimpsed as if it were the genuine article through the openings in the inner dome. Other openings serve as skylights, brightly illuminating the sugary angels and cream-puff clouds. **Pollenzo** itself retains a circular funerary monument, the foundations of the forum, amphitheatre and theatre; Roman *Pollentia* was known for its textiles, and judging by the size of its amphitheatre, with seating for 17,000, it must have been very prosperous. **Cherasco**, on the cliffs south of Brà, is smaller and more atmospheric, a strange and dusty town of broad straight streets and Baroque churches and gates. The local museum (Museo G. B. Adriani) houses an interesting collection of historical and archaeological items. The 'castle' outside town is really a lovely Renaissance château, built by the Visconti in the 14th century.

North of the Tanaro river, between Brà and Alba, is a separate region called the Roero: a humble corner of Italy, known for its peaches, strawberries and asparagus, and also (you are surprised, of course), for its wines—red *Roero* and white *Arneis*, and a *Dolcetto* for dessert. None of the Roero villages really stand out, but you can have a pleasant time exploring quiet, lovely places like Santo Stefano Roero, Vezza d'Alba, and Guarene, where there is an unusual 18th-century palace with topiary gardens.

WHERE TO STAY AND EATING OUT

In Asti (tel prefix 0141): near the Campo del Palio, the ******Aleramo**, Via E. Filiberto 13, tel 55 661, is one of the city's finest hotels, each room furnished with private bath, TV, and air conditioning; reserve well in advance for the Palio (L130 000). Just outside the city, convenient for the motorist, the ******Hasta Hotel**, at Valle Benedetta 25, tel 213 312, is tranquil and very cosy, with tennis courts, garden, and TVs and air conditioning in every room (L140 000). The Hasta also has a good restaurant, featuring local dishes for L45–60 000. *****Rainero**, Via Cavour 85, tel 353 866, is an older, medium-sized, central hotel, also with air conditioning (L40 000 without bath, L64–74 000 with). In Asti you can dine extremely well at **Gener Neuv**, Lungotanard 4, tel 57 270, overlooking the river. This is the elegant gourmet haven of Asti, where you can order a *menu degustazione* and enjoy a superb meal based on Piedmontese traditions, but prepared in an imaginative and exquisite manner. The desserts are light and beautiful to behold, and the list of Piedmontese wines is matchless. Closed Sun eve, Mon and in Aug; reservations suggested (L70–80 000). Less expensive, **La Greppia**, Corso Alba 140, tel 53 262, is another gastronomic rendezvous, with delicious truffled dishes in season. (Closed Mon; L40–50 000.) **Il Cenacolo**, Viale Pilone 59, tel 511 10, is an attractive, atmospheric old place with delicious savoury dishes based on local ingredients (closed Tues; L35 000).

In Barolo, the classic place to dine among numerous restaurants is **Del Buon Padre**, Via delle Viole 2, in the outskirts at Vergne, tel (0173) 56 192, where the Piedmontese cuisine is solid and simply very good, and the wines are divine (closed Wed; around L40 000, depending on the wine). Another choice in Barolo, **Brezza**, Via Lomondo 2, tel (0173) 56 161, is the local choice for big parties; if you can avoid the weddings, try its delicious ravioli, rabbit, guinea fowl, and polenta dishes (L35–50 000, closed Tues). Costigliole d'Asti has one of the top restaurants in all Piedmont: **Guido**, Piazza Re Umberto 1, tel (0141) 966 012, where reservations are essential to partake of the beautiful masterworks of the kitchen, all made of the freshest local ingredients, with a predilection for *porcini* mushrooms and truffles. The wine cellar is one of the best endowed in the entire country. (Closed Sun and holidays; the fixed price menu for L100 000, service included.)

Alba has a large selection of restaurants. One of the best, **Osteria dell'Arco**, Vicolo dell'Arco 2, tel (0173) 363 974, is in the very centre of town, in a historic building. The small menu includes a tasty *vitello tonnato*, stuffed guinea fowl, and a good selection of wine, all for L30–35 000 (closed Sun). La Morra's **Belvedere**, Piazza Castello 5, tel (0173) 50 190, is where, according to many, Piedmont's finest *agnolotti* is served; it is also a lovely place to try *finanziera*. Good mushroom and truffle dishes in the autumn, and naturally, fine wines (L45 000; closed Sun eve, Mon, Jan and Feb). In Verduno you can eat in Carlo Alberto's castle, the **Real Castello**, Via Umberto I 9, tel (0172) 459 125, and dine like a king on the region's favourite pasta, *tajarin* (tiny tagliatelle), roast guinea fowl, and hazelnut torte. (Open mid-April to Nov, L40–55 000.) **Il Falstaff**, also in Verduno at Via Scavino 1, tel (0172) 459 244, is another good bet, offering delights like shellfish soup and stuffed pigeon and goose; L60 000, closed Mon and Jan.

Southwest Piedmont: the Saluzzese

Southwest of Turin is the Saluzzese, from 1142 an independent marquisate which managed to retain enough of its autonomy to print its own postage stamps in the 19th century. It's a land of jagged mountains, rural pastures and mountain villages, and some lovely memories of ancient chivalry.

TOURIST INFORMATION
Saluzzo: Via Griselda 2, tel (0175) 46 710

South from Turin to Saluzzo

Students of the French Revolution will recognize the name of one of the first towns south of Turin, **Carmagnola**, as the origin of the popular Parisian song of that period, the '*Carmagnole*'. The song was originally sung by Piedmontese minstrels about an early 15th-century *condottiere* nicknamed Il Carmagnola; how it made Danton's hit parade is anyone's guess. In the same area, 12 km south of Turin on the N. 20, is **Carignano**, a town most noteworthy for the first church by Bernardo Vittone, the bright white **Sanctuary at Vallinotto**, built in 1739 as the chapel for the farm workers employed by a banker in Turin. Vittone had just finished editing Guarini's papers when he received his first commission, and the result is extraordinary, especially for its obscure location. From the outside its four tiers rise in diminishing undulating hexagons, a cake-like pagoda; if you're lucky, the chapel will be open so you can see Vittone's complex dome with its daringly innovative four separate vaults—a unique fusion of models left by Guarini and Juvarra (especially the latter's Carmine in Turin). **Racconigi**, a silk-making town further south, is the site of the **Castello Reale** of the Savoys, begun in 1676 and finished in 1842; behind the castle extends a beautiful park with ancient trees and a lake (guided tours at weekends and holidays 2–5 in the winter, 2–6 in the summer, free).

Saluzzo

Mellow, old **Saluzzo** was the capital of the marquisate, and that knew its most prosperous period in the 15th century. The upper town retains much of its character from that period, especially in the lanes below the castle. The church of **San Giovanni** has a good 14th-century Romanesque-Gothic campanile; the church itself was built in 1280, and contains among its treasures the tomb of Saluzzo's great Marquis Ludovico II, who died in 1503. The choir stalls and cloister are also worth a look. On Via San Giovanni, the charming 15th–16th-century **Casa Cavassa** has a lovely courtyard, given more than a touch of the William Morris in its 19th-century restoration. It is now used as the **Museo Civico**, with some of the treasures gathered by the lords of Saluzzo, documents from their reign, and a memorial room dedicated to patriot writer Silvio Pellico, author of *I miei prigioni* (open Oct–Mar 9–12:15 and 2–5:15; Apr–Sept 9–12:15 and 3–6:15, closed Mon, Tues, Jan & Feb; adm).

Four kilometres south of Saluzzo, in **Manta**, the marquises had one of their favourite castles. It's not much to look at, but contains in its baronial hall excellent frescoes of the 1420s by Giacomo Jaquerio of Turin, of nine heroes and nine heroines, believed by some to be portraits of the marquises and their wives, all posing by the Fountain of Youth (open Mar–Sept 10–12:30 and 2:30–6; Oct–Jan 10–12 and 2–4, closed Mon and Feb; adm). Some 8 km north of Saluzzo, on the Po plain, is **Staffarda** and the well-preserved complex of the 12th–13th-century Cistercian **Abbazia di S. Marta**, at Piazza Roma 2 (guided tours 9–12:30 and 2:30–6; closed Mon; adm.).

Western Valleys: the Po, Varaita and Maira

Buses calling at Saluzzo ascend the rugged Upper Valley of the Po just to the west. **Revello**, near the entrance of the valley, was fortified by the first Marquis of Saluzzo. Part of their palace has been incorporated in the **Municipio**, including their chapel, containing intriguing 16th-century portraits of the marquises by Hans Clemer and a Leonardoesque fresco of the *Last Supper* (open Mon–Fri 8–1, also Tues, Wed, and Thurs from 2:30–5:30, free). The fine 15th-century **Collegiata** has a Renaissance marble portal by Matteo Sanmicheli and some good art inside.

According to ancient tradition, when Charlemagne exiled the last old Lombard king, Desiderius, in 774, he took refuge in **Ghisola**, a tiny, ancient hamlet near Paesana, at the valley crossroads. Further up the valley, **Crissolo** is a small resort under the attractive pointed peak of **Monviso** (3841 m), the highest peak in the Maritime Alps. From Crissolo, with a guide and a sense of adventure, you can visit the stalactite **Grotta del Rio Martino**. The valley road ends at the **Piano del Re**, the source of the Po, Italy's longest river (652 km). If you've always wanted to drink a glass of pure Po, this is the place to do it; by the time it flows out into the Adriatic it becomes one of the most toxic substances in Europe. Above Piano del Re, you can walk through the curious **Pertuis de la Traversette** (2882 m), a tunnel, 75 m long, dug in 1480 by the Marquis Ludovico II, a remarkable feat of Renaissance engineering, built to facilitate mule caravans passing between Saluzzo and the Dauphiny. The pass above Piano del Re is believed by some to have been used by even bigger freight—Hannibal's elephants.

From **Verzuolo** (south of Manta) you can take a lovely detour or an entire holiday in the pretty and luxuriant **Valle Varaita**, a Languedoc-lovely valley retaining many of its ancient handicrafts and folklore. The most interesting villages include **Sampeyre**, manufacturer of ironwork and eiderdowns, where early frescoes have recently been discovered in its parish church of **SS. Pietro e Paolo**. During Carnival Sampeyre celebrates the *Baio*, a thousand-year-old lay custom, featuring a variety of historical characters and dramatic scenes with Napoleonic-era costumes, topped with hats made of bright ribbons. Another village, **Casteldelfino**, in its name recalls the days in the 14th century when it was the headquarters of the Dauphin's Cisalpine lands; and then there's the small summer and winter resort of **Pontechianale**. Above it, in good weather, an asphalted road leads into France at the **Colle dell'Agnello**. The **Valle Maira**, the next valley to the south, is known for its lush fruit orchards. It begins at **Dronero**, with an attractive 15th-century bridge, yet another one named the Ponte del Diavolo. Some 3 km from Dronero, **Villar San Costanzo** has a beautiful 12th-century crypt, a survivor of an ancient Benedictine Abbey, entered from the parish church of San Pietro in Vincoli. It is also the base for visiting the unusual chimney rocks, the *Ciciu*, on the slopes of the Pragamonti ridge. The upper part of the valley, around **Acceglio**, is completely unspoiled.

WHERE TO STAY AND EATING OUT

Like the rest of Piedmont, the southwest corner is a happy hunting ground for the galloping, or even the bus-riding gourmet. This is the region to look for Castelmagno cheese, considered by many the finest cheese in Italy but hard to find outside of its home ground.

In Carmagnola, there's **La Carmagnole**, Via Chiffi 31, tel (011) 971 2673, a lovely restaurant in a 17th-century Piedmontese mansion, featuring dishes based on the freshest of fresh ingredients, offering a delicious *menu degustazione*—exotic dishes like pheasant galantine in Sauternes and raspberry vinegar, and local specialities like *osso buco*, stewed in the ancient Piedmontese manner, marinated with an onion stuffed with chocolate(!) and *porcini* mushrooms in cream. The desserts are exceptional, the wines from Le Langhe and Friuli (*menu degustazione* L80 000; closed Sun eve, Mon and some of Aug). **Trattoria del Bollito**, Via Racconigi 206, tel 97 70 658, has tastier fare than its name ('Boiled') suggests. The cuisine is essential Piedmontese, with heavy emphasis on meat in all its variety. Try to eat here at the weekend, when the atmosphere is livelier, L30–40 000, closed Mon eve and Tue.

Cuneo and the Maritime Alps

Despite the long frontier this district shares with France, the difficult mountainous terrain has made it one of the least known corners of Italy. The French influence is strong, both in the dialect and kitchen. Traditions in handicrafts, costumes, and festivals have lingered longer than almost anywhere else on the peninsula. The Maritime Alps, which form the border between Piedmont and Liguria, are one of Italy's wettest but botanically most interesting regions, and velvet green the whole year round.

GETTING AROUND

Cuneo is linked by rail with Turin via Saluzzo and Carmagnola, and with Genoa, via Ceva and Mondovi. It also linked on one of Italy's most spectacular railways to southwest Piedmont's main resort, Limone Piemonte, and through France to Venti-miglia, a 98 km stretch that reopened in 1979 after suffering grave damage in World War II. The journey takes roughly three hours with all its windings and hairpin bends over the mountains.

TOURIST INFORMATION
Cuneo: Corso Nizza 17, tel (0171) 693 258
Limone Piemonte: Piazza Municipio, tel (0171) 92 101
Lurisia Terme: Via Radium, tel (0174) 683 119
Garéssio: Via del Santuario, tel (0174) 81 122
Frabosa Soprana: Piazza del Municipio, tel (0171) 34 010

Cuneo

The provincial capital, Cuneo is an important market town at the confluence of the rivers Gesso and Stura, which here form a wedge, or in Italian, a *cuneo*, which lends the city its unusual triangular shape. If you're approaching by rail, you'll pass over the impressive **Viadotto Soleri**, built in the early 1930s. Although mostly rebuilt in the 18th and 19th centuries, Cuneo is a pleasant city, built around its vast porticoed main square, the **Piazza Galimberti**, site of an enormous market every Tuesday. Via Roma, leading off from the piazza, and Via Mondovi, are the town's most characteristic streets, with their old porticoes built to shelter merchants from the snow. Of the churches, the most interesting is the **San Francesco**, built in 1227, with a good Gothic portal from 1481. Recently restored, it now houses the small collection of the local museum. In the first part of November, Cuneo hosts the Piedmontese Cheese Exhibition, starring the celebrated 'art cheeses' from the region—Castelmagno, Brà, Murazzano, Rashera, etc., which you can nibble on while sipping the vintages of Le Langhe.

Buses from Cuneo will take you up any of the surrounding valleys, the closest of which, the little **Valle Grana**, is reached by way of Caraglio. Here the tiny village of **Monterosso Grana**, spread under its ruined watchtower, has a chapel with good 15th-century frescoes and a small ethnographic museum, with a school aimed at reviving the old crafts of furniture-making and weaving. **Pradleves** is a small summer resort, while **Castelmagno** is the producer of a famous cheese named after the village. A serpentine road leads up and up to the austere and lonely **Santuario di San Magno**, dedicated to a Roman legionary martyred on this site. Its oldest section, the choir, dates back to the 15th century.

Borgo San Dalmazzo, named for another martyr, Dalmatius (3rd century), is more famous these days for its snails, the main attraction of the *Fiera Fredda* (the Cold Fair), an early December market founded by Emanuele Filiberto. Borgo's most notable monument, the **Santuario della Madonna del Monserrato**, a miniature version of the famous Catalan shrine, can be reached on foot in 20 minutes along the chapel-dotted Via Crucis.

Three Valleys

Borgo San Dalmazzo lies at the junction of three valleys. The longest, the wooded **Valle Stura**, is a botanical paradise for its rare flowers and throughout history was a major

117

route of salt merchants and armies. **Demonte** is the chief town of the valley, retaining a number of medieval buildings; on the mountain Podio stand the ruins of the once mighty **fortress of Consolata**, destroyed by the French in 1796. Further up the valley, **Terme di Vinadio** is a small, hot sulphur-spring spa, open summers only; at Pietraporzio begins the **Stretta della Barricate**, a narrow ravine closed in by tall walls on both sides. **Argentera**, the last and highest *comune* is a cool summer resort; between May and mid-October the pass above Argentera, the Colle della Maddalena, is open, lined with pastures and meadows brimful of flowers in the late spring.

The second valley, the **Valle Gesso**, leads from Borgo San Dalmazzo into the heart of the Maritime Alps, the southernmost to have snow year round, with three peaks—Argentera, Gelas, and Matto—at over 3000 m. Much of the region lies within the boundaries of the **Parco Naturale dell'Argentera**, with Alpine refuges and huts for hikes and ascents. The main resort is the **Terme di Valdieri**, in the middle of the park—a spa favoured by the Savoys but rebuilt in the 1950s. Terme di Valdieri is famed for its hot sulphur springs; near the pool the waters flow down a series of steps covered with a rare, multi-coloured alga called 'muffa' (*ulva labyrinthiformis*), which has special healing properties when applied to wounds or inflammations. From here you can walk up to the pretty **Pian del Valasco**. **Entracque** is a small resort in a branch of the valley.

To the southeast of Borgo, the **Valle Vermenagna** is steep and wooded. From Vernante, an 8 km side road leads up to **Palanfre**, a small Alpine village on the fringe of an enchanting beech forest, itself a nature reserve. The unusual circumstance of mountains over 3000 m so close to the sea and the high level of rainfall, combine to create a lush climatic environment of extraordinary richness; within the not large confines of Palanfre Natural Park alone, there are over 650 different trees and flowers. Back in the main valley, and not far from the French frontier, **Limone Piemonte**, where the natives speak Provençal, is a popular winter sports centre with chair lifts. Its name derives not from 'lemon' but from the Greek for meadow, *leimon*, one of the village's most charming features. Amidst the new development stands the Gothic parish church, **San Pietro in Vincoli**, with good examples of local 17th-century woodcarving.

There's another natural park at the head of the **Valle del Pesio**, the next valley, with interesting karst formations and pine forests, spread under the loftiest peak, Marguareis. In the spring be sure to look for what the Italians call the 'Piss del Pesio', a spectacular 30 m jet of subterranean water into a void which resembles just what it sounds like. In the centre of the valley is the **Certosa di Pesio**, founded in 1173 and dominated by its large cloister. Although abandoned after Napoleon, the *certosa* is once again used as a religious house, and the monks take in guests.

Mondovì

Like several other towns in Piedmont, **Mondovì** is divided into two sections, an older, upper half called Piazza, and a lower part known as Preo. Piazza's heart beats in the attractive, asymmetrical **Piazza Maggiore**, where in contrast to the older, Renaissance buildings, the elegant **Chiesa della Missione** (or San Francesco Saverio, 1675–1733) adds an elegant Baroque touch. The florid interior is topped by a vault frescoed with *trompe-l'oeil* figures by the 17th-century Tridentine painter Andrea Pozzo. The **Cathedral** (1763), also up in Piazza, has a chapel dedicated to Suffrage—one of the few, if not only, secular chapels in Italy. Suffrage was introduced in Italy by Mondovì native Giovanni Giolitti, five times Prime Minister of Italy and godfather of 'Italietta', the Italy of Puccini, Liberty art, and Sunday afternoons in the park. At Piazza's highest point, the **Giardino del Belvedere** is planted about the old civic tower, affording excellent views over the countryside. Down in mostly 18th-century Preo, the city's symbol, the 'Moor', sounds the hours atop the church SS. **Piero e Paolo**.

Mondovì is the base for visiting a number of interesting sites in its mountainous environs. Near Bastia Mondovì, the 11th–15th-century church of **San Fiorenzo** is covered inside with a series of 51 late Gothic frescoes in the Provençal style. Just east in **Vicoforte**, the huge 16th–18th-century **Sanctuary** has an unusual, enormous dome and an impressive interior. Southwest of Mondovì, **Villanova Mondovì** has yet another Rococo extravaganza by Vittone: the 1755 **Santa Croce**, where the square crossing of high arches below the dome is converted into an octagon by the vaulting and the architect's unique use of 'inverted squinches', as Baroque master Rudolf Wittkower calls them—a form Vittone invented by hollowing out the usual convex pendentive to create interesting new spaces and bring more light into the dome.

To the south lies yet another hot-spring spa, **Lurisia** (open between June and Sept). **Frabosa Soprana** is a popular winter/summer resort with ski slopes; from here the road continues south over the hills to Bossea (bus from Mondovì), site of the **Grotte di Bossea**, among the most interesting and important caves in Italy, with a wide variety of beautiful stalactite formations, narrow passages and huge caverns, an underground river and lakes, and the skeleton of a prehistoric bear, *Ursus Spelaeus*. The caves maintain a year-round temperature of 9°C, and can be visited daily with a guide.

From the rail junction at **Ceva**, you can take a train south along the Tanaro river as far as Ormea. **Garéssio**, a collection of four little hamlets, is a picturesque hill resort, with ski slopes, mineral water cures, and a summer palace of the Savoys, the **Castello di Casotto**. Pretty **Ormea** is a bosky summer resort, its ruined castle once a nest of Saracen corsairs in the 10th and 11th centuries, when they controlled the Ligurian coast. Ormea is the base for lovely walks into the mountains.

WHERE TO STAY AND EATING OUT

Cuneo is a good base if you intend to explore several of the region's valleys. ***Royal Superga**, Via Pascale 3, tel (0171) 693 223, is a comfortable, medium-sized hotel, with a garage (L85 000). In the oldest quarter of Cuneo, **Ligure**, Via Savigliano 11, tel (0171) 61 942, is a good place both to sleep and eat, a bit old and worn at the edges, but brightened with old-fashioned courtesy. Rooms range from L45–65 000, depending on the plumbing; tasty meals of homemade pasta and roast meat or trout, L35–45 000. Another old favourite in old Cuneo is the historic **Tre Citroni**, near Piazza Galimberti on Via Bonelli 2, tel (0171) 62 048, a family-run citadel of fine dining, with delightful *agnolotti* and roast lamb, among other dishes (L40–60 000; closed Wed and last two weeks of June and Sept).

There are also two superb restaurants near Cuneo: in Centallo, 14 km to the north, **Due Palme**, located in an old postal relay station at Via Busca 2, tel (0171) 211 366, serves mouthwatering *agnolotti*, lamb chops with *porcini* mushrooms, duck à l'orange and other delicacies (L55 000; closed Sun eve, Wed, part of July and Aug). In Boves, 9km south of Cuneo, **Rododendro**, in a mountain cul-de-sac at Frazione San Giacomo, tel (0171) 88 03 72, is the wood-surrounded atelier of one of Italy's finest woman chefs, attracting hungry customers from hundreds of miles around. Her leek soup, her truffles with eggs, and exquisitely tender chateaubriand have put her restaurant on Italy's gourmet map, with an extensive wine list of French and Italian bottles (seasonal *menu degustazione*, L100 000).

In the Cunean valleys there are many, often simple and rustic, places to stay and eat at. A couple of suggestions: **Tre Verghe d'Oro**, Via IV Novembre 131, tel (0171) 98 516, in Pradleves in the Valle Grana, a long-established, old-fashioned mountain inn, in a pretty setting (L40 000 without bath, L55 000 with). Its restaurant features *gnocchi al Castelmagno* and other mountain specialities (L30 000; closed Tues in winter, and in Jan). In Limone Piemonte, ****Principe**, tel (0171) 92 389, is a fine hotel in a scenic position; each room has a private bath and TV. The hotel is open from 15th Dec–April and end of June–10th Sept; L120 000. *Mignon, in town at Via S. Giovanni 3, tel (0171) 92 363, has seven simple rooms without bath (L38 000) and a good restaurant, where Piedmontese specialities are complemented by the cosy atmosphere (L30 000).

Part IV

LIGURIA
(THE ITALIAN RIVIERA)

Lerici

Riviera in Italian simply means shore, but in Liguria the shore is THE Riviera, a rugged, rock-bound rainbow of coast linking France to Tuscany, endowed with what is surprisingly one of the rarer Italian commodities—beautiful beaches. Usually not large, buxom, sandy beaches, but rather refined, slender strands in magical settings, under the swaying palms and bright gardens, backed by old fishing towns tumbling down the hillsides, or resorts that fit as comfortably as an old pair of shoes. After Liguria, you'd have to continue all the way down to the Bay of Naples to find a shore comparable in interest and beauty. And if you're approaching from the haughty French Riviera, the Italian Riviera comes as a pleasant surprise, wonderfully relaxed and ever so gently faded—no one cares if your socks don't quite match or you've brought the children along. There are splendid grand hotels, but they are outnumbered by small and unpretentious *pensioni*.

Although August is peak season on the Riviera these days, people first came to this fabled shore for its sunny and mild winter climate. Sheltered by the Maritime Alps from inclement weather from the north, Liguria enjoys a sensuously lush growth of lemons, oranges, and flowers—one of the region's principal exports. The oil from its ancient groves is legendary. Bathed in a luminous, warm light, the Riviera's colours are dazzling, the reds, blues, yellows and greens like glistening new-borns to the beleaguered, mist-shrouded vision of the northerner.

Whether you linger on the rugged and romantic Riviera di Levante east of Genoa, or on the luxuriant Riviera di Ponente to the west, or in Genoa itself, Italy's vivacious and largest port, the delights of sun and sea are only part of what the region has to offer.

121

Liguria has a distinct regional identity and a distinct language. Poor in resources but full of intrepid, tenacious seamen and merchants, it has always looked to the sea for its survival, its commerce; early on, the native Ligurians traded with the Phoenicians and the Greeks, before Genoa became an important Roman seaport. In the Middle Ages, after ejecting the Saracen pirates who had long harassed the coast, Genoa grew to become a seapower rivalled only by Venice, the bitterest of its many enemies. And although its importance declined in the 15th century, the Ligurian character had been formed by then—frugal, feisty, shrewd, adventurous, but not without a sense of humour. Columbus, of course, came from Liguria, as did the great admiral Andrea Doria, and Risorgimento heroes Garibaldi and Mazzini.

In Liguria look for ancient popular festivals and folk traditions, for great regional cuisine, especially fish dishes prepared in a hearty style similar to neighbouring Provence (try *cacciucco*, Ligurian bouillabaisse, or *cappon magro*, pickled fish with vegetables); or *brasato di manzo alla genovese*, braised beef with vegetables and mushrooms in red wine. Even the snacks are different, like *focaccio*, Ligurian pizza, but with a softer dough than the Neapolitan version and the ingredients baked inside; and *farinata*, a mixture of baked, ground chickpeas best eaten hot from the oven. Pasta (especially *trenette*, similar to linguine) is often served with Genoa's famous *pesto* sauce of basil, garlic, pine nuts, olive oil and parmesan, ground with a mortar and the pestle which gave it its name. Although Liguria isn't one of Italy's great wine-growing regions, you may want to try its best, *Pigato*, a fine, dry white, or *Rossese*, a fine dry red.

Ligurian Itineraries

The **Via Aurelia**, successor to the Roman road, runs along the coast offering the finest scenery, although the **A10** between Ventimiglia and Genoa, and the **A12** from Genoa to Pisa, both have lovely stretches overlooking the coast. Transport, especially buses along the coast, is especially good. The best thing to do on the Riviera is to base yourself in one place and explore from there, at least once venturing into the green mountains behind the beaches. The most scenic mountain routes include the **S28** from Imperia to Ormea and Garessio in Piedmont, from where you can circle back down on the **S582** to Albenga on the coast. Between Savona and Millesimo runs the **A6** to Turin, more or less following the prettier old route. The **A22** or **S456** from Pegli towards Milan, is attractive at least as far as Vignole Barbera; the **A7**, however, is much faster. East of Genoa, the ideal way to see the most stunning scenery—the Monte di Portofino and the Cinque Terre, is by boat and on foot.

The highlights of the Riviera, from west to east, include the fascinating prehistoric caves of **Balzi Rossi**, the medieval hill villages of **Dolceacqua** and **Taggia**, and the ghost town of **Bussana Vecchia**, all near the Riviera's old capital of fun, **San Remo**. Further along the coast is the almost undiscovered village of **Cervo** and ancient **Albenga**, near the beautiful caves of **Toirano**. And in the great embrace of the Genoan metropolitan area, **Pegli**, with its museums, villas, and gardens.

Genoa has several palaces full of art, including a great oriental museum, and a wonderfully evocative old quarter, worth a couple of days. East of Genoa there are more villas and gardens at **Nervi**, then the magnificent promontory, the **Monte di Portofino**. Here are a number of beautiful places—the charming fishing village of **Camogli**, the

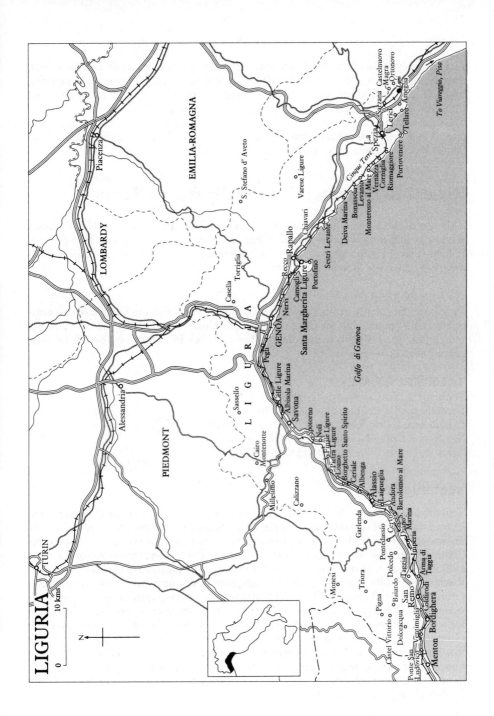

123

ancient abbey of **San Fruttuoso**, and the ultra-chic international resort and yacht port, **Portofino**, a base for beautiful walks. **Chiavari** is an interesting old seamen's town, and beyond it are the **Cinque Terre** villages, hanging on cliffs or below them, immersed in vineyards and laced together by a stunning seaside footpath. **La Spezia** has a good naval museum, and nearby, beautiful old **Portovenere** is almost as chic as Portofino these days. The whole Gulf of La Spezia, known as the 'Gulf of Poets', is enchanting, and can be combined in a boat excursion with the Cinque Terre.

Riviera di Ponente: Ventimiglia to San Remo

This part of the Riviera, especially the coast west of Imperia, enjoys one of the mildest winter climates in the country. Flowers thrive here even in February, and are cultivated in fields that dress the landscape in brilliant patchwork, lending this stretch the well-deserved name, the 'Riviera of Flowers'.

GETTING AROUND
Trains run frequently up and down the coast from Ventimiglia to Genoa; from Ventimiglia a line branches off for Cuneo, in Piedmont, one of the country's most scenic rail routes (see pp. 116–17). Inland the hill towns are easily reached by bus, from their nearest coastal towns.

TOURIST INFORMATION
Ventimiglia: Via Cavour 61, tel (0184) 351 183
Bordighera: Via Roberto 1, tel (0184) 262 322
Ospedaletti: Corso Regina Margherita 1, tel (0184) 59 085
San Remo: Corso Nuvoloni 1, tel (0184) 85 615
Arma di Taggia: Villa Boselli, tel (0184) 43 733

Ventimiglia

Ventimiglia is tricky: if you arrive by train it can seem seedy and dull. On the other hand, if you come by the coastal road from the west it is pure enchantment, a garden town by the sea where roses and carnations are the main crops, and in June the main festival is the 'Battle of the Flowers'. Ventimiglia is also a garden of history, with some of the most ancient roots in Liguria, as evinced by the relics left by Neanderthal man in the **Balzi Rossi** ('Red Cliffs') caves, near the French frontier, on the beach below the village of Grimaldi. Here, between 40,000 and 100,000 years ago, thrived one of the most sophisticated prehistoric societies discovered in Europe. In the caves themselves there are several elaborate burials, the dead adorned with seashell finery; and in one cave, the Grotto del Caviglione, is an etching of a horse, of a breed now common only on the Russian steppes. The **Museo Preistorico**, at the caves' entrance, displays the most important finds from within—ornaments, tools, weapons and some of the earliest works of art ever discovered—palaeolithic 'Venuses' (museum and caves open 9–12:30 and 2:30–6, closed Mon; adm).

In the same area at Mortola Inferiore (and reached by the same municipal bus from Ventimiglia) you can take in the world-famous **Hanbury Gardens**, an enchanted botanical paradise founded in 1867 by Sir Thomas Hanbury and acquired by the Italian state in 1960. Spread out on the slopes around a castle-like villa, planted with some 5000 rare and exotic plants that Sir Thomas acclimatized from Africa and Asia to co-exist with native Mediterranean flora, the gardens are among the most important in Italy. Part of the ancient Via Aurelia exposed near the gardens has a plaque listing the famous who have passed this way, from St Catherine of Siena to Napoleon (open 10–4, closed Wed; expensive). The main road, passing underneath the gardens, leads to the Customs Post at Ponte San Ludovico with its landmark, the **castle** where Serge Voronoff performed his experiments, seeking the Fountain of Youth in monkey glands.

In ancient times Ventimiglia was an important Ligurian capital which the Romans called *Albintimilium*, a name corrupted over the centuries into 'Ventimiglia'. An important station on the Via Aurelia and the birthplace of Agricola, the ruins of **Albintimilium** stand 1 km east of the modern town; best preserved here is the small 2nd century AD **theatre** (open afternoons, except Sun). Ventimiglia itself is divided into old and new by the river Roia: the modern town is built around the great winter flower market and lined with typical Riviera seaside promenades, while the old town, with its medieval plan of twisting lanes, has the attractive ensemble of an 11th–12th-century **Cathedral** and **Baptistry** for its focal point; the latter still shows vestiges of the Byzantine and Lombard original. Another fine Romanesque church of the same period, **San Michele**, was built with Roman columns and milestones. Overlooking the coast west of Ventimiglia are the ruins of the 12th-century **Castel D'Appio**, former headquarters of the piratical Counts of Ventimiglia.

Dolceacqua

Inland from Ventimiglia there are several pretty valleys, the Val Nervia perhaps the most appealing (buses hourly from Ventimiglia). The gem here is the picturesque old stone village of **Dolceacqua** occupying both banks of the river, spanned by the single arch of a medieval bridge and crowned by a 16th-century and reputedly haunted **Doria Castle**, where the lords are said to have taken full advantage of their droit du seigneur to spend the first night with local brides (open 9–12 and 3–7, closed Tues; adm). On St Sebastian's Day (20 January) Dolceacqua celebrates a unique religious procession, led by the 'tree man' who bears a huge tree branch hung with large, coloured communion hosts, a curious mixture of Christianity with ancient fertility rites. The hillsides around Dolceacqua are terraced with vineyards producing the good red wine, *Rossese*, available in the local cafés. Further up, **Pigna**, cradled in the foothills of the Maritime Alps, is another pretty village with an adjacent thermal spa; some 3 km away you can visit **Castel Vittorio**, a fortified hamlet that has changed little since the 13th century, when its thick walls defended it from predatory Saracen raids. From here you can circle back, by way of Baiardo (see below), to the coast at San Remo.

Bordighera

Once a favourite winter residence of Europe's pampered set, and of literati like Katherine Mansfield, blessed with a good beach and regal promenades, Bordighera is now one of the most jovial resorts on the Riviera: from the end of July until the end of August its International Humour Festival does everything possible to make you laugh, with films, comedy acts and routines. Like Ventimiglia the environs contain vast fields of cultivated flowers, but here the speciality is palms; Bordighera has had the monopoly in supplying the Vatican with fronds during Easter week since Sant'Ampelio brought the first seeds from Egypt. Or so they say, though the 16th-century story of the raising of the obelisk in front of the Vatican is more famous (no obelisk had been raised in Rome since antiquity, and no one remembered how it was done; the ropes supposedly were on the point of breaking when a sailor from Bordighera broke the silence imposed on pain of death on the watching crowd: 'Water on the ropes!' he shouted, saving the day. The grateful pope awarded Bordighera the palm frond concession.) but apparently none of the story is true.

You can learn all about the ancient Ligurians at the **Museo dell'Istituto Internazionale di Studi Liguri** (open 9–1 and 3–6, closed Sat and holidays, and the first two weeks of Aug). There are plaster casts of the curious Neolithic rock engravings from the Valle delle Meraviglie (part of France since World War II) and finds from Roman *Albintimilium*. The tiny medieval nucleus, above the Spianata del Capo, is shoe-horned behind its gates; further up the flower-bedecked **Via dei Colli** there are excellent views of the shimmering coast. Below, the Romanesque chapel of **Sant'Ampelio** stands on its little cape, over the grotto where the saint lived; from here you can walk along the pleasant Lungomare Argentina west to the spa, or east along the seaside Via Arziglia to Bordighera's palm and mimosa plantations at the **Winter Garden** and the **Giardino Madonna della Ruota**, a 45-minute walk. At Via Aurelia 1, 2000 species of cacti and other succulents are the cast at the **Giardino Esotico Pallanca**; to visit, tel (0184) 266 344.

San Remo

San Remo is the opulent, ageing queen of the Italian Riviera, her grand hotels and aristocratic villas as beautiful and out of date as antimacassars on an armchair. Yet even if the old girl isn't young, she's still a game corker with a Mae West twinkle in her eye. Other resorts may be more glamorous, but few have more character. San Remo also has considerable bargains, both in hotels and in the shops—the French pour over from the Côte d'Azur to purchase designer clothes and furnishings that cost 20–30 per cent more in Paris.

San Remo stands on a huge, sheltered bay and was long a favourite watering-hole for a variety of drifting aristocrats, most famously Empress Maria Alexandrovna, wife of Czar Alexander II, who was soon followed by a sizeable Russian contingent, including Tchaikovsky, who composed *Eugene Onegin* and the Fourth Symphony during his San Remo stay in 1878. The duke of nonsense, Edward Lear, ended his lifelong travels through the Mediterranean here in 1888, as did the father of dynamite and founder of the famous prizes, Alfred Nobel, who died in 1896 in the **Villa Nobel** (on the eastern edge of town, near the Parco Ormond; open Thurs–Sat 10–12).

A legacy from these golden days of fashion, the white, brightly-lit, Liberty-style **Municipal Casino**, is still the lively heart of San Remo's social life, with its gaming rooms (the French room, with a jacket-and-tie dress code and cover charge, or the free,

126

un-dress-coded American room), roof-garden cabaret and celebrated restaurant with a live orchestra. It is also, in February, the setting for the biggest pop song event in Italy, the unabashedly tacky 'Festival della Canzone', an extravagant, five-day-long-lip-synch ritual built of glitter and hype, where this once gloriously musical nation parades its contemporary talents with all the self-confidence of the Emperor in his new clothes.

From the Casino you can take the famous *passeggiata* down the lovely, palm-lined **Corso dell'Imperatrice**, named for Maria Alexandrovna; here, springing out of luxuriant, almost tropical, foliage are the utterly incongruous onion domes of the dainty **Russian Orthodox Church**, built in the 1920s by the exiled nobility, who lavished a considerable sum on this bright little jewel-box. It contains the tombs of more deposed blue-bloods, the royal house of Montenegro (open Sun mornings and most afternoons). On the other side of the Casino, the Corso becomes Via Matteotti, San Remo's main shopping street. Early risers can take in the almost intoxicating colour and scent of the **San Remo Flower Market** on Corso Garibaldi, just off Piazza Colombo.

The old town, **La Pigna**, has been called San Remo's 'casbah', a tangled, mystery-laden mesh of steep lanes and stairs weaving under archways and narrow tunnels. From above the vegetable market, a *funavia* ascends to **Monte Bignone**, the highest in the amphitheatre of hills wrapped around San Remo (1305 m), with great views of the Riviera. Below lies the 18-hole **Ulivi golf course**, and the most panoramic road in San Remo, the **Corso degli Inglesi**.

Around San Remo

San Remo has several interesting neighbours, all easily reached by buses departing from the train station. Just to the west, the quieter, seaside resort of **Ospedaletti** is shaded by a luxuriant ensemble of pines, palms, and eucalyptus; its name is said to derive from the Knights Hospitallers of Rhodes, who had a pilgrims' hospice here in the 14th century. They are also said to have bestowed their name on the nearby hill town of **Coldirodi**, known for its small art gallery (with paintings by Veronese and Guido Reni) and library.

Most unusual is **Bussana Vecchia**, Italy's trendiest ghost town. On 23 February 1887, a mighty earthquake shook Bussana, killing and turning the town into the picturesque ruin you see today, while the inhabitants rebuilt a new Bussana 2 km closer to the sea. It is a rather typical Italian contradiction that although Bussana Vecchia officially no longer exists, it has a number of artistically-minded inhabitants who equally officially are non-existent but have restored the interiors (but not the exteriors) of the ruined houses and have been hooked up with water, lights and a telephone service and, somehow, with two mild-mannered llamas from Peru. The earthquake knocked in the roof of the Baroque church (packed at the time for the Ash Wednesday service) but nearly all the parishioners managed to escape death in the side chapels; one survivor, Giovanni Torre detto Merlo, went on to invent the ice cream cone in 1902. The church is open to the sky behind its façade, the stucco decorations are now planters for weeds, trees grow in the nave and apse, and cherubs smile down like broken dolls on a shelf.

Further inland, **Baiardo**, spread out over its conical hill with a grand backdrop of mountains and forests, was also devastated by the earthquake. An intriguing relic is the ruined church at the top of the town, with 13th-century capitals carved roughly with the head of Mongols, some of whom are believed to have accompanied the Saracens to

Liguria. Baiardo, unlike Bussana, was rebuilt on the same site as the old town, and its reputation for healthy air has made it a modest summer resort. Baiardo celebrates an ancient rite, the 'Festival della Barca' (of the boat) on Pentecost Sunday, when a large tree trunk topped by a smaller pine tree is erected in the middle of the piazza, around which the people dance and sing—a rare survival of a pagan fertility rite left almost untouched by the Church.

To the east, **Arma di Taggia** has one of the finest sandy beaches in the area, lying at the mouth of the Valle Argentina; 3 km inland, picturesquely medieval **Taggia** is the site of a popular antiques fair held on the fourth Saturday and Sunday of every month. The **Dominican Convent**, founded in 1400 and now a national monument, contains a number of fine paintings of the local Ligurian school (open 9–12 and 3–6, closed Thurs). A pretty drive or walk from Taggia is up to the **Sanctuary of the Madonna di Lampedusa**, a fine viewpoint, reached via the remarkable, dog-leg 16-arched **medieval bridge** at Castellaro. Come on the third Sunday of July for the ancient Festival of Mary Magdalen, who according to tradition once paid Taggia a call, and is remembered by members of her red-capped confraternity with an eerie Dance of Death, performed by two men, one playing the role of 'the man', and the other of Mary Magdalen, who dies and is brought back to life with a sprig of lavender—Taggia's principal cash crop for centuries.

There are a number of attractive old villages dotting the Valle Argentina, most intriguing of which is **Triora**, a fortified 15th-century village high in the mountains. This is a small summer resort, also visited in the winter for skiing at **Monesi**, just under the lofty Cima di Piano Cavallo.

WHERE TO STAY AND EATING OUT (tel prefix 0184)

Ventimiglia: Although midway between Monte Carlo and San Remo, prices here are reasonable. The top hotel choice has to be *****La Riserva**, up in the olive groves at Castel d'Appio (5 km west of town, on Via Peidaigo 71, tel 39 533), a fine family-run inn with magnificent views, a pool, and very comfortable rooms (open Christmas holidays, and from April–Sept; L85–90 000, all rooms with bath). In town, *****Sea Gull**, Via Marconi 13, tel 351 726, is a comfortable establishment on the waterfront, with a bit of garden, parking, and private beach (L40–60 000 without bath, L58–65 000 with). ***Lido**, Via Marconi 11, tel 351 473, is another pleasant beachfront choice, open April–Sept; L45 000, less without bath.

For meals, the premier restaurant in the area is right on the frontier at San Ludovico: the **Balzi Rossi**, Piazzale De Gasperi, tel 38 132, has an almost seaworthy dining room overlooking the Mediterranean. The cuisine magnificently blends the best of France and Liguria, and includes a legendary *terrina di coniglio*, pasta dishes with fresh tomatoes and basil, scallops of sea bass, divine desserts and excellent wines (lunch menu, L40 000, dinner *menu degustazione* L70 000). Definitely reserve. Ventimiglia's other restaurants, most of them on the sea, aren't anything special. **Baia Beniamin**, west of Ventimiglia in Grimaldi Inferiore (Corso Europa 63, tel 38 002), will charm you with its fresh seafood and out of the ordinary dishes like zucchini stuffed with salmon mousse and pasta dishes like tagliolini with lobster and *pappardelle al pesto*. Top it off with a strudel—and a *conto* up to L80 000, very much depending on what you order. In Dolceacqua **Gianni**, Via della

Liberazione 35, tel 36 136, has good Ligurian and mountain specialities, which go down easily with a bottle of Rossese (L35 000).

Bordighera: Excellently equipped with hotels in all price ranges, you can go for elegance at the modern ****Del Mare, Via Portico della Punta 34, tel 262 201, in a beautiful panoramic position over the sea, with such amenities as private beach, sea water pool, gardens, tennis courts, and air conditioning. Closed Nov–Christmas; L165–230 000. Just as luxurious, the ****Cap Ampelio, Via Virgilio 5–11, tel 264 333, overlooks both Bordighera and the sea, with designer furnishings and heated pool, garden, air conditioning, and Italian or French TV; L160–165 000. The ***Britannique & Jolie, Via Reg. Margherita 35, tel 261 464, is a more traditional favourite, with a garden near the sea (closed Oct and Nov; L85–110 000, all rooms with bath). ***Villa Elisa, Via Romana 70, tel 261 313, is an inviting villa above the town, located in pretty gardens. Very nice rooms, open year round; L45–55 000 without bath, L50–95 000 with, depending on the season. Further up, *Virginia, Via Romana 55, tel 260 447, has pleasant rooms in a garden; L33–35 000 without bath, L38–45 000 with.

For meals, the most spectacular choice, inserted in the cliffs, is La Reserve Tastevin, at Capo Sant'Ampelio, Via Arziglia 20, tel 261 322. The views are fantastic, and so is the food, a delightful combination of ingredients from the sea and the Valle Argentina; L50 000. The very elegant and tiny La Chaudron, Piazza Bengasi 2, tel 263 592, will win your heart with delicious dishes like spaghetti with artichokes and the Ligurian speciality, *pesci al sale* (fish baked in a bed of salt, skinned, then dressed with olive oil). Be sure to reserve (L60 000). There are many cheaper choices in the old part of town: Degli Amici, Via Lunga 2, tel 260 591 has well-prepared seafood and rabbit dishes (L22 000).

San Remo: If you arrive in San Remo without booking, there's a hotel-finding service in the station (tel 80 172; closed Sun). On the whole, though, you shouldn't have too much trouble finding lodgings outside of July and August.

The top hotel in San Remo is more of a palace than rented accommodation: the *****Royal, near the Casino, Corso Imperatrice 80, tel 5391. Surrounded by lush gardens, with palms, flowers, tennis court, and an enormous heated sea-water pool, this turn-of-the-century *grande dame* has rooms that vary from imperial suites to more modest, refurbished bedrooms, all equipped, however, with bath, air conditioning, colour TV and frigo bar. And, true to tradition, the hotel orchestra serenades guests in the afternoon and gets them dancing in the evening (L190–380 000, depending on room). One of the oldest hotels, the ****Astoria West End, Corso Matuzia 8, tel 66 77 01, sounds as if it belongs in New York, but instead sits in all its confectionery elegance opposite the sea in San Remo. Although recently renovated, its grand chandeliers, elaborate stucco ceilings, and carved elevators have been left unchanged. Set in luxuriant gardens with a pool and pretty outdoor terrace, the hotel is open all year: rooms, all with bath, from L120–200 000. If you prefer something with a Liberty-style touch, the Astoria's neighbour, the ****Grand Hotel Londra, Corso Matuzia 2, tel 668 000, obliges. Built around the turn of the century, it has a lovely garden, pool, and fine original interior details (closed Oct and Nov; L165 000). If you seek peace and quiet, ***Paradiso, Via Roccasterone 12, tel 53 24 15, may be your paradise, located above most of the hurly-burly, enveloped with flowers on the terrace and balconies, with a distinguished salon, glass-enclosed dining room, and well-furnished rooms, all with bath and many with TVs (closed Nov and half of Dec; L60–100 000). In the centre of the action, the

***Eletto**, Via Matteotti 44, tel 531 548, is a very pretty 19th-century hotel, furnished with antiques and blessed with a welcoming little garden (open all year; L40–70 000 without bath, L50–80 000 with). The **Sole Mare**, Via Carli 23, tel 577 105, is a comfortable choice, especially popular with Italians. Open all year, all rooms have bath, and there's parking as well (L45–65 000). Cheaper hotels abound on Corso Matteotti, Via Roma, Corso Mombello, and Corso Massini, where rooms go for around L15–20 000 a head.

For a splurge at the table in San Remo, **Giannino**, Lungomare Trento e Trieste 23, tel 70 843, offers exquisitely prepared dishes based on fresh, natural ingredients; they include a speciality of the region, *tagliolini al sugo di triglia* (wholewheat pasta with red mullet sauce), polenta with cheese and vegetable sauce, pigeon with ginger, and much more. An excellent wine list accompanies it all; L80–100 000. The **Pesce d'Oro**, Corso Cavallotti 300, tel 66 332, is one of the most famous restaurants in San Remo, although one would never guess from the rather funky location. Inside, however, the *lasagnette al pesto, zuppa di frutti di mare*, and sea bass in lobster sauce will make you a convert to the Pesce d'Oro's numerous fans (L50–70 000). Just outside San Remo, at Verezzo Cava (Sta. Carr. Verezzo 172), **Silvestro**, tel 559 066, is an alternative to the constant barrage of seafood, featuring delicious homecooked meat, chicken, and rabbit dishes, for L30 000. In Arma di Taggia, **La Conchiglia**, Via Lungomare 33, tel 43 169, serves Ligurian delights, based on seafood, local cheese, and delicate olive oil—the shrimp and white bean salad is delicious. Reservations recommended; L65 000, closed Wed and part of Nov and Dec.

Riviera di Ponente: Imperia to Savona

Imperia divides the Riviera of Flowers from the more rugged, silvery Riviera of Olives. Connoisseurs of olive oil rate Liguria's tops in Italy, although of course there are plenty of other regions ready to dispute this most slippery of crowns.

TOURIST INFORMATION
Imperia: Viale G. Matteotti 54bis, tel (0183) 24 947
Diano Marina: Corso Garibaldi 60, tel (0183) 496 956
Cervo: Piazza S. Caterina 2, tel (0183) 408 197
Alassio: Viale Gibb 26, tel (0182) 40 346
Albenga: Viale Martiri della Libertà 17, tel (0182) 50 475
Finale Ligure: Via San Pietro 14, tel 692 581
Savona: Via Paleocapa 59, tel (019) 825 305

Imperia

In 1923 two towns, Porto Maurizio and Oneglia, were married by Mussolini to form a provincial capital, Imperia. The bustling oil port (olive oil, that is) of Oneglia was the birthplace of the great Genoese Admiral Andrea Doria, while the old quarter of Porto Maurizio (connected by city bus) has most of Imperia's charm, with steep lanes and steps, but even here lacks the typical Riviera resort ambience, for better or worse.

Cathedral at Cervo

Imperia is also the base for exploring old villages in the hinterland, like **Dolcedo**, the centre of the most renowned olive groves in the region, with its medieval bridges, one carved with the cross of the Knights of Malta. Another valley, further east, leads to **Pontedassio**, site of the **History of Spaghetti Museum** (yes, there had to be one!). Run by one of Italy's pasta dynasties, the Agnesi family, the museum seeks to prove that spaghetti is Genoese after all and not Chinese or Neapolitan; at least it is mentioned in a 1244 document from the Genoese archives. Other exhibits include those on the evolution of spaghetti-making machines, photographs, drawings and books; open on request, tel (0183) 21 651.

East of Imperia is a string of popular resorts: **Diano Marina** with its famous olives, modern **San Bartolomeo al Mare**, and prettiest of the three, **Cervo**, a curl of white, cream, and pale yellow houses sweeping up from the sea. At the top of the curl stands the pretty, cream-pastry Baroque **Church of the Corallini** (of the coral fishermen), with a distinct concave façade emblazoned with a stag, or *cervo* in Italian. The old town has a delightful, sunny, Moorish atmosphere. Although it hosts a chamber music festival in July and August, with only five small hotels near its shingle beach it is hardly spoiled. **Andora**, next on the coast, consists of a Marine Quarter with a beach and up in the Merula valley, the fortified medieval hamlet, reached by way of an ancient bridge. The old town is dominated by its picturesque, ruined castle and the lovely 13th-century Romanesque-Gothic Church of **SS. James and Peter**. On the other side of Capo Mele ('Cape Apple') lies the attractive old fishing town of **Laigueglia**, with its majestic Baroque church of 1754.

Alassio and Albenga

With one of the best beaches on the Riviera, and one of the mildest climates, **Alassio** has long been a popular winter resort. Of pre-resort Alassio little remains to be seen but

131

some old *palazzi* on its main street, the pretty 1597 church of **Sant'Ambrogio** with a Romanesque campanile, and a defence tower. Visiting celebrities have autographed the 'Muretto', or little wall, Alassio's version of Hollywood Boulevard; in August there's even a 'Miss Muretto' beauty contest. Summer excursion boats make the short trip to the tiny islet, **Isola Gallinara**, especially popular with skin-divers; another pleasant outing is up the **Roman Road** to the 13th-century Benedictine church of **Santa Croce**, one of the best viewpoints in the area.

Ancient **Albenga** is the most historic and interesting town on the Riviera di Ponente. Once the Roman port *Album Ingaunum*, Albenga was prosperous throughout the Middle Ages, until its harbour shifted away with the course of the Centa river; nowadays Albenga stands a kilometre from the sea, and grows asparagus in the old river bed. Albenga's impressive collection of 13th-century brick towers, built during its day as a *comune*, stand like bridesmaids around the elegant 1391 campanile of the Romanesque **Cathedral**. One of the towers (*c.* 1300) belongs to the Palazzo Vecchio del Comune and now houses the **Museo Civico Ingauno** (10–12 and 3–6, closed Mon) with archaeological odds and ends and a good view from the top floor.

Steps lead down from the piazza to Albenga's most celebrated monument, the 5th-century **baptistry** (same hours as museum). In the 5th and 6th centuries there was a great fondness for geometrical forms, for whatever obscure Dark Age reason, and as such Albenga's baptistry is a minor *tour de force*, its architects devising an unusual 10-sided exterior with an octagonal interior. Original mosaics remain in blue and white stone, depicting 12 doves, symbols of the Apostles.

To the north of the cathedral, the Piazzetta dei Leoni is named after the three mysterious lions who stand guard here. Nearby on Via Episcopio, the Bishop's Palace with exterior frescoes houses the **Diocesan Museum** (10–12 and 3–6, closed Mon), with 17th-century tapestries, paintings, reliquaries and illuminated manuscripts. The 13th-century Loggia dei Quattro Canti, nearby, marks the centre of the Roman town.

Another tower, on Piazza San Michele, belongs to the Palazzo Peloso Cipolla ('Hairy Onion Palace'), built in the 14th century, with a Renaissance era façade; it now contains the **Roman Naval Museum** (open 10–12 and 3–6, closed Mon; adm). It features rows of amphorae and other items salvaged from a 1st-century BC Roman shipwreck discovered near the Isola Gallinara, as well as 16th–18th-century blue and white pharmacy jars from Albisola.

From Albenga you can take a walk to the west and along the Centa, near the scattered remains of Roman *Album Ingaunum*—the old Roman road and tombs on the hill, the amphitheatre below, and the foundations of the city on the river banks. Towards the east stands the 13th-century bridge, the Ponte Lungo, spanning the former course of the Centa. **Garlenda**, some 12 kilometres further inland, is a pretty hill resort, with a fine 18-hole golf course.

Inland: the Grottoes of Toirano

Heading east of Albenga, **Ceriale** is a small seaside resort with a famous Good Friday procession. **Borghetto Santo Spirito**, the next coastal town, is mainly of interest as the junction (and bus pick-up point) for **Toirano**, a medieval hill village that seems spanking new compared with the relics of its Middle Palaeolithic inhabitants (80,000 BC), discovered in the two large caves nearby—the **Grotta della Basura** and the **Grotta di Santa Lucia**. The Grotta della Basura has a section called the Bear Cemetery because of all of the bones found there, and a 'Room of Mystery', with animal and human footprints as if left from a ritual dance. Near the entrance to the grottoes the **Prehistoric Museum of the Val Varatella** (10–11:30 and 3:30–6; adm) contains remains found in these and other caverns in the valley, and a reassembled bear skeleton. Like modern Italians, Toirano's ancient cave dwellers had excellent taste, and chose as their abode one of the loveliest caves in the region, where Mother Nature, their interior decorator, added draperies and designs of pastel-coloured stalactites (guided tours, 9:30–11:30 and 2:30–6; adm). Another medieval village nearby, **Balestrino**, is still defended by a picturesque Del Carretto castle; other castles constructed by the same clan of local lordlings may be seen further up the Val Varatella at cheese-making **Bardineto** and at a popular summer resort—the mountain village of **Calizzano** which besides the castle, has a small zoo with a contemporary descendant of the carnivorous cave bear and a flock of Tibetan goats.

The Coast: Loano to Noli

Loano is an attractive, palm-shaded town and resort best known for its 16th-century **Palazzo Doria** (now the Municipio), containing a rare 3rd-century AD mosaic pavement, and for the fine views to be had from its 1608 Carmelite convent. Another old seaside town, **Pietra Ligure**, has the ruins of a Genoese fortress; from Borgio, the next tiny resort, you can turn off for Valdemino and the **Grotta di Borgio**, with more good stalactites (open 9–11:30 and 2:30–5; adm).

Finale Ligure is yet another pleasant garden resort, spread out between Finale Marina and the medieval village of Finalborgo, 2 km inland. This area is especially rich in caves, many of which contain fascinating traces of Palaeolithic man—most famously the Grotta delle Arene Candide. Although none of the caves are open to visitors, pottery, tools, tombs, Venuses, and another huge bear skeleton found inside them are on display in the **Finale Civic Museum**, housed in the cloister of the convent of Santa Chiara in **Finalborgo** (open 10–12 and 3–6, Sun 9–12, closed Mon). Finalborgo itself is dominated by an impressive if derelict **castle**, another property of the Del Carretti, and a splendid 13th-century octagonal campanile of the Basilica di San Biagio. One of the prettiest excursions from Finalborgo is to make your way along the old Roman Via Aurelia which here weaves through the Valle di Ponci (near Finale Pia) and the Val Quazzola, traversing a dozen Roman bridges.

Noli thrived as a small maritime republic before its bigger neighbours elbowed it out of business. Lying under the **Castello di Monte Ursino** and still protected by its medieval walls, gates, and towers, its more important monument is the 11th-century **Church of San Paragorio**, founded in 820; its treasures include a 13th-century bishop's throne and a 12th-century crucifix called a *Volto Santo* after the picture on it, said to be a true portrayal of Christ—similar to the more famous one in Lucca. Be sure to note Noli's antique street lamps. There's a good beach here, and an even better one nearby at **Spotorno**.

Savona

The provincial capital, Savona is a working city rather than a resort, as well as one of Italy's busiest ports; one of the most amusing things to do is hang around the docks and watch the aerial cable cars unload coal for the ironworks at San Giuseppe di Cairo. The harbour tower, the **Torre di Leon Pancaldo** dates from the 13th century, but was renamed to honour Magellan's Savonese pilot, Leon 'Hot bread'. Other natives of Savona include the della Rovere family, which gave the world two popes, Sixtus IV (who built the Sistine Chapel at St Peter's) and his nephew, Julius II, who hired Michelangelo to paint the thing. Sixtus and Julius left their mark on the old quarter of Savona (take pretty Via Pia from the harbour); their **Della Rovere Palace** (now the law courts) faces the 16th-century **Cathedral**, flanked by another **Sistine Chapel**. This contains a marble tomb with two fine statues of the popes. The cathedral contains a few relics of its medieval predecessor, which the Genoese demolished in 1528 to build a fortress—not to protect Savona, but to put a damper on its considerable ambition. The best art is tucked away in the **Cathedral Museum** (9–12 and 3–7), with a fine *Adoration of the Magi* by the Hoogstaeten master, 14th-century English alabaster statues, and items donated by the popes. Near the quay, at Via Quadra Superiore 7, the medieval Palazzo Pozzobonello houses the **Museo Civico** (9–12 and 3–6, closed Mon and Sun afternoons), with a good collection of Ligurian Renaissance works by Donato De Bardi, Lodovico Brea, and Taddeo di Bartolo, as well as a polyptych by Vincenzio Foppa.

From Savona rail lines branch off for Turin (also linked by the A6 autostrada) and Milan. Along the first route you'll pass through the traditional boundary between the Alps and the Apennines at **Bocchetta di Cadibona**, and stop off at **Millesimo** (connected by bus from Savona), a charming, fortified hill town, where even the bridge, the **Gaietta**, has a watch tower. It is a popular excursion destination, with a clutch of artisans' workshops and pastry shops selling scrumptious rum chocolates called *millesimini*.

Savona to Genoa

Although the bathing quality declines the closer you get to the big city, there are some tempting stopovers: **Albisola**, Liguria's most important ceramics centre, or **Celle Ligure** and **Varazze**, popular resorts, the latter still partly surrounded by its walls which incorporate the façade (but nothing else) of the 10th-century church of **Sant'Ambrogio**. Rebuilt in 1535, the present Sant'Ambrogio, with a lovely medieval campanile, contains some fine Renaissance and Baroque art. Further east, **Cogoleto**, according to one tradition, was the birthplace of Columbus. At least, everyone in the village thinks so, and they've erected a statue and plaque to him in the main piazza.

Pegli, long a weekend retreat of the Genoese, has been sucked into the metropolis, but like Nervi to the east, maintains its beauty and most of its tranquillity. The grounds of two seigneurial villas are now used as parks. One park, the **Villa Doria**, was formerly the gardens of the interesting, frescoed 16th-century Villa Centurione Doria, now used as the **Naval History Museum**, with a fine collection of artefacts relating to Genoa's proud, maritime traditions, including ships' models, paintings (among them, a portrait of

Columbus) and compasses (9–1 and 3–6, Sun 9:15–12:45, temporarily closed for restoration). Another park in Via Pallavicini, the magnificent **Villa Durazzo-Pallavicini** is an elegantly arranged garden with statuary, rotundas, temples, and ponds, designed in the 19th century; installed in the house is the **Museum of Ligurian Archaeology** (open 9–1:15 and 3–6, Sun 9–1:15, closed Mon), with an interesting collection of pre-Roman and Roman finds from Genoa, and especially from the prehistoric caves of the Riviera di Ponente. The star exhibit is the so-called 'Young Prince', a burial discovered in the Grotta delle Arene Candide, with a seashell headdress and a dagger in his hand.

The most attractive detour inland between Savona and Genoa is to **Campo Ligure**, up winding N. 456, a mountain town famous for its silver filigree. Prime examples of the art are displayed in the **Museo della Filigrana**, in the Casa della Giustizia (Tues–Fri. 3–6, Sat & Sun 9–12 and 3–6), or you could pop into the local workshops and watch how it's done. Besides its castle and Spinola tower, Campo Ligure has a **Botanical Garden** in nearby Pratorondanino, run by the Orchid Lovers of Liguria, who grow flowers from the Apennines, Alps, and the mountains of the world. The garden is open during daylight hours, but is at its most glorious between late May and early September.

WHERE TO STAY AND EATING OUT

Imperia (tel prefix 0183): If the rest of the Riviera is booked up, look here for accommodation. Most people may just want to stop for lunch or dinner at one of the city's fine restaurants, like the **Lanterna Blu**, Via Scarincio 32 in Porto Maurizio, tel 63 859. The ingredients for its fine dishes come directly from two local farms; be sure to try the hot seafood antipasti, a splendid accompaniment to the views from the seaside veranda (L80–100 000; closed Wed, part of Nov and Dec). Excellent seafood is the top billing at **Nannina**, Viale Matteotti 56, tel 20 208, a haven for lovers of scampi and prawns (L80 000; closed Sun eve, Mon). The Imperia-ites are also quite proud of their prize-winning pizzeria, **Uobo**, at Via Rimaldo in Porto Maurizio, where an exquisite *Quattro Stagione* with a beer is L8 500.

Diano Marina (tel prefix 0183): The ****Bellevue & Méditerranée**, Via Gen. Ardoino 2, tel 402 693, is one of the most pleasant hotels on the beach, with a pool and garden in addition to its beach facilities (L94–100 000, all rooms with bath). The ***Caprice**, Corso Roma 19, tel 495 061, is a fairly classy place, also with a garden and beach, and with some of the best hotel dining on the Riviera (L58–64 000, all rooms with bath).

Cervo (tel prefix 0183): Accommodation is measly here compared with the rest of the Riviera, but the ***Columbia**, Via Aurelia 71, tel 400 079, does its best to please, with 20 comfortable rooms, a garden, and private beach (closed Oct and Nov, L32–47 000 without bath, L40–58 000 with). In the old town, *Bellavista**, Piazza Castello 2, tel 408 094, has pleasant enough rooms, without bath, for L28–35 000. Those who reserve in advance can enjoy a meal at **San Giorgio**, in the old town on Via Volta 19, tel 400 175, where in an intimate, art-filled setting, you can dine on well-prepared Ligurian specialities like *trenette al pesto* or *verdure ripiene* (stuffed vegetables) for around L50–60 000.

Albenga (tel prefix 0182): Not much here, but prices are convivial. For beach views, there's the ***Sole e Mare, Lungomare Colombo, tel 51 817, where a simple but pleasant room is L60–80 000 with bath; or *Il Bucaniere, Lungomare Colombo 8, tel 50 220, with a garden (L45–55 000, depending on the plumbing). There are a couple of restaurants worth testing a fork in: Italia, Via Martiri della Libertà 8, tel 50 405, has good home cooking, featuring *scaloppine* with artichokes or asparagus and a busy grill; L40 000, closed Mon, and Oct and Nov. The second, with the dubious name of Mini Sport, Viale Italia 35, tel 53 458, is a seafood lover's heaven, with fish in the first course (stuffed mussels, *risotto al frutta del mare*), and fish in the second, especially grilled (L35–50 000).

Garlenda (tel prefix 0182): ****La Meridiana, Via ai Castelli, tel 580 271, is a golfer's paradise, amid the pretty olive groves, ancient oaks, and vineyards. A member of the Relais et Châteaux chain, it is a contemporary building constructed with traditional stone walls, wooden ceilings, and with simple but very attractive furnishings. Besides the golf course, there is a large pool in the grounds, tennis, and a riding school, and the sea is only 10 km away. The really adventurous can even take parachuting lessons at the little airport nearby. The food is excellent. Open all year, L260–350 000. Duffers with smaller budgets can be just as near the links at the ***Foresteria Golf Club, at Brà, tel 580 013, which has all of seven simple but nice rooms, all with bath, for L95 000.

Alassio (tel prefix 0182): At the biggest resort in the area, you can stay at the ****Grand Hotel Diana, Via Garibaldi 110, tel 42 701, one of the finest hotels in town, facing the sea, as are the best rooms (cheaper ones are at the back). All have private bath, and there's an indoor pool as well as a private beach; prices range from L148–170 000. The very comfortable ****Ambassador, Corso Europa 64, tel 43 957, is one of the more popular choices with comfortable rooms and private bath; L135 000. Directly on the beach, ***Beau Séjour, Via Garibaldi 102, tel 40 303, has well-furnished rooms, good for a prolonged stay, and a fine terrace and garden for dawdling (open April–Sept; L55–80 000 without bath, L65–97 000 with). The ***Majestic, Corso Leonardo da Vinci 300, tel 42 721, is a good resort hotel, with beach facilities, open mid-April–mid-Oct, L60–90 000. The pleasant, beachfront **Eden, Passeggiata Cadorna 20, tel 40 281, also has beach facilities (L45–70 000 with bath, L35–45 000 without).

What Alassio may lack in grand hotels it makes up for with a gourmet palace, La Palma, Via Cavour 5, tel 40 514, where you can choose between two daily *menu degustazione*, one highlighting basil, the sacred herb of Liguria, and the second, Provençal-Ligurian specialities with an emphasis on seafood. La Palma is not large, so be sure to reserve; around L80 000. For a seafood orgy, head out to the local yacht club's Al Mare, Porticciolo Ferrari, tel 44 186, where each course (except the delicious ice cream for dessert), is delightfully fishy (L50 000).

Finale Ligure (tel prefix 019): Hotels here mainly cater to families. Among the best are the ***Park Hotel Castello, Via Caviglia 26, tel 691 320, a pleasant hotel near the top of the town, with more character than most and a pretty garden; it's also one of the few that remains open all year; L78–90 000, with bath. Nearby, at the castle itself, there's a fine Youth Hostel with a pretty garden, tel 690 515; L10 000 a person, including breakfast.

GENOA

There's always a tingling air of danger, excitement, unexpected fortune or sudden disaster in real port cities. The streets are enlivened with sailors, travellers, and vagrants of all nationalities, and there's the volatility of the sea itself, ready to make or break a fortune. Of the country's four ancient maritime republics (Venice, Amalfi, and Pisa are the others), only Genoa (Genova in Italian) has retained its salty tang and thrill. It is Italy's largest port, and any possible scenographic effect it could have, enhanced by its beautiful location of steep hills piling into the sea, has been utterly snuffed out by the more important affairs of the port; an elevated highway, huge docks, warehouses, stacks of containers and unloading facilities hog the shoreline for miles so that from many points you can't even see the sea. And behind the docks wind the dishevelled alleys lined with typical piquant portside establishments that cater to weaselly men of indeterminate nationality, old pirates, and discreetly tattooed ladies.

Counterbalancing this fragrant zone of stevedores is the Genoa that Petrarch called *La Superba* (the 'Proud', as in one of the Seven Deadly Sins, or the Superb City) of palaces, gardens, and art; the city whose merchant fleet once reigned supreme from Spain to the southern Russian ports on the Black Sea, the city that gave the Spaniards Columbus but in return controlled the contents of Spain's American silver fleets, becoming the New York City of the 16th century, flowing with money, ruled by factions of bankers and oligarchs, populated by rugged individualists and entrepreneurs, and leaving a mark on the fashion industry with its silks and a sturdy blue cotton cloth the French called *de Gênes*, which came to be made into jeans.

Modern Genoa is a teeming, neon-flashing, kinetic antidote to the Riviera's resorta-rama. Even its impossible topography is exciting: squeezed between mountains and sea, greater Genoa stretches for 30 km—there are people who commute to work by elevator or funicular, tunnels bore under green parks in the very centre of the city, apartment houses hang over the hills so that the penthouse is at street level. The old quarter is a bustling warren of alleys, or *carugi*, miniature canyons under eight-storey palaces and tenements, streaming with banners of laundry. There are fine streets of Renaissance palaces and Art Nouveau mansions, fine art (though the Genoese produced no painters or sculptors of note themselves, they amassed some fine collections), and one of the most amazing cemeteries on earth.

History

Genoa's destiny was shaped by its position, not only as the northernmost port on the Tyrrhenian sea, but as a port protected and isolated by a ring of mountains. It was already a trading post in the 6th century BC when the Phoenicians and Greeks bartered with the native Ligurians. Later the city was a stalwart member of the Roman Empire, and as such suffered the wrath of Hannibal; rebuilt after his sacking, it remained relatively happy and whole until the Lombards took in it 641, initiating a dark, troubled period. While the merchants of Amalfi, Pisa, and Venice were creating their maritime republics in the 10th and 11th centuries, Genoa was still an agricultural backwater, far from the main highways of the Middle Ages, its traffic dominated by Pisa, its coasts prey to Saracen corsairs.

Adversity helped form the Genoese character. Once it rallied to defeat the Saracens, the city began a dizzily rapid rise to prominence in the 12th century, capturing the islands of Sardinia and Corsica, and joining the Normans to conquer Antioch, where Genoa established its first of many trading colonies in the Middle East. The city walls had to be enlarged in 1155, as the city quickly expanded and competition with Pisa grew into a battle of blows as well as of trade. The turning point in their duel for supremacy of the Western Mediterranean came in 1284, when Genoa soundly pummelled Pisa into naval obscurity at the battle of Meloria—a victory Genoa followed up with another over a more troublesome rival, Venice, at the Curzonali islands in 1298. By this time Genoa had merchant colonies stretching from the coast of North Africa, to Syria, along the Black Sea, and in Spain, where Genoese captains became the first to sail to the Canary and Azore islands. Genoa itself was the most densely populated city in Europe, as its patricians constructed their towering houses that seemed so 'superb' to visitors; its fame was so widespread that Genoa served as a setting for a tale in the Arabian Nights, the only Western city to be so honoured.

The Famous Insult to the Genoese

It was during this period, in 1316, that one of the most beloved anecdotes of Genoese history occurred, a story the Genoese like to tell for its perfect evocation of their proud, stubborn character: a Genoese merchant, by name, Megollo Lercari, was the guest of the Eastern Emperor at Trebizond, when he disagreed with one of the emperor's pages, who slapped him across the face. The emperor refused to let the Genoese strike back, though he apologized for the youth's behaviour. It was not enough. Seething, Megollo returned to Genoa, got up a private fleet, sailed back to Trebizond, and demanded the page. When the emperor refused, the Genoese besieged the city, capturing whoever they could and chopping off their ears or noses. Finally his subjects' despair made the emperor give in, and he handed over the youth, and watched, first in trepidation and then amazement, as Megollo made the page stoop over, then gave him a smart kick in the seat of the pants. Honour thus regained, the merchant returned the youth, lifted the siege and sailed back to Genoa.

But Genoa's first golden age was marred, as all subsequent ones were to be, by civic strife and turmoil that were disgraceful even by Italian standards. The individualistic, stubborn Genoese refused to accept communal unity; nearly every enterprise was privately funded, including even most of the city's military expeditions. The city itself was divided into factions, nobles against each other, nobles against the mercantile classes, the merchants against the artisans—while the ruling families each dominated their own quarter of the city, forming *alberghi*, or brotherhoods, of their partisans, running their own prisons and armies and fighting for political control of their city. In 1339 the popular classes won a victory by electing Genoa's first doge, Simone Boccanegra, the hero of Verdi's opera. But Genoa's doges were figureheads from the beginning, and Boccanegra's victory was Pyrrhic; the nobles responded to his election by inviting in the Visconti of Milan, Boccanegra was exiled to Pisa, the Visconti were thrown out, Boccanegra returned—for nearly two centuries Genoese civic history is an ignoble chronicle of one faction momentarily gaining the upper hand, and all the others doing everything to undermine it, even inviting in a foreign lord.

The Bank of St George

The real power in Genoa turned out to be a bank. When the city sank deep into debt during its prolonged war with Venice for the Eastern Mediterranean (ending in Genoa's traumatic defeat at Chioggia in 1380), its creditors—Genoa's oligarchs—formed a syndicate, the Banco di San Giorgio, to guarantee their increasingly precarious loans. This the bank did by gradually assuming control of the city's overseas territories, castles, towns, and even its treasury. Genoa from then on, for all practical purposes, was run as a business proposition—once, in 1421, when the bank was short of cash, it sold Livorno to Florence for a tidy sum. The Genoese never had any reason to identify with their municipal government like the Venetians did, but, as Machiavelli noted, they were very loyal to their bank.

Genoa recovered quickly from the defeat at Chioggia, by transforming its economy from the mercantile sphere to the financial. The cinquecento found the city Europe's leading economic power, a position Genoa maintained for a long time thanks to the foresight of Andrea Doria (1468–1560), the 'Saviour of Genoa' and the greatest admiral of his day. In the 16th century, during the Wars of Italy between Charles V of Spain and Francis I of France, Doria drove Genoa's traditional French allies from the city and welcomed Spanish protection, then wrote a new Republican constitution for the strife-torn city, institutionalizing the shared rule of the 28 *alberghi*. Charles V rewarded Doria with the title of Prince of Melfi, and he and other Genoese took prominent posts throughout the Empire. Meanwhile at the close of the 16th century the Bank of St George became fat and sleek financing the wars in the Low Countries for Charles V and Philip II, processing Spain's silver, and taking over the international money market from Besançon and Antwerp: millions of *scudi* passed through Genoa every year. Andrea Doria was also Genoa's first great patron of the arts, introducing the High Renaissance to the city that had formerly managed without.

But after the crusty old admiral, Genoa began to decline. Spain's bankruptcies came all too frequently, Atlantic ports overtook the importance of the old Mediterranean trade, the Ottoman Empire gobbled up Genoa's last trade colonies in the east, forcing many of the port's old salts into a life of piracy (mainly at Venice's expense). The French (1668), then the Austrians (1734), took the city; Corsica, Genoa's last colony, revolted in 1768, and the Bank of St George could do nothing but sell it to France.

By the 1815 Treaty of Vienna, Genoa and Liguria joined Piedmont and almost at once the city became a hotbed of unification sentiments, led by the conspiring philosopher of the Risorgimento, Giuseppe Mazzini, and such patriot luminaries as Nino Bixio, Goffredo Mameli, the Ruffini brothers, and of course, Garibaldi himself. In 1992 the city is due to hold a major fair and exhibition in honour of the famous discovery of its most famous son: Christopher Columbus (Cristoforo Colombo in Italian).

GETTING AROUND

Genoa's international airport, Cristoforo Colombo in Sestri Ponente, has direct flights to London as well as Italian cities. For information, tel (010) 2690. Buses to the airport depart an hour before each flight from the terminal at Via Petrarca, near Piazza De Ferrari. Genoa has two main train stations: Principe, in Piazza Acquaverde, just west of the centre, and Brignole, to the northeast. Principe in general handles trains from the north and France, while Brignole takes trains from the south. Most trains call at both;

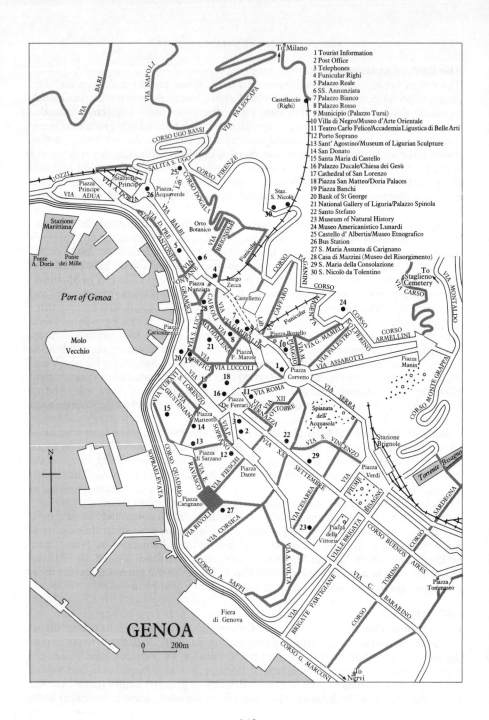

1 Tourist Information
2 Post Office
3 Telephones
4 Funicular Righi
5 Palazzo Reale
6 SS. Annunziata
7 Palazzo Bianco
8 Palazzo Rosso
9 Municipio (Palazzo Tursi)
10 Villa di Negro/Museo d'Arte Orientale
11 Teatro Carlo Felice/Accademia Ligustica di Belle Arti
12 Porto Soprano
13 Sant' Agostino/Museum of Ligurian Sculpture
14 San Donato
15 Santa Maria di Castello
16 Palazzo Ducale/Chiesa dei Gesù
17 Cathedral of San Lorenzo
18 Piazza San Matteo/Doria Palaces
19 Piazza Banchi
20 Bank of St George
21 National Gallery of Liguria/Palazzo Spinola
22 Santo Stefano
23 Museum of Natural History
24 Museo Americanistico Lunardi
25 Castello d' Albertis/Museo Etnografico
26 Bus Station
27 S. Maria Assunta di Carignano
28 Casa di Mazzini (Museo del Risorgimento)
29 S. Maria della Consolazione
30 S. Nicolò da Tolentino

GENOA

0   200m

140

city bus No 37 links the two. Buses to the rest of the province and the Riviera depart from the Piazza della Vittoria, near Brignole, and from Principe's Piazza Acquaverde.

Ferries: From Genoa you can sail away to exotic lands from the Stazione Marittima (tel 261 466), just below Stazione Principe. Nearly any travel agency in Genoa can sell you a ticket, or you can make reservations by phone. **Grandi Traghetti** sails several times a week to Palermo and Porto Torres in Sardinia (tel 589 331); **Tirrenia** has ferries to the Sardinian ports of Porto Torres, Cagliari, and Olbia, as well as Palermo and Tunis (tel 258 041); **Sardinia Ferries**, tel 593 301, links several points on that island with Genoa; **Corsica Ferries** sails to Bastia (tel 585 496). From October to May, **Transmediterranea Ferries** sails to Palma de Mallorca, Malaga, and the Canary Islands (tel 284 181).

Chances are you won't need a **city bus**, as most of Genoa's points of interest are in the centre, between the two train stations—main thoroughfares are Via XX Settembre, running from near Brignole to main Piazza De Ferrari; and Via Balbi, from Stazione Principe to Piazza di Nunziata. The local bus company, AMT, does, however, offer three-hour-long daily tours of Genoa's highlights, departing from the depot in Piazza Acquaverde at 2:30 in winter and spring, and at 3 in the summer and autumn (tel 261 550 for information). Funiculars from Piazza Portello and Larga della Zecca ascend to the city's upper residential quarters; the former, **Righi**, has a splendid belvedere over the city and harbour. A lift from Piazza Portello will take you up to the nearer belvedere at Castelletto. For a radio taxi, call 2696.

Driving in Genoa isn't much fun. The old quarter is closed to traffic, and the street plan is chaotic. Three major *autostrade* meet just north of the centre—the A10 to the Riviera di Ponente, the A12 along the Riviera di Levante, and the A7 to Milan, with a branch (A21) to Turin. The elevated branch of the A10, the *Sopraelevata* circles along the old port before ending near the Fiera di Genoa; use it to get on all three highways.

Genoa is one of several Italian cities with an unnecessarily complicated street-numbering system: any commercial establishment receives a red number, any residence (r) a black or blue numberplate.

TOURIST INFORMATION
Main office is at Via Roma 11, tel (010) 581 407. Branch offices are at Stazione Principe, tel 262 633, Stazione Brignole, tel 562 056, and at the airport, tel 600 7247.

Stazione Principe to Via Garibaldi

Both of Genoa's two main stations are lovely—the Stazione Principe could serve as a setting for a fancy-dress ball. In its Piazza Acquaverde visitors are greeted by a **statue of Columbus**, a view of the port, and the stately Via Balbi. If you're catching a ferry, Via Andrea Doria will take you down to the Stazione Marittima, but even if you're not you may want to wander down to take in Genoa's most celebrated landmark, the **Lanterna**, a medieval lighthouse standing 117 m high, last restored in 1543. In the old days a huge fire would be ignited on top to guide vessels into the port. Near the Stazione Marittima there are two other ancient monuments: the **Commandery**, a loggia belonging to the Knights of St John, who used Genoa as a Crusader port, and the 12th-century church of **San Giovanni di Pré**, with an attractive spire-clustered campanile.

Via Balbi, designed by Bartolomeo Bianco and opened in 1616, has some fine late Renaissance palaces, among them, Bianco's **University** (1650), which takes full advantage of Genoa's hilly topography to create an extraordinary courtyard of four levels, visually linked by twin staircases. Also on Via Balbi is the yellow and red **Palazzo Reale**, residence of the Savoy kings in Genoa, with its hyper-decorated 18th-century ballroom and Hall of Mirrors, works by Parodi, Strozzi, and Carlone, and a *Crucifixion* by Van Dyck, who spent several years working in Genoa (daily, 9–1:30). Via Balbi gives on to Piazza Nunziata, named after its 16th-century **Annunziata Church**, with a façade almost Puritan in its austerity, hiding a voluptuous Rococo interior. From the next square, the **Largo della Zecca** you have several options: the thrilling funicular ride up to Righi, where you can dine at the top of the town, or the elevator up to Castelletto, or the tunnel through to Piazza Portello, or a browse through the district's antique shops; or you can continue along the Via Cairoli to Genoa's most famous street, **Via Garibaldi**.

Via Garibaldi, the former Strada Nuova, was laid out in 1558 by Galeazzo Alessi and for centuries was Genoa's 'Millionaires' Row,' with its uninterrupted lines of 16th- and 17th-century *palazzi*. Many have since been converted into banks and municipal offices, but the street's unique and elegant character has been carefully maintained. Two of the palaces hold important art collections: the **Palazzo Bianco**, former residence of the Grimaldi (no longer very white; No 11, Tues-Sat 9–7, Sun 9–12; adm), has the most noteworthy collection in the city, with a good assortment of Italian paintings, including Filippino Lippi's *Madonna with Saints*, Pontormo's *Florentine Gentleman*, Veronese's *Crucifixion*, and an even more impressive collection of Flemish art; Gerhard David's sweetly domestic *Madonna della Pappa*, paintings by Cranach, Van der Goes, Van Dyck and Rubens (who also worked for a while in Genoa), and a fine *San Bonaventura* by the Spaniard Zurbaran. The portrait of Andrea Doria by Jan Matsys has remarkable hands. Across the street, the **Palazzo Rosso** (the Red Palace; No 18, same hours as Palazzo Bianco), still maintains some of its palatial fittings as a well as a picture gallery, with an especially good collection of portraits by Van Dyck, Pisanello, Dürer, and works by Caravaggio and his pupil Mattia Preti; here, too, is *La Cuoca*, a favourite work by Genoa's own Bernardo Strozzi.

Next to the Palazzo Rosso, the former **Palazzo Tursi**, designed by Rocco Lurago, is now Genoa's Municipio, with the city's most beautiful courtyard and such municipal treasures as native son Paganini's violin in the Sala della Giunta and three letters from Columbus in the Sala del Sindaco. You can enter the courtyard of No 7, the **Palazzo Podestà**, with an elaborate fountain in the shape of a grotto. The façade of No 3, the 16th-century **Palazzo Parodi-Lercari**, was built by the descendants of Megollo Lercari, who recalled the 'Insult to the Genoese' at Trebizond with ear-less and nose-less caryatids.

The Villa di Negro
Via Garibaldi ends at Piazza Marose, with more palaces, especially the 15th-century **Palazzo Spinola dei Marmi**, embellished with black and white bands and statues of the Spinola family. From here Salita Santa Caterina leads into the circular **Piazza Corvetto**, a major junction of the city bus lines and the entrance to the **Villa di Negro**, an urban oasis that takes full advantage of Genoa's crazy topography, with streams,

cascades, grottoes and walkways, culminating at the top with the **Museo d'Arte Orientale**, Italy's finest museum of Oriental art, a lovely collection of statues, paintings, theatre masks, and an extraordinary set of Samurai helmets and armour, all well displayed in a sun-filled modern building (Tues–Sat 9–5, Sun 9–12; adm).

At the corner of Piazza Corvetto and Via Roma you can stop off for a history-imbued break at the early 19th-century **Caffè Mangani**. Via Roma continues down to tumultuous **Piazza De Ferrari**, on one side marked by a crumbling but imposing façade—all that remains of the neoclassical **Teatro Carlo Felice**, built in 1829 and bombed in 1944. At no. 5, Ligurian paintings from the 15th–19th centuries are hung in the **Pinacoteca dell'Accademia Ligustica di Belle Arti** (daily 9–1, closed Sun). From Piazza De Ferrari you can descend into Old Genoa; the most picturesque way is to head down Via Dante to Piazza Dante and the **Porta Soprana**, the tall twin-towered 1155 gateway, where, according to documents, Columbus' father was gatekeeper; his 'boyhood home', smothered in ivy, is nearby, as are the 12th-century ruins of the **Cloister of Sant'Andrea**, set out on the lawn.

Porta Soprana

The Old City

Within the Porta Soprana are the tall houses sliced by the corridor-like alleys of the old city, some so narrow that they live in perpetual shade. Partly bombed and mostly unrepaired after the War, leaning ever so gently towards the harbour below, many houses have white marble and black slate portals, permitted only to those families who have performed a deed to benefit the city, while corners and wall niches are decorated with hundreds of little shrines known as *madonnettes*, the little madonnas.

The old town is for exploring, although single women should exercise caution, especially after dark. To see the highlights of the quarter, take the Via Ravecca down from Porta Soprana to the 13th-century Gothic **Church of Sant'Agostino**, its ruined cloisters converted into the well-designed **Museum of Ligurian Sculpture and**

Architecture (open 9–7; Sun 9–12; adm) containing art and architectural fragments salvaged from Genoa's demolished churches. One of the finest works is the 1312 fragment of the tomb of Margherita of Brabant, wife of Emperor Henry VII, sculpted by Giovanni Pisano. Margherita died suddenly in Genoa while accompanying her husband to Rome for his coronation, and Henry, whom Dante and many others had hoped would be able to end the feud between Italy's Guelphs and Ghibellines, died in Siena two years later, many believe of sorrow; his last request was that his heart be taken to Genoa to be interred with his wife. There are also Roman works, Romanesque sculpture, frescoes (some as old as the 6th century), the 14th-century wooden *Christ of the Caravana*, and much more.

From Sant'Agostino, the Stradone di Sant'Agostino leads to another good church, the 12th-century Romanesque **San Donato**, with an exceptionally lovely octagonal campanile, portal and interior, combining a pleasant mix of Roman and medieval columns. The nearby Via San Bernardo, one of the few straight streets in the old city, was laid out by the Romans. Their *castrum* up the hill (take the Salita della Torre degli Embriaci) provided the foundations for Genoa's most venerable church, the evocative **Santa Maria di Castello** (Tue–Sat 9–7, Sun 9–12), founded in the palaeo-Christian era and incorporating numerous Roman columns and stones in its Romanesque structure. The crusaders used Santa Maria's complex as a hostel. Fairest of its art treasures is the 15th-century fresco of the *Annunciation* in the cloister, strangest is the *Crocifisso Miraculoso* in a chapel near the high altar—miraculous in that the Christ's beard is said to grow whenever Genoa is threatened with calamity.

Around Piazza Matteotti

Another entrance into the historic centre from Piazza De Ferrari is by way of Piazza Matteotti, site of the grandiose **Palazzo Ducale**, once residence of Genoa's doges, and renovated in the 17th century to serve as the city law courts. You can walk through its attractive courtyards, one adorned with a fountain. Also sharing the square is the Baroque **Church of the Gesù**, designed in the late 16th century by Pellegrino Tibaldi. The interior is a colourful Baroque fantasia, all *trompe-l'oeil* stage effects that highlight its frothy Baroque treasures: a *Circumcision* and *St Ignatius Exorcising the Devil* by Rubens, and an *Assumption* by Guido Reni, briefly known as 'Divino' in the 18th and 19th centuries.

Just off the square stands the jauntily black and white striped **Cathedral of San Lorenzo**, begun in the 12th century, and modified several times; the façade was last restored in 1934. Odds and ends from the ages embellish the exterior: two kindly 19th-century lions by the steps on the main façade, a carving of St Lawrence toasting on his grill over the central of three French Gothic-style portals. On the north side there's a pretty 12th-century **Portal of San Giovanni**, on the south, Hellenistic sarcophagi, another Romanesque portal, and a 15th-century tomb. The rather morose interior also wears jailbird stripes. The first chapel on the right contains a good marble *Crucifixion* of 1443 and an English shell fired from the sea 500 years later that hit the chapel but miraculously failed to explode. On the left, note the sumptuous Renaissance Chapel of St John the Baptist, with fine sculptures and marble decorations, and a 13th-century sarcophagus that once held the Baptist's relics.

The well-arranged **Cathedral Treasury** (Tues–Sat 9:30–11:45 and 3–5; adm) in the vaults off the nave to the left, contains a number of genuine treasures, acquired during the heyday of Genoa's mercantile empire: a crystal dish said to have been part of the dinner service of the Last Supper, the blue chalcedony dish on which John the Baptist's head was supposedly served to Salome, an 11th-century arm reliquary of St Anne, the golden, jewel-studded Byzantine *Zaccaria Cross*, and an elaborate 15th-century silver casket built to hold St John the Baptist's ashes.

The Salita del Fonaco follows the back of the Palazzo Ducale, then veers right for the **Piazza San Matteo**, a beautiful little square completely clothed in the honourable black and white bands of illustrious civic benefactors—and it's no wonder, for Piazza San Matteo was the public foyer of the Doria family, encompassed by their proud palazzi and their 12th-century church of **San Matteo**, inscribed with their great deeds. Inside the church, the highlight is the early 14th-century cloister, with charming capitals on twinned columns. Andrea Doria's palace was No 17 on the square, while No 14, belonging to Branca Doria, has a beautiful portal with Genoa's patron St George.

Between Via San Lorenzo and Via Garibaldi

This northern section of the historic centre, built up mostly in the Renaissance, has survived somewhat better than the area around Porta Soprana, and has, amid its monuments, fine shops, pubs, restaurants, and cafés. From Piazza San Matteo it's a short walk to the **Campetto**, a lovely square adorned with the ornate 16th-century Palazzo Imperiale; in the nearby Piazza Soziglia you can take a break at one of the oldest coffee houses in Genoa, **Kainguti**, at No 98r, or **Romanengo**, at No 74r, both founded by a Swiss at the beginning of the 19th century. From the Piazza Soziglia and the Campetto, the pretty Via degli Orefici meanders down to the major intersection of medieval Genoa, the **Piazza Banchi**, with its Renaissance Loggia dei Mercanti. From here Via Ponte Reale descends to the harbourside **Piazza Caricamento**, lined with the ancient arcades of Via Sottoripa and dominated by the rather plain, grey **Palazzo di San Giorgio**. This was built originally in 1260 for the Capitani del Popolo, but was taken over in 1408 by the famous Bank of St George, the shrewd Genoese bankers requiring a headquarters from where they could scrutinize the comings and goings of the port. Now occupied by the Harbour Board, you can ask the guard to show you some of the rooms refurbished in their original 13th-century style.

Via San Luca, the main street passing through Piazza Banchi, was the principal thoroughfare of medieval Genoa and, in its day, home turf of another prominent Genoese family, the Spinola. One of their palaces, just off Via San Luca in little Piazza di Pellicceria, now houses the **National Gallery of Liguria** (closed until late 1992 for restoration). Most of its paintings were donated by the Spinola, along with the palace, which retains most of its 16th–18th-century decor (ring 294 661 to see if it's reopened). The paintings are arranged as in a private residence, and include Antonello da Messina's sad, beautiful *Ecce Homo*, Joos Van Cleve's magnificent *Adoration of the Magi*, works by Van Dyck (*Portrait of a Child* and the *Four Evangelists*), and another fragment of Giovanni Pisano's tomb of Margherita di Brabante, a statue of Justice.

East Genoa

East of the Piazza de Ferrari runs the arcaded **Via XX Settembre**, the main thoroughfare of 19th-century Genoa, adorned here and there with Liberty-style touches. This street, and the area around Brignole station, is one of the city's most lively and genteel neighbourhoods, aglow with neon lights. Via XX Settembre is traversed by the Ponte Monumentale, which carries the Corso A. Podestà overhead. Next to the bridge a lane leads up to another of Genoa's striped medieval churches, **Santo Stefano**, containing a *Martyrdom of St Stephen* by a less flamboyant than usual Giulio Romano. Beyond the bridge the avenue continues to the large Piazza della Vittoria, site of a 1931 War Memorial Arch and the nearby **Giacomo Doria Museum of Natural History** (Via Brigata Liguria 9, open 9–12 and 3–5:30, closed Mon and Fri), an interesting collection garnered by 19th-century Genoese noblemen in their travels abroad, with two rooms chock full of minerals, one of palaeontology and one of zoology.

The Hills and Staglieno Cemetery

Some of the loveliest corners of Genoa are up in the surrounding hills. The **Circonvallazione a Monte** is the scenic route made up of several *corsos* skirting the slopes, a route followed by city bus No. 33, departing from Stazione Brignole or Piazza Manin, to Corso Armellini and Corso Solferino, where at No. 39, in the 17th-century Villa Grüber, the **Museo Americanistico F. Lunardi** has been installed, with an important pre-Colombian collection, especially strong in Mayan art (9:30–12, 3–5:30, Sun 3–5:30, closed Mon). The route continues along Corsos Magenta, Paganini, Firenze, and U. Bassi, passing by the imposing Castello D'Albertis (medieval, but rebuilt in the 19th century), housing the **Museo Etnografico**, with another pre-Colombian collection (Corso Dogali 18; with vague re-opening date).

Just over the mountains, along the Torrente Bisagno lies Genoa's famous **Staglieno Cemetery** (daily 8–5, bus 34 from Piazza Acquaverde or Piazza Corvetto). Founded in 1844, the cemetery covers 160 hectares and even has its own internal bus system. The Genoese have a reputation for being tight-fisted, but when it comes to post-mortem extravagance, they have few peers. Staglieno is a veritable city of the dead, with miniature cathedrals, Romanesque chapels, Egyptian temples, and Art Nouveau palaces and statuary—a fantastic, almost surreal ensemble. In the centre of the hills, Genoa's great revolutionary idealist of the Risorgimento, Giuseppe Mazzini, is buried in a simple tomb behind two massive Doric columns, surrounded by laudatory inscriptions by Tolstoy, Lloyd George, D'Annunzio and others. After a life of plots, conspiracies, and exile, Mazzini died, exiled in Pisa, hiding out under the assumed name of American abolitionist John Brown. Mrs Oscar Wilde is buried in the Protestant section.

Nervi

Nervi, one of the oldest resorts on the Riviera, is just east of Genoa and has been incorporated into the metropolis (to get there, take bus No. 17 from Piazza De Ferrari, or bus No. 15 from the portside Piazza Caricamento). Two of the oldest Genoese villas here have been converted to museums: in the Parco Municipale, the **Galleria d'Arte Moderna** in the former Villa Serra (Via Capolungo 3, closed for works until 1992/3) contains a large collection of 19th- and 20th-century Italian art, especially by Ligurians, who went through every convulsion of every international art movement. The other, the **Villa Luxoro**, is further east in one of the Riviera's loveliest parks (Via Aurelia 29, Tues–Sat 9–5, Sun 9–12; closed Mon). It, too, has a small modern art collection, but is especially noteworthy for its decorative arts: clocks (some of the first luminous time-pieces), furniture, fabrics and lace. Nervi's seaside promenade is named after the hard-riding, pistol-slinging Mrs Anita Garibaldi of Brazil, who helped her husband reunite Italy while being pregnant nearly all the time.

There are two popular excursions into the hinterland from Genoa: **Casella**, a small mountain resort reached by a small electric train from Piazza Manin, and **Torriglia** (reached by bus), with an impressive if utterly derelict medieval castle, a small resort offering skiing in winter and pretty walks in summer.

ACTIVITIES

There are three good sources of information on current events in Genoa—the city's daily paper, *Il Secolo XIX*, the detailed monthly calendar, *L'Agenda*, and the less detailed monthly booklet, *Genova per Voi*, partially in English. The latter two are distributed at the tourist offices.

In Paganini's home town, there is bound to be plenty of music. The **Genoa Opera Company**, homeless since the levelling of the Teatro Carlo Felice, performs from January to April in the Teatro Margherita, Via XX Settembre 16a, and in the summer sponsors the prestigious **Ballet Festival** in Nervi's park. In the summer there's also a full schedule of music and theatre in the city itself; all year round there's jazz every Thursday at the **Louisiana Jazz Club**, C. Saffi, tel 585 067. **The Cotton Club**, Via C. Cabella 5, is a nostaglic reminder of 30s New York, with live jazz, American bar and restaurant; closed Mon.

Sea-bathing around Genoa being a dubious proposition, you may want to take advantage of municipal pools—there's a lake-sized one at the Lido d'Albaro on the east side of town, on the sea, or in Nervi. Every year Genoa competes with Venice, Pisa, and Amalfi in the **Regatta of the Ancient Maritime Republics**, to be held next in Genoa in 1990. For less glamorous but fascinating boating, take the **tour of Genoa's port**. Excursions are run by the Cooperative Battellieri, tel 265 712 for reservations; boats depart from the Calata Zingari, near the Stazione Marittima.

There are frequent flower shows in the Fiera district, and a lively flea market in Piazzetta Lavagna. English books are available at **Bozzi**, on Via Cairoli 2; English drinking at the **Britannia Pub** on Vico della Casana 76, near the bottom of Via Roma.

WHERE TO STAY   (tel prefix 010)

Genoa's hotels range from the fabulous to the scabrous. Most are near one of the two train stations—Brignole has the better neighbourhood if you're looking for something cheap. Only crusty sailors and bodyguards would feel comfortable in the establishments near the port.

The top choice, *******Colombia**, Via Balbi 40, tel 261 841, is also the largest. Genoa's address for visiting nabobs since 1926, it was commandeered as the German, then American headquarters during World War II. Now owned by the luxurious CIGA chain, both its public and private rooms are as vast and palatial as those in the nearby

Palazzo Reale. Rooms, air-conditioned, with TV, magnificent bathrooms, and nearly every other luxury you could ask for, are priced from L220 000 up to L380 000 for a princely suite. ******Bristol Palace**, Via XX Settembre 35, tel 592 541, is near the Brignole station, an elegant choice with sumptuous, antique furnishings and beautiful air-conditioned rooms, and a pleasant English bar downstairs (L170–240 000). In the centre, near Piazza Corvetto and the pretty Villa di Negro park—the ******Plaza**, Via Martin Piaggio 11, tel 893 641, is a very pleasant modern choice, with large cosy rooms, all with frigo bars and air conditioning (L200–270 000).

The *****Agnello d'Oro**, Via Monachette 6, tel 262 084, is housed in a 17th-century property of the Doria family, near Via Balbi. Although most of the old-fashioned charm is concentrated in the lobby, the rooms are very comfortable, and all have private bath (L80–95 000). *****Vittoria Orlandini**, Via Balbi 33–45, tel 261 923, is not far from the Principe station, with good rooms and optional air conditioning (L80–95 000).

Among the less costly and still hygienic, ****Della Posta e Nuova Genoa**, Via Balbi 24, tel 262 005, has the best lodgings in a pensione-filled building (L55 000 without bath, 68 000 with). ****Rex**, with a garden on Via de Gasperi 9, tel 314 197, is near the pool on Genoa's 'lido'. The location is quiet, but convenient only for the motorist (rooms, all with bath, range from L36–55 000). ***Carletto**, Via Colombo 16 (signposted off Via XX Settembre), not far from the Brignole station, tel 546 412, has good rooms in a fine neighbourhood, and lots of *focaccia* stands nearby (L40–50 000).

Nervi means 'nerves' in Italian, but here you can escape the hurly burly of Genoa at the fashionable elegant ******Astor**, Viale delle Palme 16, tel 328 325, in an enchanting garden near the sea (L125–200 000). ****Villa Bonera**, Via Sarfatti 8, tel 326 164, has 26 charming rooms in a 17th-century villa, in another pretty garden (L45 000 without bath, L58 000 with).

EATING OUT   (tel prefix 070)

Besides various forms of pasta with *pesto*, the Genoese are fond of putting basil in numerous other dishes. Another popular pasta dish, *pansotti* are little ravioli filled with spinach and served in a walnut sauce. *Torta pasqualina* consists of vegetables and hard-boiled eggs rolled in a pastry; *Cima alla Genovese* is breast of veal filled with similar ingredients.

One of Genoa's most famous restaurants, **Toe Drue**, is in the working-class district of Sestri Ponente, west of the centre, at Via Corsi 44, tel 671 100. Toe Drue means 'hard table', and this very fashionable restaurant has kept the furnishings of the rustic inn that preceded it. On these hard tables are served an array of delightful and unusual Ligurian specialities, many featuring seafood (definitely reserve; L50 000; closed eve, Sun and Mon). **Gran Gotto**, Via Fiume 11 (near Piazza della Vittoria), tel 564 344, is one of the city's classic eateries, featuring imaginative and delicately prepared seafood like turbot in radicchio sauce, warm seafood antipasti, famous kidney (*rognone*) dishes, and delectable desserts (L80 000). In the same price range, but enjoying a romantic sea view over the cliffs, is **Vittorio al Mare**, at Boccadasse (east of the Lido, Belvedere Firpo 1, tel 312 872), and featuring good pasta and seafood (closed Sun eve, Mon and holidays). In the historic centre, near the Piazza Banchi, **Trattoria del Mario**, Via Conservatori del Mare 35r, tel 298 467, is an old Genoese favourite, featuring the freshest of fish prepared in the authentic Genoese style, pasta with *pesto* as well as *cima*; the delicious seafood salad is a popular starter (closed Aug and Sat; L35–40 000). Also in the maze of the southern old city, **Da Franco**, Archivolto Mongiardino 2, tel 203 614, is the place to go for lobster (*aragosta*) and other excellent seafood dishes. Interior decoration is not Da Franco's forte, but the prices are among the most reasonable anywhere for the type and quality of the seafood (L50 000; closed eve, Mon, and mid-July–mid-Sept). Another traditional choice in the old city, **Pacetti Antica Osteria**, Borgo Incrociati 22r, tel 892 848, offers *pansotti*, chick pea soup, and other Ligurian classics that are rarely prepared elsewhere, accompanied by the region's best vintages (L30–40 000, closed Mon).

Less expensive restaurants abound, especially in the old town. Try the fresh fish in the **Trattoria Da Pino** (L25 000), in Piazza Caricamento, tel 326 395, in one of Genoa's top greasy spoon districts. **Orlando Vegia Zena**, on Vico del Serriglio 15, tel 299 891, features Sard as well as Ligurian specialities (L11 000). **Trattoria del Castello**, Salita Santa Maria di Castello has some of the best cheap food in town, with good Genoese specialities (L18 000).

Riviera di Levante: Recco to Santa Margherita

East of Genoa, the coast, fairly tame up to this point, metamorphoses into a creature of high drama and romance. The beaches aren't as prominent, nor the climate quite as mild, but from the Monte di Portofino to the once inaccessible fishing villages of the Cinque Terre, the mountains and sea tussle and tumble in voluptuous chaos of azure, turquoise, and piney green. Against these deep-coloured coves, cliffs, and inlets, rise the villages of weathered pastels and ochres, originally painted even brighter, surrounded by silvery groves of olives, and gazing out over bobbing fleets of fishing craft, sailing boats, and sleek white yachts.

GETTING AROUND
The Genoa–Pisa railway hugs the coast, but in many places you can only get glimpses of the scenery between the tunnels. The same holds true of the autostrada (A12, between Genoa and La Spezia); most scenic of all is the old coastal road, used by most of the buses. Portofino, Santa Margherita, San Fruttuoso and the Cinque Terre are linked by boat services.

TOURIST INFORMATION
Camogli: Via XX Settembre 33, tel (0185) 770 235
Portofino: Via Roma 35, tel (0185) 269 024
Santa Margherita Ligure: Via XXV Aprile 2, tel (0185) 287 495

Recco and Camogli

Of all the nubs and notches in the Italian coastline, one of the best beloved is the squarish promontory of Monte di Portofino, which comes into view as you leave Nervi, and forms, on its western side, the Gulf of Paradiso. **Recco**, at the crossroads to Camogli, was bombed into dust during World War II, and has since been completely rebuilt, but **Camogli**, only a kilometre or so away on the promontory was spared. Built on a pine-wooded slope, it is an old sea town, once home port of a renowned fleet that fought with Napoleon; its fishing and merchant vessels were equally prominent along the Riviera. Its name derives from *Casa Moglie* (home of wives), since the menfolk were almost always at sea. The wonderfully picturesque old harbour, piled high with tall, faded houses with dark green shutters, is the site of Camogli's famous *Sagra del Pesce*, an ancient festival that takes place on the second Sunday in May, where Italy's largest frying-pan (4 m across) is used to cook up thousands of sardines, distributed free to all comers—a display of generosity and abundance that carries with it the hope that the sea itself would be equally generous and abundant in the coming year. Another popular festival, the *Stella Maris* (first Sunday of August), honours those lost at sea and features a nautical procession to Punta Chiappa.

A small promontory separates Camogli's little pebble beach from its fishing port. Near here, **Dragonara Castle**, originally built in the Middle Ages to defend the port from Saracens, now contains the **Tyrrhenian Aquarium** (10–12 and 2–6 winter; 10–12 and 3–7 summer), with 22 tanks of Mediterranean creatures. Camogli recalls its history in the **Maritime and Archaeology Museums** (Mon, Thurs, Fri 9–12; Wed, Sat, Sun 9–11:45 and 3–5.45; closed Tues; free) on Via Gio Bono Ferrari 41. The archaeological section contains artefacts from, and a reconstruction of, an Iron Age settlement discovered nearby; the Marine section contains an interesting array of ship's models, nautical instruments, maps, paintings, and documents that recall Camogli's thrilling days as a rough-and-tumble sea power.

From Camogli there's a regular boat service to the tiny fishing hamlet of **San Fruttuoso** on the seaward side of the promontory, inaccessible save by sea or on foot (from Camogli, it's a three-hour hike; there are also boats from Portofino, Santa Margherita, and Rapallo, so in summer it can be elbow-room only). On the way from Camogli, the boats pass **Punta Chiappa**, a rockbound tentacle stretching into the sea, a point famous for the changing colours of the water. San Fruttuoso is named after its famous abbey, according to legend founded by two of Fruttuoso's disciples in 259, as they fled the persecutions in Spain with their leader's remains. They were shipwrecked here, where they were met by three lions, who marked out with their paws the limits of the saint's shrine.

More prosaically, it is said that San Fruttuoso was founded in 711 by the bishop of Tarragona, who fled Spain from the Moors, bringing with him the relics of San Fruttuoso. After the Saracens destroyed the abbey in the 10th century, the Benedictines rebuilt it, with the special protection of Genoa's powerful Doria family. In the 13th century six of the Dorias were buried in the abbey (while their home church of San Matteo was being done up), and in 1550 Andrea Doria added the **Torre dei Doria** to defend the abbey from Turkish corsairs, who plagued the coast in the name of the king of France. In 1983 the Doria-Pamphili family donated the abbey, tower, and surrounding land to an environmental conservation group; you can stroll through the complex of palace, pretty white 11th-century church, and cloister. San Fruttuoso is surrounded by a lush growth of pines and olives, and through these it's a two-hour walk to Portofino. Another sight, best appreciated by skin-divers, is the 1954 bronze **Cristo degli Abissi** (Christ of the Depths), off shore, eight fathoms under the sea, a memorial for those lost at sea and protector of all who work under water.

Portofino and Santa Margherita

The stunning **Monte di Portofino** (610 m) is easiest reached from **Ruta** and **Portofino Vetta** (buses from Camogli). Protected as a natural park, there are several lovely walks, especially up to the summit, with its priceless views of the Riviera and out to sea as far as Elba (one hour from Ruta). From the summit, one hour's walk will take you to the lighthouse on the cliffs (Semaforo Nuovo), or two hour's walk to Portofino.

One of Italy's most romantic little nooks, **Portofino**, set in the beautiful Golfo di Tigullio, was discovered long ago by artists, and then by the yachting set, who fell in love with its delightful little port framed by mellowed, narrow houses, then by the rich and trendy, who fell in love with its spectacular emerald beauty and seclusion and made it a favourite setting for illicit trysts and such, far from the clicking cameras of the *paparazzi*. The exclusiveness still exists to a certain extent—if you don't sleep on your yacht, there are only a handful of small hotels—but the seclusion vanishes every weekend and every day in summer, when thousands of trippers pour in for an afternoon's window-shopping in the smart boutiques (some selling the district's famous lace) and a drink in the port-side bars. But in the evening the yachtsmen and the residents of the hillside villas descend once again to their old haunts and reclaim Portofino as their own.

Portofino's name is derived from the Roman *Portus Delphini*, which had a *mithraeum* (an initiatory sanctuary dedicated to the popular Persian god Mithras, a favourite of Roman soldiers). This is now the site of the **Castle and Church of St George**, the latter housing the supposed relics of the officially defrocked saint. The castle, built against the Turks, affords a fine view of the little port (open 9–5, closed Tues; adm). Another lovely walk, beyond the castle, is to the Faro, taking in magnificent views of the Gulf of Tigullio through the pine forest. Boats travel to San Fruttuoso and Santa Margherita.

If you're driving to Portofino, you'll have to take the narrow road from **Santa Margherita Ligure**, passing by way of the **Abbey of La Cervara**, where King Francis I was imprisoned for a while after the Battle of Pavia. Santa Margherita (or just Santa, to her friends) is a thoroughly pleasant resort with a beautiful harbour, folded in the green hills—not as spectacular as Portofino, but friendly and lively, a popular winter hideaway for the British, and a summer resort with accommodation priced for all budgets. If it rains, visit the old defence tower by the sea with its **Museum of Local History**, or the **Museo Vittorio G. Rossi** in the 16th-century Villa Durazzo, on a hill surrounded by formal gardens; Rossi (d. 1978) was a reporter for the *Corriere della Sera* and a fiendish sailor (daily 8:30–6). Among the churches, there's **Basilica di Santa Margherita**, a 16th-century proto-Rococo extravagance by Galeazzo Alessi, decorated with Italian and Flemish art, and the black and white striped **Church of the Cappuccini** (1606), with a 12th-century wooden Madonna and child by the steps. In **S. Lorenzo della Costa**, 3 km from Santa Margherita, the Romanesque parish church contains a fine 1499 triptych of *S. Andrea*, attributed to Quentin Matsys and two paintings by Luca Cambiaso.

WHERE TO STAY AND EATING OUT (tel prefix 0185)

Camogli: The top hotel here is the ******Cenobio dei Dogi**, Via Cuneo 34, tel 770 041, a former palace belonging to Genoa's doges, enjoying a tranquil, secluded location overlooking the gulf, immersed in a splendid flower-filled park. The rooms are well appointed and comfortable, many with balconies enjoying the charming view. There's a salt-water pool, tennis, and pebble beach. Closed Jan and Feb; L250–320 000. The **Pensione La Camogliese**, Via Garibaldi 55, tel 771 402, is very nice and not far from the sea (L50 000 without bath, L65 000 with). The pensione's restaurant, with an attractive veranda overlooking the port, has good, reasonably priced fish dishes; full meals around L20 000. Near Camogli, up at Portofino Vetta, the small ****Portofino Vetta**, Viale Gaggini 8, tel 772 281 is a wonderfully peaceful little hotel, set in a charming garden, a great base for walks. Rooms are very cosy, equipped with private bath and air conditioning. (Closed Jan and Feb; L160 000.) Among the numerous restaurants, **Rosa**, Largo Casabona 1, tel 771 088, enjoys some of the finest views and prepares some of the finest seafood brought in the morning's catch (L65 000; closed Tues, Nov–mid-Dec). A tiny, charming place, which bases its existence entirely on the luck of Camogli's fleet, is **Vento Ariel**, Calata Porto, tel 771 080. Reservations required in the summer, and there's a daily menu offered in the L50–80 000 range, as well as à la carte choices; closed Wed and Feb.

Nearby Recco is a bit of a gourmet mecca, famous for its *foccacia* with cheese and *trofie*, a helix-shaped pasta made of chestnut flour and wheat. The mayor of Recco runs two of the best places to eat: the celebrated **Manuelina**, Via Roma 278, tel 74 128, located just outside the centre, where you can try *trofie* with *pesto* and seafood prepared in a variety of styles for the *secondo* (L55–75 000; closed Wed and mid-Jan–mid-Feb); in the adjacent **Focacceria**, tel 731 019, you can dine on Recco's other speciality, as well as such Ligurian dishes as *cima*, for a lot less—L20–25 000 for a full meal.

Portofino: Nothing stays inexpensive when the jet set comes to town, but the *****Splendido**, Viale Baratta 13, tel 269 551, is worth every lira; the view alone from every balcony of every room over Portofino, its tiny harbour and the deep blue sea beyond, is priceless. Rose and white, the Splendido is adorned with a huge terrace, large heated pool, tennis courts, and splendid garden. Each of the 67 spacious, very comfortable rooms has a hydromassage bath, air-conditioning and everything else you might desire. Open April–Oct; L420–530 000. The ****Nazionale**, smack on the port in the centre of the action (Via Roma 2, tel 269 575) has a certain, slightly faded charm to it, furnished with antiques or reproductions, with modern baths. The best rooms, rather more expensive, have Venetian furniture and overlook the harbour. No parking though, which can be a big problem in Portofino, but it's open year round (L158–190 000). The *Eden**, Vico Dritto 21, tel 269 091, is Portofino's charming budget choice, a 9-room hotel in the centre of town, but endowed with a fine garden and good Ligurian restaurant. All rooms have private bath, and the hotel is open all year; L65–90 000.

Dining out in Portofino can be a rarefied experience at **Il Pitosforo**, Molo Umberto I, tel 269 020, located on Portofino's famous little piazza. The view, the bouillabaisse, the pasta, the sea bream with olives, and the bill (around L100 000) are all guaranteed outstanding (closed Tues, Wed lunch, and Jan & Feb). Another ravishing restaurant, but one that does a bit less ravishing wallet-wise, is **Da Puny**, Piazza Martire Olivetta 7, tel 269 037, with delicious pasta and seafood dishes for starters and well-prepared fish, like sea bass baked in salt (L75 000). For chic drinking, two port-side establishments have long competed for the biggest celebrities: **La Gritta American Bar** and **Scafandro American Bar**, both elegant and glamorous in Portofino's studied, laid-back and very expensive style.

Santa Margherita: Two hotels have long rivalled one another in the luxury category, although the *****Imperial Palace has been rated one more star (Via Pagana 19, on the edge of town, tel 288 991). Formerly a private villa, it was converted into a hotel at the turn of the century; the original villa contains the palatial marble and gilt-encrusted public rooms, in one of which, in 1922, the Weimar Republic signed an agreement with Russia to reopen diplomatic relations. Concerts are frequently performed in the afternoons in the music room. Even the rooms are furnished with Genoese antiques, some more elaborately than others, and each has colour TV, private bath, frigo-bar. There's a heated pool and tennis amid the hotel's semi-tropical garden, and a private beach. Open March–Oct; L380–420 000. The shining white ****Grand Hotel Miramare, Lungomare Milite Ignoto 30, tel 287 013, is almost as palatial, built as a posh winter hotel in the early 1900s. Surrounded by a lovely garden, containing a heated salt-water pool (in addition to the pebbly beach across the road), the air-conditioned rooms are lovely, many with balconies enjoying fine views of the gulf. The Miramare's water-skiing school is one of the best in Italy (L300–350 000).

Less extravagant choices include the ***Mediterraneo, Via della Vittoria 18a, tel 286 881, located in the middle of town; a fine old villa, with a garden (L65–75 000 without bath, L80–95 000 with). Another former villa, ***La Vela, Corso Cuneo 21, tel 286 039, is located a bit above Santa Margherita and enjoys good sea views. With only 16 rooms, it has a friendly, intimate atmosphere (L80–100 000; all rooms with bath). Another former villa, the **Conte Verde, Via Zara 1, tel 287 139, is in the centre, a short walk from the sea. Cheerful, with a small terrace, garden, and bar, it is closed Nov–Christmas (prices vary from L55 000 to L75 000 depending on whether or not they have a sea view). *San Giorgio, a bit outside the centre at Via Cuneo 59, tel 286 770, has nine pleasant rooms and a garden (L49–70 000, all with bath).

If you can escape the board requirements of your hotel, try the finest restaurant in Santa Margherita, Cesarina, Via Maragliano 7, tel 286 059, located under an arcade in the old part of town. The decor is fresh and modern, and goes down well with such specialities as *zuppa di datteri* (razor clam soup) or Liguria's famous spaghetti with red mullet sauce (*triglie*). Reservations suggested; L70–85 000; closed Wed, 2 weeks in Dec. In the same place Ancora, Via Maragliano 7, tel 280 599, offers delicious seafood specialities (especially the *insalata di pesce*). More seafood is on tap at Dei Pescatori, Via Bottaro 44, tel 286 747, where a tasty fresh fish dinner will cost around L65 000.

Rapallo to Sestri Levante

TOURIST INFORMATION
Rapallo: Via A. Diaz 9, tel (0185) 54 573
Uscio: Via IV Novembre 96, tel (0185) 91 101
S. Stefano d'Aveto: Piazza del Popolo 1, tel (0185) 98 046
Zoagli: Piazza S. Martino 8, tel (0185) 259 127
Chiavari: Piazza G. Mazzini 1, tel (0185) 310 241
Lavagna: Piazza Libertà 40, tel (0185) 392 797
Sestri Levante: Via XX Settembre 33, tel (0185) 41 422

Rapallo

At the innermost corner of the Gulf of Tigullio, Rapallo is perhaps the most famous resort on the Riviera di Levante, synonymous in history with the 1920 Treaty deciding the borders of Yugoslavia, signed in the **Villa Spinola** (on the S. Margherita road). Otherwise it's synonymous with leisure, boasting a mild year-round climate, a fairly good beach, an 18-hole golf course, busy tourist harbour, indoor swimming-pool, tennis, riding-school and stables, and marvellous natural surroundings. Rapallo was the long-time home of Max Beerbohm, who lived in the Villino Chiaro and attracted a notable literary circle to the resort; Yeats and his wife came, and experimented with automatic writing, which resulted in the poet's oddest book, *A Vision*.

In Rapallo itself, the **Castle**, surrounded by the harbour's waters, is used for changing exhibitions; and there's a **Museo Civico**, in the Oratorio della Santissima Trinità in Piazza delle Nazioni, with religious art, *presepi* figures, and antique lace (at the time of writing closed for restoration). There's a funicular (which probably won't be working, so you'll have to drive or take the bus) up to the 16th-century **Sanctuary of Montallegro**, with a Byzantine icon which miraculously flew here from Dalmatia. Above the church it's a short walk up to Monte Rosa for a spectacular view; another excursion is to the church of **San Michele di Pagana** (just west of Rapallo); it contains a *Crucifixion* by Van Dyck, and is the site of large firework-popping festivals in July and September.

Inland from this stretch of coast there are two hill resorts: **Uscio**, reached by road from Recco, a health spa and manufacturer of large campanile clocks. From Rapallo and the Montallegro, a long winding road reaches in about an hour **Santo Stefano d'Aveto**, up in the Ligurian Apennines, where Rapallo's wintertime visitors can head for a taste of snow and a bit of skiing at just over 1000 m, as well as a scenic 8 km cable car excursion. Santo Stefano's landmark is the imposing **Castello Malaspina**.

Chiavari and Lavagna

East of Rapallo, **Zoagli** is a small seaside village that has produced patterned velvets ever since they were fashion's rage in the Middle Ages, although nowadays people prefer it to dress their furniture instead of themselves; most of the velvet factories are open for visits on request. Dominating the shoreline is a curious, eclectic castle-villa with a red tiled roof. **Chiavari**, the next town, is another specialist craft centre in ship building, fine wooden and straw chairs, and macramé, an art brought back by the town's sailors from the Middle East, and still used to adorn towels and tablecloths with intricate fringes and tassels. Orchids are another local speciality, their blooms best seen at the annual show at the end of February.

Chiavari has a quaint main street, called in dialect the 'Carruggio Drittu', lined with a couple of kilometres of medieval arcades. One of the most interesting buildings in the historic centre, the 17th-century **Palazzo Torriglia** in Piazza Mazzini, houses both the tourist office and a picture gallery (Mon–Fri, 9–12 and 3–6), with art by the Genoese school and a *Pietà* by Quentin Matsys. Also to see are two museums in the Palazzo Rocca, surrounded by beautiful gardens: the **Civico Museo Archeologico** on Via Costaguta 24 (Tues–Thurs 9–1:30, Fri–Sat 2–7:15), with items discovered in the nearby 8th–7th-century BC necropolis, proving trade links with the Phoenicians, Greeks, and Egyptians; and the **Civica Galleria**, containing tapestries and paintings from the

16th–20th centuries (Sat & Sun 10–12 and 4–7). In Chiavari's newer quarters, there's a small pleasure port, near the long sandy beach. A road leads from here to the ski resort of Santo Stefano d'Aveto.

Lavagna, separated from Chiavari by a bridge over the Entella, has an equally long beach. It was ruled in the Middle Ages by the Fieschi, who produced a 13th-century pope, Innocent IV, and Count Opizzo Fieschi, whose marriage to Bianca dei Bianchi in 1230 made such an impression on Lavagna that the anniversary (14 August) is annually re-enacted, a ceremony climaxing in the communal eating of the gargantuan *Torta dei Fieschi*. Innocent IV, on the other hand, is remembered by the beautiful early Gothic church he built, the **Basilica di San Salvatore dei Fieschi**, a half-hour's walk inland near Cogorno.

Sestri Levante and Varese Ligure

Sestri Levante is endowed with a lovely, curving peninsula called the Isola, dividing the 'Bay of Silence' from what Hans Christian Andersen himself christened the 'Bay of Fables'. It has a picturesque sandy beach, and perhaps more than its share of touristic development. There is a magnificent garden on the peninsula, the **Parco Naturale dei Castelli**; in its tower Marconi performed his first experiments with radio waves. Below it stands the good Romanesque church of **San Nicolò** and the Piazza Matteotti, with fine views of the two bays. The **Galleria Rizzi**, on the Bay of Silence (Via Cappuccini 10, open May–Sept, Thurs, Sat and Sun 4–6), containing works of the Florentine, Emilian, and Ligurian schools, ceramics, bronzes, sculptures, and a small furniture collection. Just outside of Sestri, the **Villa Tassani** is a rock hound's paradise, housing the most complete collection of minerals in Liguria (open daily).

From Sestri a bus heads inland along the N. 523 to Borgo Val di Taro in Emilia, passing by way of **Varese Ligure**, the chief town of the mountainous Val di Vara. Like many villages in the region, its medieval architecture and town design are interesting for their adaptation to the hilly terrain in Varese, typified by the ancient **Borgo Rotundo**, a carousel of pastel arcades. Its great 15th-century **Castle** belonged to the Fieschi clan of Lavagna.

WHERE TO STAY AND EATING OUT (tel prefix 0185)
Rapallo: Rapallo has more hotels than any resort on the Riviera di Levante. The ******Eurotel**, Via Aurelia Ponente 22, tel 60 981, overlooks Rapallo and the sea. A modern building, with pretty gardens and pool, all rooms have a balcony as well as private bath, frigo-bar, and air-conditioning (L190–220 000). *****Moderno & Reale**, Via Gramsci 6, tel 50 601, is a lovely villa built in the '30s with a Liberty-style flair on Rapallo's seafront promenade, with a pretty garden and terrace. Rooms have been renovated, and all have private bath (L70–100 000). The *****Riviera**, Piazza IV Novembre 2, tel 50 248, is also a converted villa, in the centre of Rapallo, near the sea. Remodelled inside, it has a popular glass terrace in the front and a garden at the rear, and comfortable rooms, all with bath (L85–100 000; closed Nov–mid-Dec). *****Minerva**, Corso Colombo 7, tel 230 388, is a good bargain: up-to-date, near the shore, tasteful decor, garden and bar (L60 000, all rooms with bath).

Among the restaurants in Rapallo, **A Chigeugna**, up on a hill above Rapallo, at Via Sotto la Croce 1, tel 260 281, is the hardest to pronounce but one of the best known, featuring Ligurian dishes like *pansotti* with walnut sauce and *cima*, all on a fixed-price menu of L42 000. **Cuoco d'Oro**, Via della Vittoria 3, tel 50 745, is an intimate, authentic restaurant, where each order is freshly prepared (reservations suggested; L40 000).

Chiavari: Chiavari's hotels are adequate and pleasant but nothing special. You may want to eat here, however, at **Copetin**, Piazza Gagliardo 16, tel 309 064, with delicious fish and scampi dishes, *risotto mare-monti*, and fresh desserts (L60 000; closed Tues eve, Wed, Jan & Feb). At Leivi, 6 km from Chiavari, **Ca' Peo**, Strada Panoramica, tel 319 090, is one of the best restaurants on the Riviera. The atmosphere is elegant and charming, and the food imaginatively and delicately prepared, featuring ingredients like *radicchio* (red chicory) from Treviso, truffles from Alba, *porcini* mushrooms, fresh fish, followed by excellent desserts and accompanied by noble wines. (Reservations a must; L60–80 000, closed Mon, Tues lunch, & Nov.) At Lavagna there's an excellent trattoria, **Cantinna**, Via Torrente Barassi 8, tel 390 394, where fish-lovers and fish-haters can happily dine together, the former on shrimp and scampi, the latter on roast veal (L35–40 000; closed Tues, Nov and mid-Feb–mid-March).

Sestri Levante: Sestri competes with Rapallo for being the most touristy resort of the Eastern Riviera, but you'll never notice it if you stay at the *****Hotel dei Castelli**, Via Penisola 26, tel 485 780, occupying the tip of the peninsula. Built in the '20s on the site of a Genoese castle, it was constructed from the castle's stone. The views of both bays and the sea crashing against the cliffs all around the hotel's park are magnificent, especially from the dining terrace. There's a natural sea pool cut into the rock for safe swimming. Open 10 May–10 Oct, rooms are air-conditioned, and all have private bath (L190–240 000). The seaside ****Grand Hotel Villa Balbi**, Viale Rimembranza 1, tel 42 941, is a pink palace, its core an 18th-century Genoese villa. Rooms are large, many with views of the sea, and public rooms are palatial. In the garden there's a heated sea-water pool. (Open April–Sept; L94–100 000 without bath, L115–160 000 with.) On the less expensive side, the ***Metropole**, at Via Sertorio 7, tel 43 914 is a comfortable choice. Rooms with bath come to a reasonable L70 000. ***Helvetia**, Via Cappuccini 43, tel 41 175, is a fine welcoming little hotel in the prettiest part of town, right on the Bay of Silence. There's a large terraced garden (open March–Oct; L75 000).

There are a number of good restaurants in Sestri. For excellent seaside dining, **Angiolina**, Viale della Rimembranza 49, tel 441 198, is the place to go for an exquisite *zuppa di pesce* and other delicious denizens of the deep (L70–100 000; closed Tues & Nov). Seafood and Ligurian traditional cuisine comprise the menu at **Fiammenghilla Fieschi**, Via Pestella 6, tel 481 041, housed in an old patrician villa. Open evenings only, it's a great place to try marinated swordfish, lobster, *focaccia*, or *pansotti*. Good Ligurian wine list; reserve (L70 000; closed Mon & Tues).

Riviera di Levante: The Cinque Terre and La Spezia

Before sliding down to the comparatively dull and flat coast of Tuscany, the Riviera bows out with a dramatic flourish, around the rugged, almost inaccessible cliffs of the Cinque Terre, the rocky peninsula of Portovénere, and La Spezia's lovely Gulf of Poets.

GETTING AROUND

The easiest way to reach the Cinque Terre is by train from Genoa or La Spezia. Each of the five towns has a station, only a few minutes apart and separated by long tunnels; afterwards the train drills through the mountains straight to La Spezia and Sarzana, from where you can continue on towards Parma or Pisa.

The A12, beyond Sestri Levante, heads inland to avoid the wild coast until it arrives at La Spezia. The controversial coastal road to the Cinque Terre (*Litoranea delle Cinque Terre*; Italian engineers' bulldozers begin to twitch at the mention of the word 'inaccessible') has succeeded so far in reaching Monterosso (approaching from Genoa) and Riomaggiore and Manarola (approaching from La Spezia). There are buses from Piazza Chiodo in La Spezia to Riomaggiore and Manarola, Portovénere (every 15 minutes), Lerici, Sarzana, and Florence.

There are seven ferry companies serving the area (tel prefix 0871). Corsica Ferries (tel 21 282) and NAVARMA (tel 21 855) make the five-hour run between La Spezia and Bastia in Corsica daily in the summer, less so at other times. In-Tur (tel 24 324), Navigazione Golfo dei Poeti (tel 967 676) and Battellieri del Golfo (tel 28 066) sail between La Spezia, Lerici, Portovénere, and the Cinque Terre; NGP goes as far as Portofino, Marina di Massa and Marina di Carrara. Another company, Verde Azzurro (tel 967 860) runs similar itineraries based from Lerici; another, Filli Rossignoli (tel 817 456) sails between Monterosso and Viareggio.

TOURIST INFORMATION

Levanto: Piazza C. Colombo 12, tel (0187) 807 175
Monterosso al Mare: Via Fegina 38, tel (0187) 817 506
La Spezia: Viale Mazzini 47, tel (0187) 36 000
Portovénere: Piazza Bastreri, tel (0187) 900 691
Lerici: Via Roma 47, tel (0187) 967 346

Sestri Levante to the Cinque Terre

After Sestri Levante, the Apennines move in and crowd the coast, admitting here and there little glens and sandy strands—at **Monéglia** with its two castles, **Déiva Marina** (near the pretty village of Framura), **Bonassola**, and most importantly, **Levanto**, with a good sandy beach, flower gardens, and several monuments from the 13th century—the **Loggia** (town hall), the **Church of Sant' Andrea**, and chunks of its walls.

Next on the coast, **Monterosso al Mare** is the first of the five towns of the **Cinque Terre** ('The Five Lands'), as they've been known since the Middle Ages. Perched wherever the cliffs and hills permitted enough space to build, surrounded by steep slopes corrugated by hundreds of terraces, laboriously carved out of the earth and rock, the Cinque Terre towns are visually stunning. They also enjoy a fine, mild climate, and the vineyards that occupy the near-vertical terraces produce the region's finest, most fragrant, and most potent wines—those labelled *Sciacchetrà* are made from raisins, and can be either dry or sweet. As wines go, they are unusually addictive—Dante consigned Pope Martin IV to fast in the Inferno for his passion for Cinque Terre wines. Formerly accessible only by sea or by a spectacular series of cliff-skirting footpaths, the Cinque

Manarola

Terre villages have maintained much of their charm, even though nowadays they are far from being undiscovered.

Monterosso, attainable by car, is the largest and the most touristy of the five, with beaches (free and 'organized'), hotels, rooms in private houses, etc., and boats to hire for personal tours of the coast. Most of the facilities are in the new half of town called Fegina, separated from the old by a hill crowned with the 1622 **Convento dei Cappuccini** and a medieval tower; the 18th-century **Sanctuary of Soviore**, built over an older church, hosts a music festival in the summer. From Monterosso it's a momentary train ride or a lovely hour-and-a-half walk to the next town, **Vernazza**, founded by the Romans on a rocky spit, a striking vision from the footpath above. Its parish church, **Santa Margherita of Antioch**, was built in 1318.

The hour-and-a-half walk from Vernazza to **Corniglia** is one of the most strenuous, for Corniglia, unlike the other towns, is high up on the cliffs and not on the sea, though it does have the longest (though pebbly) beach. From Corniglia another hour's walk through splendid scenery leads to **Manarola**, at the terminus of the coastal road from La Spezia. Manarola is a colourful fishing village built on steep lanes. It is linked in 20 minutes or so to **Riomaggiore** by the most popular section of the footpath, the *Via dell'Amore*, carved into the cliff face over the sea. Riomaggiore, one of the prettiest towns, also sees plenty of visitors, who crowd its lively cafés and rocky beaches.

La Spezia

The largest city in the region, provincial capital, and one of Italy's most important naval bases, La Spezia owes its livelihood to its modern Arsenale, conceived by Count Cavour in the 1860s. This, however, also caused the town to be bombed heavily in the last war, and today La Spezia presents a modern, but cheerful face to the world, standing at the head of one of Italy's prettiest gulfs. Mostly used as a base for visiting the Cinque Terre and Portovénere, it has a number of attractions in its own right—a promenade of swaying palms and lush public gardens. At Via Curtatone 9, the **Museo Civico** (9–1 and 3–7, Sun 9–1, closed Mon) contains an important archaeological section, with prehistoric finds from Palmaria's Grotta dei Colombi, pre-Roman and Roman material from Luni, and most notably Ligurian statue steles from the Bronze and Iron Ages. Another section is ethnographic, with costumes and tools from villages in the province. The excellent **Naval Museum** is in Piazza Chiodo, next to the Naval Arsenal (open Tues–Thurs and Sat 9–12 and 2–6; adm), containing a fine collection begun in 1560 by Emanuele Filiberto, with relics of the Savoy Navy in the Battle of Lepanto; there are models, a gallery of figureheads, and relics from Italy's naval battles. In the church of **Santa Maria Assunta** there's a terracotta *Coronation of the Virgin* by Andrea della Robbia.

Portovénere and Palmaria

The road between La Spezia and Portovénere is lovely and winding (if you're prone to motion sickness you may want to take the equally scenic boat), and passes by way of the pretty cove of **Le Grazie**. At the end of the road stands ancient, fortified **Portovénere**, with its long promontory, castle, and tall pastel houses, one of the loveliest towns on the Riviera. Named after the goddess of love herself, protectress of fishermen, her legendary temple stood at the tip of the promontory, on the site of the **Church of San Pietro**, another patron of fishermen. This is a strange little church, of black and white striped marble dating from 1277, built over a few colourful marble remains of a 6th-century predecessor. There are splendid views from here, of Palmaria and the coast of the Cinque Terre; the pretty cove below once held the Grotta Arpaia, where Byron wrote *The Corsair*, and from where he swam across the gulf to Lerici and Shelley's villa. The Grotta collapsed in the 1930s.

The best thing to do in Portovénere is wander through its narrow cat-crowded lanes (Portovénere is Italy's champion kitty city): past tall ancient houses on the waterfront, built under the Genoese, who fortified the town in the early 12th century (as the Pisans had fortified Lerici across the gulf), with interesting details on the doorways. From the port a narrow lane leads up to the lovely **Church of San Lorenzo**, with a bas-relief over the door of St Lawrence being toasted on his gridiron, built in 1130; inside is a marble retable attributed to Mino da Fiesole and Portovénere's most precious relic, the *Madonna Bianca*, said to have floated to the town, encased in a cedar log, in the 13th century (the log, too, is on display). Further up, a steep but worthwhile walk leads to the 16th-century Genoese **Castello**, with marvellous views (open April–Oct 10–12 to 2–6, other times 3–5).

From Portovénere you can cross the 400 m channel to **Isola Palmaria** and visit its famed **Grotta Azzura**—a much cheaper proposition is to book a passage from La Spezia. Palmaria produces the black, gold-veined marble you may have noticed in Portovénere, and was the site of a Neolithic settlement. A much smaller islet, **Isola del Tino**, with a lighthouse and ruins of an 8th-century monastery, and the tinier **Tinetto**, lie further out.

Lerici

Lerici, on its own little bay, is the most important town and resort on the east shore of the Golfo dei Poeti. Lerici is dominated by its imposing **Castello**, towering up on its promontory (9–12:30 and 2:30–5, later in the summer; adm). Built by the Pisans, it was enlarged by the Genoese in the 15th century; inside you can visit the Chapel of Sant'Anastasia (1250). Lerici has a nice beach and mild winter climate, and its environs were beloved by Shelley, whose last home was the Casa Magni in **San Terenzo**, the charming fishing village across the bay from Lerici: it was from here that he sailed, in 1822, to meet Leigh Hunt at Livorno, only to be shipwrecked and drowned on the way home near Viareggio. To the south is the enchanting, tranquil, tiny cove and beach of **Fiascherino**, where D. H. Lawrence lived in 1913–14; beyond is the unspoiled medieval hamlet of **Tellaro**. Another road continues around the gulf and begins to climb up the Val di Magra to **Ameglia**, with its remains of the Roman port of Luni, its 10th-century castle, and the slate portals of the older houses.

Sarzana and Ancient Luni

From La Spezia, trains and the autostrada cross the Val di Magra for **Sarzana**, on the easternmost edge of the Republic of Genoa. An ancient, fortified town dominated by the **Fortezza di Sarzello**, a sharp-walled citadel built in the early 14th century by the tyrant of Lucca, Castruccio Castracani. The 14th-century **Cathedral** contains one of the best works of Master Guglielmo, a painted wooden *Crucifixion* of 1138, one of the oldest in existence; other churches of note include **Sant'Andrea**, where the remains of a much earlier church have recently been discovered, and **San Francesco**, with fine sculptures. To the north in **Fosdinovo**, the Malaspina castle hosted Dante in 1306; he is also said to have visited the ruined 13th-century castle in **Castelnuovo Magra**. The parish church contains an *Ascent to Calvary* by Brueghel the Younger.

Ortonovo lies near the site of the ancient Roman town of the moon, **Luni**. Luni was built as a colonial bulwark against the fierce Ligurians as well as a port for Carrara marble (or Luni marble), and it gave its name to the Lunigiana, the northernmost finger of Tuscany. The city survived until the Middle Ages; the bishopric of Luni survived until 1929, when it was combined with that of La Spezia. Excavations have revealed a sizeable amphitheatre (used for summer performances), a forum, houses, temples, etc.; on the site there's the **Museo Nazionale di Luni** (9–12 and 4–7, 2–5 winter, closed Mon), with an interesting collection of marble statuary, coins, jewellery, portraits, etc., as well as a display of archaeological techniques used in excavating the site, which can be toured with a guide.

WHERE TO STAY AND EATING OUT (tel prefix 0187)
Local dishes to look for around La Spezia include *lattughe ripiene* (stuffed lettuce), *mes-ciua* (a healthy, whole-grain soup), vegetable pies, and codfish fritters; local wines are all of the white variety: try *Marinasco*, *Bianca di Biassa*, and *Campiglia*.

In the Cinque Terre: of the five towns, Monterosso has the best accommodation with the ******Porto Roca**, tel 817 502, as the top choice, located in a prominent position on the headland, with lovely views of the sea from the rooms. All rooms have bath (L140 000). The largish, modern *****Cinque Terre**, Via IV Novembre 21, tel 817 543, has a private beach and plain but comfortable rooms; L50–60 000 without bath, L65–80 000 with. Large, friendly ****Villa Adriana**, Via IV Novembre 5, tel 818 109, is also on the waterfront, with a beach as well. Rooms are simple (without bath L40 000, with L55 000). The best food in Monterosso is served at **Il Gigante**, Via IV Novembre 9, tel 817 401, with especially good Ligurian specialities—*pansotti, trenette al pesto* and fresh fish (L45–50 000). There's one hotel at Manarola, the *****Marina Piccola**, tel 920 103, with all of six simple rooms—a good place to get away from it all, even if you may not feel especially pampered (L65–70 000). **Aristide**, Via Discovolo, tel 920 000, is Manarola's choice trattoria, serving a delicious *minestra* and exquisite fish dishes, but also rabbit, game, and other dishes when in season (L50 000; closed Mon). In Vernazza, there's the ****Sorriso**, Via Gavino 4, tel 812 224, an honest little inn with rooms for L35 000 without bath, L40 000 with, and a well-known restaurant, the **Gambero Rosso** in Piazza Marconi 16, tel 812 265, partly carved out of rock; try the *tegame di acciughe*, a tasty dish made with anchovies, a Cinque Terre speciality. There's also plenty of less piquant seafood, too (L40–55 000, closed Mon).

La Spezia: The finest lodgings in La Spezia are at the ******Jolly del Golfo**, Via XX Settembre 2, tel 27 200, a modern and rather stylish member of the original Italian hotel chain, up on a slope, with views stretching to the gulf. Each room has air-conditioning, TV, and private bath (L160–220 000). Near the station, the *****Firenze & Continental**, Via Paleocapa 7, tel 31 248, is comfortable and convenient for making rail hops into the Cinque Terre (L65–70 000, all rooms with bath). It has a cheaper annexe (*dipendenza*) nearby on Via Fiume 60. Among the bargains the best is ***Flavia**, Vicolo dello Stagno 7 (not far from the station, off Via del Prione, tel 27 465, with rooms for L30 000 without bath, L35–40 000 with).

La Posta, in the centre of town on Via Don Minzoni 24, tel 34 419, has some of the city's most diverse and expert cuisine, with game, truffles and mushrooms in season, and good pasta dishes. Closed weekends & Aug; L50 000. **Rossetto**, Via dei Colli Cacciagone 105, tel 29 393, has good views, up on a hillside over the gulf; its menu features beef, chicken, rabbit and boar, but not a minnow in sight. Its hearty roast and grilled meats are accompanied by good red Tuscan wines (L40 000).

Portovénere: Large and modern ******Hotel Royal Sporting**, tel 900 326, is Portovénere's finest hotel, with a fantastic location overlooking sea and town, a salt-water pool, beach, garden, tennis, and air-conditioning in every room. There is also a place to park—an important consideration in this little town (L110–170 000, all with bath). *****San Pietro**, tel 900 616, has hardly any of the facilities of the Royal, but a lot more character. Located up at the old castle, it has charming 1920s Liberty-style decor, and superb views (L75 000 with bath). ****Genio**, Piazza Bastreri 8, tel 900 611, has the cheapest rooms in town, and a nice little garden, too; L60 000, all rooms with bath. You can dine in a former fisherman's house in the picturesque Calata Doria, at **Al Gavitello da Mario**, tel 900 215. The menu—surprise!—is devoted to seafood, but prepared in unusual ways—for *primo*, try ravioli filled with fish with prawn sauce; for *secondo*, scampi with pear brandy (L60 000). At the beginning of the promontory, **La Taverna del Corsaro** (Lungomare Doria 102, tel 900 622) has one of the most delightful addresses in Portovénere, where you can savour delicacies like shrimp in bell-pepper sauce, *zuppa dei datteri* (razor clams) and well-prepared seafood. Good selection of wines and desserts (L65 000; closed Thurs, 25 May–mid-June, and Jan).

Lerici: *****Shelley & Delle Palme**, Lungomare Biaggini 5, tel 967 127, is one of the largest and most comfortable hotels on the Gulf of Poets, with fine views of the sea (L80–95 000, all with bath). ****Panoramic**, above most of the resort hubbub at

Carbagnano, tel 967 192, has more good views, a garden, and simple but good rooms (all with bath: L65 000). **Paolino**, Via S. Francesco 14, tel 967 801, offers three dining choices—light, medium, and full, depending on your appetite—good salads, pasta dishes (L40–60 000; closed Mon).

In the more laid-back San Terenzo, ***Elisabetta**, tel 970 636, is tiny but comfortable, with a garden (L60 000 with bath). **Palmira**, Via Trogu 13, tel 971 094, is a very popular restaurant, serving delightful *zuppa di datteri* and other seafood, though meat dishes are available as well(L50 000; closed Wed, Sept, & Oct).

On the cove of Fiascherino, **Il Nido**, Via Fiascherino 75, tel 967 286, enjoys a lovely location, with enchanting views over the sea and beach. Good rooms (but not so good in the annexe) are perfect for rest and relaxation (L80 000). The nearby restaurant, **Miranda**, Via Fiascherino 92, tel 968 130, serves mouthwatering seafood dishes with a French touch, like shrimp flan in white truffle sauce, fish gnocchi with *pesto*, or linguine with scampi and asparagus (L70 000).

Ameglia: This is the site of the most famous hotel and restaurant in the region, the ****Paracucchi Locanda dell'Angelo**, at Ca' di Scabello, Via XXV Aprile, tel 64 391, owned and run by a master chef. The hotel is modern, stylish, and slick, each room furnished with private bath, air-conditioning, TV; the sea is only a couple of minutes away (L140 000). The restaurant is one of the finest in the country, a haven for gourmets. The menu changes often, but each and every dish is a superb and often amazingly simple example of pure wizardry. The desserts are exquisite, and the wine list contains many a rare and prestigious vintage (L80–100 000; closed Mon & 10–31 Jan). Near Ameglia at Fiumaretta, **Il Veliero**, Viale Litoranea 50, tel 64 347, offers tempting pasta dishes (including one with cognac), and landlubber dishes like kid, wild boar or hare; (L40 000, closed Mon).

Part V

LOMBARDY AND THE LAKES

Tremezzina, Como

Of all the barbarians who desecrated the corpse of the Roman Empire none were more barbaric than the Lombards (or Longobards), a tall Germanic tribe of violent heretics who bled much of the peninsula before settling down in the region that still bears their name. Even today the Milanese are taller than the average Italian, though whether it's because of their Lombard blood or general prosperity is anyone's guess. For Lombardy, since the Middle Ages, has been the most developed region in Italy, in its industry and agriculture, commerce and transport. The complaint that Milan makes money while Rome wastes it is almost as old as the city itself.

Frenetic Milan, the pounding, racing economic heart of modern Italy, is the transport node for the entire north. It always has been; geography has placed Lombardy, more than any other Italian region, at the crossroads of European history. The destinies of entire empires and kingdoms were decided on the plains and cities of Lombardy; Christianity was declared the official religion of the Empire in Milan; princes, from Charlemagne to Barbarossa to Napoleon, came to Lombardy to be crowned King of Italy; it was a prize that kept Spain, France, and the Holy Roman Emperors of Germany and Austria fighting like cats and dogs.

Lombardy has its gentle side as well. This was the homeland of two of Rome's greatest poets, epic Virgil and lyric Catullus, of composers Donizetti and Monteverdi, of the great violin masters, Amati, Guarneri and Stradivarius. And since the 18th century countless poets, composers and weary aristocrats have come for the solace and beauty of the Italian Lakes, one of the most charming districts in the country (which, though partially in Piedmont, Switzerland, and the Veneto, have all been included here for convenience's sake).

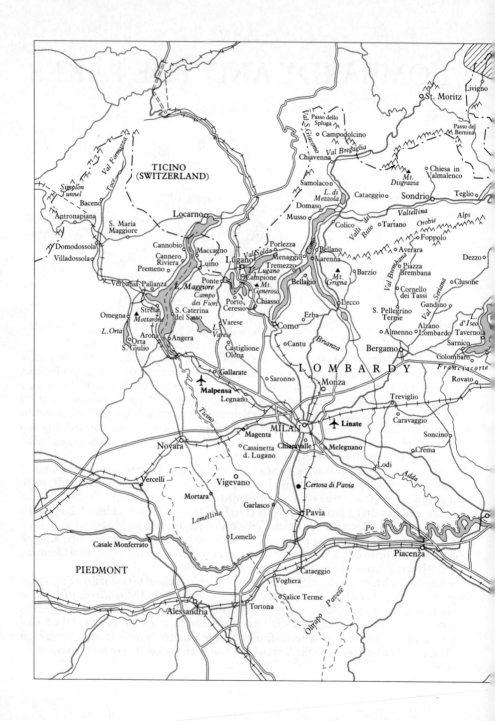

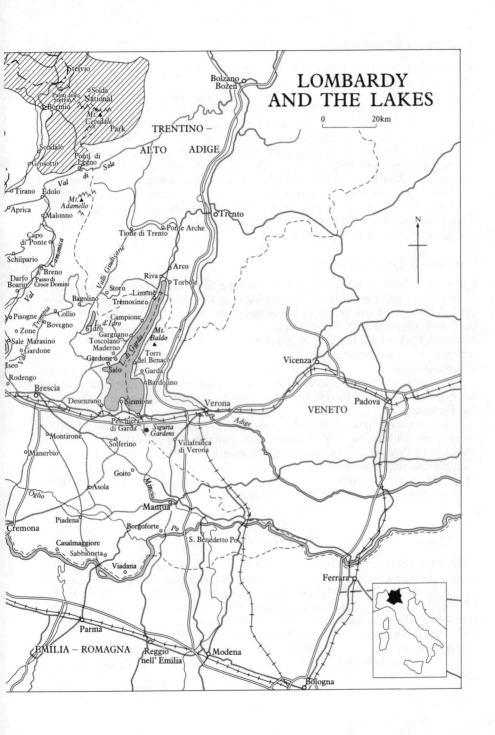

The Best of Lombardy

Milan is far more than a centre of finance and fashion, but an art city in its own right, where you can easily spend three days, taking in nearby **Pavia** and its famous **Certosa** as a day trip. The famous gardens and villas of **Lake Como** (Villa Carlotta and Bellagio) or of **Lake Maggiore** (Stresa and the Borromean isles) can also be seen in rather hurried day trips from Milan, though it's far more pleasant to spend at least a night on their shores, even better to linger and relax. Spectacular **Lake Garda** is a bit far for a day trip, but rates as the liveliest for a prolonged stay and a good stopover if you're headed towards Venice; on Garda don't miss Sirmione with its Romantic ruins of the Grotte di Catullo and Gardone Riviera with Gabriele D'Annunzio's kitsch palace. Both **Bergamo** and **Mantua** are top-notch art cities, the former for its medieval *Città Alta* and the Carrara Academy, the latter for the Renaissance palaces of the Gonzaga dukes. Silk-weaving **Como**, violin-making **Cremona**, and Roman **Brescia** all have fine cathedrals and enough sights to occupy at least half a day.

Unknown Lombardy

Unknown, at least, to most foreigners. Besides the three main lakes, the lesser lakes of **Orta** and **Iseo** are charmers and fine choices for a quiet sojourn. The Bergamask valleys, the **Val Brembana** and the upper **Val Seriana** offer great Alpine scenery without the hype, while the beautiful **Val Camonica**, above Lake Iseo, is the home of the remarkable **National Park of Prehistoric Engravings**. The rugged Alpine valleys of Sondrio province, the **Valchiavenna** and the **Valtellina**, are dotted with castles and quiet villages; **Bormio**, at the top of the Valtellina, is one of Italy's top winter-sports centres and the gateway to glacier-encrusted **Stelvio National Park**. More splendid scenery lies to the north of Lake Maggiore, especially around **Domodossola** and the Romantic **Val Formazza**.

Artistic treasures pale before Lombardy's natural wonders, but certainly worth a mention are **Sabbioneta**, an ideal Renaissance town near Mantua; the lovely frescoes of Masolino da Panicale in **Castiglione Olona**, east of Lake Maggiore; **Lugano**, with its Villa Favorita with a fine art collection and Santa Maria degli Angioli, with the remarkable frescoes of Leonardo's pupil Luini; the ancient cathedral of **Monza**, with the treasure of the ancient Lombard Queen Theodolinda.

MILAN

Most tourists don't come to Italy looking for feverishly slick and beaverishly busy Milan (in Italian *Milano*), and most of those who somehow find themselves here take in only the obligatory sights—Leonardo's *Last Supper*, La Scala, the Duomo, and the Brera Gallery—before rushing off in search of designer millinery, itself a word derived from this metropolis of fashion. Most Italians (apart from the almost 2,000,000 Milanese, that is), have little good to say about their second city, either: Milan just isn't very Italian, or polite or charming, and where are the chunky ochre buildings with the fountain in the piazza? All the Milanese do is work, all they care about is money, and they defiantly refuse to indulge the myth of *la dolce vita*.

The Italians who deride Milan (most of whom work just as many hours) are mostly envious, and the tourists who whip through it in a day are mostly ignorant of what this great city has to offer. Milan is indeed atypical, devoid of the usual Italian daydreams and living-museum mustiness. Like Naples it lives for the present, but not in Naples' endearing total anarchy; as one of Europe's major financial centres and a capital of fashion in the '80s, Milan dresses in a well-tailored, thoroughly cosmopolitan three-piece suit. And yet, as the Milanese will be the first to admit, Milan has made its way in the world not so much by native talent but through the ability to attract and make use of that from other places, from St Ambrose and Leonardo da Vinci to its most celebrated designer of the moment. It is Italy's New York, its greatest melting pot, the Italians' picture window on the modern world, more European than Italian, where the young and ambitious gravitate to see their talents properly appreciated and rewarded. Here history seems to weigh less; here willowy Japanese models slink down the sidewalk with natty young gents whose parents immigrated from Calabria.

Milan has produced no great music of its own, but its La Scala opera house is one of the world's most prestigious places to sing; it has produced but one great artist (the extraordinary Arcimboldi), but managed to amass enough treasures to fill four first-class galleries. It is the one great Italian city that isn't finished, a Renaissance waiting in the wings, a potential Golden Age lurking around the corner. Luigi Barzini complained that foreigners are interested only in dead Italians, but Milan is one city where the live ones are equally captivating and overflowing with ideas.

Beware that in August Milan turns into a veritable ghost town, when only a handful of restaurants remain open. On the other hand, during its great fairs (especially the big fashion show in March and autumn, and the April Fair) you may find no room at the inn.

History

Milan was born cosmopolitan. Located far from any sea or river, in the middle of the fertile but vulnerable Lombard plain, it nevertheless lies at the natural junction of trade routes through the Alpine passes, from the Tyrrhenian and Adriatic ports, and from the river Po. While an advantage commercially, its strategic position put Milan square in the path of every conqueror tramping through Italy.

Mediolanum, as it was originally called, first became prominent in the twilight of the Roman Empire, when, as the headquarters of the Mobile Army and the seat of the court and government of the West, it became the de facto capital; Diocletian preferred it to Rome, and his successors spent much of their time here. The Christianization of the Empire became official in 313, when Constantine the Great proclaimed the Edict of Milan.

St Ambrose (Sant'Ambrogio)

No sooner had Christianity received the stamp of approval than it split into two camps, the orthodox and the Arian, which held that Christ was not of the same substance as God. The bishop of Milan was an Arian and persecutor of the orthodox, and a schism seemed inevitable when he died. When the young consular governor Ambrose spoke to calm the crowd during the election of the new bishop, a child's voice suddenly piped up: 'Ambrose Bishop!' The cry was taken up, and Ambrose, who hadn't even been baptized, suddenly found himself thrust into a new job.

167

According to legend, when Ambrose was an infant in Rome, bees had flown into his mouth, attracted by the honey of his tongue. Ambrose's famous eloquence as bishop (374–397) is given much of the credit for preserving the unity of the Church; when the widow of Emperor Valentine desired to raise her son as an Arian, demanding a Milanese basilica for Arian worship, Ambrose and his supporters held the church through a nine-day siege, converting the Empress's soldiers in the process. His most famous convert was St Augustine, and he also set what was to become the standard in relations between Church and Empire when he refused to allow Emperor Theodosius to enter church until he had done penance for ordering a civilian massacre in Thessalonika. St Ambrose left such an imprint on Milan that even today genuine Milanese are called Ambrosiani; their church, practically independent from Rome until the 11th century, still celebrates Mass according to the Ambrosian rite. The Milanese even celebrate their own civic carnival of Sant'Ambrogio in March.

The Rise of the *Comune*

During the barbarian invasions of the next few centuries 'Mediolanum' was shortened to Mailand, the prized Land of May, for so it seemed to the frostbitten Goths and Lombards who came to take it for their own. In the early 11th century Milan evolved into one of Italy's first *comuni* under the another great bishop, Heribert, who organized a *parlamento* of citizens and a citizen militia. The new *comune* at once began subjugating the surrounding country and especially its Ghibelline rivals Pavia, Lodi, and Como, and to inspire the militia Heribert also invented that unique Italian war totem, the *carroccio*, a huge ox-drawn cart that bore the city's banner and an altar into battle, to remind the soldiers of the city and church they fought for.

It was Lodi's complaint about Milan's bullying to Holy Roman Emperor Frederick Barbarossa that first brought old Red Beard to Italy in 1154. It was to prove a momentous battle of wills and arms between the emperor and Milan, one that would define the relationship of Italy's independent-minded *comuni* towards their nominal overlord. Barbarossa besieged and sacked Milan in 1158; the Ambrosiani promised to behave but attacked his German garrison as soon as the Emperor was back safely over the Alps. Undaunted, Barbarossa returned again, and for two years wasted the countryside around Milan, then grimly besieged the defiant city. When it surrendered he was merciless, demanding the surrender of the *carroccio*, forcing the citizens to kiss his feet with ropes around their necks, and inviting Milan's bitterest enemies, Lodi and Como, to raze the city to the ground, sparing only the churches of Sant'Ambrogio and San Lorenzo.

But this total humiliation of Milan, meant as an Imperial example to Italy's other *comuni*, had the opposite effect to that intended; it galvanized them into forming the Lombard League against the foreign oppressor (only Pavia hated Milan too much to join). Barbarossa, on his next trip over the Alps, found the *comuni* united against him, and in 1176 was soundly defeated by the Lombard League at Legnano. Now the tables had turned and the empire itself was in danger of total revolt. To preserve it, Barbarossa had to do a little foot-kissing himself, in Venice, the privileged toe in this case belonging to Pope Alexander III, whom Barbarossa had exiled from Rome in his attempt to set up a pope more malleable to his schemes. To placate the Lombard *comuni*, the Treaty of Constance was signed after a six-year truce in 1183, in which the signatories of the Lombard League received all that they desired: their municipal autonomy and the

THE LORDS OF MILAN (* = ruler)

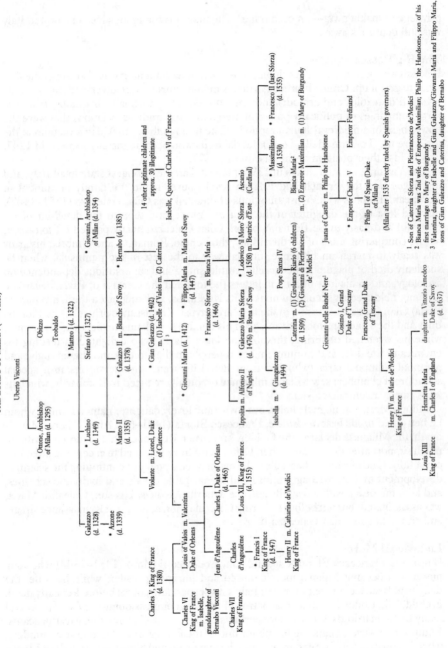

1 Son of Caterina Sforza and Pierfrancesco de'Medici
2 Bianca Maria was 2nd wife of Emperor Maximilian; Philip the Handsome, son of his first marriage to Mary of Burgundy
3 Valentina, daughter of Isabelle and Gian Galeazzo/Giovanni Maria and Filippo Maria, sons of Gian Galeazzo and Caterina, daughter of Bernabo

privilege of making war—on each other! The more magnanimous idea of a united Italy was still centuries away.

The Big Bosses

If Milan was precocious in developing a *comunale* government, it was also one of the first cities to give it up. Unlike Florence, Milan's manufacturers were diverse (though mainly involved in textiles and armour) and limited themselves to small workshops, failing to form companies of politically powerful merchants and trade associations that were the power base of a medieval Italian republic. The first family to fill Milan's vacuum at the top were the Torriani (della Torre), feudal lords who became the city's *signori* in 1247, only to lose their position to the Visconti in 1277.

The Visconti, created dukes in 1395, made Milan the strongest state in all Italy, and marriages into the French and English royal houses made the family prominent in European affairs as well. Most ambitious of them all was Gian Galeazzo (1351–1402), married first to the daughter of the king of France, and then to the daughter of his powerful and nasty uncle Bernabò, whom Gian Galeazzo neatly packed off to prison, before conquering most of northern Italy, the Veneto, Romagna, and Umbria; his army was ready to march on Florence, the gateway to the rest of the peninsula, when he suddenly died of plague. In his cruelty, ruthlessness, and superstitious dependence on astrology, and in his love of art and letters (he founded the Certosa of Pavia, began the Duomo, held a court second to none in its lavishness, and supported the University of Pavia) Gian Galeazzo was one of the first 'archetypal' Renaissance princes. The Florentines and the Venetians took advantage of his demise to pick up the pieces of his empire, while his wretched offspring, the obscene Gian Maria (who delighted in feeding his enemies to the dogs and hunting innocent people in the streets) and the fat, ugly, and paranoid Filippo Maria (who hid from his visitors and thunderstorms in a special soundproof chamber) saw Milan's influence eventually reduced to Lombardy, which its lords ran as a centralized state.

Filippo Maria left no male heirs, but a wise and lovely daughter named Bianca, whom he betrothed to his best *condottiere*, Francesco Sforza (1401–66). After Filippo Maria's death, the Milanese declared the Golden Ambrosian Republic, which crumbled without much support after three years, when Francesco Sforza returned to accept the dukedom peacefully. One of Milan's best rulers, he maintained a policy of continuing the scientific development of Lombard agriculture and its navigable canals and hydraulic schemes, and kept the peace with a friendly alliance with the Medicis. His son, Galeazzo Maria, was assassinated, but not before fathering Caterina Sforza, the great Renaissance virago, and an infant son, Gian Galeazzo II.

Lodovico il Moro

But it was Francesco Sforza's second son, Lodovico il Moro (1451–1508) who took power and became Milan's most cultured and intriguing leader, while his wife, the delightful Beatrice d'Este ran one of Italy's most sparkling courts before her early death in childbirth. Lodovico was a great patron of the arts, commissioning the *Last Supper* and many of Leonardo da Vinci's engineering schemes, as well as his theatrical pageants. Lodovico, however, bears the blame for one of the first great Italian political blunders, when his quarrel with Naples grew so touchy that he invited King Charles VIII of France to march through the peninsula to claim the Kingdom of Naples. Charles took him up on it and marched unhindered through the country. Lodovico soon realized it was all a terrible mistake, and joined the last-minute league of Italian states that united to trap and destroy the French at Fornovo. They succeeded, partially, but the damage was done: the French invasion had shown the Italian states, beautiful and rich and full of treasures, to be divided and vulnerable. Charles VIII's son, Louis XII, took advantage of a claim on Milan through his grandmother and captured the city and Lodovico as well, who died a prisoner in France. After more fights between French and Spanish, Milan ended up a strategic province of Charles V's empire, ruled by a Spanish Viceroy. Yet even then Milan was wealthy enough to survive a fierce rapacity that brought about the saying: 'In Sicily the Spaniards nibble, in Naples they eat, but in Milan they devour.'

In 1712 the city came under the Habsburgs of Austria, and like the rest of Lombardy profited from the enlightened reforms of Maria Theresa, who did much to improve agriculture (especially the production of rice and silk), rationalize taxes, and increase education; under her rule La Scala opera house was built, the Brera Academy founded, and most of central, Neoclassical Milan built. After centuries of hibernation the Ambrosiani were stirring again, and by the time Napoleon arrived, the city welcomed him fervently and with a huge festival became the capital of the Cisalpine Republic, linked with Paris via the new Simplon Highway. Milan rebelled against the subsequent rule of the repressive Austro-Hungarian Empire in 1848, and joined the kingdom of Italy.

The city rapidly took its place as the new country's economic and industrial leader, attracting thousands of workers from the poorer parts of Italy. Many of these workers joined the new Italian Socialist Party, which was strongest in Lombardy and Emilia-Romagna. In Milan, too, Mussolini left behind his job as editor of the Socialist paper *Avanti!* to found the Fascist party and ran its first campaign in 1919. The city was bombed heavily in air raids during World War II. Its well-organized partisans liberated it from the Germans before the Allies arrived, and when Mussolini's corpse was hung up on a meat-hook in a city service station, the Milanese turned out to make sure that the duke of delusion was truly dead before beginning to rebuild their battered city on more solid ground.

GETTING AROUND

With two international airports, several train stations, an expanding Metro, and efficient tram and bus lines, Milan is not a difficult place to get to or around in—unless you've brought the car. Driving in the city requires chutzpah, luck, and good navigation skills. One-way streets are the rule, signs are confusing, parking impossible (barring a handful of usually full underground garages), and bringing a private vehicle into the city centre between 7 and 10 am or trying to park during rush hour is not only foolhardy but illegal. Also remember that even though Milan looks like a bloated amoeba on the map, having grown outward like a tree in concentric circles, most of the sights are in the highly walkable innermost ring, the 'Cerchia dei Navigli' which follows the former medieval walls and now buried canals; the second ring, the 'Viali', follows the line of the Spanish walls built in the 16th century. The Metro is also a highly useful navigational guide; stops (MM) are listed in the text.

By Air

Both of Milan's airports, **Linate** (8 km from the centre) and **Malpensa** (50 km to the west) receive national and international flights. As a rule, intercontinental flights use Malpensa, while Linate handles most of the European and domestic traffic—but be sure to check (both share the same tel (02) 748 52 200). Linate may be reached by bus every 20 minutes from Corso Europa or from Piazza Luigi di Savoia, next to the Stazione Centrale, or on city bus 73 from Piazza San Babila (MM1) in the city centre. For Malpensa, buses also depart from Piazza Luigi di Savoia 2½ hours before each flight; check the schedule in the nearby Agenzia Dorea.

By Train

Milan's splendiferous main **Stazione Centrale** (MM2), designed in the '30s with the travelling satrap in mind, dominates the Piazza Duca d'Aosta northeast of the centre. Centrale handles nearly all the international trains as well as most of the domestic; for information dial 67 500. From Centrale tram No. 1 goes to Piazza Scala and Nord Station, and No. 33 to Stazione Garibaldi, Cimiterio Monumentale; bus No. 60 goes to Piazza Duomo and Castello Sforzesco and 65 down Corso Buenos Aires, Corso Venezia, Via Larga, Corso Italia.

    Stazione Garibaldi (MM2) is the terminus for car-train services, as well as trains for Pavia, Monza, Varese, Como, and Bergamo; **Stazione Lambrate** (MM2) has connections to Genoa, Bergamo, and towards the Simplon Pass. **Milan Nord** (MM: Cadorna) is the main station of Lombardy's regional railway network, with connections to Lake Como, Varese, Novara, Lake Maggiore, etc.

By Bus

Most intercity buses depart from the Piazza Castello (MM: Cairoli). Autostradale is the main company (tel 801 161), and it's worth giving them a call if you're aiming for one of the less frequented lake shores or Alpine valleys with no train link.

    City buses and the rather dashing, Art Deco trams (ATM) are convenient and their routes well marked. As usual you must purchase tickets in advance at tobacco shops, news-stands, or in the coin-gobbling machines at the main stops, and validate on board; one ticket lasts 75 minutes, regardless of how many transfers you make. If you plan to do a lot of riding, buy a one-day pass valid on both buses and the Metropolitana, available at the tourist office or ATM's information office in the Piazza del Duomo, tel 875 495; be sure to get their large map with all the buses and metro stops, the *Guida Rete dei transporti pubblici*.

By Metro

The **Metropolitana Milanese** (MM), begun in the '60s, is sleek and well run, and a boon for the bewildered tourist. There are three lines, the Red (MM1) and Green (MM2), with a new north–south Yellow line (MM3). Junctions of the Red and Green Lines are at Cadorna and Loreto, Yellow and Red at Duomo; tickets are the same as those used for the buses or trams.

Taxis

In Milan they are yellow and the drivers mostly honest. They're easy enough to flag down in the centre; otherwise call 8585.

TOURIST INFORMATION
The main tourist office is in the Piazza del Duomo on Via Marconi 1, tel (02) 809 662; others are at the Stazione Centrale, tel 669 04 32 and in Linate Airport, tel 744 065. All three will make free hotel reservations on the spot and distribute good city maps and other practical information; they also sponsor daily coach tours of the city departing from the Piazza Duomo and boat rides in season on the canals. The municipal office in the Piazza del Duomo is especially good for information on exhibits, concerts, and other special events. Other good sources are Milan's excellent daily *Corriere della Sera*, and the weekly tabloid *Viva Milano*.

Piazza del Duomo

In the exact centre of Milan towers its famous **Duomo**, a monument of such imposing proportions (third-largest in the world after St Peter's and Seville Cathedral) that on clear days it is as visible from the distant Alps as the Alps are visible from its dome. Bristling with 135 spires, defended by 2244 marble saints and one sinner (Napoleon, who crowned himself King of Italy here in 1805), guarded by some 95 leering gargoyles, energized by sunlight pouring through the largest stained-glass windows in Christendom, Milan Cathedral is a remarkable bulwark of the Faith. And yet for its monstrous size, for all the hubbub of its Times Squarish piazza of throbbing neon signs, traversed daily by tens of thousands of Milanese and tourists, the Duomo is utterly ethereal, a rose-white vision of pinnacles and tracery woven by angels.

Gian Galeazzo Visconti founded it in 1386 as a votive offering to the Mother of God, hoping in return that she would favour him with a male heir. His prayers for a son were answered in the form of Giovanni Maria, a loathsome degenerate assassinated soon after he attained power; as the Ambrosiani have wryly noted, the Mother of God got the better of the deal. For, along with the money to build the church, Gian Galeazzo threw in the Candoglia quarries (source of the fine marble still used by the Cathedral Building company) and hired the finest architects and masons of the day, including the masters of Campione of Lake Lugano, who are accredited with the design, assisted by Gothic artisans from the North. But before the cathedral could be completed, the Gothic style—which the Italians never liked much to begin with—had become unfashionable, and the bewildered façade went through several overhauls of Renaissance and Baroque, then back to Gothic, with the end result, completed in 1809 under Napoleon's orders, a shotgun wedding of Isabelline Gothic with Christopher Wren. In the 1880s there were plans to tear it down and start again, but no one had the heart, and the Milanese have become used to it. But walk around to the glorious Gothic **apse**, to see what its original builders were about. The subjects of the bas-reliefs on the bronze doors, all cast in this century, are a Milanese history lesson: the Edict of Constantine, the Life of St Ambrose, the city's quarrels with Barbarossa, and the history of the cathedral itself.

The remarkable dimensions of the **interior** challenge the eyes to take in what at first seems like infinity captured under a canopy. Its tremendous volume is defined into five aisles by 52 pillars of titanic dimensions, crowned by rings of niches and statues, and is dazzlingly lit by acres of stained glass; the windows of the apse, embellished with flamboyant Gothic tracery, are among the most beautiful anywhere. In them you can see the mysterious alchemical symbol adopted as the Visconti crest, and now the symbol of

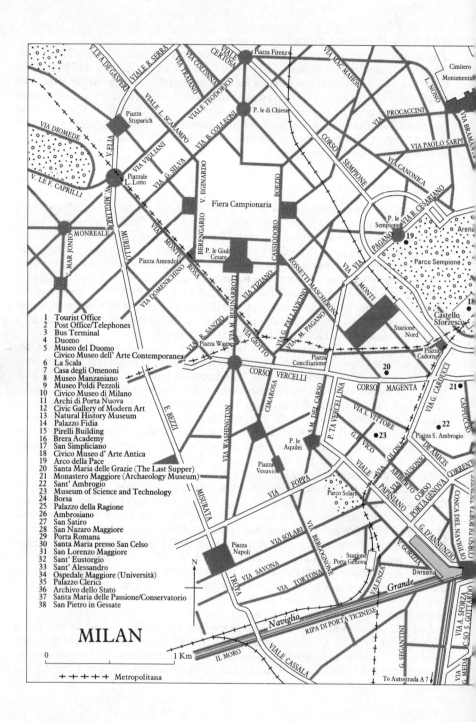

1 Tourist Office
2 Post Office/Telephones
3 Bus Terminal
4 Duomo
5 Museo del Duomo
   Civico Museo dell' Arte Contemporanea
6 La Scala
7 Casa degli Omenoni
8 Museo Manzaniano
9 Museo Poldi Pezzoli
10 Civico Museo di Milano
11 Archi di Porta Nuova
12 Civic Gallery of Modern Art
13 Natural History Museum
14 Palazzo Fidia
15 Pirelli Building
16 Brera Academy
17 San Simpliciano
18 Civico Museo d' Arte Antica
19 Arco della Pace
20 Santa Maria delle Grazie (The Last Supper)
21 Monastero Maggiore (Archaeology Museum)
22 Sant' Ambrogio
23 Museum of Science and Technology
24 Borsa
25 Palazzo della Ragione
26 Ambrosiano
27 San Satiro
28 San Nazaro Maggiore
29 Porta Romana
30 Santa Maria presso San Celso
31 San Lorenzo Maggiore
32 Sant' Eustorgio
33 Sant' Alessandro
34 Ospedale Maggiore (Università)
35 Palazzo Clerici
36 Archivo dello Stato
37 Santa Maria delle Passione/Conservatorio
38 San Pietro in Gessate

MILAN

0   1 Km

+ + + + + Metropolitana

the city: a twisting serpent in the act of swallowing a man. All other decorations seem rather small afterthoughts, but you may want to seek out in the right transept Leoni's fine Mannerist **tomb of Gian Giacomo de' Medici**, better known as Il Medeghino, the pirate of Lake Como—erected by his brother Pope Pius IV. Near Il Medeghino's tomb is the most disconcerting of the cathedral's thousands of statues: that of **San Bartolomeo** being flayed alive, with an inscription assuring us that it was made by Marco Agrate and not by Praxiteles, just in case anyone couldn't tell the difference. Other treasures include the 12th-century Trivulzio Candelabrum, by Nicola da Verdun, as well as medieval ivory, gold, and silverwork in the **treasury**, located below the main altar by the crypt, where St Charles Borromeo lies in state in an illuminated casket. Near the entrance of the cathedral is a door leading down to the **Baptistry of St Ambrose**, excavated in the 1960s, containing the octagonal baptismal font where the good bishop baptized St Augustine (10–12 and 3–5).

For a splendid view of Milan, take a walk through the enchanted forest of spires and statues on the **cathedral roof** (steps from the right transept, or elevator from outside; adm). The 15th-century dome by Amadeo, topped by the main spire with the gilt statue of La Madonnina (who at 4 m, really isn't as diminutive as she seems 100 m from the ground) offers the best view of all—on a clear morning all the way to the Matterhorn.

Museo del Duomo and Palazzo Reale

On the south side of the cathedral, the **Museo del Duomo** is housed in a wing of the Palazzo Reale, for centuries home of Milan's rulers, from the Visconti to the Austrian governors, the latter of whom are responsible for its current Neoclassical make-up. The museum (open 9:30–12:30 and 3–6, closed Mon; adm) contains artefacts related to the Duomo, including some of the original stained glass and fine 14th-century French and German statues and gargoyles, tapestries, and a Tintoretto among many other works of art. Other rooms document the history of the cathedral's building, including a magnificent wooden model built in 1519, designs from the 1886 competition for the new façade, and castings from the bronze doors.

In the main core of the Palazzo Reale, the **Civico Museo d'Arte Contemporanea** (CIMAC) has recently been installed, with temporary exhibits on the second and the main collection on the third floor (open 9:30–12:15 and 2:30–5:15, closed Mon; free). Devoted to mainly Italian art of this century, there are early works by the Futurists (especially Boccioni), as well as by Modigliani, De Chirico, Morandi, De Pisis, Melotti, the mystical Carrà, and current artists like Tancredi and Novelli.

Behind the palace, on Via Palazzo Reale, be sure to note the beautiful 14th-century **campanile di San Gottardo**, formerly belonging to the palace chapel. The main flanks of the Piazza del Duomo are occupied by porticoes sheltering some of the city's oldest bars; in the centre stands a florid equestrian statue of Vittorio Emanuele II.

The Galleria and La Scala

Opening up on the north end of the Piazza del Duomo is Milan's majestic drawing room, the elegant **Galleria Vittorio Emanuele**, a great glass-roofed arcade designed by Giuseppe Mengoni, who tragically fell from the roof the day before its inauguration in 1878. Here are more fine bars, especially the venerable Il Salotto, with some of Milan's finest coffee, and some of the city's finest shops. Under the marvellous 48-m glass dome,

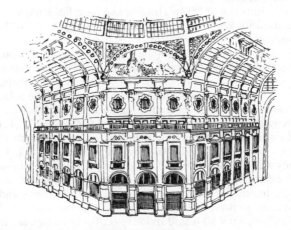

Galleria Vittorio Emanuele

you'll often be treated to a 50-man orchestra rehearsal, or even a full-blown fashion show.

At the other end of the Galleria lies the **Piazza della Scala**, address of one of the world's great opera houses, the modest looking Neoclassical **La Scala Theatre**, its name derived from the church of Santa Maria alla Scala which formerly stood on the site. Inaugurated in 1778 with Salieri's *Europa Riconosciuta*, La Scala saw the first perform-ances of most of the 19th-century classics of Italian opera, and when bombs smashed it in 1943, it was rebuilt as it was in three years, reopening under the baton of its great conductor Arturo Toscanini. The **Museo Teatrale alla Scala**, entered through a door on the left, has recently been rearranged to better house its excellent collection of opera memorabilia, scores, letters, portraits and photos of legendary stars, and set designs; there's even an archaeological section with artefacts related to ancient Greek and Roman theatre. From the museum you can look into the beautiful 2800-seat theatre with its great chandelier; try to imagine the scene in 1859, when the crowded house at a performance of Bellini's *Norma* took advantage of the presence of the Austro-Hungarian governor to join in the rousing war chorus (open 9–12 and 2–6, closed Sun from Oct to April; adm).

An unloved 19th-century statue of Leonardo stands in the middle of the Piazza della Scala, while opposite the theatre the imposing **Palazzo Marino** is a fine 16th-century building hiding behind a 19th-century façade; now the Palazzo Municipale, it has one of the city's loveliest courtyards. A few steps away, on Via Catena, the unusual 1565 **Casa degli Omenoni** is held up by eight uncomfortable giants; around the corner on the lovely cobblestoned Piazza Belgioioso, the **Museo Manzoniano** (9–12 and 2–4, closed Sat–Mon) is located in the fine old house where Manzoni lived, and contains items relating to the novelist's life and work, including illustrations from his classic novel, *I Promessi Sposi* and an autographed portrait of his friend Goethe. For more on the man and his works, see Lecco (p. 248).

The Museo Poldi-Pezzoli

In front of La Scala runs one of Milan's busiest and most fashionable boulevards, **Via Manzoni**. Verdi lived for years in the Grand Hotel (No. 29); at No. 10 is the lovely 17th-century palace of Gian Giacomo Poldi-Pezzoli, who decorated his home to fit his fabulous art collection, then left it to the State in 1879. Repaired after bomb damage in World War II, the **Museo Poldi-Pezzoli** houses one of Italy's best-known portraits, the 15th-century *Portrait of a Young Woman*, by Tuscan Antonio Pollaiuolo, depicting an ideal Renaissance beauty. She shares the most elegant room of the palace, the Salone Dorato, with the other jewels of the museum: Mantegna's Byzantine *Madonna*, Giovanni Bellini's *Pietà*, Piero della Francesca's *San Nicolò* and from a couple of centuries later, Guardi's *Grey Lagoon*. Other outstanding paintings include Vitale da Bologna's *Madonna*, a polyptych by Moretti, and works by Luini, Foppa, Turà, Crivelli, Lotto, Cranach (portraits of Luther and wife) and a crucifix by Raphael. The museum also has a fine Islamic collection of metalwork and rugs, including a magnificent 1532 Persian carpet, depicting a hunting scene (in the Salone Dorato); medieval and Renaissance armour; Renaissance bronzes; Flemish tapestries, Murano glass, and more (open 9:30–12:30 and 2:30–6, Sat 9:30–12:30 and 2:30–7:30, closed Sun & Mon in summer; adm).

Via Montenapoleone

A couple of blocks up Via Manzoni from the museum is Milan's high fashion vortex, the palace-lined **Via Montenapoleone** and a bit beyond, the elegant, pedestrian-only **Via della Spiga**. Even if you're not in the market for astronomically priced clothes by Italy's top designers, these exclusive lanes make good window shopping and perhaps even better people-watching. It's hard to remember that until the 1970s Florence was the centre of the Italian garment industry. When Milan inherited it, thanks mainly to its international airport, it added the essential ingredient of public relations to the Italians' innate sense of style to create a high-fashion empire rivalling Paris, London and New York.

There are two recently established museums in the sumptuous 18th-century Palazzo Morando Bolognini, on Via S. Andrea 6, between 'Montenapo' and Via della Spiga: the **Civico Museo di Milano** and the **Civico Museo di Storia Contemporanea**, the first documenting the story of the city, the second devoted to Italian history between the years 1914 and 1945 (both 9:30–12:15 and 2:30–5:15, closed Mon; free).

Near the intersection of Via della Spiga and Via Manzoni, the **Archi di Porta Nuova**, the huge stone arches of a gate, are one of the few survivals of the 12th-century walls. The original moat that surrounded the walls was enlarged into a canal to bring in the marble for the construction of the cathedral; it was covered in the 1880s when its stench became greater than its economic benefits. (A convenient bus, No. 96/97, from the Piazza Cavour makes the circuit of the former canal, convenient for reaching the Castello Sforzesca, Santa Maria delle Grazie, or Sant'Ambrogio.)

Giardini Pubblici

From Piazza Cavour, Via Palestro curves between the two sections of Milan's Public Gardens. The Romantic **Giardini di Villa Reale** (MM: Palestro) were laid out in 1790 for the Belgioioso family by Leopoldo Pollak, who also built the Villa Reale, Napoleon's residence while in town. This is now the **Civic Gallery of Modern Art** (open 9:30–

12:15 and 2:30–5:30, closed Tues; free); it specializes in Lombard art of the 19th century, in which local artists reflected international movements and invented one of their own, the self-consciously Romantic *Scapigliati* (the 'Wild-haired Ones'). Besides the Italians, there are works by Millet, Corot, Cézanne, Gauguin, Manet, and Van Gogh. A third section contains early 20th-century works by the Futurists and others, while a recent donation has added paintings by Picasso, Renoir, and Matisse.

The **Giardini Pubblici** proper, with its fine old trees, lies between Via Palestro and the Corso Venezia; laid out in 1782, artificial rocks were added to this shady corner of arcadia to compensate for Milan's flat terrain. A good place to take the children, with its zoo, swans, pedal cars, and playgrounds, it is also the site of Italy's premier **Natural History Museum**, near the Corso Venezia; another victim of the War, it has been rebuilt in its original neo-medieval style (open 9:30–12:30 and 2:30–5:30, Sun 9:30–7; closed Mon). Look out for the Canadian *Cryptosaurus*, the stuffed white rhino, the Colossal European Lobster, the Madagascar *aye-aye* and the 40-kilo topaz.

Corso Venezia itself is one of Milan's most interesting thoroughfares, with its Neoclassical and Liberty-style palaces—most remarkably, the 1903 **Palazzo Castiglioni** at No. 47 and the Neoclassical **Palazzo Serbelloni**, Milan's press club, on the corner of Via Senato. The quarter just west of the Corso Venezia was the most fashionable in the 1920s. It has a smattering of unusual buildings: on Via Malpighi 3, off the Piazza Oberdan, the **Casa Galimberti** with a colourful ceramic façade; the good Art Deco foyer at Via Cappuccini 8; the eccentric houses on Via Mozart (especially No. 11); and the romantic 1920s **Palazzo Fidia** on Via Melegari 2.

Northwest of the Giardini Pubblici, the **Piazza della Repubblica** has many of the city's hotels; the Mesopotamian Stazione Centrale, blocking the end of Via Vittorio Pisani, is the largest train station in Italy. The nearby skyscraper, the **Pirelli Building**, is one that the Milanese are especially proud of: built in 1960 by Gio Ponti, Pier Luigi Nervi designed its concrete structure. Now the seat of Lombardy's regional government, you see most of the city from its terrace (call ahead, tel 85 351).

Brera and its Accademia

Another street alongside La Scala, Via G. Verdi, leads into the **Brera**, one of the few old quarters to survive in the central city. Although some of the old cobblestone streets of Brera have maintained their original flavour (especially the Corso Garibaldi), local trendies are busily turning the remainder into Milan's version of Greenwich Village, full of antique and curiosity shops, late night spots, and art galleries.

At the corner of Via Brera and the pungently named Via Fiori Oscuri ('Street of the Dark Flowers') is the elegant courtyard of the **Brera Academy**, one of Italy's most important hoards of art. Credit for the collection goes mainly to Napoleon, whose bronze statue, draped in a toga, greets visitors as they enter; a firm believer in centralized art as well as central government, he stripped northern Italy's churches and monasteries of their treasures to form a Louvre-like collection for Milan, the capital of his Cisalpine Republic. The museum first opened in 1809 (open 9–2, Sun 9–1, closed Mon; adm expensive, but free on 1st and 3rd Sun and 2nd and 4th Sat of each month).

Perhaps the best-known of the Brera's scores of masterpieces is Raphael's *Marriage of the Virgin*, a Renaissance landmark for its evocation of an ideal, rarefied world, where

179

even the disappointed suitor snapping his rod on his knee performs the bitter ritual in a graceful dance step, all acted out before a perfect but eerily vacant temple in the background. In the same room hangs Piero della Francesca's last painting, the *Pala di Urbino*, featuring among its holy personages Federico da Monfeltro, Duke of Urbino, with his famous nose. The Venetian masters are well represented, Carpaccio, Veronese, Tintoretto, Jacopo Bellini and the Vivarini, but especially Giovanni Bellini, with several of his loveliest Madonnas and the great *Pietà*, as well as a joint effort with his brother Gentile, of *St Mark preaching in Alexandria*; there are luminous works by Carlo Crivelli and Cima da Conegliano; and several paintings by Mantegna, including his remarkable study in foreshortening, the *Cristo Morto*. Other Italian works include a unique panel painting by Bramante, Caravaggio's striking *Supper at Emmaus*, the *Pala Sforzesca*, by an unknown 15th-century Lombard artist, depicting Lodovico il Moro and his family; a polyptych by Gentile da Fabriano; and fine works by the Ferrarese masters, del Cossa and Ercole de'Roberti. Outstanding among the foreign artists are Rembrandt's *Portrait of his Sister*, El Greco's *St Francis*, and Van Dyck's *Portrait of the Princess of Orange*. When the Great Masters become indigestible, take a breather in the new 20th-century wing of the gallery, populated mainly by Futurists like Severini, Balla, and Boccioni, who believed that to achieve speed was to achieve success, and the metaphysical followers of De Chirico, who seem to believe just the opposite.

Brera's other principal monument is **San Simpliciano**, just off the Corso Garibaldi to the north. Founded perhaps by St Ambrose, it retains its essential palaeo-Christian form in a 12th-century wrapping, with an excellent fresco in the apse by Bergognone, one of the leading 15th-century Lombard painters.

Castello Sforzesco

Delimiting the western boundaries of the Brera quarter, the **Castello Sforzesco** (MM: Cairoli) is one of Milan's best-known monuments. Originally a fortress in the walls, the Visconti made it their castle, and as a symbol of their power it was razed to the ground by the Ambrosian Republic in 1447. Three years later, with the advent of Francesco Sforza, it was rebuilt, though since then its appearance has suffered many vicissitudes. Air raids damaged it and its treasures, and when it was rebuilt, its stout towers were made to double as cisterns. Today it houses the city's main art collection, the **Civico Museo d'Arte Antica del Castello** (open 9:30–12:15 and 2:30–5:15, closed Mon; adm). The entrance is located across the vast Piazza d'Armi, in the lovely Renaissance Corte Ducale. Housed in what was the principal residence of the Sforzas, the well-displayed collection contains intriguing odds and ends from Milan's history—the equestrian tomb of Bernabò Visconti and a beautiful 14th-century monument of the Rusca family; reliefs of Milan's triumph over Barbarossa, and the city's gonfalon. Leonardo designed the ilex decorations of the **Sala delle Asse**. The next room, the **Sala dei Ducali**, contains a relief by Duccio from Rimini's Tempio Malatestiano; the Sala degli Scarlioni contains the two finest sculptures in the museum, the *Effigy of Gaston de Foix* (1525) and Michelangelo's unfinished *Rondanini Pietà*, a haunting work that the artist laboured on for nine years, off and on, until his death.

Upstairs, most notable among the fine collection of Renaissance furnishings and decorative arts, are the 15th-century Castello Roccabianca frescoes illustrating the tale of Patient Griselda. The **Pinacoteca** contains a tender *Madonna with Child* by Giovanni

Bellini, his brother-in-law Mantegna's more austere, classical Madonna in the *Pala Trivulzio*, and the lovely *Madonna dell'Umiltà* by Lippi. From Lombardy there are several fine works by Bernardino Bergognone (especially the serene *Virgin with SS. Sebastian and Gerolamo*) and Bramantino (Bramante's pupil Bartolomeo Suardi, also one of the strangest of Mannerists) whose *Noli me tangere* is the eeriest painting in the collection. There's a roomful of Leonardo's followers, then a painting by Milan's own Giuseppe Arcimboldi (1527–1593), who was no one's follower at all, but the first Surrealist. Although Arcimboldi went on to become court painter for the Habsburgs in Prague, he left behind this *Primavera*—a portrait of a woman made up entirely of flowers. From 18th-century Venice, Francesco Guardi's *Storm* could be the precursor of another school—Impressionism.

The castle's third court, the beautiful **Cortile della Rochetta**, was designed by the Florentines Bramante and Filarete, both of whom worked several years for Francesco Sforza. Filarete also built Milan's great Ospedale Maggiore (1450s, the centrepiece of the Università degli Studi) with ornate brickwork and terracotta and the first cross-shaped wards, and wrote an architectural treatise on the ideal city he called *Sforzinda* in honour of his patron. The basement of the *cortile* is filled with the *comune's* extensive **Egyptian collection** of funerary artefacts and the **Prehistoric collection** of items found in Lombardy's Iron Age settlements. The first floor houses the **Museum of Musical Instruments** with a beautiful collection of string and wind instruments, and a spinet once played by Mozart. The **Sala della Balla**, where the Sforzas played ball, now contains the Tapestries of the Months designed by Bramantino.

Parco Sempione and Cimiterio Monumentale

Behind the Castello lies the **Parco Sempione**, Milan's largest city park, with De Chirico's **Metaphysical Fountain**, the 1930s **Palazzo dell'Arte**, used for exhibitions; the **Arena**, designed in 1806 on Roman models, where 19th-century dilettantes staged mock naval battles, and the imposing triumphal arch, **Arco della Pace**, marking the terminus of Napoleon's great highway (Corso Sempione), extending from Milan to the Simplon Pass. The arch, originally meant for him, was instead dedicated to peace by the Austrians. The **Casa Rustici** at Corso Sempione 36, designed in 1931 by Terragni, has proportions following Euclid's Golden Rule; many consider it Milan's finest modern building.

Further out (tram 4 from Piazza Scala) lies the **Cimiterio Monumentale**, the last rendezvous of Milan's well-to-do burghers. Their lavish monuments—Liberty-style temples, ancient columns and obelisks—are only slightly less flamboyant than those of the Genoese. The cemetery-keeper has guides to the tombs—Manzoni, Toscanini, and Albert Einstein's father are among the best-known names; the memorial to the 800 Milanese who perished in German concentration camps is the most moving (open 8:30–5, closed Mon).

THE LAST SUPPER

Milan's greatest painting, Leonardo da Vinci's *Last Supper* (or the *Cenacolo*), is in the refectory of the convent of **Santa Maria delle Grazie** (MM: Cadorna, then Via Boccaccio and left on Via Caradosso, open 9–1:15 all year round; adm expensive). But before entering, get into the proper Renaissance mood by first walking around the

15th-century church and cloister. Built by Guiniforte Solari, with later revisions by Bramante under Lodovico Il Moro, it is perhaps the most beautiful Renaissance church in Lombardy, its exterior adorned with fine brickwork and terracotta. Bramante's greatest contribution is the majestic Brunelleschi-inspired tribune, added in 1492; he also designed the choir, the unusual crossing under the dome, the sacristy, and the elegant little cloister, the **Chiostrino** (open 7–12 and 3–7).

Leonardo painted two of his masterpieces in Milan, the mystery-laden *Virgin of the Rocks* and *The Last Supper*. The former is in the Louvre and the latter would have been, too, had the French been able to figure out a way to remove the wall. Unfortunately, the ever-experimental artist was not content to use proper, established fresco technique (where the paint is applied quickly to wet plaster), but painted with tempera as if on a wood panel (*fresco secco*), enabling him to return over and over again to achieve the subtlety of tone and depth he desired. The result was exceedingly beautiful, but almost immediately the moisture in the walls began its deadly work of flaking off particles of paint. As the painting deteriorated, various restorers through the centuries came to try their hand at the most challenging task in their profession, with mixed success. In World War II the refectory was heavily damaged by a bomb, and the *Last Supper* only preserved thanks to precautionary padding measures taken in advance. Since 1977 restorers have been at work once again, this time cleansing the work of its previous restorations, and stabilizing the wall to prevent further damage; scaffolding will hide portions of the work until the 1990s.

Deterioration or no, the *Last Supper* still thrills, especially in the mellow, afternoon light. Painted at the moment when Christ announces that one of his disciples will betray him, it is a masterful psychological study, a single instant caught in time, the apostles' gestures of disbelief and dismay captured almost photographically by one of the greatest students of human nature. According to Vasari, the artist left the portrait of Christ purposely unfinished, believing himself unworthy to paint divinity; Judas was another problem, but Leonardo eventually found the proper expression of the betrayer caught guiltily unawares but still nefariously determined and unrepentant.

Monastero Maggiore

From Santa Maria delle Grazie the Corso Magenta leads back towards the centre; at the corner of Via Luini stands the Monastero Maggiore. The monastery's pretty 16th-century church of **San Maurizio** contains exceptional frescoes by Bernardino Luini, one of Leonardo's most accomplished followers; unfortunately the church is only open on Wednesdays, 9:30–12 and 3:30–6:30. The former Benedictine convent (entrance at Corso Magenta 15) houses the city's Etruscan, Greek, and Roman collections in the **Civic Archaeological Museum** (open 9:30–12:15 and 2:30–5:15, closed Tues, adm free), with good Greek vases, Roman glass, a 1st-century AD head of Jove discovered under the Castello Sforzesca, finds from Caesarea in the Holy Land, and Etruscan funerary objects. As important as Milan was in the late Empire, next to nothing has survived the city's frequent razing and rebuilding.

Sant'Ambrogio

The last resting-place of Milan's patron saint, the ancient church of Sant'Ambrogio, lies just off San Vittore and Via Carducci (MM: Sant'Ambrogio) behind the restored medieval gate, the **Pusterla di Sant'Ambrogio**. Founded by St Ambrose in 379, it was enlarged and rebuilt several times, lastly in the 1080s; the result became the prototype of Lombardy's Romanesque basilicas.

The church (open 7–12 and 2–7, Sun 7–1 and 3–8) is entered through a porticoed **Atrium** lined with tomb fragments, which sets off the simple, triangular façade with its rounded arches and ancient towers; the one to the right, the Monks' Campanile, was built in the 9th century, while the more artistic Canons' Campanile on the left was finished in 1144. The bronze doors, in their decorated portals, date from the 10th century. In its day the finely proportioned **interior** was revolutionary, for its newfangled rib vaulting; rows of arches divide the aisles, supporting the women's gallery, or *Matroneum*. On the left, look for the 10th-century bronze serpent (said to symbolize Moses' staff) and the **pulpit**, one of the masterpieces of Italian Romanesque. The apse is adorned with 10th–11th century mosaics of the Redeemer and saints, while the sanctuary contains two ancient treasures: the 9th-century *Ciborium* (a casket on columns containing the Host) and a magnificent gold, silver, enamel, gem-studded **altar** (835), portraying scenes from the lives of Christ and St Ambrose. In the crypt below moulder the bones of SS. Ambrose, Gervasio, and Protasio. At the end of the south aisle the 4th-century **Sacello di San Vittore in Ciel d'Oro** ('in the sky of gold') contains brilliant 5th-century mosaics in its cupola and an authentic portrait of St Ambrose.

After working on Santa Maria delle Grazie, Bramante spent two years on Sant' Ambrogio, contributing the unusual **Portico della Canonica** (entered from the door on the left aisle) and the two cloisters, now incorporated into the adjacent Università Cattolica; these display Bramante's new interest in the ancient orders of architecture, an interest he was to develop fully when he moved on to Rome. The upper section of the Portico houses the **Museo della Basilica di Sant' Ambrogio** (open 10–12 and 3–5, closed Tues and weekend mornings; adm); this contains illuminated manuscripts, medieval capitals and other architectural fragments, as well as ancient fabrics and vestments, some dating back to the 4th century, known as the 'Dalmatiche di Sant' Ambrogio', tapestries, and paintings by Luini and Bergognone. The 1928 **War Memorial** in the Piazza Sant'Ambrogio was designed by Giovanni Muzio and inspired by Athens' Tower of the Winds.

Museum of Science and Technology

From Sant'Ambrogio Via San Vittore leads to the former Olivetan convent of San Vittore, repaired after World War II to house the **Leonardo da Vinci Museum of Science and Technology** (open 9:30–4:50; closed Mon; adm). Most of this vast and diverse collection, still arranged in its original 1950s format, is rather mysterious for the uninitiated, and if you're not keen about smelting and the evolution of batteries you may want to head straight for the **Leonardo da Vinci Gallery**, lined with wooden models and explanations of his machines and inventions; his knowledge of hydraulic engineering was put to good use in canal-building Milan. 'I work for anyone who pays me,' said Leonardo, who after his Milan period worked for the nefarious Cesare Borgia and Francis I; and work he did, though most of his notes and discoveries didn't see the light of day until decades after his death.

Other rooms include musical instruments and displays on optics, radios, computers, clocks and astronomy; among the highlights here is a reconstruction of a revolutionary astronomical clock by the great Giovanni Dondi of Padua (1320–89) and the 1709 'arithmetical machine', a precursor of the modern calculator, built by a Venetian merchant, Giovanni Poleni. Downstairs you can push buttons and make waterwheels turn. Another building is devoted to trains, another to ships and naval history.

Milan's Financial District

Between Sant'Ambrogio and the Duomo lies what has been the centre of Milan's merchant guilds, bankers, and financiers for centuries: the bank-filled **Piazza Cardusio** (MM: Cardusio), Via degli Affari ('Business Street') and Via Mercanti, which gives onto the Piazza del Duomo. Milan's imposing **Borsa** (stock exchange), was founded by Napoleon and is now the most important in the nation. On Via Mercanti, the 13th-century **Palazzo della Ragione**, the old Hall of Justice, was given an extra floor with oval windows by Maria Theresa. It has recently been restored, and is adorned, on the Via Mercanti side, with a curious statue of a sow partly clad in wool, recalling the city's Roman name, Mediolanum, which could be translated as 'half-woolly', while on the Piazza Mercanti side the building is adorned with beautiful early 13th-century equestrian reliefs.

The Ambrosiana

In the Piazza Pio XI (off Via Spadari and Via Cantù) is the most enduring legacy of the noble Borromeo family, the **Ambrosiana** (closed for works, but due to reopen in late 1992). The building was founded by Cardinal Federico Borromeo (cousin of Charles), who amassed one of Italy's greatest libraries here in 1609, containing 30,000 rare manuscripts, including ancient Middle Eastern texts collected for the Cardinal's efforts to produce a Counter-Reformation translation of the Bible, a 5th-century illustrated *Iliad*, Leonardo da Vinci's famous *Codice Atlantico*, containing thousands of his drawings, early editions of *The Divine Comedy*, and much more.

Of more interest to non-scholars, however, is the Cardinal's art collection, the **Pinacoteca**, housed in the same building. Although a number of paintings have been added over the centuries, the gallery is a monument to one man's taste—which showed a marked preference for the Dutch, and for the peculiar; the art here ranges from the truly sublime to some of the funniest paintings ever to grace a gallery: here are Botticelli's lovely *Tondo* and his *Madonna del Baldacchino*, nonchalantly watering lilies with her milk; a respectable *Madonna* by Pinturicchio and the strange, dramatic *Transito della Vergina* by Baldassare Estense. Further along an *Adoration of the Magi* by the Master of Santo Sangue is perhaps the only one where Baby Jesus seems thrilled at receiving the wise men's gifts. A small room is illuminated by a huge pre–Raphaelitish stained-glass window of Dante by Giuseppe Bertini (1865), and contains the glove Napoleon wore at Waterloo, a 17th-century bronze of Diana the Huntress, so ornate that even the stag wears earrings, and a number of entertaining paintings by Cardinal Borromeo's friend Jan Brueghel the Younger, who delighted in a thousand and one details and wasn't above putting a little pussy cat in Daniel's den of lions.

These are followed by more masterpieces: Giorgione's *Page*, Luini's *Holy Family with St Anne* (from a cartoon by Leonardo), Leonardo's *Portrait of a Musician* and a lovely portrait, attributed to Ambrogio De Predis of Beatrice d'Este, and then Bramantino's *Madonna in Trono fra Santi*, a scene balanced by a dead man on the left and an enormous dead frog on the right. Challenging this for absurdity is the nearby *Female Allegory* of 17th-century Giovanni Serodine, where the lady, apparently disgruntled with her lute, astrolabe, and books, is squirting herself in the nose.

The magnificent cartoon for Raphael's *School of Athens* in the Vatican is as interesting as the fresco itself; the copy of Leonardo's *Last Supper* was done by order of the Cardinal, who sought to preserve what he considered a lost work (the copy itself has recently been restored). A 16th-century *Washing of Feet* from Ferrara has one Apostle blithely clipping his toenails. Another room contains pages of drawings from Leonardo's *Codice Atlantico*. The first Italian still-life, Caravaggio's *Fruit Basket*, is also the most dramatic; it shares the hall with more fond items like Magnasco's *The Crow's Singing Lesson*. Further on is Titian's *Adoration of the Magi*, painted for Henri II, and still in its original frame.

San Satiro

On the corner of Via Spadari and busy Via Torino is the remarkable Renaissance church of **San Satiro** (officially Santa Maria presso San Satiro), rebuilt by Bramante in 1476, his first Milanese project, with a mostly 19th-century façade. Faced with a lack of space in the abbreviated, T-shaped interior, Bramante came up with the ingenious solution of creating the illusion of an apse with *trompe-l'oeil* stucco decorations. Bramante also designed the beautiful octagonal **Baptistry** off the right aisle, decorated with terracottas by Agosto De Fondutis; to the left the **Cappella della Pietà** dating from the 9th century is one of the finest examples of Carolingian architecture in North Italy, even though it was touched up in the Renaissance, with decorations and a Pietà by De Fondutis. San Satiro's 11th-century **Campanile** is visible on Via Falcone.

South of the Duomo: Porta Romana

This corner of Milan, at the time of writing further dishevelled with the construction of the city's third Metro line, is the main traffic outlet of Milan towards the autostrada to the south. Tram 13 will take you past its two monuments, firstly, **San Nazaro Maggiore** on Corso Porta Romana, a church that has undergone several rebuildings since its 4th-century dedication by St Ambrose, and was last restored in the Romanesque style. The most original feature of San Nazaro is the hexagonal **Cappella Trivulzio** by Bramantino, with the tomb of the *condottiere* Giangiacomo Trivulzio, who had inscribed on his tomb, in Latin: 'He who never knew rest now rests: Silence.' Trivulzio did have a busy career; a native Milanese who disliked Lodovico Sforza enough to lead Louis XII's attack on Milan in 1499, he became the city's French governor, then went on to lead the League of Cambrai armies in thumping the Venetians at Agnadello (1509), when they threatened to create a land empire as great as the one they already possessed on the sea. Further down Corso Porta Romana, in the Piazza Medaglie d'Oro, is one of the original Renaissance gates, the **Porta Romana** (1598).

Corso Italia, another main artery to the south, leads to **Santa Maria presso San Celso**, finished in 1563; its façade is a fine example of the Lombard love of ornament, which reaches almost orgiastic proportions in the Certosa di Pavia (see below). Within, beyond an attractive atrium, the interior is paved with an exceptional marble floor and decorated with High-Renaissance paintings by Paris Bordone, Bergognone, and Moretto. The adjacent 10th-century church of **San Celso** has a charming interior restored in the 19th century and a good original portal.

Ticinese Quarter

Southwest of the city centre, Via Torino leads into the artsy quarter named after the Ticino river, traversed by the main thoroughfare, Corso di Porta Ticinese (tram 15 from Via Torino). In the Ticinese you can find pieces of Roman Mediolanum, which had its centre in modern **Piazza Carrobbio**: there's a bit of the Roman circus on Via Circo, off Via Lanzone, and the **Colonne di San Lorenzo**, on the Corso: these 16 Corinthian columns, now a rendezvous of Milanese teenagers but originally part of a temple or bath, were transported here in the 4th century to make a portico in front of the **Basilica di San Lorenzo Maggiore**. This is considered the oldest church in Milan, perhaps dating back to the palaeo-Christian era and taking its octagonal form, encircled by an ambulatory, in the 4th century. Along with Sant' Ambrogio it was preserved when Barbarossa sacked the city in 1164, but since then it has suffered severe fires, and in the 16th century came near to total collapse. The dome and interior were then rebuilt, conserving as much of the old structure as possible. The most interesting section of the church is the **chapel of Sant' Aquino** (adm) with beautiful 5th-century mosaics of Christ and his disciples and an early Christian sarcophagus.

Near the Neoclassical **Porta Ticinese** built in the Spanish walls, stands another 4th-century church, **Sant'Eustorgio**, rebuilt in 1278 and modelled along the lines of Sant'Ambrogio, with its low vaults and aisles. The pillars have good capitals, and the chapels are finely decorated with early Renaissance art. One chapel is dedicated to the Magi, and held their relics until Frederick Barbarossa took them to Cologne. The highlight of the church, however, is the pure Tuscan Renaissance **Cappella Portinari**, built for Pigello Portinari, an agent of the Medici bank in Milan. Attributed to Michelozzo and often compared with Brunelleschi's Pazzi Chapel in Florence in its elegant simplicity and proportions, the chapel is crowned by a lovely dome, adorned with stucco reliefs of angels. This jewel is dedicated to one of the more dreadful saints, the Inquisitor St Peter Martyr (who was axed in the head in 1252), whose life was frescoed on the walls by Vincenzo Foppa and whose remains are buried in the magnificent tomb in the centre, the Arca di San Pietro Martire by the Pisan Giovanni di Balduccio in 1339.

The Navigli District

Beyond Porta Ticinese is Milan's Navigli district (MM: Porta Genova, or tram 9 or 15) which takes its name from the navigable canals, the **Naviglio Grande** and **Naviglio Pavese** that break up the endless monotony of streets, and meet to form the 'Darsena' near the Porta Ticinese. Until the 1950s Milan, through these canals, handled more tonnage than seaports like Brindisi, and like any good port, the Navigli was a funky working-class district of warehouses, workshops, sailors' bars, and housing projects. Although some of this lingers, Navigli is Milan's up-and-coming trendy area, where many of the city's artists work, and many of the city's new night spots are opening up.

A popular bicycle excursion from Milan is to pedal along the Naviglio Grande to the Ticino river (around 40 km), passing by way of **Cassinetta di Lugagnano**, which has one of Italy's finest restaurants (see below). Like the Venetians with their villas along the Brenta canal, the 18th-century Milanese built sumptuous summer houses along the Naviglio. Unfortunately, none are open for visits. Bicycles can be rented for any period of time from Vittorio Comizzoli's shop in Via Washington 60, tel 498 4694 (MM: Wagner).

ACTIVITIES
A dip in one of Milan's public swimming-pools can make a hot day of summer's sight-seeing far more tolerable: two of the nicest and most convenient are situated in the **Parco Solari**, Via Solari and Montevideo (MM: San Agostino), and the outdoor **Lido di Milano**, Piazzale Lotto 15 (MM: Lotto). East of town, the **Parco dell'Idroscalo**, built around an artificial lake designed as a 'runway' for hydroplanes in the '20s, has a lovely complex of three pools known as Milan's Riviera (Viale dell'Idroscalo 1), reached by a special bus departing from Piazza Cinque Giornate.

Milan has two first-division football clubs, Milan and Inter, which play alternate Sundays at **San Siro stadium** (arrive early to be sure of getting a ticket). American football (the 'Rhinos') and rugby are semi-professional and can often be seen at the Giurati sports centre. Milan has a good basketball team, which plays in the Super Palatenda sports facility, on Via Sant'Elia. There are two race tracks, the Ippodromo and the Trottatoio for trotters, both near San Siro. For a real escape, travel agencies throughout Milan can book you a week's package holiday in the mountains, for skiing or hiking.

NIGHTLIFE
For many people, an evening at **La Scala** is one of the major reasons for visiting Milan. The season traditionally opens on 7 December, St Ambrose's Day, and continues until July, while a symphony concert season runs from September until November. The programme is posted outside the theatre, and the box office is located on the left side of the façade. For information, call 807 041; for reservations tel 809 126, but beware, finding a good seat at a moment's notice is all but impossible. You can try through your hotel's concierge, or show up at the box office an hour before the performance to see what's available. Chances are it'll be a vertiginous gallery seat, just squeezed in under the ceiling, but what you can't see you can at least hear. More **classical music** is performed in the Giuseppe Verdi Conservatorio, Via del Conservatorio 12, tel 7600 1755), and at the Angelicum, Piazza Sant'Angelo 2, tel 659 2748. The city of Milan sponsors a series of **Renaissance and Baroque music concerts** in the lovely church of San Maurizio on Corso Magenta, while the province puts on, between October and June, a series of contemporary concerts called *Musica nel nostro tempo*. Keep an eye peeled for posters and bannners.

Milan is also the home of Italy's best theatre company, the **Piccolo Theatre**, Via Rovello 2, near Via Dante, tel 877 663. Founded after World War II and run for years by brilliant director Giorgio Strehler, the Piccolo is ideologically sound, with a repertory ranging from Commedia dell'Arte to the avant-garde. Tickets are priced low so anyone can go—but reserve in advance as far as possible. Sometimes the Piccolo performs at the much larger **Teatro Lirico**, near the Duomo at Via Larga 14, tel 866 418. Even if your Italian is only so-so you may enjoy a performance at the **Teatro delle Marionette**, Via Olivetani 3/b, tel 469 4440, near Piazza Sant'Ambrogio. **Films** in English are the fare of the Angelicum, tel 659 9832, Piazza Sant'Angelo 2. The *Corriere della Sera* has complete listings of theatre and films, but if the films aren't listed under '*In Originale*' you can be sure they've been dubbed.

The *Corriere* also lists under '*Ritrovi*' the cabarets and nightclubs with live music; for **jazz** Milan's best club is **Scimmie**, Via Ascanio Sforza 45, in Brera, with diverse but high-quality offerings from Dixieland to fusion. **Tangram**, Via Pezzotti 52, attracts a varied crowd; live jazz Mon–Wed, Rock and Blues at the weekend. Near Cerso Vercelli, the long-time favourite **Magia** caters to the musical tastes of the younger generation (Via Salutati 2), and at Viale Monza 140, **Zelig** presents a zippy, amusing nightly cabaret.

Milan's very fashion-conscious rock 'n' rollers get down to the **Rolling Stone**, Corso Marzo XXII 32 (closed Mon–Wed), or the accepted cornerstone of Italian rock **Sorpasso**, Via General Govone 42 (closed Sun), or, chicest of all, Milan's version of Studio 54, **Plastic**, on Viale Umbria 120—and yes, you must meet with the doorman's approval to enter (closed Sun). Discotheques are pricey: **Lizard**, Largo La Foppa, is one of the trendiest discos in town, and, in the heart of Milan, in the Galleria Manzoni, **Stage** is a great place to dance with a cabaret and live music. During the day it is an elegant restaurant with an emphasis on *nouvelle cuisine*. Brazilian music and drinks are on tap at **Berimbao**, Via De Andreis 13, closed Monday.

Milan has some good, lively bars, concentrated in the Brera, Navigli and Ticinese quarters. The old rendezvous of artists and intellectuals in the '20s and '30s, the **Bar Giamaica**, is still open for business at Via Brera 32, as is another old bar, **Moscatelli**, Corso Garibaldi 93, a beloved Milanese oasis for the fashion weary, so out of fashion. **El Tombon de San Marc**, Via San Marco 20, serves some of Milan's best beer, but for a hearty atmosphere, and a balm to the heart of a homesick Brit, try the **Racanà Pub**, Via Sannio 18, near the Porta Romana Station, open 9 am–2 am. In the Piazza Mirabello, artists, writers and professional people gather to enjoy the cocktails and homemade pasta at the bar/restaurant **Café Milano**; exquisite ice cream concoctions, as well as drinks, are served up at the **Osteria del Pallone**, Alzaia Naviglio Grande. In the Ticinese **Pois**, by the Colonne di San Lorenzo, is a place for the young and stylish. If you have James Bondish tastes and the wallet to match, the exclusive **Champagneria**, Via Clerici 1 (near La Scala), will soothe your palate with 850 labels of champagne to wash down the vast selection of caviares. The **Magenta** Bar, Via Carducci 13, still draws the crowds, after 80 years in business. Students, models and yuppies all rub shoulders happily here.

As in the rest of Italy, a favourite evening activity is a promenade topped off with a stop at the *gelateria* (ice-cream parlour). Traditional favourites include **Pozzi**, Piazza Gen. Cantore 4, in the Navigli and **Passerini**, Via Hugo 4, near the Duomo. **Viel** in Piazza Castello (Corso Buenos Aires 15) has the most surprising flavours, while totally natural ingredients go into the treats at the **Ecologica**, Corso di Porta Ticinese 40.

SHOPPING

Milan is the cloud-cuckoo-land of conspicuous consumption, where buying and selling is a veritable art form, a city that can wilt the strongest-backed credit card in the solar system. Few places on earth offer such a variety of designs and goods, especially in clothes and home furnishings. There are few bargains to be had, but a couple of interesting weekly markets which offer high-fashion for terrestrial prices. In Milan shops are closed all day Sunday and Monday morning; food stores closed Monday afternoons.

Many of the big names in designer apparel and jewellery have their boutique 'headquarters' in what is known as the **Quadrilatero**, defined by Via Montenapoleone, Via della Spiga, Via Sant' Andrea and Via Borgospesso. Nearly all the shops here have branches elsewhere in Milan and in other cities; some of the better established, like Gucci, Armani, and Krizia, are glorified international chain stores. You may just find the latest of the latest prêt-à-porter designs on Montenapoleone, but be assured they'll soon show up elsewhere, expensive enough, but without the high snob surcharges. The aura and status created around the Italian garment industry is as much due to quality as to a certain wizardry with words and images; a language of gloss and glamour that could provide the subject for the doctoral thesis of an anthropologist from New Guinea. But then again, Italians have always liked to put on the dog, *la bella figura*; it's in their blood. The hype machine has turned this national trait into a national obsession—there are countless Italian fashion magazines (most of them emanating from Milan, naturally), and a weekly television programme devoted to *La Moda*. The bright lights and glitter of modern Milan, with its celebrity designers, resemble those of Hollywood in its glory days; this is an Italian fantasyland that dreams are made of, diverting the attentions of thousands whose attentions might otherwise be unoccupied. But for all this, are Italian designers making genuine inroads in fashion? Are their clothes as well designed as the classics of the post-War era? The verdict has yet to come in—check it out for yourself.

In the Quadrilatero

The **jewellers** were here first, in the 1930s; since then, to have an address on Via Montenapoleone has meant status and quality. Among the most interesting on the street are **Buccellati** (No. 4), considered by many the best jewellery designer in Italy, featuring exquisitely delicate gold work and jewels, each piece individually crafted. **Calderoni** (No. 8) is fun for lavishly kitsch creations; **David Colombo** (No. 12) specializes in fine antique jewellery, while another shop, **Trabucco** (No. 5) creates more trendy, modern styles.

The artsy displays of clothing and, increasingly, shoes (in 1987 the Milanese staged a demonstration protesting against the takeover of their sacrosanct Montenapo by such 'Millipedes') are a window shopper's paradise. **Missoni's** ravishing knits for women and men are at Montenapoleone 1; **Valentino** and his classics are at Via Santo Spirito 3; **Krizia** sells her famous knits, evening dresses, and children's wear at Via della Spiga 23. **Armani's** chief Milanese outlet is at Via Sant'Andrea 9, featuring his famous 'unstructured' jackets for men and women, while **Mila Schön** sells her women's styles at Montenapoleone 2, and her men's at No. 6. For quiet sophistication from a designer who has an 'architectural' approach, visit **Gianfranco Ferré**, who was the first Italian in years to branch out from prêt-à-porter into individualist *haute couture* (women's clothes, Via della Spiga 11). **Gianni Versace** displays his innovations on Via della Spiga 4, **Adriana** at Via della Spiga 22, and **Gaultier** at Via della Spiga 20.

Lace and leather are also well represented. For lingerie and linens, **Jesurum**, Via Verri, offers handmade Venetian embroideries and laces, as well as bathing-suits, robes, etc. Italian leather goods are known in most of the world simply as **Gucci** at Montenapoleone 5. **Ferragamo** sells his famous designs and shoes for men and women at Montenapoleone 3; **Mario Valentino**, Montenapoleone 10, has stylish shoes and leather fashions; **Trussardi**, another famous name in leather, has shoes, bags, and gloves at Via S. Andrea 5, while **Beltrami**, Montenapoleone 16, has the most outrageous and colourful women's shoes in Italy.

Amongst the treasure-troves of jewels, clothes, leathers and shoes are antique dealers and furriers; among the latter, **Furs Bazaar**, Via Sant'Andrea 8, specializes in high-fashion 'almost new' furs at reasonable prices. **Lorenzi**, Montenapoleone 9 is the city's most refined pipe and male accessories shop. The **Salumaio di Montenapoleone**, at No 12, has an infinite array of hams, salamis, pasta, and cheeses, and nearly every gourmet item imaginable. If you need a break from shopping, **Café Cova** on Via Montenapoleone 8, or **Baretto**, Via Sant'Andrea 3 will keep you up in the ozone of chic.

City Centre

Besides the great Galleria Vittorio Emanuele, several minor *gallerias* branch off the Corso Vittorio Emanuele, each a shopping arcade lined with good quality and reasonably priced shops. In Piazza Duomo a monument almost as well known as the cathedral itself is Milan's biggest and oldest department store, **La Rinascente**; it's also the only one to have been christened by Gabriele D'Annunzio. La Rinascente has six floors of merchandise, with especially good clothing and domestic sections, offering a wide array of kitchen appliances dear to the heart of an Italian cook. There's a cafeteria on the top floor with great views over the cathedral. Other central shops include those of **Fiorucci**, who has his main headquarters in the Galleria Passerella; **Mandarina Duck**, Galleria San Carlo, with a vast variety of totes and travelling cases; **Fratelli Prada**, Galleria Vittorio Emanuele, with classically and beautifully crafted leather goods; and **Guenzati**, Via Mercanti 1, which will make a velvet-lover's heart flutter; they also do made-to-order clothes. Cheeses, the most exotic and the most everyday, have been sold since 1894 at the **Casa del Formaggio**, Via Speronari 3, near the Duomo. **Rizzoli**, in the Galleria Vittorio Emanuele, is one of the city's finest and best-stocked bookshops (with many English titles), owned by the family that founded the *Corriere della Sera*. Also in the Galleria, **Messaggerie Musicali** is one of the best in town for musical scores. On Sunday morning, a **Stamp and Coin Market** is held in Via Armorari, behind the Central Post Office.

The shops on busy **Via Torino** have some of Milan's more affordable prices, especially in apparel. **Frette**, at No. 42 has an excellent section of moderately priced household linens, while **La Bottega del Tutu'**, No. 48, has everything for your favourite ballerina; at **Medolla**, No. 23, you can find those Franciscan sandals you've always wanted, as well as fine children's shoes.

Brera District
Besides the Monday market in the Piazza Mirabello and the **Antiques Fair** (every third Saturday of the month, off Via Fiori Chiari) Brera offers some of Milan's most original shops. Unusual and bizarre antiques are the mainstay of **L'Oro dei Farlocchi**, Via Madonnina 5; **Naj Oleari**, Via Brera 8, has unusual children's clothes and household items; **Piero Fornasetti**, Via Brera 16, has rather eccentric home decorations; exotic handmade papers are to be found in the **Legatoria Artistica**, Via Palermo 11; **Surplus**, Corso Garibaldi 7, has a marvellous array of second-hand garments. The latest Italian fashions are also reasonably priced at the big COIN department store, Corso Garibaldi 72 (Piazza 5 Giornata).

Elsewhere in Milan
On **Corso Buenos Aires**, one of Milan's longest and densest shopping thoroughfares, you can find something of every variety and hue; an unusual one is **Le Mani D'Oro**, Via Gaffurio 5 (near Piazalle Loreto), which specializes in *trompe-l'oeil* objects and decorations, while **Guerciotti**, Via Tamagno 55 (parallel to Corso Buenos Aires), makes bicycles to order. Another shopping street with excellent merchandise and reasonable prices is **Via Paolo Sarpi** (near MM: Moscova), formerly the city's Chinatown. Other interesting shops: **Faenze di Faenza**, Via Stoppani 10, with faience ware; **Franco Leoni**, Via Urbano III 1 (just off Corso Porta Ticinese), has antique Italian dolls; and Il **Discanto**, Via Turati 7, sells exotic instruments and jewellery from Asia and Africa. For an excellent selection of books in English, try either **The English Bookshop**, Via Mascheroni 12 (MM: Conciliazione) or **The American Bookstore**, Largo Cairoli, near the castle. If you're interested in the latest designs in all kinds of furniture, Milan has a major concentration of showrooms and stores near the centre: well worth a look are **Artemide**, Corso Monforte 18; **De Padova**, Corso Venezia 14; **Dilmos**, Piazza San Marco 1; and **Alias**, Via Respighi 2.

Perhaps the best place to hunt for designer bargains in Milan is the Saturday market in **Viale Papiniano**, in the Navigli. On December 7 (St Ambrose's Day), there's a fine market, the **O Bei, o Bei** with antiques in the Piazza Sant'Ambrogio.

WHERE TO STAY   (tel prefix 02)
Milan has basically two types of accommodation: smart hotels for expense-accounted business people and seedy dives for new arrivals from the provinces, still seeking their first job in the city. This bodes ill for the pleasure-traveller, who has the choice of paying a lot of money for an up-to-date modern room with little in the way of atmosphere, or paying less for some place where he/she may not feel very comfortable (or worse, very safe). Reserve in advance if possible, because the exceptions to the rule are snapped up fast: you can do so through the Innkeepers' Association, **Hotel Reservation Milan**, Via Palestro 24, tel 706 095. The tourist offices (see above) can also make pot-luck on-the-spot reservations—both services are free.

The deluxe hotels are clustered between the centre and the Stazione Centrale; four are owned by the reliable and imaginative CIGA chain, with the *******Hotel Principe di Savoia**, Piazza della Repubblica 17, near the Giardini Pubblici, tel 62 30, the most elegant and prestigious of them all, originally built in 1927 and since lavishly redecorated. Rooms and service are designed to pamper and please even the most demanding clients—when Margaret Thatcher or Jerry Lewis are in Milan, they stay here. The hotel has its own buses to the airports, a good bar, and private garage; L320–625 000. Another CIGA hotel, the *****Palace, Piazza della Repubblica 20, tel 63 36, caters primarily to executives who demand heated towel racks in addition to very tasteful bedrooms and public rooms; many have balconies, and there's a nice roof garden as well; L300–590 000. Another deluxe hotel near the Stazione Centrale, the *****Excelsior Gallia, Piazza Duca d'Aosta 9, tel 67 85, hosted most of Milan's visiting potentates when it first opened in 1932. Lately spruced up with briarwood furnishings and oriental rugs, its spacious, elegant, and air-conditioned rooms are equipped with satellite television that receives English channels; the Health Centre offers Turkish baths, massages, solarium and beauty treatments, and the Baboon Bar (ask how it got the name during World War II) is a mellow place to while away the evening (L422 500–566 000). Visiting nabobs, however, may prefer the lingering Belle Epoque atmosphere and more central location of the *****Grand Hotel de Milan, Via Manzoni 29 (at the corner of Via Montenapoleone), tel 801 231. Verdi lived here for years (the room he died in has been carefully preserved as it was), and while the exterior and the delightful decor of the interior have remained unchanged, the creature comforts have been updated; it is especially popular among fashion executives, who often preview their collections in its elegant salon (L300–384 000).

Another CIGA hotel, ****Diana Majestic, Viale Piave 42 (MM: Porta Venezia), tel 295 134 04, is a stylish hotel built at the turn of the century, with charming rooms and views over a garden (L190–360 000). Another good choice in the same category, the elegantly furnished ****Cavour, Via Fatebenefratelli 21, tel 657 2051, is in the Brera, a few blocks from the Giardini Pubblici and Via Montenapoleone (L214 500). Even more central, between the Duomo and La Scala, ****De La Ville, Via Hoepli 6, tel 867 651, is a modern hotel with antique furnishings and courteous service (L350–380 000), while the comfortable ****Manin, Via Manin 7, tel 659 6511, faces the shady Giardini Pubblici, in one of central Milan's quieter corners; reception is friendly and the rooms modern (L250 000).

***Ariosto, Via Ariosto 22, tel 481 7844, has more character than most Milanese hotels of its class, and is conveniently close to MM: Conciliazione stop. An early 20th-century mansion converted to a hotel in 1969, it has a lovely little courtyard, overlooked by the nicer rooms (L145 500). Pleasant and tranquil ***Hotel Manzoni, Via Spirito Santo 20, tel 7600 5700, enjoys one of the most privileged locations in Milan—on a quiet street within easy walking distance of Montenapoleone and La Scala, with the plus of a private garage. Its cheap prices for its location, however, make it extremely popular, so book well in advance (L145 500).

Among the less expensive offerings, the most delightful is the **Antica Locanda Solferino, Via Castelfidardo 2, tel 659 9886, a 19th-century inn in Brera brought back to life, complete with its former furnishings. All 11 rooms are different in shape and decoration, though the baths are modern. This is another place that requires advance reservations (L86 000). The **London, Via Rovello 3, tel 7202 0166, between the castle and the cathedral, lacks the charm of the Solferino, but offers a good room with bath and breakfast for L96 000. Near the London there's the wholesome *Giulio Cesare, Via Rovello 10, tel 876 250, among the more pleasant of Milan's budget accommodation; it even has air-conditioning (L46 000–64 000). Another respectable place, the ***Pensione Londra**, Piazza Argentina 4, tel 228 400, is up on the 7th floor near Corso Buenos Aires. The building's a bit on the shabby side, but it's a lively place, and a favourite of models who have yet to make it big (L48 500–67 500). Two blocks east of the Stazione Centrale, the ***Pensione Valley**, Via Soperga 19, tel 669 2777, is one of the best bargains in the area, with good, safe rooms for L62 500.

Milan also has a youth hostel, the modern **Ostello Riero Rotta**, Via Salmoiraghi 2, tel 3926 7095, near San Siro stadium and MM1: QT8. IYHF card required; open all year, 7–9 am and 5–11 pm, L14 000 per person, per night, including breakfast.

EATING OUT

In moneyed Milan you'll find some of Italy's finest restaurants, and some of its most expensive; an average meal will cost you considerably more than it would almost anywhere else. Butter is preferred to oil in local cooking, and polenta appears more often on the menu than pasta. Perhaps the best-known Milanese speciality, found even in the most obscure corners of Calabria, is the breaded cutlet (*cotoletta alla milanese*), with *risotto alla milanese* (prepared with broth and saffron) a close second. The Lombards also favour hearty dishes like *osso buco alla milanese* (veal knuckle braised with white wine and tomatoes, properly served with risotto) and *cassoeula* (a stew of pork, cabbage, carrots and celery). Milan also claims minestrone and *busecca*, tripe soup with eggs and cheese. The Milanese cake, *panettone* filled with raisins and fruit, is a Christmas tradition all over the country.

Good Lombard wines include the reds from the Valtellina (*Grumello, Sassella*, or the diabolical-sounding *Inferno*); the various wines from *Oltrepó Pavese* or *Franciacorta*'s crisp dry whites or mellow reds. Visconti's *Lugana* is a very pleasant, dry white; *Barbacarlo*, a dry, fruity red; *Buttafuoco*, a dry, heartier red.

In August (and Sundays, for that matter) so few restaurants remain open that their names are printed in the paper; in the past few years the *comune*, taking pity on the famished hordes, has operated an open-air mess hall in August in the Parco Sempione with inexpensive meals.

Expensive

The best-known gourmet enclave in Milan, and one of the top restaurants in all Italy, is **Gualtiero Marchesi**, Via Bonvesin de la Riva 9, tel 741 246, named after its innovative master chef and the city's Pied Piper of *la nuova cucina*, who takes his inspiration from the freshest and best ingredients available. Marchesi is a celebrity in Italy and author of several cookbooks, and composes unusual marriages of flavours—pigeon and lobster with ravioli, or ratatouille of sweet and sour aubergines with salted shrimp, or bass in creamy sea urchin sauce, or for dessert, figs in Marsala with almond mousse. The restaurant has a variety of fixed-price menus to choose from, ranging from L55 000 to more than double that, depending on which you order (always prepared for two people). The wine list is as superlative as the food. Reservations essential; closed Sun and Mon lunch. In contrast, **Savini**, in the Galleria Vittorio Emanuele (since 1867), tel 7200 3433, is considered the most traditional Milanese restaurant of all, a cultural institution where you can try Lombard classics at the pinnacle of perfection—here the often-abused *cotoletta* and *risotto* retain their primordial freshness, as do the more earthy *cassoeula* and *osso buco*. Oenophiles will appreciate the vast cellar of Italian and French wines. Closed Sun & Aug; L80–120 000. Another culinary bastion, **La Scaletta**, is located in one of the city's more banal corners, in the Piazzale Stazione Porta Genova 3, tel 835 0290. But don't let the location fool you; this little restaurant is the workshop of Italy's *nuova cucina* sorceress, Pina Bellini, who does exquisite things to pasta and risotto, to fish and rabbit, all beautifully presented. Excellent desserts and wines finish off a truly memorable meal; closed Mon and Sun, reservations strongly advised; L70–95 000. If you prefer the ultimate in traditional Italian cuisine, **Aimo e Nadia**, Via Montecuccoli 6 (in another dull out-of-the-way corner north of the Stazione San Cristoforo), tel 416 886, will serve you such mouth-watering delights as hot ricotta with radicchio (that slightly bitter red chicory from the Veneto), an exquisite liver pâté, risotto with zucchini and white truffles, sole tarragon, and pigeon with artichokes. Fantastic light desserts top off the meal; L100 000; closed Sat lunch and Sun.

Although it's 20 km from Milan, along the Naviglio Grande in Cassinetta di Lugagnano, the **Antica Osteria del Ponte**, Piazza G. Negri 9, tel 942 0034, is known as a holy temple of Italian cuisine and shouldn't be missed by any serious gourmet, featuring heavenly dishes like ravioli filled with lobster and zucchini, fresh foie gras, marvellously prepared fish, cassata with pistachio sauce and perfect little pastries—nearly every dish is based on Italian traditions. The decor is beautiful, intimate and elegant. The fixed-price menu in the evening will set you back L110 000; add 10 000 for wine and cover charge—closed Sun and Mon.

Moderate

For a glimpse at Milanese intellectuals like Umberto Eco and fashion's trend-setters, dine at their favourite restaurant, **Decio Carugati** in the Navigli at Via Vigevano and Via Corsico, tel 4895 2361, where *la cucina nuova* is as interesting as its elegant patrons (L50 000; closed Sun). A relative newcomer, **La Zelata**, Via Anfossi 10 (off Corso Porta Vittoria) tel 548 4115, is a quiet and refined place run by the former head chef of the Palace hotel. Specialities here include the unusual *raviolone* (one big ravioli, with a delightful sauce) and turbot in a delicate sauce of zucchini flowers; great desserts and French and Italian wine list (closed Sat lunch and Sun; around L60 000). **Trattoria del Ruzante**, Corso Sempione 17, tel 316 102, is gaining a reputation for its exquisite and utterly simple approach to Lombard dishes, especially their famous *tagliatelle alle verdure* (L65 000). **Aurora**, Via Savona 23 (in the Navigli), tel 8940 4978, has lovely Belle Epoque dining rooms and an equally lovely cuisine, with an emphasis on mushrooms and truffles; another speciality is the trolley of boiled meats, from which you can choose a vast array of sauces, or the salad trolley, which offers a quick lesson in Italian olive oil and vinegar dilettantism—the former especially is treated as circumspectly as vintage wine. Yet another trolley will overwhelm you with its bewildering choice of cheeses. (Closed Mon; fixed lunch L25 000, otherwise L45 000.) For delectable gourmet treats, **Peck**, Via Victor Hugo 4, tel 876 774, is a name that has denoted the best in Milan for over a hundred years, either in its epicurean delicatessen and shop at Via Spadari 9, or here, at its restaurant, offering different tantalizing fixed-price menus every week (L60–70 000; closed Sun and first 3 weeks of July). If you need a break from Italian cuisine, **Suntory**, Via G. Verdi 6, Mazoni, tel 862 210, serves some of the best Japanese food in all Italy, patronized by Milan's large Japanese business community (L75–90 000; closed Sun and part of Aug).

Inexpensive
Inexpensive by Milanese standards, anyway. Besides the places listed below, Milan is well endowed with American and Italian fast-food joints, for those without the money or time for a genuine Italian sit-down feast.

A good, but again out-of-the-way place, **Osteria del Binari**, Via Tortona 1 (by the Porta Genova station), tel 8940 9428, has delightful Lombard and Piedmontese specialities, served outdoors in a shady garden in the summer, complemented by homemade bread and pasta and fine wines, for L35–40 000 (closed lunchtime and Sun). **Pizzeria Carmignani Angelo e Gianfranco**, Corso S. Gottardo 38 (Navigli district), tel 839 1959, offers excellent value and tasty pizza from a wood oven as well as fish, pasta, and other dishes for around L15 000 (closed Tues and Wed). Spaghetti-lovers will want to try one of the over 100 varieties offered at **Emilio**, Viale Piave 38, tel 2940 1982 (closed Mon, Tue lunch; L25 000). Late-night eaters, except on Sun, can find delicious victuals at **Topkapi**, Via Ponte Vetero 21, in Brera, tel 808 282—good pizza, risotto, involtini and more, topped off with homemade pies (closed Wed; L25 000). Championship pizzas are the speciality at **Vecchia Napoli Da Rino**, Via Chavez 4 (between Stazione Centrale and Parco Lambro), tel 291 9056; besides pizzas, they do good antipasti, gnocchi, and fish dishes. Closed Mon; L40 000. One of the best bargains in town, **Grand'Italia**, Via Palermo 5 in Brera, tel 877 759, serves up good pizza and *focacce* (Ligurian pizza), as well as a daily if limited choice of first and second courses that will set you back L15 000 (closed Tue and Sat lunch), with a bottle of beer or glass of wine.

Short Excursions from Milan: Monza

Monza, only 15 minutes by train from the Porta Garibaldi Station, or 20 minutes by bus from Piazza Quattro Novembre, is synonymous with the Italian Grand Prix, which runs in early September on the famous Monza race course. The course, built in 1922, lies in the heart of one of greater Milan's 'lungs', the beautiful Parco di Monza, formerly part of the Villa Reale of the kings of Italy. It includes the 27-hole Golf Club Milano as well as other recreational facilities in its acres and acres of greenery; the single sombre note is struck behind the 18th-century residence—an expiatory chapel built by Vittorio Emanuele III that marks the spot where his father Umberto was assassinated by an anarchist in 1900.

Monza itself is a pleasant if industrial town, once highly favoured by the Lombard Queen Theodolinda, who founded its first cathedral in the late 6th century after being converted to orthodoxy by Gregory the Great. The present **Duomo** on Via Napoleone, dates from the 13th century, and bears a lovely if crumbling multi-coloured marble façade by the great Campionese master, Matteo (1390s), who also did some of the fine carvings inside. Theodolinda's life is depicted in a series of 15th-century frescoes near her tomb, honouring the good queen who left Monza its most famous relic, preserved in the high altar: the **Iron Crown of Italy**, a crown believed to have belonged to the Emperor Constantine, named after the iron strip in the centre said to be one of the nails from the True Cross. In the old days, new emperors would stop in Monza or Pavia to be

195

crowned King of Italy, before heading on to Rome to receive the Crown of Empire from the Pope. The cathedral's precious treasury is displayed in the **Museo Serpero** (open 9–12 and 3–6, closed Mon; adm) and includes many objects once belonging to Theodolinda: a processional cross given her by Gregory the Great, her crown and her famous silver hen and seven chicks symbolizing Lombardy and its provinces.

Lodi

The southeast corner of the province of Milan, watered by the river Adda, is called La Bassa. La Bassa's main city, **Lodi**, was a fierce rival of Milan, until the year 1111 when the Milanese ended the feud by decimating Lodi, leaving only the ancient church of San Bassiano intact; they then forbade the citizens of Lodi ever to return. Even in the cruel and bitter period of inter-city rivalries Milan's treatment was unduly harsh, and in 1153 Lodi brought a formal complaint to the newly elected Emperor Frederick Barbarossa, hoping he would act as a referee. The emperor warned Milan to leave Lodi alone, and when the proud Ambrogiani mocked his threats, he levied a terrible penalty, the brutal sacking of Milan. He also founded a new city of Lodi, but it showed its gratitude by joining Milan in the Lombard League as soon as the Emperor was safely back over the Alps—the first Italian city to learn that calling in foreign intervention was a Pandora's box best left closed. But history was to repeat itself over and over again before 1796, when another emperor, Napoleon, won his important battle over the Austrians here.

Besides the ancient church of **San Bassiano** in Lodi Vecchio (5 km to the east of the modern town), Lodi's greatest monument is its elegant Renaissance church of the 1490s, **L' Incoronata**, an octagon in the style of Bramante, lavishly decorated within with blue and gold and paintings by Bergognone. It is located near the city's large central arcaded Piazza della Vittoria, site of its Broletto and 12th-century **Duomo**, with a fine porch and Romanesque statuary within; another church, **S. Francesco**, has a lovely rose window and 14th–15th century frescoes.

Saronno

Northwest of Milan, on the road and rail line to Varese, lies industrial **Saronno**, synonymous with *amaretti* biscuits, but also in Italian art scholarship with its **Santuario della Madonna dei Miracoli**, built by Giovanni Antonio Amedeo, begun in the 1430s and finished in 1498, and decorated with major frescoes by Gaudenzio Ferrari and Bernardino Luini, including the former's innovative and startling *Assumption* (1535).

The Lombard Plain:
Pavia, Cremona and Mantua

The three small capitals of the Lombard plain are among Italy's most rewarding art cities, each maintaining its individual character: Pavia, the capital of the ancient Lombards and the region's oldest centre of learning, embellished with fine Romanesque churches and its famous Renaissance Certosa; Cremona, the graceful city, where the raw medieval fiddle was reincarnated as the lyrical violin; and Mantua, the dream-shadow capital of the wealthy Gonzaga dukes and Isabella d'Este.

Pavia

Pavia (pronounced pa-VEE-a) is one of those rare cities that had its golden age in the three-digit years before the millennium, that misty half-legendary time that historians have shrugged off as the Dark Ages. But these were bright days for Pavia, when it served as capital of the Goths, and saw Odoacer proclaimed King of Italy after sending Romulus Augustulus, bewildered, teenage, and last Roman Emperor of the West, off to a forced early retirement in Naples. In the 6th century the heretical Lombards led by King Alboin captured Pavia from the Goths and formed a state the equal of Byzantine Ravenna and Rome, making Pavia the capital of their *Regnum Italicum*, a position the city maintained into the 11th century; Charlemagne came here to be crowned (774), as did the first King of Italy, Berenguer (888), and Emperor Frederick Barbarossa (1155). At the turn of the millennium, the precursor of Pavia's modern university, the 'Studio', was founded, and among its first students of law was the first Norman Archbishop of Canterbury, Lanfranc, born in Pavia in 1005.

Pavia was a Ghibelline *comune*, the 'city of a hundred towers' and a rival of Milan to whom it lost its independence in 1359. It was favoured by the Visconti, especially by Gian Galeazzo, who built the castle housing his art collection and founded the Certosa di Pavia, one of the most striking landmarks in Italy. It, and many other churches in the city bear the mark of Pavia's great, half-demented sculptor-architect of the High Renaissance, Giovanni Antonio Amadeo.

Pavia

197

GETTING AROUND

There are buses nearly every 45 minutes or so between Milan and Pavia, which is the best way to stop off and visit the Certosa, some 8 km north of Pavia. Frequent trains link Pavia to Milan (30 min) and Genoa (1½ hours), less frequently to Cremona and Mantua, Alessandria and Vercelli, and Piacenza. The train station is an easy walk from the centre, at the end of Corso Cavour and Via Vittorio Emanuele II; buses depart opposite the station and from Viale G. Matteotti, not far from the Castello.

TOURIST INFORMATION

Via Fabio Filzi 2, tel (0382) 22 156

The Duomo and San Michele

Pavia retains its street plan from the days when it was the Roman city of *Ticinum*, the *cardus* (Corso Cavour) and the *decumanus* (Strada Nuova) intersecting by the town hall, or **Broletto**, begun in the 12th century, and the **Duomo**. Begun in 1488, the cathedral owes its overcooked design to Amadeo, Leonardo da Vinci, Bramante, and a dozen other architects, and its strange, unfinished appearance (from a distance it looks as if it's covered with corrugated cardboard) to the usual lack of funds and interest—a curious Renaissance trait. The last two apses in the transept were added only in 1930, while the vast cupola that dominates the city skyline was added in the 1880s. Next to the cathedral rises the singularly unattractive 12th-century **Torre Civica**.

From the Duomo, the Strada Nuova continues south down to the river and the pretty **Covered Bridge**, which replaces the Renaissance version damaged during the last war; it is the only one in Italy, if not anywhere, with a church (S. Giovanni Nepomuceno) built into its centre. From Strada Nuova, Via Maffi leads to the small brick, 12th-century **San Teodoro**, notable for its early 16th-century fresco of Pavia when it still had a forest of a hundred towers and its original covered bridge.

East of the Strada, Via Capsoni leads in a couple of blocks to Pavia's most important church, the Romanesque **Basilica di San Michele**, founded in 661 but rebuilt in the 12th century after its destruction by lightning. Unlike the other churches of Pavia, San Michele is made of sandstone, mellowed into a fine golden hue, though the weather has been less kind to the intricate friezes that cross its front like a comic strip, depicting a complete 'apocalyptic vision' with its medieval bestiary, mermaids, monsters, and human figures involved in the never-ending fight between Good and Evil. The solemn interior, where Frederick Barbarossa was crowned Emperor, contains more fine carvings on the capitals of the columns; the most curious, the fourth on the left, portrays the 'Death of the Righteous'. Along the top runs a Byzantine-style women's gallery, while the chapel to the right of the main altar contains the church's most valuable treasure, a 7th-century silver crucifix.

The University and Castello Visconteo

The great yellow Neoclassical quadrangles of the **University of Pavia**, famous for law and medicine, occupy much of the northeast quadrant of the Roman street plan. The ancient Studio was officially made a university in 1361. St Charles Borromeo, a former student, founded a college here (still supported by the Borromeo family in Milan), while Pope Pius V founded another, the Collegio Ghislieri, in 1569. In the 18th century Maria

Theresa worked hard to bring the university back to life after scholarship had hit the skids, and financed the construction of the main buildings. Three of Pavia's medieval skyscrapers, called the **Torri**, survive in the middle of the university, in the Piazza Leonardo; the roof in the piazza shelters what is believed to be the crypt of the demolished **Sant' Eusebio**. This, in the 7th century, was Pavia's Arian church, and the columns in the crypt retain their quaint capitals from the period. Nearby you can meet some of the university's 17,000 students (many of whom commute from Milan), at the Bar Bordoni, on Via Mentana. In the Piazza Cairoli, northeast of the main university, **San Francesco d'Assisi** was one of the first churches in Italy dedicated to the saint (in 1228); it has an unusual façade, adorned with lozenge patterns and a triple-mullioned window.

At the top of Strada Nuova looms the mighty **Castello Visconteo** built in 1360 by the Campionese masters for Gian Galeazzo II, but partially destroyed in the Battle of Pavia (February 24, 1525) when Emperor Charles V captured Francis I of France, who succinctly described the outcome in a letter to his mother: 'Madame, all is lost save honour'. Three sides of the castle, and its beautifully arcaded courtyard with terracotta decorations managed to survive as well, and now house Pavia's **Museo Civico** (open 9–1 Jan, July, Aug, and Dec; 10–12 and 2:30–4 otherwise, closed Mon; adm). The archaeological and medieval sections contain finds from Roman and Gaulish Pavia, as well as robust Lombard and medieval carvings salvaged from now-vanished churches, and colourful 12th-century mosaics. One room contains an impressive wooden model of the cathedral, built by the architect Fugazza in the early 16th century. The picture gallery on the first floor contains works by Giovanni Bellini, Correggio, Foppa, van der Goes and others.

San Pietro in Ciel d'Oro

Behind the castle, Via Griziotti (off Viale Matteotti) leads to Pavia's second great Romanesque temple, **San Pietro in Ciel d'Oro** ('St Peter in the Golden sky'), built in 1132 and so named because of its once-glorious gilded ceiling, mentioned by Dante in Canto X of the *Paradiso*. The single door in the façade is strangely off-centre; within, the main altar is one of the greatest works of the Campionese masters: the **Arca di Sant' Agostino** is a magnificent 14th-century monument built to shelter the bones of St Augustine, which, according to legend, were retrieved in the 8th century from Carthage by the Lombard king Luitprand, staunch ally of Pope Gregory II against the Iconoclasts of Byzantium. Luitprand himself is buried in a humble tomb to the right, while in the crypt lies another Dark Age celebrity, the philosopher Boethius, who wrote his *Consolation of Philosophy* in the dungeons of Emperor Theodoric, before being executed for suspected intrigues with Byzantium in 524.

There are two other notable churches in Pavia. In the centre of town (walk down the Piazza Petrarca from Corso Matteotti), **Santa Maria del Carmine** (1390s) is an excellent example of Lombard Gothic, with a fine façade and rose window, and inside, a beautifully sculptured *lavabo* by Amadeo. Away from the centre, to the west (Corso Cavour to Corso Mazzoni and Via Riviera), it's a 15-minute walk to the rather plain vertical, 13th-century **San Lanfranco**, especially notable for its lovely memorial, the *Arca di San Lanfranco*, sculpted by Amadeo in 1498, his last work (though Archbishop Lanfranc was actually buried in Canterbury); the same artist helped design the church's pretty cloister.

The Certosa di Pavia

The pinnacle of Renaissance architecture in Lombardy, and according to Jacob Burckhardt, 'the greatest decorative masterpiece in all of Italy', the Certosa, or Charterhouse of Pavia, is a splendid symphony of design built over a period of 200 years. Gian Galeazzo Visconti laid the cornerstone in 1396, with visions of the crown of Italy dancing in his head, and the desire to build a splendid pantheon for his hoped-for royal self and his heirs. Although many architects and artists worked on the project (beginning with the Campionese masters of Milan cathedral), it bears the greatest imprint of Giovanni Antonio Amadeo, who with his successor Bergognone, worked on its sculptural programme for 30 years and contributed the design of the lavish façade.

Napoleon disbanded the monastery, but in 1968 a small group of Cistercians reoccupied the Certosa. The monks of today live the same style of contemplative life as the old Carthusians, maintaining vows of silence. A couple, however, are released to take visitors around the complex (open all year, Tues–Sun 9–11:30 and 2:30–5:30; until 5 pm in the spring and autumn, and until 4 pm in the winter; try to avoid the crowded weekends). If you arrive by the Milan-Pavia bus, the Certosa's a 1.5 km walk, a beckoning vision at the end of the straight, tree-lined lane, surrounded by groomed fields and rows of poplars, once part of the vast game park of the Castello Visconteo in Pavia.

Once through the main gate and **vestibule** adorned with frescoes by Luini, a large grassy court opens up, lined with buildings that served as lodgings for visitors and stores for the monks. At the end rises the incredibly sumptuous, detailed façade of the **church**, a marvel of polychromatic marbles, medallions, bas-reliefs, statues, and windows covered with marble embroidery from the chisel of Amadeo, who died before the upper, less elaborate level was begun. The interior plan is Gothic but the decoration is Renaissance, with later Baroque additions. Outstanding works of art include Bergognone's five statues of saints in the chapel of Sant'Ambrogio (sixth on the left); the tombs of Lodovico il Moro and his young bride Beatrice d'Este, a masterpiece by Cristoforo Solari; the beautiful, inlaid stalls of the choir, and the tomb of Gian Galeazzo Visconti, all works of the 1490s and surrounded by fine frescoes. The old sacristy contains a magnificent, early cinquecento ivory altarpiece by the Florentine Baldassare degli Embriachi, with 94 figures and 66 bas-reliefs.

From the church, the tour continues into the **Little Cloister**, with delicate terracotta decorations and a dream-like view of the church and its cupola, a rising crescendo of arcades. A lovely doorway by Amadeo leads back into the church. The **Great Cloister** with its long arcades, is surrounded by the 24 house-like cells of the monks—each contains a chapel and study/dining room, a bedroom upstairs and a walled garden in the rear. The frescoed **Refectory** contains a pulpit for a monk who reads aloud during otherwise silent suppers.

Lomello and Vigevano

West of Pavia and the Certosa lies the little-known Lomellina, a major rice-growing and frog-farming district, irrigated by canals dug by order of the Visconti in the 14th century. The feudal seat, **Lomello**, retains some fine early medieval buildings, most notably a lovely little 5th-century polygonal **Baptistry** near the main church, the 11th-century **Basilica di Santa Maria**.

Also in the Lomellina is the old silk town of **Vigevano** (known better these days for its high-fashion footwear manufacturers), the site of another vast **castle** of the Visconti and Sforza clans; it was the birthplace of Lodovico il Moro and is now undergoing a lengthy restoration process. Before it lies the majestic rectangular **Piazza Ducale**, designed in 1492 by Bramante (with help from Leonardo) as Lombardy's answer to Venice's Piazza San Marco. Originally a grand stairway connected the piazza to one of the castle towers, though now the three sides are adorned with slender arcades, while on the fourth stands the magnificent concave Baroque façade of the **Cathedral**, designed by a Spanish bishop, Juan Caramuel de Labkowitz. Inside there's a good collection of 16th-century paintings and a 15th-century Lombard polyptych on the life of St Thomas of Canterbury and an especially rich treasury (opened holidays 3–5, or upon request), containing illuminated codices, Flemish tapestries, and golden reliquaries and artefacts.

WHERE TO STAY (tel prefix 0382)
Most people visit Pavia as a day trip from Milan, but for light sleepers or budget-minded souls, there's always the possibility of taking in Milan as a day trip from Pavia. Most comfortable is the centrally located ******Ariston**, Via A. Scopoli 10d, tel 34 334, with air conditioning, private bath, and television in each room, for less than you'd pay in Milan (L100 000). The ******Albergo Moderno**, Viale V. Emanuele II 45, tel 303 401, next to the railway station, has recently been completely remodelled: L130 000 with bath. Less costly choices include the ****Aurora**, Via V. Emanuele II 25, tel 23 664, close to the station, and with a shower in each room (L75 000), or the elderly and not very ***Splendid**, Via XX Settembre 11, tel 24 703, with plenty of rooms, none with bath, L45 000.

EATING OUT
Pavia is well endowed with good restaurants. Specialities include frogs, salami from Varzi and *zuppa di pavese* (a raw egg on toast drowned in hot broth); good local wines to try are from the Oltrepò Pavese region, one of Lombardy's best. *Cortese* is a delicious dry white wine, *Bonarda* a meaty, dry red, *Pinot* a fruity white. For excellent innovative cuisine, eat at the small but chic **Locanda Vecchia Pavia**, right under the cathedral on Via Cardinal Riboldi 2, tel 304 132; its young chefs base the day's menu on what looks good in the market, with some surprising but delicious results like salmon and caviar tartare, truffle-filled ravioli, and equally fine desserts; closed Mon and Aug (L65–70 000). Pavia'a other gastronomic temple is **Al Cassinino**, Via Cassinino 1, tel 422 097, just outside the city on the Giovi highway. Sitting on the Naviglio, the restaurant is done out in the style of a medieval inn, complete with rare antiques, and is finely furnished. Dishes are whatever the market provides—from truffles to frogs' legs, oysters to caviar (L70 000; closed Wed and Christmas). **Osteria della Madonna**, Via Liguri 28, tel 302 833, is a lively place featuring good, solid lunches for around L20 000 and more elaborate dinners, often with live entertainment, for L30 000 (closed Sun, Mon and all of Aug).

In the old 16th-century mill of the Certosa, the **Vecchio Mulino** (Via Monumento 5, tel 925 894) serves up delicious food with ingredients garnered from the fertile countryside—foie gras, risotto with crayfish or asparagus, frogs' legs, *coniglio al Riesling* (rabbit in wine), crêpes filled with artichokes, and much more. The wine list has nearly every label produced in Lombardy; closed Sun night and Mon, L50 000.

Cremona

Charming Cremona is famous for two things: the stupendous complex of its Romanesque cathedral and its equally stupendous violins. It has been the capital of the latter industry since 1566, when Andrea Amati developed the modern violin in his Cremona workshop, an instrument so superior in tone and grace to the medieval fiddle that even the king of France heard tell and ordered a dozen for his court. Amati's followers perfected the violin, and the next two centuries were a musical golden age for the city, when the workshops of Andrea's son Nicolò Amati, and his famous pupils Antonio Stradivarius and Giuseppe Guarneri produced the masterpieces of their craft. Their modern heirs continue to produce 800–1000 instruments a year in some 60 workshops (*Bottege Liutarie*), in La Bottega, the EEC school for violin masters, and in Cremona's International School of Violin-making. To celebrate the instrument that put it on the map, the city hosts a festival of stringed instruments every third October (next in 1994). Violins even seem to be reflected in the curving spiral cornices and pediments that adorn Cremona's elegant brick and terracotta palaces, while the sweetness of their tone is recalled in the city's culinary specialities—*torrone*, a nougat made of almonds and honey and sold in bars throughout the city, and *Mostarda di Cremona*—candied cherries, apricots, melons, etc. in a sweet mustard sauce.

In the 14th century the *comune* of Cremona was captured by Milan, and from then on played second fiddle to the Lombard capital. In 1441, it was given to Bianca Maria Visconti as her dowry when she wed Francesco Sforza, marking the change of the great Milanese dynasties. The city enjoyed a happy, fruitful Renaissance as the apple of Bianca's eye; the fertile countryside is littered with lovely villas and castles.

GETTING AROUND
Even Cremona's railway station is delightful; you can get there frequently from Milan (around 2 hours), Pavia, Mantua, Brescia, and Piacenza, as well as four times a day from Bergamo. If you approach from Parma or Bologna, change in Fidenza. Cremona's station lies north of the centre, at the end of Via Palestro. Buses depart from Piazza Marconi, southeast of the Piazza del Comune, for Genoa, Trieste, Mantua, Brescia, Bergamo, Padua, Milan, Iseo and towns in the province; for information, call 28 859.

TOURIST INFORMATION
Piazza del Comune 5, tel (0372) 23233. If you're in the market for a violin or just want to visit a workshop, ask for their list of *Bottege Liutarie*; they also have a special itinerary called 'Cremona in Violin Terms.'

Via Palestro to the Piazza del Comune

Cremona can be easily covered on foot in a day, starting from the station and the Via Palestro. Here, behind a remodelled Baroque façade at No. 36, the 15th–16th-century **Palazzo Stanga**'s courtyard is an excellent introduction into the Cremonese fondness for elaborate terracotta ornament. The **Museo Stradivariano** nearby at No. 17 (open 9:30–12 and 3–5:45, Sun 9:30–12, closed Mon; adm) is an equally good introduction to the cream of Cremona's best-known industry, featuring casts, models, and drawings explaining how Stradivarius did it. Just around the corner, in Via Dati, the Palazzo Affaitati (begun in 1561) houses a grand theatrical stair of 1769 and the **Museo Civico** (same hours), that has sections devoted to art; there are paintings by the Cremonese school (Boccaccino and the Campi clan), and one of the 16th-century Surrealist Arcimboldi's most striking portraits, *Scherzo con Ortaggi*, a vegetable face with onion cheeks and walnut eyes spilling out of a bowl; also look for a fine anonymous and very Tuscan-looking Madonna. The interesting archaeology section includes a fine labyrinth mosaic and a fierce lion-topped column from the Roman colony of Cremona; another section houses the Cathedral Treasury with some fine Renaissance illuminations.

Via Palestro becomes Via C. Campi, and at an angle runs into the boxy, Mussolini-era Galleria Venticinque Aprile, leading to the **Piazza Roma**, a little park; along Corso Mazzini, **Stradivarius' tombstone** has been transferred from a demolished church. Corso Mazzini forks after a block; near the split, at Corso Matteotti 17, is Cremona's prettiest palace, the 1499 **Palazzo Fodri** (now owned by the Banca d'Italia; ask the guard to unlock the gate) with a courtyard adorned with frescoed battle scenes and terracottas. Via Gerolamo da Cremona, the other street forking off Corso Mazzoni, leads to the city walls and the Romanesque brick church of **San Michele**, founded back in the 7th century, but rebuilt after a fire in 1113. The crypt is especially interesting for its capitals, uncouth survivors of the original church.

The Duomo and its Torrazzo

By now you've probably caught at least a glimpse of the curious pointy crown of the tallest bell tower in Italy, the 112 m **Torrazzo**, looming high over Cremona's equally remarkable Duomo in Piazza del Comune, itself a square seductive enough to compete in any urban beauty pageant.

The Torrazzo, only slightly shorter than Milan Cathedral, was built in the 13th century, a time when it never hurt to have a spare tower—this one even has battlements as well as bells, though any warlike intentions it may have had are belied by a fine astronomical clock, added in 1583 by Giovanni Battista Divizioli, and the twin 'wreaths' and spire on top. The stout-hearted may ascend to the top for an eye-popping view of Cremona. An added attraction is a violin workshop, reproducing a *Bottega Liutaria* from the time of Stradivarius, where a violin maker often works and explains his art (March–Oct 10–12 and 3–6; winter, Sat only 3–6; adm).

The **Cathedral**, visually linked with the Torrazzo in the early 1500s by a double loggia, nicknamed the Bertazzola, is the highest and most exuberant expression of Lombard Romanesque, with a trademark Cremonese flourish in the façade's graceful curls; from a distance the façade could be a stubby primordial version of a lute, with two rows of blind arches as its strings and its immense, beautiful rose window as a sounding board of resonant grace. Built by the Comacini masters after an earthquake in 1117 destroyed its predecessor, the cathedral's details are just as captivating, especially the main door, the **Porta Regia**, flanked by two nearly toothless lion telamones and four flat prophets, and crowned by a small portico, known as the Rostrum, where 13th- and 14th-century statues of the Virgin, S. Imerio and S. Omobono silently but eloquently hold forth above a frieze of the months by the school of master Antelami.

The Cathedral was begun as a basilica, but as Gothic became the rage it was decided to add arms to make a Latin cross; the new transept façades, especially the one facing north is almost as splendid as the main marble-coated front. Inside, the nave and apse are opulently frescoed (early 1500s) by Romanino, Boccaccino, Pordenone, and others, and decorated with fine Flemish tapestries. The twin pulpits, facing each other across the nave, have reliefs attributed to Amadeo or Pietro da Rho. Among the individual paintings, look for the *Pietà* in the left transept by Antonio Campi—not a great painter, but a strange one. The choir has stalls inlaid in 1490 by G. M. Platina.

Before leaving the cathedral, find the medieval capital in the presbytery supported by a band of tired telamones, while behind them an impassive mermaid holds up her forked tail—a Romanesque conceit nearly as popular as the two hungry lions by the main door. Such mermaids, displaying the entrance to the tomb, with birds or dragons whispering in their ears, are steeped in medieval mysticism, perhaps a symbol of the cosmic process: such sirens, representing desire, become the intermediaries by which nature's energy and inspiration (here represented by the birds) are conducted into the conscious world.

Completing the divine ensemble in Piazza del Comune is the octagonal **Baptistry di San Giovanni** (1167), with another pair of lions supporting the portico, and two sides of marble facing to match the cathedral. Across from the cathedral is the fine Gothic **Loggia dei Militi** (1292) where Cremona's citizen militia had their rendezvous in the days of the *comune*; the outdoor pulpit between two of the arches is a relic of the charismatic, itinerant preachers like San Bernardino of Siena, whose sermons were so popular they had to be held outside. Behind the Loggia the 13th-century **Palazzo del Comune** (1206–45), still the town hall, preserves some of its original frescoes; one room has been converted into a **Saletta dei Violini** (9–12 and 3–7, Sun mornings only; free); this contains the municipal collection, where you can see some of the greatest products of Cremona's greatest craftsmen, such as Stradivarius' golden 'Cremonese 1715', that retains its original varnish—is as mysterious as the embalming fluids of ancient Egypt. Another of Stradivarius' secrets was in the woods he used for his instruments; like Michelangelo seeking just the right piece of marble in the mountains of Carrara, Stradivarius would visit the forests of the Dolomites looking for perfect trees that would one day sing. Other violins on display are 'Charles IX of France' by Andrea Amati, one of 24 violins commissioned in the 1560s by the French sovereign from the father of modern fiddles; the 'Hammerle', by Nicolò Amati (1658); Giuseppe Guarneri's 'Del Gesù' (formerly owned by Pinchas Zukerman) and the 1689 'Quarestani' also by Guarneri.

Piazza del Comune to San Luca

Behind the Palazzo del Comune lies Piazza Cavour and Corso Vittorio Emanuele, leading to the River Po. En route it passes one of Italy's earliest and most renowned small town theatres, the **Teatro Ponchielli**, built in 1734, and rebuilt after a fire in 1808; its name recalls composer Amilcare Ponchielli (see below) who premiered several of his operas on its little stage. A street to the left of the theatre leads back to **San Pietro al Po**, coated with 16th-century stuccoes and paintings, none individually as effective as the sum.

North of the Corso Vittorio Emanuele, on Via Plasio, stands the 14th-century church **Sant'Agostino**. Its Gothic façade has fine terracotta decorations, and within are good Renaissance frescoes by Bembo, one of which, in the Cappella Cavalcabò, contains a matronly portrait of Bianca Maria Visconti. The highlight, however, is the fifth chapel on the left with its luminous *Madonna with two Saints* (1494), by Perugino, a painting which he was quite pleased with, judging by his prominent signature; also look for the fine bas-reliefs by Bonino di Campione. Further up Via Plasio joins the Corso Garibaldi, address of the church of **Sant'Agata**, hiding an 11th-century structure behind a Neoclassical temple façade; inside are more frescoes and a medieval masterpiece, the 13th-century wooden panel painted with the life of St Agatha. Across the street stands (just barely) the dilapidated 1256 **Cittanova**, former headquarters of the Guelph party in Cremona, now attached to the flamboyant but phoney Gothic façade of the **Palazzo Trecchi**. Further up Corso Garibaldi, the pink and white **Palazzo Raimondi** (1496), is the home of the **International School of Violin-making** (currently under restoration), while across the street stands the city's most peculiar palace, crowned with strange iron dragons. Further up, near the station, the church of **San Luca** (1270s) has a beautiful terracotta façade of 1471 and a little detached octagonal baptistry.

One other church of interest, **San Sigismondo**, lies to the east of the centre, a kilometre beyond Corso Matteotti and the Piazzale Libertà, on Via A. Ghisleri (take bus 3 from the station or Piazzale Libertà). Built by Bartolomeo Gadia for Bianca Maria Visconti in 1463, S. Sigismondo celebrates the Duchess' marriage to Francesco Sforza on this site in an uniquely harmonious marriage of art and architecture. The church is completely covered within by frescoes of the Cremonese school, with a generous dollop of the kind of ambiguous *trompe-l'oeil* scenes that would be perfected by Veronese, like Giovanni Campi's Pentecost scene on the ceiling. There are fine sculptural details in the choir (including a portrait of the bride); other Campi frescoes, by Antonio this time, are precisely that, with their overwrought protruding eyeballs.

Soncino, Paderno and Crema

Lying between the rivers Po and Oglio, the mainly agricultural province of Cremona is fortified by a number of castles and towers that recall the days when the Italians had nothing better to do than beat each other up. The best surviving one, the **Castello Sforza** is in **Soncino** on the river Oglio. It was originally built in the 12th century, but expanded in 1473 by Galeazzo Maria Sforza as an advance base against the Venetians, who possessed the Brescian-built fortified town of Orzinuovi directly across the river. The castle's now-dry moat and dungeons survive, as well as its imposing quadrangle of towers (open for visits, but check at Cremona's tourist office for details before setting out).

Between Cremona and Crema (the two Italian towns that most sound like dairy products), lies **Paderno**, birthplace of 'the Italian Tchaikovsky', Amilcare Ponchielli (1834–86). Italy has produced scores of 'one opera' composers, but Ponchielli can claim two that are performed with some frequency: *La Gioconda* and *Marion Delorme*; and as the teacher of Puccini and Mascagni can claim to be grandfather of many others. His humble birthplace is now the **Museo Ponchielliano**, devoted to his life and works (Mon–Fri, 3–7).

Crema, also west of Cremona, is an attractive town that belonged to Venice for three centuries and still bears a Lion of St Mark on its town hall. In the same piazza stands the 14th-century Lombard Romanesque **Duomo**, especially notable for its finely worked windows and tower. The **Museo Civico di Crema** on Via Dante (open 3–6, Sat 10–12 and 3–6, Sun 10–12) has an interesting collection of Lombard armour discovered in local tombs, housed in the former convent of Sant'Agostino; the Refectory contains 15th-century frescoes by Da Cemmo. A kilometre or so north of Crema, the rotund **Santa Maria della Croce** is a lovely Renaissance church inspired by Bramante, with three orders of loggias encircling the façade, and four polygonal chapels with spherical cupolas. Crema also has a number of fine palaces and villas dating from its Venetian period; the 18th-century **Villa Ghisetti-Giavarina** in nearby Ricengo is the most interesting and stately with its arches and statues.

WHERE TO STAY (tel prefix 0372)

Cremona has a small selection of fairly good hotels, with the ******Continental** on top of the list (Piazza della Libertà 26, tel 434 141), modern and comfortable and near the centre, featuring a display of its own collection of Cremona-made fiddles. All rooms have bath and television, and there's parking in the garage (L150 000). The *****Astoria** at Via Bordigallo 19, tel 22 467, is a very pleasant, recently remodelled hotel in a quiet street near the Duomo and the Piazza Roma, with bathless rooms for L61 000, with bath L78 000. ***Albergo Touring**, Via Palestro 3, tel 21 390, is a good, simple choice midway between the centre and the station (L37 000 without bath, L45 000 with). On Via Dante Alighieri 51, the ***Casere** has bathless doubles for L35 000, tel 996 300.

EATING OUT

Cremona is not one of Italy's gastronomic capitals, but you can dine very well at the elegant **Ceresole**, at Via Ceresole 4, tel 23 322, near the Piazza del Comune. Recently remodelled, it serves a balance of traditional and innovative dishes—eel with leeks, gnocchetti with ricotta and herbs, and duck are among the specialities; reservations suggested (L65 000). An older, more traditional restaurant, the **Trattoria Bissone**, Via F. Pecorari 3, tel 23 953, features boiled meats with *mostarda di Cremona* and other hearty fare for around L30 000. On Via Bordigallo, a Chinese restaurant, **Amicizi**, tel 412 030, offers full meals adapted for Italian tastes for L20–30 000; closed Mon.

On the northwest outskirts of Crema, in Via Crocicchio, the **Trattoria Guada 'L Canal**, tel (0373) 200 133, is considered the finest restaurant in the whole province, with a warm, country atmosphere. The cuisine is based entirely on seasonal availability, and though the menu is usually brief, everything is sublime, from the pâtés to the various pasta dishes (try the *tagliolini* with scallops and broccoli), to the well-prepared seafood, succulent rack of lamb with thyme, and more (L60–70 000).

Mantua

Mantua's (*Mantova* in Italian) setting hardly answers to many people's expectations of Italy, sitting as it does in a fertile, table-flat plain, on a wide thumb of land protruding into three swampy, swollen lakes formed by the River Mincio. Its climate is moody, soggy with heat and humidity in the summer and frosty under blankets of fog in the winter. The local dialect is harsh, and the Mantuans, when they feel chipper, dine on braised donkey with macaroni. Verdi made it the sombre setting of his opera *Rigoletto*. And yet this former capital of the art-loving, fast-living Gonzaga dukes is one of the most atmospheric old cities in the country, masculine and stern, dark and handsome with none of neighbouring Cremona's gay architectural arpeggios, melancholy with memories of past glories, poker-faced but holding in its hand a royal flush of dazzling Renaissance art.

History

Mantua gained its fame in Roman times as the beloved home town of the poet Virgil, who recounts the legend of the city's founding by the Theban soothsayer Manto, daughter of Tiresias, and her son, the hero Ocnus. Virgil was born around 70 BC, and not much else was heard from Mantua until the 11th century, when the city formed part of the vast domains of Countess Matilda of Canossa. Matilda was a great champion of the Pope against the Emperor; her adviser, Anselmo, Bishop of Lucca, became Mantua's patron saint. Even so, as soon as Mantua saw its chance it allied itself with the opposition, beginning an unusually important and lengthy career as an independent Ghibelline state, a *comune* that became dominated first by the Bonacolsi family, and then the Gonzaga.

Naturally defended on three sides by the Mincio, enriched by river tolls, Mantua became prominent as a neutral, buffer state between the expansionist powers of Milan and Venice. The three centuries of Gonzaga rule, beginning in 1328, brought the city unusual peace and stability, thanks to the prudent and delicate balancing act of the marquesses, who at various times served as *condottieri* not only for Venice and Milan, but for the popes and emperors—whoever would continue to support Mantua's independence. Their enlightened patronage brought in artists, singers, and composers of the highest calibre from all parts of Italy: Pisanello, Alberti, and especially Andrea Mantegna, who was court painter from 1460 until his death in 1506. Gianfrancesco I Gonzaga invited the great Renaissance teacher, Vittorino da Feltre, to open a school in the city in 1423, where his sons and courtiers, side by side with the children of Mantua's poorer families, were taught according to Vittorino's humanist educational theories which gave equal emphasis to the intellectual, the physical, and the moral.

Vittorino da Feltre's star pupil was Lodovico (1412–78), who was considered one of the most just princes of the Renaissance, and one with the good taste to hire the great Leon Battista Alberti to improve Mantua according to Renaissance Tuscan principles, inspired by a lengthy visit of the papal court of the Sienese humanist, Pius II in 1459–60. Lodovico's grandson, Gianfrancesco II, was a military commander, leading the Italians to victory over the French at Fornovo, but is perhaps best known in history as the husband of the brilliant and cultivated Isabella d'Este, the foremost culture vulture of her day as well as an astute diplomat, handling most of Mantua's affairs of state for her not very clever husband.

The family fortunes reached their apogee under Isabella's two sons. The eldest, Federico II (1500–40), godson of Cesare Borgia, married Margherita Paleologo, the heiress of Monferrato, acquiring that duchy for the family, as well as a ducal title for the Gonzaga; he brought Raphael's pupil, the great Giulio Romano (called 'that rare Italian master' by Shakespeare in *The Winter's Tale*), from Rome, to design and adorn his pleasure dome, the Palazzo del Tè. When he died his worthy brother, Cardinal Ercole,

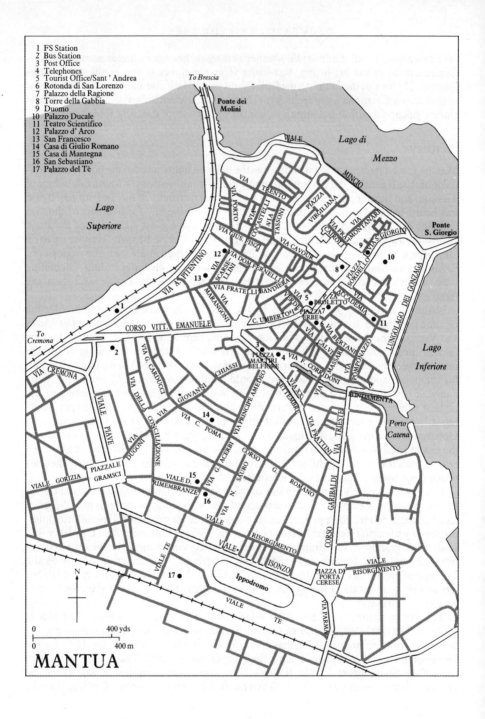

served as regent for the young Duke Guglielmo; both were busy builders and civic improvers. The last great Gonzaga, Vicenzo I, was a patron of Rubens and Claudio Monteverdi (1567–1643) who composed the first modern opera, *L'Orfeo*, for the Mantuan court in 1607, as well as the second, *L'Arianna*, the following year.

The Gonzaga and Mantua suffered a mortal blow in 1630 when their claims for Monferrato came into conflict with the Habsburgs, who sent Imperial troops to take and sack the city. The Gonzaga's rich art treasures were stolen or sold, including Mantegna's great series, the *Triumphs of Caesar*, now at Hampton Court. The duchy, under a cadet branch of the family, limped along until the Austrians snatched Mantua in 1707, eventually making it the southwest corner of their Quadrilateral.

GETTING AROUND
Mantua is linked directly by train with Verona, Milan, Modena, and Cremona, and indirectly with Brescia and Parma (changing at Piadena or Suzzara). There are also buses to Lake Garda and towns in the province, frequently to Sabbioneta. Both the bus and train stations are near Piazza Porta Belfiore, at the end of Corso Vittorio Emanuele, about 10 minutes from the centre.

TOURIST INFORMATION
Piazza A. Mantegna 6, tel (0376) 350 681

Piazza Mantegna
From the station, Corso Vittorio Emanuele and Corso Umberto I lead straight into the Renaissance heart of Mantua, where the narrow cobbled streets are lined with heavy porticoes. Rising up above the rest of the city, in Piazza Mantegna, is the lofty dome of Mantua's great basilica, **Sant'Andrea**, built by Leon Battista Alberti in 1472 to house the Gonzaga's most precious holy relic, a chalice of Christ's blood, said to have been

Cathedral of Sant'Andrea, Mantua

given to St Andrew by St Longinus, the Roman centurion who pierced Christ's side with his lance. Ludovico Gonzaga had asked Alberti to create a truly monumental edifice to hold the relic and form a fitting centrepiece for the city, and Alberti complied. In Florence Alberti had found himself constrained as an architect by his patrons' tastes, but in Mantua he was able to experiment and play with the ancient forms he loved. Sant'Andrea is based on Vitruvius's idea of an Etruscan temple, with a single barrel-vaulted nave supported by side chapels, fronted with a unique façade that combines a triumphal arch and a temple. Inside, Andrea Mantegna is buried in the first chapel on the left, beside a rather stern self-portrait in bronze. He designed much of the decoration in the spacious interior, later executed by his pupils.

On the east, the unfinished flank of the basilica is lined with the porticoes and market stalls of the **Piazza delle Erbe**. Across the square is the attractive 1082 **Rotunda di San Lorenzo**, built by the Countess Matilda over an earlier Lombard structure, and restored in 1908 after many centuries of neglect; fragments of medieval frescoes in the beautiful apse were discovered by the restorers. Also on the Piazza delle Erbe, the lovely **Casa di Boniforte** has delicate stucco decoration, almost unchanged since it was built in 1455, while the 13th-century **Palazzo della Regione** has a stout clock tower topped by an odd little temple and astronomical clock, added during Lodovico's restoration of the palace. The adjacent **Broletto**, built in 1227, faces the Piazza del Broletto, with a medieval figure of Virgil seated near the door.

An archway leads into the grand, cobbled **Piazza Sordello**, traditional seat of Mantua's ruling lords. On one side rise the sombre palaces of the Bonacolsi, the Gonzaga's predecessors, with their **Torre della Gabbia**, named after the iron torture cage (*gabbione*) they kept to suspend prisoners over the city (though the Mantuans claim it was only used once). At the head of the piazza stands Mantua's **Duomo**, with a silly 1756 façade topped with wedding-cake figures that hides a lovely Renaissance interior by Giulio Romano. The 15th-century house at No. 23 has been restored as the official **Casa di Rigoletto**, and contains a little exhibit on the opera.

Palazzo Ducale

Opposite the Bonacolsi palaces stands that of the Gonzaga, its unimpressive façade hiding one of Italy's most remarkable Renaissance residences, both in its art and sheer size—the never-satisfied Gonzaga kept on adding on until they had some 500 rooms in three main structures—the original **Corte Vecchio** first built by the Bonacolsi in 1290, the 14th-century **Castello**, with its large towers overlooking the lake, and the **Corte Nuovo**, designed by Giulio Romano. Throw in the Gonzaga's **Basilica di Santa Barbara** and you have a complex that occupies the entire northeast corner of Mantua. (Open Tues–Sat 9–3, Sun and Mon 9–1, guided tours every half hour; adm expensive. If you go in the winter, dress warmly—it's as cold as a dead duke.)

Although stripped of its furnishings and much of its art, the palace is still imposing, majestic, and seemingly endless. One of the first rooms on the tour, the former **chapel**, has a dramatic if half-ruined 14th-century fresco of the Crucifixion, attributed by some to Tommaso da Modena, while another contains a painting of a battle between the Gonzaga and the Bonacolsi in the Piazza Sordello, in which the Gonzaga crushed their rivals once and for all, in 1328—although the artist, Domenico Monore, painted the piazza as it appeared later in 1494. More fascinating than this real battle is the vivid fresco of **Arthurian knights** by Pisanello, Italy's master of Gothic painting. For centuries the work was believed lost until layers and layers of plaster were stripped away in 1969, revealing a remarkable, if unfinished, work, commissioned by Gianfrancesco Gonzaga in the mid-15th century in honour of receiving from Henry VI the concession to use the heraldic collar of the House of Lancaster, insignia that form the border of Pisanello's mural, mingled with the marigold motif of the Gonzaga.

Beyond this are the remodelled **Neoclassical rooms**, holding a set of Flemish tapestries based on Raphael's Acts of the Apostles cartoons (now in the Victoria and Albert Museum). Woven in the early 1500s, these copies of the Vatican originals are in a much better state of preservation; note the curious pagan borders. Beyond these lies the **Sala dello Zodiaco**, with vivacious 1580 frescoes by Lorenzo Costa il Giovane, and the **Sala dei Fiume**, so called because of its fine views over the river, and the **Galleria degli Specchi**, with its mirrors and mythological frescoes, and, by the door, a note from Monteverdi on the days and hours of the musical evenings he directed there in the 1600s.

The Gonzaga were mad about horses and dogs, and had one room, the **Salone degli Arcieri**, painted with *trompe-l'oeil* frescoes of their favourite steeds standing on upper ledges; they were used in a family guessing game, when curtains would be drawn over the figures. Sharing the room are works by Tintoretto and a painting by Rubens of the Gonzaga family, so large that the French cut it into pieces to carry it off. Further on lie the duke's apartments, with the family's fine collection of classical statuary, including busts of the emperors, a Hellenistic torso of Aphrodite, and the 'Apollo of Mantova', a Roman copy of a Greek original. The **Sala di Troia** has vivid 1536 frescoes by Giulio Romano and his pupil, Rinaldo Mantovano, while another ducal chamber has a beautiful seicento labyrinth on the ceiling, each path inscribed in gold with 'Maybe yes, maybe no'. From some of the rooms you can look out over the grassy **Cortile della Cavallerizza**, with rustic façades by Giulio Romano.

The **castle** is reached by a low spiral ramp, built especially for the horses the Gonzaga apparently could never bear to be long without. Here, in the famous **Camera degli Sposi**, are the remarkable frescoes by Mantegna, who like a genie captured the essence of the Gonzaga in this small bottle of a room. Recently restored to their brilliant, original colours, the frescoes depict the life of Lodovico Gonzaga, with his wife Barbara of Brandenburg, his children, dwarfs, servants, dogs, and horses, and important events— greeting his son Francesco, recently made a cardinal, and receiving Emperor Frederick III and King Christian I of Denmark. The portraits are unflattering and solid, those of real people not for public display, almost like a family photo album. The effect is like stumbling on the court of the Sleeping Beauty; only the younger brother, holding the new cardinal's hand, seems to suspect that he has been enchanted. Wife Barbara and her stern dwarf stare out, determined to draw the spectator into the eerie scene. And in truth there is a lingering sorcery here, for these frescoes are the fruit of Mantegna's fascination with the mysterious new science of perspective that gave artists the power to recreate three-dimensional space. The beautiful backgrounds of imaginary cities and ruins reflect Mantegna's other love, classical architecture, and add another element of unreality, as do his *trompe-l'oeil* ceiling decorations.

From here the tour continues down to the **Casetta dei Nani**, residence of the dwarfs, tiny rooms with low ceilings and shallow stairs, although there are bookish party-poopers who say the rooms had a pious purpose, and were meant to bring the sinning duke and his courtiers to their proud knees.

The last stop on the tour is the **suite of Isabella d'Este**, designed by her as a retreat after the death of her husband. In these little rooms Isabella held court as the Renaissance's most imperious and demanding patroness of art, practically commanding Leonardo and Titian to paint her portrait; at one point she commissioned an allegorical canvas from Perugino so exacting that she drew a sketch of what she wanted and sent spies to make sure the painter was following orders. Given an excellent classical education in her native Ferrara, she surrounded herself with humanists, astrologers, poets, and scholars. Her fabulous art collection has long gone to the Louvre, but the inexplicable symbols or 'inventions' she devised with her astrologist remain like faint ghosts from a lost world on the walls and ceilings.

Other Sights

There are several sights within easy walking distance of the Palazzo Ducale. On Via Accademia, just east of the Broletto, lies the Piazza Dante, with a monument to the poet and the **Teatro Scientifico** (3–5:30 except Sun; adm), built by Antonio Galli Bibiena, a member of the famous Bolognese family of theatre builders. Mozart, at the age of 13, performed the inaugural concert in 1770; father Leopold thought it was the most beautiful theatre he had ever seen.

West of the Piazza Sordello, Via Cairoli leads to the city's main park, the **Piazza Virgiliana** with a Mussolini-era statue of Virgil. Further west, in the Piazza d'Arco, the 18th-century **Palazzo d'Arco** has been opened to the public; former residence of the Counts d'Arco, it contains period furnishings, instruments, and a section of the original 15th-century palace, with beautiful zodiac frescoes. The nearby 1304 church of **San Francesco** was rediscovered in 1944, when a bomb hit the arsenal that disguised it for a century and a half. It was restored to its original state in 1954, and contains interesting frescoes attributed to Tommaso da Modena.

South of the medieval nucleus lies Mantua's second great sight, the Palazzo del Tè; on the way there, just off the main Via Principe Amedeo, you can take a look at **Giulio Romano's House**, designed by the artist, as was the quaint palace decorated with monsters opposite. Mantegna also designed his dream house in the same neighbourhood, at Via Acerbi 47, (open daily 8–1, also Mon and Thurs from 3–6). Designed as a cube built around a circular courtyard, he intended it partially as his personal museum. Embellished with classical 'Mantegnesque' decorations, the house is used for frequent art exhibitions. Nearby stands the rather neglected **San Sebastiano**, the second church in Mantua designed by Alberti, this one in the form of a Greek cross.

Palazzo del Tè

At the end of Via Acerbi is Giulio Romano's masterpiece, the marvellous Palazzo del Tè, its name derived, not from tea, but from *tejeto*, a local word for a drainage canal—formerly the palace grounds were swampland, drained for a Gonzaga horsy pleasure ground. In 1527 Federico II had Giulio expand the stables to create a little palace for his mistress, of whom his mother, Isabella d'Este, disapproved. The project expanded over the decades to become a guest house suitable for Emperor Charles V, who checked in twice, in 1530 and 1532 (open 10–6; adm expensive).

In the Palazzo del Tè Giulio Romano created one of the great Renaissance syntheses of architecture and art, combining *trompe l'oeil* with a bold play between the structure of the room and the frescoes; in the **Sala dei Giganti** the Titans, wrestling with pillars, seem to be bringing the ceiling down upon the spectator's head. Another room has more life-size Gonzaga horses up on ledges, and another, the **Camera di Psiche**, is painted with lusty scenes from *The Golden Ass* of Apuleius, all in contrast with the serene Pompeii-style decorations in between. In the garden Giulio Romano added the little **Casino della Grotta**, adorned with pretty stuccoes.

Around Mantua

Although the Po plain isn't famous for its natural beauty, Mantua's western lake, Lago Superiore makes a tempting diversion for its delicate lotus blossoms, planted experimentally in the 1930s. Since then they have thrived, and in July and August turn the city's park, the **Valletta Belfiore** into a veritable lotus land. On the banks of Lago Superiore at Curtatone, Francesco Gonzaga built the **Sanctuary of the Madonna delle Grazie** in 1399, in thanksgiving for relief from the plague; and the church is chock-full of lesser votive offerings, some curious, and some, like the stuffed crocodile, inexplicable. It's especially fun in mid-August when there's an art competition between Italy's professional *madonnari* (artists who draw chalk masterpieces on the sidewalks).

The whole length of the river Mincio, north of Lago Superiore all the way to Lake Garda, has been declared a natural park, including the rare **Bosco della Fontana**, 5 km from Mantua. The Bosco's ancient, broad-leafed trees are believed to be a relic of the ancient forest that once covered the Po plain, and its shady paths, ruins of a 12th-century Gonzaga castle, and streamlets are a tempting retreat from the afternoon heat.

San Benedetto Po

Some 22 km southeast of Mantua (connected in the summer by small tourist boats, sailing down the Mincio to the Po), San Benedetto Po grew up around the Benedictine abbey Polirone, the 'Monte Casino of the North,' established in the year 1007. San Benedetto enjoyed the special favour of the famous Countess Matilda of Canossa (died 1115); in the abbey's **Basilica**, rebuilt in the 1540s by Giulio Romano, her alabaster sarcophagus survives in the apse, though in 1635 her remains were relocated to St Peter's in acknowledgement of her great services to the papacy. The basilica is connected to the 12th-century church of **Santa Maria**, which has a fine contemporary mosaic. There are several cloisters from various periods, and a refectory with recently discovered frescoes attributed to Correggio. Another part of the monastery contains the **Museo Civico Polironiano**, devoted to the country life and culture (all open for visits 10–12 and 1:30–5, Sun 10–12 and 3–6, closed Mon; adm). In winter call ahead 615 911.

213

Sabbioneta

An hour's bus ride southwest of Mantua on the Parma road, Sabbioneta was built as a capital and ideal dream city by the prince of Bozzolo, Vespasiano Gonzaga, member of a cadet branch of the Gonzaga family. Vespasiano was a firm believer that the city should be a rational expression of the measure of man, and he had the streets of his 'Little Athens' laid out straight and square within its irregular hexagonal walls; his humanistic philosophy attracted many Jewish settlers, who founded a famous printing press in town. To see the interiors of the historic centre, contact the Pro Loco on Via V. Gonzaga 31, tel (0375) 52 039 (open Nov–March 10–12:30 and 2:30–5, and April–Oct 10–12:30 and 3–6:30, closed Mon; adm).

The classical, Utopian vision of Vespasiano was out of fashion before Sabbioneta was even built, and its spark died with its creator, leaving a silent little museum city with a declining population. Around the central Piazza Castello, Vespasiano constructed a lengthy frescoed corridor, the **Galleria degli Antichi** to display his collection of classical statues (now in Mantua's Palazzo Ducale). At one end of the galleria lies the **Palazzo del Giardino**, the prince's pleasure palace, richly adorned with frescoes and stuccoes by the school of Giulio Romano. The next piazza contains the symmetrical **Palazzo Ducale** with its five arches, housing wooden equestrian statues of Vespasiano and his kin; other rooms, with fine frescoes and ceilings, include the **Sala d'Oro**, with its golden ceiling, the **Sala degli Elefanti**, with elephants, and the **Sala delle Città Marinare**, with paintings of port towns. Behind the palace, the 1586 church **dell'Incoronata** houses Vespasiano's mausoleum, with a bronze statue of the prince in classical Roman garb. The last stop on the tour is the small 1588 **Teatro Olimpico**, designed by Vincenzo Scamozzi after Palladio's theatre in Vicenza. Twelve plaster statues of the ancient Olympians grace the balcony and some of the original Venetian frescoes have recently been rediscovered. Also in the centre of town is the 16th-century **Synagogue**, derelict for the past 50 years.

WHERE TO STAY (tel prefix 0376)

Mantua has a small selection of typical hotels, the best of which is the ******Rechigi**, conveniently located in the historic centre at Via Calvi 30, tel 320 781. All rooms have private bath and air-conditioning, comfortable furnishings and parking (L140 000). Another fine choice, ******San Lorenzo**, Piazza Concordia 14, tel 220 500, is housed in a restored late Renaissance building, with all modern comforts, in the centre's pedestrian zone; many rooms have views over the Piazza delle Erbe (L210 000). Another pleasant hotel housed in an older building, *****Due Guerrieri**, overlooks the Piazza Sordello and the Ducal Palace, tel 325 596, with baths in every room; parking nearby (L95 000). Near the station, the *****Albergo Bianchi**, Piazza Don E. Leoni 24, tel 321 504, is recently remodelled and handy for train travellers; rooms without bath L63 000, with bath L95 000.

Mantua has an exceptional youth hostel, the **Ostello Sparafucile**, located just outside the city at Lunetta di San Giorgio, tel 372 465 (to get there, take bus No. 2 or 9 from Piazza Cavallotti). The hostel is in a cinquecento castle, popularly believed to be the headquarters of the baddie in Rigoletto. The interior has been remodelled, without losing any of its character. L14 000 a person a night with breakfast, cheap meals available. Closed Oct 15–March.

A recently inaugurated programme has developed five old country villa-farmhouses as inexpensive accommodation, averaging around L15–20 000 per person per night. One, the **Villa Schiarino-Lena**, is only a few kilometres from Mantua, on the other side of Lago Superiore (tel 398 238); the rooms surrounding a 16th-century agricultural courtyard have been converted to apartments. Another farmhouse, **Corte Baghina** is 6 km from San Benedetto Po, in a setting evocative of the film *1900*, a typical estate of the lower Po. It has only 10 beds, cooking facilities, etc. (tel 558 568). Another, fully functioning farm near the shores of the Mincio, the **Feniletto**, is 13 km from Mantua at Rodigo, in the midst of the Regional Park of the Mincio; boating excursions are possible on the river. Reserve well in advance, as there are only 5 beds (tel 650 262). For more information on stays in traditional buildings in the Mantuan countryside, write to the tourist office.

EATING OUT

During the long reign of the Gonzaga the Mantuans developed their own cuisine, which other Italians regard as a little peculiar. The notorious *stracotto di asino* (donkey stew), heads the list, together with the Mantuan predilection for adding Lambrusco to broth and soup. The classic Mantuan *primi* include *agnoli* stuffed with sausage and cheese in broth, *risotto alla pilota*, with sausage sauce and local grana cheese, or *tortelli di zucca* (little caps stuffed with pumpkin, served with melted butter). The local lake and river fish—deep-fried frogs' legs, catfish, eel, crayfish, pike and bass, are traditional second courses.

Long considered Mantua's finest restaurant, **Il Cigno**, Piazza dell'Arco 1, tel 327 101, does many local specialities in a very elegant setting. The menu changes according to season—when it's cold, the *agnoli* in broth with Lambrusco will take off the chill; the eel in balsamic vinegar is a delicious second course (closed Mon, Tues, and first part of Aug; L60 000 and up). The lovely **Aquila Nigra**, Vicolo Bonacolsi 4, tel 350 651, offers both local dishes, and dishes based on regions, including seafood and risotto with scampi. There's a large selection of Italian and French wines, and delicious desserts like chestnut torte (L55 000; closed Sun, Mon and Aug). **Al Garibaldini**, Via S. Longino 7, tel 328 263, is right in the historic centre of Mantua, in a fine old structure with a shady garden for al fresco dining in the summer. The menu features many Mantuan dishes, with especially good risotto and *tortelli di zucca*, fish, and meat dishes (closed Wed and most of Jan; L50–65 000).

For no atmosphere but delicious Mantuan cooking, try the **Trattoria al Lago**, Piazza Arche 5, tel 323 300, with full meals for L25 000, or the **Due Cavallini**, tel 322 084, Via Salnitro 5 (near Lago Inferiore, off Corso Garibaldi); if you want to bite into some donkey meat, this is the place—but there are other, less piquant dishes as well. (Closed from the first part of July; L28 000.)

In Sabbioneta, the **Ca' d'Amici**, tel (0375) 52 318, is the best restaurant, featuring local and national specialities for around L55 000. For a real treat, however, drive 20 km north to Canneto sull'Oglio (just beyond Piadena), where you can feast at one of Lombardy's finest and most tranquil restaurants, **Dal Pescatore**, Via Runate 13, tel (0376) 70 304, located in an old and elegant country house. The menu and its preparation are authentic and delightful; offerings include tortelli with pumpkin, grilled eel, delectable fish dishes and magnificent desserts and wines. (Closed Mon, Tues, mid-August and first two weeks in Jan; L70–90 000.)

The Italian Lakes

Just to mention the Italian Lakes is to evoke a soft, dreamy image of romance and beauty, a Latin Brigadoon of consumptive gentlemen and gentle ladies strolling through gardens, sketching landscapes, and perhaps indulging in a round of whist on the villa veranda in the evening. Gracing their fond pleasures are scenes woven of poetry, of snow-capped peaks tumbling steeply into ribbons of blue, trimmed with the silver tinsel of olives and the daggers of dark cypress; of mellow villas gracing vine-clad hillsides and gold-flecked citrus groves; of spring's excess, when the lakes become drunken with colour, as a thousand varieties of azaleas, rhododendrons, and camellias spill over the banks. For even though the Swiss border is just around the corner, the three largest lakes—Maggiore, Como and Garda—cover a large enough area to create their own climatic oases of Mediterranean flora, blooming even at the foot of the star-lit Alps.

Lake holidays faded from fashion in the post-War era, when a suntan became a symbol of leisure instead of manual labour and summer's mass trek to the seashore became a ritual as necessary as the annual exodus of lemmings. But the lakes are simply too lovely to stay out of fashion for long, and now a new generation is busily rediscovering what their grandparents took for granted, polishing up the old Belle Epoque fixtures of the villas and grand hotels. For better or worse, the Italians have ringed the lakes with finely engineered roads, making them perhaps too accessible, whereas before, visitors had to make do with small boats or leisurely steamers. Prices have risen with demand, and between July and September rest and relaxation, or even peace and quiet, may seem a Victorian relic, unless you book in at one of the grander villa hotels. Quiet havens, however, still exist on the smaller, less developed lakes of Iseo and Orta, on the east shores of Lakes Maggiore and Como, and in the mountain valleys to the north of the lakes, around Domodossola and in the beautiful Valtellina.

Lake resorts generally stay open between April and October. The best times to visit are in spring and autumn, not only because there are fewer crowds, but because the lakes themselves are less subjected to winter mists and summer haze. In the restaurants, look for, obviously, lake fish and trout, served either fresh or sun-dried. The finest wines from the Lake District come from Bardolino on the east shore of Lake Garda, or the reds from the Valtellina, or the vintages from Franciacorte near Lake Iseo or La Brianza near Lake Como.

Below, the lakes are described geographically from west to east, from Piedmont's Lake Orta and the valleys around Domodossola, through Lombardy's lakes and the Valtellina, through the art cities, Bergamo and Brescia, then to Lake Garda on the border of the Veneto.

Lake Orta

Westernmost of the Italian Lakes, Orta (the Roman *Lacus Cusius*) is neither a contender for the largest, stretching a mere 13 km at its longest point, nor the most majestic—its mountains aren't as high, nor are its villas as opulent as some of its neighbours. But what Orta does have is an exceptional dose of charm; a lake 'made to the measurements of man', that can be encompassed by a glance, surrounded by hills made soft with greenery,

216

a haven from the worst excesses of international tourism that sometimes scar the major lakes. Nietzsche, who never fell in love, did so on its shores, and although it seems he didn't get the girl, the rest of the world got *Thus Spake Zarathustra*. The green waters of Lake Orta run still and quiet, and in the centre they hold a magical isle, illuminated on summer nights to hang like a golden fairy castle in the dark. On a more mundane level, the villages around the lake produce most of Italy's kitchen and bathroom taps, and some of its finest chefs; so many come from Armeno that in November it holds an annual reunion of cooks and waiters.

GETTING AROUND
The main resorts on Lake Orta, Orta San Giulio and Omegna are easily reached from Turin or Milan on trains heading north to Domodossola and the Simplon Pass. There are frequent buses from Orta to Arona on Lake Maggiore, and from Omegna to Verbania. On the lake itself, Navigazione Lago d'Orta provides service between the ports of Oria, Omegna, Punta di Crabbia, Pettenasco, L'Approdo, Orta, Isola S. Giulio, Pella, S. Filiberto, and Lagna—at least twice a day, if not more often. The company also offers a midnight cruise from Orta, Pella, and Pettenasco on Sat and Sun in July and Aug.

TOURIST INFORMATION
Orta San Giulio: Via Olina 9/11, tel (0322) 90 355

The east bank of Lake Orta is dominated by the district's highest peak, the 1491 m **Mottarone**; under its shadow, on its own little garden peninsula, is the lake's charming main village, **Orta San Giulio**. Life in Orta is centred in its sombrely handsome main square, dominated by the little 1582 **Palazzotto** of faded frescoes, where art exhibitions are frequently held. Among the villas in town, look for **Villa Crespi**, done in the Alhambra style. Orta San Giulio also has its own acropolis, **Sacro Monte**; its 20 chapels, built between the 1590s and the 1770s, contain yet more 3-D Piedmontese art, this time frescoes and terracotta statues by different artists relating to the life of Italy's patron saint, St Francis. A path from the village follows the lake for about a kilometre.

According to legend, **Isola San Giulio**, the pretty islet facing the Orta, was once inhabited by loathsome serpents and monsters. In the year 390 Julius, a Christian preacher from Greece, showed up on the shores of Orta and asked to be rowed to the island. The local fishermen, fearing that he would anger the dragons, refused; Julius, undeterred, spread his cloak on the waters and floated across. He sent the dragons packing and built the precursor to the island's **Basilica**, by yoking a team of wolves to his cart—a feat good enough to make him the patron saint of builders. Most of what you see today dates from around the 12th century, including the giant eagle, griffons, and serpents carved on the black marble pulpit. There are some good 15th-century frescoes by Gaudenzio Ferrari and his school, and a marble sarcophagus with ancient carvings, believed to have belonged to the Lombard Duke Meinulphus, who had betrayed the island to the Franks and was beheaded by King Agilulf; and indeed a decapitated skeleton was found inside in 1697. Pride of place, however, goes to the big vertebrae displayed in the sacristy, belonging to one of the dragons Julius dismissed from the island.

Just above Orta town is the village of **Ameno**, site of a museum of contemporary art, the **Fondazione Calderara**, founded by painter Antonio Calderara in a 16th-century

217

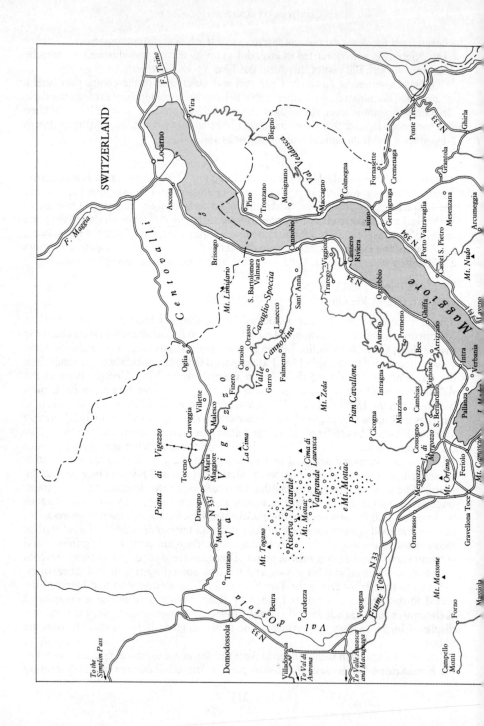

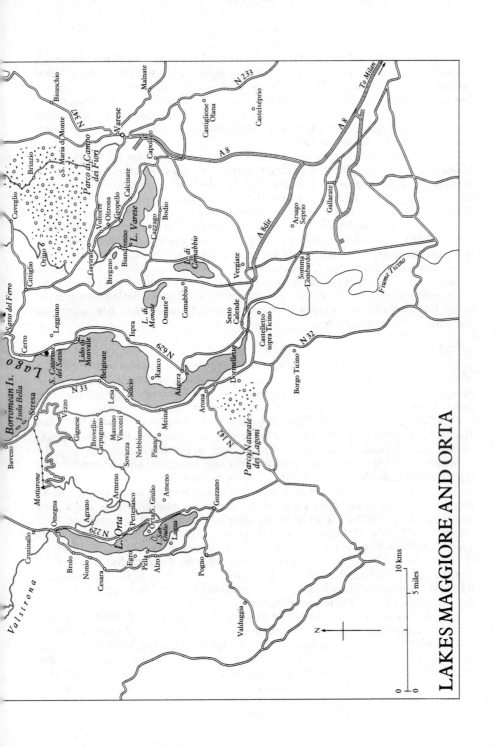

LAKES MAGGIORE AND ORTA

villa. Calderara collected paintings and sculptures by 133 artists from all over the world, but some of his own contributions are the most memorable—still-life landscapes that capture the spirit of the lake better than any photograph. The south point of Orta, by **Gozzano**, is overlooked by the **Torre di Buccione**, first built in the 4th century and rebuilt by the Lombards in the Dark Ages; in times of trouble its bells were loud enough to warn all the communities on the lake. **Villa Junker**, near Gozzano, has the finest garden on the lake, despite its name.

Round on the west shore, a majestic rocky outcrop supports the **Santuario della Madonna del Sasso**, which isn't as impressive as the rocks, but affords a grand view over the lake and the villages of Pella and Alzo near the shore. On the northern tip of the lake, the main town and port is **Omegna** (Roman *Vomenia*), where you can stand in the Piazza del Municipio and look for the famous contrary river, the Nigoglia, the only one in Italy to flow *towards* the Alps. From Omegna a road curls up in ringlets through chestnut forests to **Quarna**, divided into Sotto and Sopra (lower and upper). Quarna Sotta has been manufacturing musical instruments for over 150 years, and has a small museum devoted to them; Quarna Sopra has spectacular views over Lake Orta. A second valley radiating from Omegna, the **Valstrona** is less intensely spectacular, but **Forno** is a fine sleepy little place where dogs can sleep in the middle of the street; the last hamlet in the valley, **Campello Monti**, is another kind of Sunday afternoon destination, where you can walk off too many tortellini.

WHERE TO STAY AND EATING OUT

Watch out for *tapulon*—minced donkey stewed in red wine. Local wines worth trying that offer their kicks without the donkey include *Barengo Bianco* or *Greco*, both whites, and *Faro DOC, Gattinara* and *Caramino*, all three reds. Besides hotels, Orta has ten camp sites—Verde Lago and Riviera, both in Pettenasco, are among the nicest.

Orta San Giulio (tel prefix 0322): Orta has the most hotels, beginning with *******San Rocco**, Via Gippini 11, tel 905 632, the lake's most luxurious hotel, located in a former 17th-century monastery with a comely garden right on the water, tennis courts, and a swimming-pool. All rooms have private baths and balconies, and air-conditioning (L210–240 000, meals around L45 000). A pleasant, moderate choice, *****La Bussola**, tel 90 198, enjoys a magnificent panorama of the lake, set back on a quiet hill; its 16 rooms all have bath, and there's a pretty garden with a swimming-pool and a good restaurant (L90–100 000). Two charming older hotels in Orta have restaurants built directly over the lake: *****Leon d'Oro**, in the centre, tel 90 254, with parking and its own beach (L75 000 with bath) and *****Orta**, tel 90 253, a pretty white villa set amid the trees (L75–90 000 with bath). In the centre, ***Antica Agnello**, Piazzetta Regazzoni, tel 90 259, is a simple little inn, also with a good restaurant downstairs (L37 000, without bath). The best restaurant is **Sacro Monte**, Via Sacro Monte 5, tel 90 220, which has delicious food and wine with the Piedmontese touch; closed Tues (L45 000).

Just inland from Orta, at Miasino, ****Albergo Bellavista** tel (0322) 980 053 occupies a slightly faded Neoclassical villa, in a pretty flower-filled garden (all rooms with bath, L50–60 000). At nearby Pettenasco, the *****Hotel Giardinetto**, Via Provinciale, tel (0323) 89 118, is also right on Lake Orta, with beautiful views of the islet of San Giulio. Open April–Oct, it is a friendly, family-run hotel that offers reduced rates for children; there's a swimming-pool, private beach, and water sports facilities, and an excellent restaurant, serving seafood dishes steeped in champagne, as well as kidneys in cognac and chateaubriand. All rooms have private bath or shower (L75–90 000, with breakfast; meals L40 000). Above Pella, at Madonna del Sasso Boleto, *Panoramico, tel (0322) 981 109, is a tidy and new little hotel with only 7 rooms and views over the lake (L60 000, with bath). In Omegna, the *Vittoria, tel (0323) 62 237, is the pick of the *locande*, offering rooms for L35 000 without bath, L40 000 with. At Quarna Sopra, high above Omegna, **Belvedere, tel (0323) 826 197, lives up to its name, with its enchanting views over the lake far below; doubles only, all with bath L50 000. At Forno in the Valstrona, the little yellow *Leone, tel (0323) 85 112, is a well-run inn in the middle of the village, with a restaurant downstairs (L88 000).

From Lake Orta to Domodossola: the Ossola Valleys

Unspoiled, and mostly unnoticed by visitors plunging down the motorway to more Mediterranean delights, the Ossola valleys cut deep into the Alps, following the course of the river Toce and its tributaries on their way to Lake Orta. Napoleon drove the first road through here, from Milan to the Simplon Pass, but even the improved communications couldn't help the Fascists and Nazis when the inhabitants booted them out and formed an independent republic that lasted 40 days. Nowadays the valleys are visited for their forests, rustic hospitality, and Alpine lakelets so blue they hurt.

GETTING AROUND
A small railroad, the Vigezzina, makes the trip along the Val Vigezzo, between Domodossola and Locarno (Switzerland) while the other mountain valleys are served regularly by bus from Domodossola.

TOURIST INFORMATION
Domodossola: Via Romita 13, tel (0324) 481 308
Macugnaga: Piazza Municipio, tel (0324) 65 119
Bognanco Fonti: Piazzale Giannini 5, tel (0324) 34 127
Santa Maria Maggiore: Piazza Risorgimento 10, tel (0324) 9091

From Omegna to Domodossola

North of Omegna the main road heads north towards **Gravellona Toce**, an important crossroads in the shadow of the mighty granite dome of Mt Orfano, which the locals are slowly whittling away to make flowerpots. Mt Orfano in its turn guards an orphan lake, **Lago Mergozzo**, which formed an arm of Lake Maggiore until the 9th century, when sediment from the Toce plugged it, a loss perhaps in prestige compensated by the fact that Mergozzo is now much cleaner than its larger neighbour.

The main town on the lake, also called **Mergozzo**, lost most of its importance as a transit centre with the construction of the Simplon road. Its main attraction is the 12th-century church of **San Giovanni**, made of Orfano granite; the small **Antiquarium of Mont'Orfano** contains local pre-Roman and Roman artefacts. The next town up the valley, **Candoglia**, is the site of the quarry which for the past six centuries has been worked for the marble to build the Duomo in Milan.

221

The first valley splitting off to the west, the enchanting **Valle Anzasca** leads straight towards the steep east face of Monte Rosa (buses from Domodossola or from the station at Piedimulera at the foot of the valley). A number of attractive little villages lie scattered among the woods and vineyards—tiny **Colombetti**, its slate roofs huddled under a lofty cliff; **Bannio-Anzino**, the 'capital' of the valley, across and above the river Anza, with modest ski facilities and a 3.5-m high, 16th-century bronze Christ in its parish church, brought here from Flanders. **Ceppo Morelli** has a famous, vertiginous bridge over the Anza, which traditionally divides the valley's Latin population from the Walser. Beyond Ceppo the road plunges through a gorge to the old mining town of **Pestarena**, mining in this case meaning gold; the upper Valle Anzasca has Italy's largest gold deposits, extracted in galleries stretching 40 km.

The various hamlets that comprise **Macugnaga**, the Valle Anzasca's popular resort, lie under the majestic frowning face of **Monte Rosa** (4638 m). As in the Valle d'Aosta's Val Gressoney on the southern side of Monte Rosa, Macugnaga was settled by German-speaking Swiss from the Valais (the Walser) in the 13th century. A small museum in **Staffa**, the chief village of Macugnaga, is devoted to Walser folklore, while other old Swiss traces remain in the parish church, built in the 13th century. Macugnaga has a number of ski lifts, and a chair lift that operates in the summer as well, to the magnificent **Belvedere** with views over the Macugnaga glacier; a cableway from Staffa to the **Passo Monte Moro** (2868 m) is used by skiers in both the winter and summer seasons.

From Macugnaga, fearless alpinists can attempt the steep east flank of Monte Rosa, one of the most dangerous ascents in the Alps; walkers can make a three-day trek over the mountains to Gressoney-St-Jean and other points in the Valle d'Aosta (trail map essential).

To the north, the much less visited **Val d'Antrona** is a pretty wooded valley famed for its trout fishing. The valley begins at **Villadossola**, from where you can catch a bus to the chief village **Antronapiana**, a pleasant place lost in the trees, near the lovely lakelet Antrona, created by an avalanche in 1642. The north branch of the valley winds up and to **Cheggio**, a wee resort with refuges, restaurants, and another lake.

Domodossola

The largest town in the Valley of the River Toce, or Valle d'Ossola, Domodossola was a Roman settlement, perhaps best known in Italy as the largest town in the Republic beginning with the letter D, and for its location at the foot of the **Simplon Pass** (*Passo del Sempione*), through which Napoleon constructed his highway from Geneva to Lombardy after the Battle of Marengo; it was completed in 1805. Exactly 100 years later the even more remarkable Simplon Tunnel was completed—the longest in the world (19.8 kilometres).

Domodossola is a pleasant old town with an arcaded market square, and the **Museo Galletti**, with incorporates a medieval church and has something for every taste: natural history, paintings, Roman finds from the 3rd-century AD necropolis at Gurro, in the Val Cannobina; exhibits relating to the construction of the Simplon tunnel and the flight of the Peruvian Georges Chavez, the first man to fly over the Alps (29 September 1910), only to die in a crash near Domodossola. You can also find a monument to him in Piazza Liberazione.

The road and railway line between Domodossola and Locarno (the largest Swiss town on Lake Maggiore) pass through the extraordinary **Val Vigezzo**, a romantic beauty of woodlands and velvet pastures that has attracted and produced so many artists through the years to earn the name, the 'Valley of Painters'; it also claims to have given birth to the 18th-century formulators of the first *acqua di colonia*, or cologne. If the valley's silvan charms tempt you to linger, stay in the main town, **Santa Maria Maggiore**; its **Scuola di belle arti**, where you can see some of the paintings that gave the valley its sobriquet, or perhaps take in the odd little **Museo dello Spazzocamino** (a *chimneysweep* museum; we couldn't find it, but maybe you can). In Re the **Santuario della Madonna del Sangue** has a charming collection of naif ex votos. From nearby Malesco a road descends the Val Cannobina to Cannobio on Lake Maggiore (see below).

Buses from Domodossola also plunge north towards the San Giacomo Pass, through the spectacular scenery of the **Valli Antigorio e Formazza**, colonized in the 13th century by German families from the Valais. Their charming, scattered villages are planted with vines and figs, and offer bases for excursions to some genuinely obscure little Alpine lakes. The valley's spa, **Crodo**, is famous in Italy for bottling a ludicrously chipper soft drink called Crodino, as well as iron-laced mineral water; further north, **Baceno**'s parish church, **San Gaudenzio** (11th–16th century) is the finest church of the Ossola valleys and a national monument to boot; it has a fine front portal with sirens and a cartwheel window, and 16th-century Swiss stained-glass and carved wooden altarpiece. In **Premia**, along the Toce, you can visit the steep gorges sliced by the river over the millennia. The bus from Domodossola terminates at **Ponte** (with a chair lift), but one of the most breathtaking waterfalls in all the Alps is 6 km up the road: the **Cascata della Frua** (or del Toce) but like all of Italy's best waterfalls it is almost always dry, diverted for hydroelectric power. However, if you come between August 10 and 20, or between 9 and 5 on a Sunday or holiday from June until September, you can be overwhelmed by a thundering 300-m veil of mist, plummeting down a series of terraces.

WHERE TO STAY AND EATING OUT (tel prefix 0324)

Specialities in the valleys include gnocchi filled with pumpkin and chestnuts and *vivlin* (herbed kid). Most of the Valle Anzasca's accommodation is clustered in Macugnaga. The ****Nuova Pecetto**, in the hamlet of Pecetto, tel 65 025, is one of the most charming, a tiny, traditional hotel with a garden and fine views of Monte Rosa. Closed mid-Sept–Nov; all rooms with bath; L60–75 000. In Staffa, the largest and most luxurious choice, *****Zumstein**, tel 65 118, has attractive rooms in a pretty location; open mid-Dec–April and mid-June–mid-Sept; L70 000 without bath, L90 000 with. Also in Staffa, ***Chez Felice**, tel 65 229, is a little mountain villa which has simple but charming rooms with bath (L65 000) and the best restaurant in the valley, a lively haven of mountain *nuova cucina*, serving salmon mousse with herbs, warm artichokes with a sauce of anchovies and capers, delicious soups, risotto with almonds, cheese and herb soufflé and more; for afters, there's a magnificent array of local cheeses and exquisite desserts. (Closed Thurs, and reserve if you're not staying at the hotel; L40 000.)

In Domodossola the nicest hotel *****Europa**, tel 481 032, is above the town in the suburb of Calice, 4 km away; fine views and garden, and rooms all with private bath and toilet, L90 000. In town, try the ****Piccolo Hotel**, tel 42 351, with comfortable rooms for L60 000 without bath, L80 000 with. At Santa Maria Maggiore, ****La Jazza**, tel 94 471, is a pleasant hotel with a garden, open all year with prices suited to struggling artists; L40–55 000 without bath, L55–60 000 with. In Formazza San Michele, **San Michele, tel 63 014, is a fine tranquil, moderate-sized hotel outside the centre at Prestinone; open all year; L45–58 000 without bath, L50–60 000 with.

Lake Maggiore

Have you not read in books how men when they
see even divine visions are terrified? So as
I looked at Lake Major in its halo I also was
afraid...

Hilaire Belloc, The Path to Rome

Italy's second-largest lake after Garda, Lago Maggiore, winds majestically between Piedmont and Lombardy, its northern corner lost in the towering, snow-capped Swiss Alps. Chiselled out of the mountains in the Ice Age, the climate improved enough by Roman times to be called *Lacus Verbanus*, for the verbena that still grows luxuriantly on its shores, accompanied in the spring by a drunken profusion of camellias and azaleas. But what really sets the lake apart are its jewel-like islands, which for many people make it the best lake to visit if there's only time for one. These, the fabled Borromean isles, still belong to the Borromeo family of Milan, who also possess the fishing rights over the entire lake—as they have done since the 1500s.

The western shore of the lake, especially in the triad of resorts Stresa, Baveno, and Verbania, are the most scenic places to aim for, with the best and most varied accommodation. Unless you reserve well in advance, however, you may want to avoid July and August.

GETTING AROUND

From Milan's central station, trains to Domodossola stop at Arona and Stresa; from Milan's Porta Garibaldi Station trains go to Luino on the east shore. A third option is the Nord-Milan railway which passes by way of Varese to Laveno. Trains from Turin and Novara go to Arona and Stresa; from Lake Orta there are buses from Omegna to Verbania every 20 minutes. Other buses connect the lakes from Stresa and Arona station.

Navigazione Lago Maggiore runs steamers to all corners of the lake, with the most frequent services in the central lake area, between Stresa, Baveno, Verbania, Pallanza, and Laveno; hydrofoils buzz between Arona and Locarno (in Switzerland). Frequent service by steamer or hydrofoil from Stresa will take you out to the Borromean Isles—a ticket for the furthest, Isola Madre, entitles you to visit all. Car ferries run between Intra and Laveno. Pick up a boat schedule at one of the tourist offices, or from the company's headquarters at Viale F. Baracca 1, in Arona. On Thurs evenings in the summer the tourist office sponsors reasonably-priced night cruises with musical serenades departing from Arona, Stresa, Baveno, and Verbania-Pallanza.

TOURIST INFORMATION

Arona: Piazzale Stazione, tel (0322) 243 601
Stresa: Via Principe Tomaso 70, tel (0323) 30 150

Arona, and the World's Biggest Saint

Arona is the southernmost steamer landing and the most interesting town in the southern reaches of Lake Maggiore. Even if you're just passing through it is hard to avoid **San Carlone**, a copper colossus towering 23 m (35 m with his pedestal) above the old town, spreading a hand in blessing. San Carlone (St Big Chuck) is perhaps better known as Charles Borromeo (1538–84), born in the now ruined **Castle of Arona**; the statue, paid for by a family member, was designed by Il Cerano and cast by Bernardo Falcone in 1697.

Charles Borromeo was the most influential churchman of his day, appointed 'Cardinal Nephew and Archbishop of Milan' at the age of 22 by his maternal uncle, Pope Pius IV. In Rome he was a powerful voice calling for disciplinary reforms within the Church and an instigator of the Council of Trent, in which he played a major role. There was one legendary point in the Council when the cardinals were ready to ban all church music, which by the 16th century had degenerated to the point of singing lewd love ballads to the *Te Deum*. Charles and his committee, however, decided to let the musicians have one more go, and gave Palestrina a chance to compose a mass that reflected the dignity of the words of the service (and Charles reputedly told the composer that the cardinals expected him to fail). But to their surprise, and to the everlasting benefit of Western culture, Palestrina succeeded, and sacred music was saved.

After the death of his uncle-Pope, Charles went to live in his diocese of Milan, the first archbishop to do so in 80 years. Following the mandate of the Council of Trent to the letter, he at once began reforming the cosy clergy to set the example for other bishops. In Milan he was so hated that he narrowly escaped an assassination attempt (the bullet bounced off his heavy brocade vestments). He was a bitter enemy of original thought and not someone you would want to have over for dinner, but for a queer sensation, walk up the steps in his statue and enjoy a colossal view of Lake Maggiore through his eye sockets and ear holes. The Borromeo family's chapel in **Santa Maria**, also in the upper part of town, contains a lovely 1511 polyptych by Gaudenzio Ferrari.

More Borromeana awaits at **Angera**, across the lake in Lombardy and the first steamer call. Angera has a fascinating,well-preserved castle, the **Rocca di Angera**. The original owner, Ottone Visconti, had it frescoed in the 14th century, with battle scenes from his family's victory over the Della Torre family, still to be seen in all their medieval splendour in the Sala degli Affreschi. The Borromei picked it up in 1439, and have lately added some detached frescoes from their palace in Milan (open April–Oct 9:30–12 and 2–5).

From Arona to Stresa

From Arona the state road for the Simplon Pass hugs the lake shore, through **Meina**, the medieval **Màdina**. Màdina was owned by the Benedictines of Pavia, and latter came under the rule of Milan's Visconti and Borromeo families; from the 18th century, when it first became fashionable, it still has a sprinkling of Neoclassical villas. Meina is the base for visiting **Ghevio** and **Silvera**, little villages immersed in the green of hills of Colle Vergante. Further up the west shore lies **Belgirate**, with its Gothic church of Santa Marta and Villa Carlotta, a favourite retreat of Italy's 19th-century intellectuals, now a hotel.

Beautifully positioned between the lake and Monte Mottarone lies the 'Pearl of Verbano', **Stresa**. A holiday resort since the last century, famous for its lush gardens and mild climate, it soared in popularity after the construction of the Simplon Tunnel in 1906; Hemingway used its Grand Hotel des Iles Borromées as Frederick Henry's refuge from war in *A Farewell to Arms*. The town is also a favourite of international congresses, and from the last week of August through September sponsors a highly acclaimed series of music weeks, *Settimane Musicale di Stresa*, featuring orchestras from around the world. Among the villas and gardens, the star attraction is the Villa Pallavicino and its colourful gardens, where saucy parrots rule the roost, along with a small collection of other animals.

While Stresa itself is lovely, bursting with flowers and sprinkled with fine old villas, it serves primarily as a base for visiting the isles and **Monte Mottarone** (1491 m), via the cableway beginning on Stresa Lido. The views are famous, taking in a vision of glacier-crested Alpine peaks, stretching all the way from Monte Viso (far west) and Monte Rosa over to the eastern ranges of Ortler and Adamello by Lake Garda, as well as the Lombard plain and the miniature islands below. Stresa's golf course is on the slopes of Monte Mottarone, at **Vezzo** (9 holes); both it and **Gignese**, site of a curious little **Umbrella Museum** (with models from 1840 to 1940; mornings, April-Sept), can be reached from Stresa by bus.

The Borromean Islands

Rare and probably myopic is the visitor to Lake Maggiore who can resist a trip to at least one of these lush beauties, dotting the mouth of the wide bay of Pallanzo. Actually, the three Borromean Islands do not include the **Isola dei Pescatori** in the middle, with its almost too quaint and utterly picturesque fishing village, but a private islet called

The Amphitheatre, Isola Bella, Lake Maggiore

226

San Giovanni, just off the shore at Pallanza, with a villa once owned by Toscanini. Although Stresa has the most boats to the islands (you can even rent a rowing boat in town to avoid the crowds), there are also frequent excursions from Baveno and Pallanza. The closest island to Stresa, Isola Bella, is also the most celebrated. It was a barren rock until the 17th century, when Count Carlo III Borromeo decided to make it a garden for his wife, Isabella (hence the name of the islet), hiring the architect Angelo Crivelli to plan its impressive series of 10 terraces and formal arrangements. Later 17th-century Borromei added the palace and 'artificial grottoes,' finished the gardens, endowing them with statuary, fountains, and perhaps the first of its famous white peacocks. The only problem is that the 17th century was not an auspicious time for doing much of anything, especially art, and on Isola Bella sighs of raptures over the splendour of the views and gardens intermingle with groans of disbelief at the 'art'. The conducted palace tour goes down best after a few drinks (open March–Oct 9–12 and 1:30–5:30; adm expensive).

The delightful, larger Isola Madre stands in interesting contrast to Isola Bella, planted with a colourful and luxuriant botanical garden, dominated by a giant Kashmir cypress. On its best days few places are more conducive to a state of perfect languor, at least until one of the isle's bold pheasants tries to stare you out. Like Isola Bella, Mother Island has its palace, though smaller and more refined, with an interesting collection of Borromean family portraits, and the family's 18th-century marionette theatre, antique dolls, and puppets (same hours as Isola Bella; adm expensive).

WHERE TO STAY

Easter and July to mid-September are the high season on Lake Maggiore, when you should definitely reserve. In Arona, there are two good choices: the modern ***Giardino, Corso della Repubblica 1, tel (0322) 242 401, a largish hotel in a pretty setting (L80–130 000) or **Becco Fino del Lago, outside of Arona in Fornaci, Via Sempione 18, tel (0322) 243 364, with only 8 rooms but a nice little beach (L50 000 without bath, L65 000 with).

Meina: You can have the lake on both sides at the modern ***Paradiso, Strada del Sempione, tel (0322) 64 88, located amid the trees on a mere slip of a peninsula: 38 rooms, ranging from L60–90 000. More economically, but still right on the lake, the **Verbano, Strada del Sempione, tel (0322) 62 29 is jovial, pink, and friendly, and most of the rooms look out over Maggiore (L50 000 without bath, L60 000 with).

Belgirate: ****Villa Carlotta, Strada del Sempione, tel (0322) 76 461, is a saffron-coloured Belle Epoque gem, isolated between the lake and the rugged wooded hills; it has a beach, pool, and elegant rooms, many with an old-fashioned charm, ranging from L110–150 000 without bath, L150–195 000 with.

Stresa (tel prefix 0323): Opened in 1863, *****Des Iles Borromées, tel 30 431, has recently been smartened up by its new CIGA owners to become opulent both in its aristocratic Belle Epoque furnishings and modern conveniences. Overlooking the lake, the islands, and a lovely flower-decked, palm-shaded garden, the hotel has a pool, beach, tennis, and the Centro Benessere ('well-being') where doctors are on hand to give you a check-up, exercises, and improve your diet. The magnificent rooms all have sumptuous private baths and frigo-bars (open all year; L200–420 000). Some 40 years younger than the former, the creamy white ****Regina Palace, Lungolago Umberto I, tel 30 171, is a lovely, bow-shaped palace with Liberty-style touches, tranquil in its large park.

It has a heated swimming-pool, tennis, beach, and splendid views (open April–Oct; L170–250 000). At Stresa Lido, enjoying the most ravishing view of the islands, is the modern ****Villa Aminta, on the Sempione road, tel 32 444. In addition to its comfortable rooms, nearly all with terraces, there's a beach, pool, and tennis, and its good restaurant serves excellent lake fish and dishes from nearly every region in Italy (open mid–March to Oct, L135–180 000).

Among the more reasonably priced hotels, there's the atmospheric ***Hotel du Parc, Via Gignous 1, tel 30 335, a pretty villa set in the lofty pines (L50–65 000 without bath, or L60–90 000 with). The ***Primavera, Via Cavour 39, tel 31 191, is a friendly hotel with a touch of style, pretty balconies, but no restaurant. Open all year, doubles with bath are 50–80 000. The **Italia et Suisse, Piazza Marconi 1, tel 30 540, is near the lake and the steamer landing (open all year; doubles L50–60 000 without bath, L75–90 000 with). A bargain, the little *Paradiso, Via R. Sanzio 7, tel (0323) 30 470, has nice quiet rooms just above Stresa, L36 000, without bath. Up in Gignese, the *Vittoria, tel 20 106, is a pleasant, older hotel with a garden (L40 000 without bath, L50 000 with).

On the Isola dei Pescatori, the ***Verbano, tel 30 408, is a lovely, quiet little hotel on the lake, which offers the chance to see the picturesque island after the hordes return to the mainland; good restaurant (room with bath, L90 000). A less expensive choice on Isola dei Pescatori, *Belvedere, tel 30 047, has doubles for L40 000 without bath, L50 000 with. There's also a little 9-room hotel on Isola Bella, which quietens down completely after dark: the *Elvezia, Lungolago Vitt. Emanuele 18, tel 30 043; L40 000 for a simple room without bath.

EATING OUT

Not surprisingly, Lake Maggiore's most traditional dishes come from the water: *risotto alla tinca* (with tench); pike in a piquant sauce, marinated whitefish; also the unexpected *mortadella di fegato* (liver salami).

In Arona, ring ahead to reserve a delicious fixed price menu at Vecchia Arona, on the lake at Lungolago Marconi 17, tel (0322) 24 2469; the kitchen begins with the best and freshest ingredients to concoct delicacies like smoked goose, salmon tartare, pasta with seafood, and one of the best chocolate truffles (*tartufo*) in Italy. Closed Fri and part of June and Dec: L45 000. Just a notch higher in the *haute cuisine* category, Arona's Taverna del Pittore, Piazza del Popolo 39, tel (0322) 24 33 66, was founded by an artist who likes to cook as well as paint; its current owners concentrate, to good advantage, on producing memorable daily specials of exceptional quality. (Reservations suggested; L75–90 000; closed Mon.)

Another fine place to eat is just north of Angera, in the pretty village of Ranco: Del Sole, Piazza Venezia 5, tel (0331) 97 66 20, is the finest restaurant on the lake, in a lovely old inn with a charming terrace for outdoor dining in the summer. The exquisitely and imaginatively prepared lake fish and crayfish are worth the journey; magnificent wine lists and delicate desserts. (Closed Mon eve, Tues & Jan; L80–100 000).

Stresa's gourmet haven, Emiliano, is on the lakefront at Corso Italia 52, tel 31 396, and offers *la nuova cucina* with a Bolognese touch, with delicious seafood dishes, a beef and lobster 'mosaic', calves' liver in balsamic vinegar; excellent desserts and a superb wine list. The grand *menu degustazione* is L90 000; others are less (closed Tues, part of

Dec & Jan). **Le Chandelle**, Via Sempione 23, tel 30 097, offers a mixed Italian-French menu in an elegant atmosphere; fondues, escargot, French onion soup, and curried shrimp are only some of the choices on the menu (L50 000; closed Mon & Jan).

Beyond Stresa

TOURIST INFORMATION
Baveno: Corso Garibaldi 16, tel (0323) 924 632
Verbania: Corso Zanitello 8, tel (0323) 503 249

Baveno, Verbania, and the Villa Taranto Gardens

Baveno is Stresa's quieter sister, connected by a beautiful, villa-lined road. Known for its quarries of pink stone, it has been a fashionable international resort ever since 1879, when Queen Victoria spent a summer at the Villa Clara, now Castello Branca. In the centre of Baveno, the church of **SS. Gervasio e Protasio**, founded in the 11th century, has retained its original plain square façade, though the frescoes inside are workaday Renaissance. Next to the church stands a charming, little octagonal baptistry founded in the 5th century. A pretty road leads up **Monte Camoscio**, behind Baveno, while the main shore road carries on to **Pallanza**, with a famous mild winter climate. Along with Suna and Intra, Pallanza was united in 1939 to form **Verbania**, although each of the towns retains its own identity. Pallanza has several manmade attractions: the pretty Renaissance **Madonna di Campagna** church, inspired by Bramante, with a curious gazebo-like arcaded drum and a Romanesque campanile, and the 16th-century Palazzo Dugnani, site of the **Museo del Paesaggio**, with Renaissance frescoes and local archaeological finds.

The glory of greater Verbania is the **Villa Taranto**, built on the Castagnola promontory between Intra and Pallanza by a certain count Orsetti in 1875. In 1931, the derelict villa was purchased by a Scots Captain, Neil McEacharn, who had one of the world's greenest thumbs and pockets deep enough to afford to import exotic plants from the tropics to the tune of some 20,000 varieties, planted over 20 hectares. The aquatic plants, including giant Amazonian water-lilies and lotus blossoms, the tulips (end of April–first week of May) and autumn colour are exceptional, as are some of the more rare species—the handkerchief tree, bottle brush, and copper-coloured Japanese maple. The villa is used by the prime minister for special conferences (open April–Oct, 8:30–sunset; adm expensive).

Intra, Verbania's industrial and business quarter, has a large market each Saturday and a ferryboat across to Laveno. From here, buses wind up to the Intrasca valley, past quiet, woodsy holiday towns like **Arizzano, Bèe**, and most impor..ntly **Premeno**, a mountain resort overlooking Maggiore, with skiing in the winter and a beautiful 9-hole golf course. In 1950, some 4th-century AD Roman tombs were discovered in Premeno's **Oratorio di S. Salvatore**. The road continues up to the mountain refuge of Pian Cavallo, then across to **Aurano**, a lovely base for walks in the woods and pastures, and two fine belvederes: **Intragna**, from where you can see almost all of Lake Maggiore and **Miazzina**, an old stone village known as the Balcony of Lake Maggiore.

Back on the lake, north of Intra, **Ghiffa** is a pretty, rural place, with a waterside

229

promenade and in its suburb of Ronco, the **Trinità Sanctuary**, another 17th-century Piedmontese series of chapels. **Cannero Riviera**, further up the shore, is a quiet resort set amidst glossy green citrus groves and facing three tiny islets, formerly haunted by the five brothers Mazzarditi, medieval *banditti* defeated in 1414 by the Visconti. On the largest islet, a ruined castle surges straight out of the water; though once the Mazzarditi stronghold, in the twilight it could easily pass for a lost isle of Avalon.

Cannobio, the last stop before Switzerland, is an ancient market town, one that, though in Piedmont, is famous for adhering to the Milanese Ambrosian Rite, itself revived by Cardinal Charles Borromeo in an effort to promote local pride. It has a fine Bramante-inspired **Santuario della Pietà**, with an altarpiece by Gaudenzio Ferrari.

Cannobio lies at the foot of the sparsely populated and seldom visited **Val Cannobina**, which rises up to meet the Val Vigezzo and Domodossola. Just a few km in from Cannobio, you can hire a boat to visit the dramatic **Orrido di Sant'Anna**, a deep, narrow gorge carved by the Cannobio river and waterfall. Further up the valley lies a cluster of wee hamlets of stone houses, known collectively as **Cavaglio Spoccia**, where you can follow the valley's first road, the 'Via Borromeo', and its old mossy bridges. **Falmenta,** a tiny village on the other side of the valley, has, among its quaint black houses, a 1565 parish church with a rare wooden altarpiece, crowded with small figures, from the 1300s. The next village, **Gurro**, has retained its medieval centre and keeps alive its folk traditions, with a little museum of local customs and products. Tiny **Cursolo-Orasso**, further up, has the valley's only hotel. Orasso has a 13th-century **Visitazione** church, and another finely carved wooden altarpiece in the 15th-century parish church, **San Materno**. Buses continue to Malesco, in the Val Vigezzo.

WHERE TO STAY AND EATING OUT

Baveno (tel prefix 0323): The *Grande Dame* here is the illustrious ******Lido Palace Hotel Baveno**, Strada del Sempione 30, tel 924 444, a Neoclassical pile overlooking the lake with a pool, tennis court, beach, and plenty of atmosphere (L110–150 000, all with bath). *****Simplon**, Via Garibaldi 52, tel 924 112, another fine hotel, has the same amenities, minus the opulence; a good bet for families (open April–Oct, L45–90 000, all with bath). Another choice, ****Villa Ruscello**, Via Sempione 62, tel 923 006, offers 12 rooms, all with bath, in a comfortable lakeside villa (L65 000).

Verbania (tel prefix 0323): Right on the lake in Verbania-Pallanza the grand old ******Majestic**, tel 504 305, is very comfortable, and endowed with a good restaurant and plenty of amenities—an indoor pool, tennis, park and private beach. Open April–Oct; L180–250 000. Another good choice, the *****Belvedere**, Piazza Imbarcadero, tel 503 202, is located on the lake near the steamer landing. Open April–Sept; doubles with bath L90 000. In Verbania-Intra you can sleep more serenely in a former cloister, at *****Il Chiostro**, Via dei Ceretti 11, tel 53 151, where each room gives onto the central garden (L65–100 000). The older ***Villa Petronio**, Via Crocetta 26, in a park near the lake at Pallanza tel 506 015, has doubles without bath for L40 000. The best place to eat in Pallanza, the **Milano**, Corso Zanitello, tel 506 816, is located in a fine old villa on the lake, with dining out on the terrace for a very romantic evening. The food is some of the finest on Maggiore, with fish from the lake prepared in a number of delicious styles, and delicious antipasti (closed Tues & part of Dec and Jan; L60 000).

Ghiffa: Prices tend to be a bit lower here, whether you check in by the lake at the ***Ghiffa, tel (0323) 59 285, a comfortable sunny little hotel with a shady garden (open April–Sept, L85–120 000, depending on the room and view), or the **Castello di Frino, Via Cristoforo Colombo, tel (0323) 59 181, housed in a stately old villa, with a pool and tennis courts (L50–75 000).

Cannero Riviera: The serene ***Hotel Cannero, Lungolago 2, tel (0323) 788 046, is a fine hotel, with terraces overlooking the lake. Many rooms also have private terraces, and all have private bath. There's a swimming-pool, better than average food in the restaurant, and a garage; three days' stay minimum—open end of March–Oct (L90 000, breakfast included).

Cannobio: A nice, serene choice on the lake is the ***Lago, at Fraz. Carmine, tel (0323) 70 595—only 10 rooms, all with bath L70 000; **Magnolia, also in Cannobio at Via Giovanola 33, tel (0323) 70 393, is a stately cream-coloured Neoclassical villa, with pretty high-ceiling rooms (L70 000, all with bath).

In Cursolo-Orasso, you can eat and sleep at the friendly *Belvedere, in Orasso, tel (0323) 77 136 (rooms without bath L40 000; home-cooked mountain meals for L15 000).

Swiss Lake Maggiore, to Luino

TOURIST INFORMATION
Luino: Viale Dante Alighieri 6, tel (0332) 530 019

Beyond Cannobio and the Swiss frontier, the first town of any importance is bustling **Brissago**; from its Porto Ronco boats sail to the two little **Brissago islands**, one with the ruins of a stronghold, the other with a beautiful botanical garden. Striking lake and mountain views continue along the shore to **Ascona**, its older neighbourhoods a retreat of artists and writers from the 16th century to the present. Near the northernmost tip of Maggiore is **Locarno**, one of the chief towns of the Canton Ticino, and a well-equipped resort, its lakeside promenade lined with beautiful trees. From Locarno a rope railway ascends 365 m to the **Santuario della Madonna del Sasso**, founded in 1497, where the star work of art is a *Flight into Egypt* by Bramantino. From here, you can rise into the clouds, by way of the cableway and chair lift to **Cimetta Cardada** (1671 m) for a fabulous view of the lake and snow-capped Alps.

The Northeast Shore

Maccagno, the first sizeable town on the east shore back in Italy, is a quiet haven, with only a crenellated tower recalling its medieval heyday, when it even had the right to mint its own coins. Maccagno is the base for visiting the wild, woody **Val Veddasca**, with venerable alpine villages like **Curiglia**, accessible only on foot. Another road from Maccagno leads up to little **Lake Delio**, a pretty retreat with two small hotels.

To the south, where the river Tresa flows into Lake Maggiore—from Lake Lugano—is the most important town on the Lombard shore, **Luino** (with a big market on Wednesdays). Luino is the presumed birthplace of Leonardo da Vinci's chief follower, Bernardino Luini, who left a fresco on the campanile of the **Oratorio di SS. Pietro e**

Paolo. In the hills above Luino, a narrow road leads up to **Dumenza** and **Agra**, the latter enjoying a mighty view over Maggiore; off shore towers a photogenic rocky pinnacle called **Sas Galet**, which, depending on your point of view, could be a praying nun or the Smog Monster.

To the south is the ceramics town of **Laveno**, where boats wait to ferry your car over to Verbania-Intra; if you're taking the train from Milan or Varese, the Nord Milan line will leave you right next to the lake and quay. The best thing to do in Laveno is to take the cable car up to the **Sasso del Ferro** (1062 m), from where you can walk up for a marvellous view over the lake. In the Palazzo Perabò, in nearby Cerro, you can take in the municipal ceramics collection. Or come at Christmas-time when Laveno claims Italy's only underwater *presepio* (Christmas crib), floodlit and visible from terra firma—and no, the figures don't wear snorkles!

Santa Caterina del Sasso

Hanging—literally—further down the Lombard shore between Reno and Cerro, is the deserted Carmelite convent of **Santa Caterina del Sasso**. Suspended on the sheer cliffs of the Sasso Ballaro over the water, with grand views over the Borromean islands and mountains, the convent is visible only from the lake (boats sail there between April and September; if you're driving, follow the signs from the shore road after Leggiuno, and take the path down).

According to legend, in the 12th century a wealthy merchant and usurer named Alberto Besozzi was sailing on the lake when his boat sank. In deadly peril he prayed to St Catherine of Alexandria, who saved him from the waves and cast him upon this rock-bound shore. Alberto henceforth repented of his usury and lived as a hermit in a cave, becoming famous for his piety. When his prayers brought an end to a local plague, he asked that as an *ex voto* the people construct a church to St Catherine. Over the centuries, other buildings were added as the cave of '*Beato Alberto*' became a popular pilgrimage destination, especially after a huge boulder fell on the roof, only to be miraculously wedged just above the altar, saving the priest who was saying mass. In 1910 the boulder crashed through, without harming anyone, because nobody was there; in 1770 the monastery was suppressed by Joseph II of Austria. In 1986 a 15-year-long restoration of Santa Caterina was completed, revealing medieval fresco fragments (especially notable is one in the Sala Capitolare, of 13th-century armed men). And don't miss the 16th-century *Danse Macabre* fresco in the loggia of the Gothic convent.

WHERE TO STAY (tel prefix 0332)

Lodgings on the less fashionable Lombard side of the lake tend to be small and simple. In Maccagno, try the ****Italia**, tel 560 182, open March–Nov (L50 000 with bath) or little ***Paradiso**, tel 560 128, which steals a march on the competition with its swimming-pool (L34 500 without bath, L47 500 with). In Luino the smart ******Camin**, tel 530 118 has only 13 luxurious, well-fitted rooms (L210 000, with bath); another pleasant choice, little ****Miralago**, tel 531 492, has a little garden and better than par restaurant (L50 000, all with bath).

Between Lakes Maggiore and Lugano

The triangle formed by Lakes Maggiore, Lugano, and the Swiss border is called the Prealpi Varesine, not exactly a destination you'll see in Thomas Cook's posters. Obscure, yes, but dull, no: besides three small and hygienic lakes and the Campo dei Fiori natural park, it has villages with frescoes, ranging in date from the 8th century to last year, including some exquisite works by that Tuscan charmer, Masolino, in the early Renaissance town of Castiglione Olona.

GETTING AROUND

Varese, the main town between the lakes, is served by both FS and Nord Milano; there's also a station at Castiglione Olona, on the little line that passes from Milan through Legnano. Buses from Varese also go to Castiglione, Arsago, Castelséprio, Lake Varese, and Campo dei Fiori.

TOURIST INFORMATION

Varese: Via Carrobbio 2, tel (0332) 283 604

Lake Varese

Lake Varese, a 8.5-km long sheet of water set in its low hills, is the big sleepy-head of the minor lakes. Its main settlement, **Gavirate**, is famous for its hand-carved pipes. For carvings of a different nature, go to **Voltorre**, just south of Gavirate, where you can visit the 11th-century Cluniac monastery of **San Michele** (now a cultural centre), where the cloister has great sculpted capitals attributed to the Comacino master Lanfranco. The monastery's campanile has one of the oldest bells in Italy, and sounds like it, too.

The best thing to do at Lake Varese is catch the little boat from Biandronno on the west shore for **Isolino Virginia**, a wee wooded islet inhabited three millennia ago by a people who built their homes on pile dwellings just off the shore. The islet's **Museo Preistorico di Villa Ponti** chronicles the settlement, which endured into Roman times. Isolino Virginia is a good spot for a picnic, or you can have lunch in the little island restaurant.

The finest beaches on the lake, such as they are, are at Schiranna and Bodio, while to the southwest the lake dissolves into marshlands, not as much fun for humans as for waterfowl; the same holds true for the reed beds in Lake Varese's twin baby sisters to the west, **Lago di Monate** and **Lago di Comabbio**.

Arsago Seprio to Castiglione Olona

South of the lakelets, to the east of Somma Lombardo, **Arsago Séprio** has remains of another ancient civilization, the 9th-century BC Iron-Age Golasecca culture, the first known inhabitants of Lake Maggiore, named after their cemetery in Golasecca with their little mementos tidied off into the **Civic Museum**. Later residents in the 9th century (AD this time) gave the village a Romanesque gem of a church, the **Basilica di San Vittore**, with a lovely façade, aisles lined with Roman columns, three apses, and a 9th-century campanile that has its bells looped on top. In the 11th century, an unusual hexagonal **baptistry** was added, crowned with a round drum dressed in blind arches; it has a serenely harmonious interior. There are traces of ancient frescoes, but real fresco-lovers should carry on 19 km to the east, to **Castelséprio**, an ancient Lombard *castrum* designed on the Roman model. Ruins of the walls and castle survive, but the main reason to stop is to visit the little church of **Santa Maria Foris Portas**, once the parish church of a town destroyed in the 13th century. Its unique, 8th-century frescoes were discovered during World War II by a partisan hiding here; no one knows who painted them, but the style shows an exotic, Eastern influence.

More lovely, though, is the little Renaissance town of **Castiglione Olona**, southeast of the lake (there's a local station about 3 km away on the Nord Milano line to Varese). Castiglione Olona owes its quattrocento Florentine charm to Cardinal Branda Castiglioni (1350–1443), a native who went on to serve as a bishop in Hungary and briefly in Florence, where he was so enchanted by the blossoming Renaissance that he brought Masolino and other Florentine artists home with him to do up the town. Among their works are the frescoes in the cardinal's birthplace, the **Casa dei Castiglioni**, with Masolino's fresco of Veszprem, Hungary, as described to him by the cardinal; and the Brunelleschi-style **Chiesa di Villa** on Piazza Garibaldi, a cube surmounted by a hemispherical dome. Walk up Via Cardinal Branda to the Gothic-Lombard **Collegiata**, built over the Castiglioni castle. It contains beautiful frescoes, with Masolino contributing several on the life of the Virgin; his greatest work is in the separate **Baptistry**, the old tower of the castle. On the first Sunday of each month, Castiglione holds the *Fiera del Cardinale*, an antiques fair and flea market.

Varese and Campo dei Fiori

Varese, a pleasant little garden city of shoe-manufacturers, has had a very minor role in history; Maria Theresa gave it briefly to the Duke of Modena, Francesco III d'Este (1765–1780), whose main contribution was to build himself a suitable residence, **Palazzo Estense**, now the Municipio; usually you can visit the gaudiest room, the Salone Estense, on request. Behind the palace, the duke's formal park, modelled on the Schönbrunn gardens in Vienna, is now the **Giardino Pubblico**. Next to this garden is the pretty English garden of the eclectic **Villa Marabello**, this now the seat of Varese's **Museo Civico**, with a hotchpotch of local archaeology and art, including artefacts from the prehistoric Golasecca culture, which flourished near modern Sesto Calende (9–12 and 3–5, closed Mon). Another public park, at Biumo Superiore, is built around a quaint Neoclassical villa, **Villa Fabio Ponti**, now used as a congress centre.

Varese's landmark, the quirky garlic-domed 17th-century **Campanile del Bernascone** rings the chimes for Varese's most important church, the **Basilica di San Vittore**, an ancient foundation rebuilt on a design by Pellegrino Tibaldi, with a Neoclassical façade pasted on; inside the most important paintings are by Morazzone. The neighbouring **Baptistry**, is an austere relic of the 12th century, containing some of its original frescoes. In the far northwestern corner of Varese, on the Gavirate road, stands the small **Castello di Masnago**, containing a rare cycle of secular frescoes by the 15th-century Lombard school, including a lady with a mirror, preening her elaborate muffin of hair. In the opposite direction, the neighbouring town of **Malnate** has a **Museum of Transport** (horse-drawn trams, steam locomotives, old bicycles, etc) in its Villa Rachele-Ogliari.

Northbound buses from Varese link the city to the medieval village of **Santa Maria del Monte**, site of yet another variation on Piedmont's obsession with symbolic New Jerusalems, this **Sacro Monte** features fourteen 17th-century chapels inviting pilgrims to contemplate allegorically the Mystery of the Rosary. Above Santa Maria is the karst massif of the **Parco Naturale di Campo dei Fiori**, pocked with deep, meandering grottoes for expert potholers (spelunkers) only, especially the 480-m deep Grotta Marelli, this next to a grand but abandoned Liberty-style hotel, the **Albergo Campo dei Fiori**, built in 1912.

If you're not up (or down!) to journeying to the centre of the earth, the Campo dei Fiori offers other points of interest within easy walking distance: a botanical garden at **Zambeletti**, the path to the panoramic western peak, **Vetta Paradiso** (1227 m), with its astronomical observatory and views as far as Monte Rosa. At Brinzio the road through Campo dei Fiori forks; the left branch with some zigzags will eventually take you towards **Casalzuigno**, where Villa Bozzolo has another fine Italian garden. Just beyond Casalzuigno, a winding road cuts up the wooded flank of Monte Nudo for **Arcumeggia**, an ancient hamlet, where the stone houses are piled one atop the other, and where, after World War II, the locals decided to turn their home into a work of art by inviting Italy's best known artists to fresco the old stone walls. None of their efforts is especially rivetting, but they add a cheerful 1950s note. An easy path from Arcumeggia leads to **Sant' Antonio**, with splendid views over Lake Maggiore.

From Varese to Lake Lugano

From Varese there are two valley routes to Lake Lugano, the prettiest, N. 233, cutting through the Valganna to Ponte Tresa, a route that takes in the Liberty-style brewery at Grotte, the **Birreria Liberty Poretti**, the 11th-century **Badia di San Gemolo** at Ganna, and little **Lake Ghirla** beside a village of the same name. The second, easterly route from Varese to Porto Ceresio passes by **Bisuschio**, site of the 16th-century **Villa Cicogna Mozzoni** and its large Italian garden (open 9–12 and 2–6, closed Nov–April); the villa, a national monument, is especially interesting for its frescoes by the Campi brothers and their school, and has a good courtyard. **Viggiù**, just to the east, is a little resort and belvedere, and was the birthplace of early Baroque architect Martino Longhi, who worked mainly in Rome.

WHERE TO STAY
An attractive villa of 1821, in Induno Olona (a few km from Varese) has been converted into an elegant, beautifully restored 30-room hotel, the ******Villa Castiglioni**, Via Castiglioni 1, tel (0332) 200 201; Garibaldi and Mazzini were guests here, and as you stroll the shady park, or go for a swim or game of tennis, and doze in one of the canopy beds, you can easily forget that this is a hotel (until you have to pay the bill: L300 000).

Lake Lugano

Zigzagged Lake Lugano with its steep, wooded, fjord-like shores is more than half Swiss; the Italians, when they have their druthers, call it Lake Ceresio. Its most important town, Lugano, is the capital of the Canton Ticino. The Swiss snatched it from Milan way back in 1512, and when the canton had a chance to return to Italy a couple of centuries later it stalwartly refused. Nevertheless, Italy maintains a wee island of territory in the middle of the lake, Campione d'Italia, which is just big enough to support a prosperous casino that more than welcomes Swiss francs. If you can't beat them, soak them.

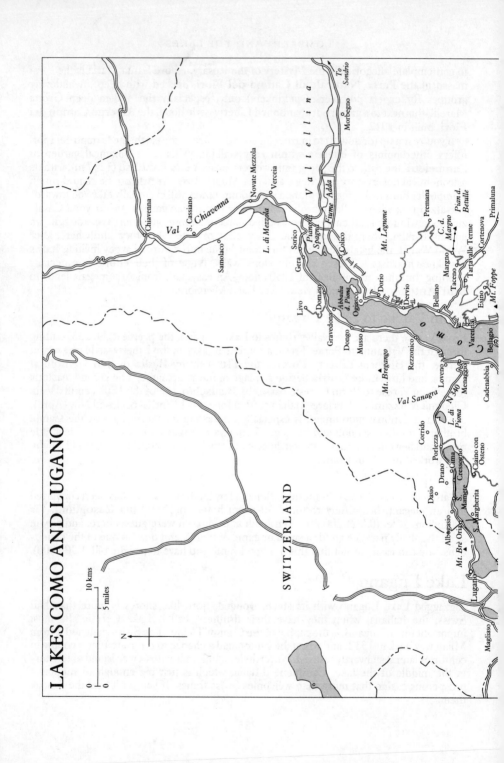

LAKES COMO AND LUGANO

SWITZERLAND

To Sondrio

Morbegno

Valtellina

Fiume Adda

Chiavenna

Val S. Cassiano

Val Chiavenna

Samolaco

Novate Mezzola

Verceia

L. di Mezzola

Gera

Sorico

Pian di
Spagna

Colico

Livo

Domaso

Gravedona

Abbadia
d. Piona

Dorio

Dervio

Mt. Legnone

Premana

C. d.
Margno

Pian d.
Betulle

Dongo

Ogiasco

Margno

Taceno

Tartavalle Terme

Cortenova

Primaluna

Musso

Rezzonico

Bellano

Esino

Mt. Foppe

Varenna

Mt. Bregango

Loveno

Menaggio

Cadenabbia

Bellagio

Val Sanagra

Corrido

L. di
Piona

Portezza

Drano

Dasio

Cima

Cressogno

Claino con
Osteno

Albogasio

Mamgie

S. Margherita

Mt. Orio

Brè

Magliaso

Lugano

N 340

Lago di Como

N

0 ——— 10 kms

0 ——— 5 miles

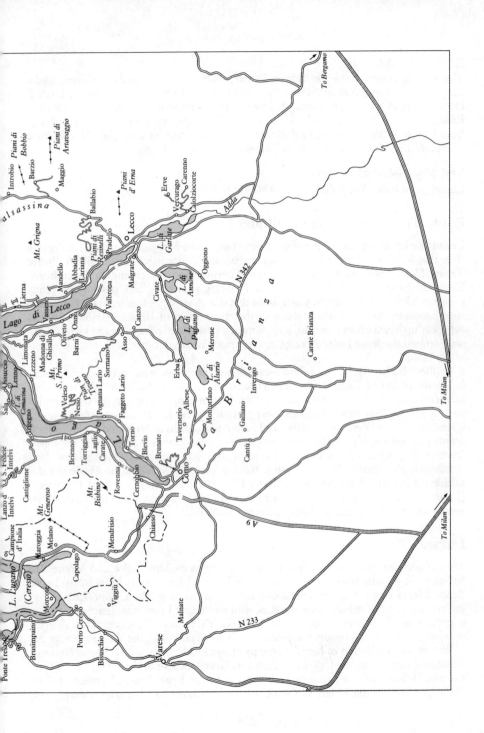

GETTING AROUND

The main approach to the lake is from Varese, which has a train to Porto Ceresio and a bus to Ponte Tresa. Both of these are steamer calls on the Società Navigazione Lago di Lugano line, with several links daily to Lugano, from where you can continue east back to Italian territory (Porlezza or Osteno). You can also approach from Lake Como; buses from Como or Menaggio go to Porlezza. Varese is served by both the FS and Nord Milano from Milan—the stations in Varese are next to each other.

TOURIST INFORMATION

Campione d'Italia: Via Volta 16, tel (004191) 685 051

Ponte Tresa to Campione d'Italia

Lugano slowly drains its rather polluted waters into Lake Maggiore through the Tresa, a river that forms the border between the Italian and Swiss halves of the village **Ponte Tresa**. There's not much to see in either half beyond the steamer landing. From **Porto Ceresio**, the steamer enters Swiss territory (bring your passport), passing the pretty village of **Morcote** en route to **Campione d'Italia**. Another option from Porto Ceresio is to continue along the south shore to the Swiss town of Brusino Arsizio, with its cableway up **Monte San Giorgio**, long, long ago a graveyard of reptiles and fish; you can walk around the fossil beds, a heady, magical place in the summer when the cyclamens are in bloom.

In the Middle Ages, before state-sanctioned gambling was invented, the once-independent fief of Campione was celebrated for its master builders, who like other medieval artists worked anonymously, and are known to history only as the the Campionesi Masters. They had a hand in most of Italy's great Romanesque cathedrals—in Cremona, Monza, Verona, Modena, and Sant'Ambrogio in Milan—and such was their reputation that when the Hagia Sofia began to sag, the Emperor hired the Campionesi Masters to prop it up. In their home town they left only a small sample of their handiwork, **San Pietro** (1326). A later, Baroque-coated church of the **Madonna dei Ghirli** (Our Lady of the Swallows), has a fine exterior fresco of the Last Judgement (1400) and several others from the same period in the interior. Campione uses Swiss money and postal services and has no border formalities.

Lugano

The scenery improves as you near Lugano, set between Monte Brè and Monte San Salvatore. A popular resort, it has two main sights, tht 16th-century Franciscan church **Santa Maria degli Angioli**, containing striking frescoes by Bernardino Luini, considered his greatest masterpiece; Ruskin, who wrote that Luini was 'ten times greater than Leonardo' saw these frescoes and declared, 'Every touch he lays is ethereal; every thought he conceives is beauty and purity....' The second sight, the **Villa Favorita**, has an exceptional collection of brand-name paintings inside, amassed by Baron Heinrich Thyssen-Bornemisza: the Italians—Bramante, Uccello, Crivelli, Veronese, Titian, Caravaggio, Bellini, and Carpaccio—share space with van Eyck, Bosch, Vermeer, Dürer, Holbein, Cranach the Elder, El Greco, Goya, Velazquez and Watteau, among many others. A popular excursion is to continue down the south arm of the lake to **Capolago** and take the rack railway up to the summit of Monte Generoso for the fabulous view. East of Lugano, the lake returns to Italy, in the province of Como. **Santa Margherita** on the south shore has a cableway up to the panoramic Belvedere; 2 km above the Belvedere, from the resort **Lanzo d'Intelvi**, there are even more wide-ranging views of Lake Lugano. **San Mamete**, a steamer landing on the north shore, is the prettiest village in the area, with its castle and the quiet Valsolda behind. **Claino con Osteno** has fine views of the lake and boat excursions up the watery ravine of the River Orrido. From **Porlezza** you can catch a bus for Menaggio on Lake Como, passing by way of the tiny but enchanting Lago del Piano.

WHERE TO STAY AND EATING OUT
In Campione d'Italia, the punters' choice is **La Taverna**, Piazza Roua 1, tel (004191) 687 201, where you can celebrate a win or console a loss at the nearby casino with good solid Italian cooking, from genuine Parma ham to a genuine *bistecca alla fiorentina*; cost around 80 Swiss francs.

In San Mamete (Valsolda), the ***Stella d'Italia**, tel (0344) 68 139, is a lovely lakeside hotel, with a lido, garden, and waterside terraces. Each room has a balcony looking over a tranquil vision of mountain and lake, and you can borrow the hotel's boat for outings. Open April–Oct, all rooms have private bath, L80 000. In Porlezza there are more choices; try **Rosen-Garden**, tel (0344) 62 228, which has ten comfortable rooms, all with bath near the lake, open all year (L40 000), or **Regina**, tel (0344) 61 228, with quiet and simple rooms on the lake, all with bath, for L80 000. Regina also has a fine restaurant, featuring good homemade pasta and specialities like breast of duck with grapes (L40 000; special price afternoon and evening menus as well).

Lake Como

Sapphire Lake Como has been Italy's prestige romantic lake ever since the earliest days of the Roman empire, when the Plinys wrote of the luxuriant beauty surrounding their several villas on its shores. It had just the right mix of wild and rugged nature, still waters and gardens, to sweep the children of the Romantic era off their feet, inspiring some of the best works of Verdi, Rossini, Bellini, and Liszt as well as enough good and bad English verse to fill an anthology. And it is still there, the Lake Como of Shelley and Wordsworth, Manzoni and Stendhal (who thought it simply 'the most beautiful place in the world'), adorned with grand villas and lush gardens, the mountains and beloved irregular shore of wooded promontories. The English still haunt their traditional English shore, but most of the visitors to Como these days are Italian, and there are times when the lake seems schizophrenic, its nostalgic romance and mellowed dignity battered by modern demands that it be the Milanese Riviera. Even so, Como is large and varied enough to offer retreats where, to paraphrase Longfellow's ode to the lake, no sound of Vespa or high-heel breaks the silence of the summer day.

Third largest of the lakes, 50 km long but only 4.4 km at its widest point, Como (or Lario) is one of the deepest lakes in Europe, plunging down 410 m near Argegno. It forks in the middle like a pair of legs, the east branch known as the Lago di Lecco after its biggest town, while the prettiest region is the centre, where Como appears to be three separate lakes and where towns like Tremezzo and Bellagio have been English enclaves for 200 years. One legacy of the English is the seven excellent golf courses in the province, while the waters around Domaso are excellent for windsurfing. As a rule, the further you go from the city of Como, the cleaner the lake, and the more likely you are to find 'Lucias', the traditional fishing boats topped with hoops, and wooden racks of fat twaite shad, drying in the sun. The winds change according to the time of day: the *breva* blows northwards from noon to sunset, while the *tivà* blows south during the night.

GETTING AROUND
There are frequent trains from Milan's Centrale or Porto Garibaldi stations, taking you in some 40 minutes to Como's main San Giovanni station. Slower ones run on the Milan-Nord line to the lakeside station Como-Lago. From Como, trains to Lugano and Lecco all depart from San Giovanni. Buses from Como run to nearly every town on the lake.

TOURIST INFORMATION
Piazza Cavour 17, tel (031) 262 091; also in Piazza S. Gottardo, by the railway station, tel 267 214.

City of Como

Magnificently located at the southern tip of the lake, Como was captured from the Gauls by the Romans in the 2nd century BC. In AD 23, it was the birthplace of Pliny the Elder, compiler of antiquity's greatest work of hearsay, the *Natural History*, and later of his nephew and heir, Pliny the Younger, whose letters are one of our main sources for the cultured Roman life of the period. In the 11th century Como enjoyed a brief period as an independent *comune*, but it was too close to Milan and the Visconti to last long, and from 1335 on it has been ruled by Milan. For centuries it has been the leading Italian silk city, and while silk worms are no longer raised on the lake, Chinese thread is woven and dyed here to the specifications of the Milanese fashion industry. Even if you're just passing through to the more serene resorts, Como is worth a brief visit; part of its charm is that the historic centre, still bearing the imprint of its Roman plan, is closed to traffic.

Life in Como centres around the busy lakeside **Piazza Cavour**, with its cafés, hotels, steamer landing, and pretty views; to the left, the city's **Giardini Pubblici**, with its two landmarks: a circular Neoclassical **Tempio Voltiano**, dedicated to native son, physicist Alessandro Volta, and containing a display of his scientific instruments, and the **War Memorial** by Futurist architect Antonio Sant'Elia, who perished in World War I at the age of 28. The gardens continue up the lake shore to the massive 18th-century **Villa Olmo**, a frequent venue of congresses, though you can visit its large formal garden, under its mighty 18th-century trees.

From Piazza Cavour, Via Plinio leads back to the elegant Piazza Duomo, adorned with the colourful striped town hall, or **Broletto**, the **Torre del Comune** (both early 13th-century), and the magnificent **Duomo**, considered Italy's best example of the transitional style from Gothic to Renaissance, begun in the 14th century and finished by Juvarra (who completed the dome) in 1700. The Gothic has its say in the lovely rose window and in the pinnacles on the main façade, while in the spirit of the Renaissance,

240

the three doors are rounded instead of pointed, and embellished with intricate carvings by two sculptors of the late 15th century, Tommaso and Iacopo Rodari, brothers from Maroggia who it seems dedicated their lives' talents to this one church. On either side of the central portal, their delicate stone canopies protect seated Renaissance statues of Pliny the Elder on the left and Pliny the Younger on the right. And what, you may well ask, are those two old pagans doing on a cathedral? Although Pliny the Younger had at least a brush with Christianity (while serving as a governor in Anatolia, he wrote a letter to Emperor Trajan, asking how to treat the local Christians; Trajan's famous reply was that they should simply be left alone), the fact is that the Renaissance liked to regard all noble figures of antiquity as honorary saints.

Inside, the three Gothic aisles combine happily with a Renaissance choir and transept. The aisles of the nave are hung with 16th-century tapestries, which lend the cathedral a palatial elegance; a pair of Romanesque lions near the entrance are survivors from the cathedral's 11th-century predecessor. But most of the art is from the Renaissance: in the right aisle six reliefs with scenes from the Passion by Tommaso Rodari, and fine canvases by two of Leonardo's followers, Gaudenzio Ferrari (*Flight into Egypt*) and Luini (*Adoration of the Magi* and the famous *Madonna with Child and four saints*). The left aisle has more by the same trio: Rodari's *Deposition* on the fourth altar; Ferrari's *Marriage of the Virgin*, and Luini's *Nativity*, as well as a 13th-century sarcophagus.

Down the main street, Via Vittorio Emanuele, the 12th-century **San Fedele** has a unique pentagonal apse and a doorway carved with portly medieval figures. Further up the street, in the Piazza Medaglie d'Oro Comasche, the **Museo Civico** is the city's attic of artefacts, dating from the Neolithic era up to World War II (open 9:30–12 and 2:30–5:30, closed Mon and Sun afternoons). From here, continue down Via Giovio to the **Porta Vittoria**, a striking gate of 1192 topped with five tiers of arches.

Como's Romanesque gem, the 11th-century **Sant' Abbondio** is a short walk from here in an industrial suburb; from the Porta Vittoria, follow Viale Cattaneo to Viale Roosevelt, cross and turn left to Via S. Abbondio. Well-restored in the 19th century, the church, as typical of the period, has five aisles, and there are some interesting 14th-century frescoes; knights in medieval armour come to arrest Christ in Gethsemane.

Also eminently worth while for the great views over the lake is the funicular up **Brunate**, the hill overlooking Como. The station is on the Lungolario Trieste; beyond, at Villa Geno, lies the main beach. The 18-hole golf course is 4 km away in Montorfano. Como's tourist office distributes the free monthly *Turismo Proposte* for a complete list of events and concerts around the lake. Shopping means silk in Como; for some of the best prices on cloth, try the two branches of *Centro della Seta*, Via Volta 64 and Via Bellinzona 3.

From Como, the lace-making town of **Cantù** is only a short hop away on the train towards Lecco. Cantù's landmark is the tall, minaret-like Romanesque campanile of its parish church, but its main point of interest, the 10th-century **Basilica di San Vicenzo** is a 20-minute walk to the east in the neighbouring hamlet of Galliano, and is decorated with a remarkable fresco cycle painted just after the millennium.

WHERE TO STAY AND EATING OUT (tel prefix 031)

On Como's main Piazza Cavour, overlooking the lake, the grand old ******Barchetta**, tel 3221, has recently renovated rooms, many with balconies over the piazza and lake.

Open all year (L142–175 000). In a garden, just out of Como on the west shore road the ****Villa Flori, Via Cernobbio 12, tel 573 105, is also open year round; all rooms with bath (L90–130 000). The ***Park Hotel, Viale Rosselli 20, tel 572 615, is a moderate-sized establishment near the lake, without a restaurant (L95 000, all with bath). The *Canova, Viale T. Gallio 5, tel 22 100, is a good budget choice near the centre (L38 000 without bath, L54 000 with).

Como is one of those towns where the restaurants tend to process clients with slipshod food and service, especially in the summer. One place that doesn't, Sant'Anna, Via Filippo Turati 3, tel 505 266, is an old family establishment, more frequented by the denizens of the silk trade than tourists, featuring well-prepared if typical Lombard specialities; good risotto with radicchio and trout with almonds (L45–60 000, closed Fri and Aug). Another choice, reasonably priced for Como, is the Trattoria della Catene, between the S. Giovanni station and S. Abbondio on Via Borsieri 18, tel 262 176; dishes here include risotto with mushrooms, sausages and beans, and if you have an iron stomach, polenta with snails; L35–40 000.

Around the Lake: Como to Tremezzo

GETTING AROUND
Steamers and hydrofoils are operated by *Navigazione Lago di Como*, based on the lake in Como at Via Rubini 20, tel (031) 273 324, where you can pick up schedules and tourist passes. Frequent connections are between Como, Tremezzo, Menaggio, Bellagio, Varenna, and Cólico, with additional services in the Centre Lake, and generally at least one boat a day to Lecco. Car ferries run between Bellagio, Varenna, and Cadenabbia. Some services cease altogether in the winter.

TOURIST INFORMATION
Cadenabbia: Via Brentano 6, tel (0344) 40 393
Cernobbio: Via Regina 33b, tel (031) 510 198
Tremezzo: Piazza Via Regina 3, tel (0344) 40 493

Cernobbio, Torno, and Argegno

Zigzagging back and forth from shore to shore, the steamer is the ideal way to travel around the lake, allowing you to drink in the marvellous scenery. The first steamer landing, Cernobbio, is an old resort, the 1816–17 retreat of Queen Caroline of England who held her wild parties in what is now the fabulous Hotel Villa d'Este. The best views in the neighbourhood are to be had from atop Monte Bisbino, a dizzy, 17-km drive up from Cernobbio.

Across the lake, above the steamer landing of ancient Torno, is Faggeto Lario and the 16th-century Villa Pliniana, which so charmed Shelley that he tried to buy it; its name is derived from its peculiar intermittent spring described in a letter of Pliny the Younger. Stendhal lived here for a period, as did Rossini who composed *Tancredi* during his stay.

Back on the west shore, across from Torno, **Villa Passalacqua** at **Moltrasio** has a lovely Italianate garden decorated with ceramics, open for visits in the spring; while nearby **Villa Salterio** is where Vincenzo Bellini lived and composed *Norma* in 1831. **Argegno** enjoys one of the privileged positions on the lake, with views of the snow-clad mountains to the north. It stands at the foot of the pretty Val d'Intelvi, which culminates at its highest point at the summer/winter resort of **Lanzo d'Intelvi**, with views over Lake Lugano.

Beyond Argegno (still on the west shore), lies the pretty islet of **Comacina**, sprinkled with the ruins of nine ancient churches, many destroyed by raiders from Como in the 1190s; by some twist of fate it was owned by the King of Belgium, who donated it as a retirement home for Milanese artists. The islet comes blazingly alive on the Saturday or Sunday nearest St John's Day for the festival of the *lumaghitti*, when hundreds of tiny lamps in snail shells decorate the lanes, followed by an immense show of fireworks and a Sunday parade of boats decked with flowers and islanders in 18th-century garb. On the east shore, you can take a boat to visit **Lézzeno**'s version of Capri's Blue Grotto, the **Grotta dei Búlberi**.

Tremezzina

In the west shore district of **Tremezzina**, the description of the lake as the 'mirror of Venus' hardly seems extravagant. Totally sheltered, the Tremezzina enjoys the most benign climate on Lake Como, lined in the spring with carpets of azaleas, agaves, camellias, rhododendrons, and magnolias under the towering cypresses and palms. **Lenno**, the southernmost village, is believed to have been the site of Pliny the Younger's villa 'Comedia'. In one of his letters he describes how he could fish from his bedroom window. No remains of the villa have ever been found, but you can visit the fine 11th-century octagonal baptistry of the parish church. It was in this lovely setting, in front of a posh villa in nearby **Mezzegra**, that Mussolini and his mistress Claretta Petacci were executed by local partisans. They had been captured along the north shore of the lake, attempting to flee in a German truck to Switzerland. Claretta was killed trying to shield Il Duce from the bullets.

Villa Carlotta

The main towns of the Tremezzina are the popular English resorts of **Tremezzo** and **Cadenabbia**, served by an old Anglican church. Between the two lies the most popular attraction on Lake Como, the **Villa Carlotta** (open March and Oct from 9–12 and 2–4:30, April–Sept 9–6; adm exp.). Originally built in 1747 for the Marquis Antonio Clerici, the villa took its name from its subsequent owner, Princess Carlotta of the Netherlands, who received it as a wedding gift from her mother upon her marriage to the Duke of Saxony-Meiningen in the 1850s. Carlotta laid out the magnificent formal gardens and park, and in April and May the thousands of azaleas and rhododendrons put on a dazzling display of colour. But no matter when you come you can also take in the Neoclassical interior with its once immensely popular, and now mostly insufferable, Neoclassical statuary; Canova's passionate *Cupid and Psyche* holds the pride of place. Ponder, if you can, the Icelander Bertel Thorvaldsen's frieze of *Alexander entering Babylon*, commissioned by Napoleon but completed after Waterloo for another client who picked up the considerable tab. In another villa in Cadenabbia, Verdi composed *La Traviata*.

WHERE TO STAY AND EATING OUT

Cernobbio: Cernobbio has the most palatial hotel on Lake Como. The famous *****Villa d'Este, Via Regina 40, tel (031) 511 471, was built originally in 1557 by Cardinal Tolomeo Gallio, the son of a local fisherman who went on to become one of the most powerful men in the Vatican—besides this villa, he had seven along the road to Rome so he never had to spend a night under anyone else's roof. Queen Caroline was not the only crowned head to make use of the Cardinal's old digs, and since 1873 it has been a hotel. Each room is individual, furnished with antique or reproductions, the public rooms are regal, the glorious gardens in themselves a reason to stay. There is a swimming-pool literally on the lake, an indoor pool, a fine golf course, squash, tennis, sailing, nightclub, dancing and more. Open March–Nov, the rooms cost a king's ransom as well—L650 000 a night. The excellent restaurant serves tagliatelle with squid and smoked salmon, veal with *porcini* mushrooms, and for something different, lamb with thyme and kidneys in Marsala (fixed menu L75 000, otherwise around L100 000). Much less exalted, **Terzo Crotto, Via Volta 21, tel (031) 512 304, offers nine rooms, all with bath, for L70 000, and delicious cooking in the hotel restaurant for around L35 000.

Comacina: Dotted with the interesting ruins of its numerous churches, the islet of Comacina is deserted, except for a restaurant, the 50-year-old Locanda dell'Isola Comacina, tel (0344) 55 083. For one price (L50 000) you are picked up in a boat at Cala Comacina or Ossuccio (near Lenno), and given a fine meal including an antipasto of vegetables, ham, and sausage, then grilled trout, followed by fried chicken, wine, and dessert, and return trip to the mainland.

Cadenabbia: Right on the lake, charmingly old fashioned, the ****Bellevue, Via Regina 1, tel (0344) 40 418, is a large but very pleasant place to stay, with plenty of sun terraces, garden, and pool (open 20 March–30 Oct, L120 000 all with bath). Another cosy old hotel, the ***Britannia Excelsior, Via Regina 41, tel (0344) 40 413, is set in a piazza overlooking the lake, and has lots of rooms with balconies. Open March–Oct; L60 000 without bath, L90 000 with.

Tremezzo: Built in the 19th century, the ****Grand Hotel Tremezzo Palace, Via Regina 8, tel (0344) 40 446, is large, comfortable, and next door to Villa Carlotta. Besides its garden and pool, it has large rooms with good views on all sides. Open April–Oct, L190 000. More intimately Victorian, the **Villa Marie, tel (0344) 40 427, has 15 pleasant rooms overlooking the lake and a shady garden (open March–Nov, L80 000). By common consent, the best place to dine in the area is 1.5 km up in the hills at Rogara di Tremezzo and is called Al Veluu, Via Rogaro 11, tel (0344) 40 510. From the terrace you can see the lake shimmering below, once home of the fish on the menu. Good basic Italian meat courses are served as well, and fresh vegetables. Closed Tues, and Nov–March; L45 000.

Bellagio, Menaggio, and Northern Lake Como

TOURIST INFORMATION
Bellagio: Piazza della Chiesa 14, tel (031) 950 204
Menaggio: Piazza Garibaldi 8, tel (0344) 32 924

Bellagio

High on the headland where the lake forks, enjoying one of the most scenic positions in all Italy, Bellagio (from the Latin *bi–lacus*) is a fine old town that has managed to maintain an air of quiet dignity through the centuries, perhaps because even now, with its silk industry, it doesn't depend totally on tourism. A bus from the pier will take you to the **Villa Serbelloni**, now the Study and Conference Centre of the Rockefeller Foundation. Most scholars believe this stands on the site of Pliny's villa 'Tragedia', higher over the lake than his villa 'Comedia', and so named not only because tragedy was considered a 'loftier' art, but because in his day tragic actors wore high-heels. The villa itself is closed to visitors, but you can walk through the park on a two-hour guided tour from April–Oct, Tues–Sun, 10–4; adm expensive but it all goes to charity. Another villa in Bellagio open for visits, the white **Villa Melzi**, topped with a score of pointy little chimneys, also has immaculate lawns, a fine terraced garden, a lake of waterlilies and a greenhouse, while the villa contains a collection of sculpture from Egypt (April–Oct, 9–6). In the centre of Bellagio, the 12th-century church **San Giacomo** has some interesting carvings.

South of Bellagio is an interesting area called the **Triangolo Lariano**, a wedge of karst that keeps Como doing the eternal splits, though millennia of dripping water have bored long caverns in its very intestines—one cave called Tacchi-Zelbio meanders for 9 km, and has yet to be explored to its end. A number of paths, best in the spring and autumn, crisscross the Triangle, especially the **Piani del Tivano**.

Menaggio, back on the west shore, is another pleasant resort, with a lovely golf course and beach. It lies at the head of two valleys: the Val Menaggio, an easy route to Lake Lugano, and the **Valle Sanagra**, from where you can make one of the finest ascents on the lake, the day-long walk up to panoramic **Monte Bregagno**, departing from the Villa Calabi.

Varenna, and its River of Milk

Varenna, a tidy row of yellow and ochre houses, is the main village on the east shore of Como, near Lake Como's most curious natural wonder, the **Fiumelatte** ('river of milk'), the shortest river in Italy, running only 250 m before hurtling down in creamy foam into Lake Como. For the Fiumelatte, as its name implies, is as white as milk. Not even Leonardo da Vinci, who studied the cavern from which it flows, could discover its source, or why it abruptly begins to flow in the last days of March and abruptly ceases at the end of October. On the north bank of Fiumelatte are the gardens of **Villa Monastero**, built on the site of a 13th-century convent, suppressed by Charles Borromeo in 1567 for the scandalous and luxurious behaviour of the nuns; its garden, adorned with statues and bas-reliefs, is especially known for its citrus trees (open April–Nov, 9–2 and 2–5; adm).

Varenna's most interesting church is the Romanesque **San Giorgio**, adorned with an exterior fresco of St Christopher (giant-sized, the better to bring luck to passing travellers) while the nearby **Oratorio di San Giovanni Battista**, built around the millennium, is one of the oldest surviving churches on the lake. High over Varenna, the ruined 11th-century **Castello Vezio**, was, according to legend, founded by Queen Theodolinda; you can drive there, or it's a 15-minute walk from Varenna.

Another east-shore village, **Bellano**, lies at the bottom of the steep gorge of the River Pioverna. It has a fine Lombard church of 1348, **SS. Nazzaro e Celso**, built by

Campionesi masters, with a rose window in majolica. A series of steps and gangways threads through the gorge and its bulging walls, offering remarkable views of the river just below (open Easter–Sept, 9:30–5:30, closed Wed; adm). **Dervio**, the next town, has some of Como's widest beaches; steps lead up to the old Castello district, marked by a massive stump of a tower. From Dervio you have the option of turning up the rustic Val Varrone (see below) or continuing north along the lake shore to **Corenno Plinio**, a town built around the impressive embattled towers of the **Castello Andreani**. Next to the castle, the early 14th-century church of **St Thomas à Becket**, has frescoes and a pretty Tuscan ancona of the Annunciation from the 1500s.

Facing Dervio on the west shore, visitors of Venice will recognize the name of the hamlet **Rezzonico**, cradle of the family that built one of the grandest palaces on the Grand Canal and produced Pope Clement XIII. Further up, above Musso, the lofty, almost inaccessible **Rocca di Musso** was the castle stronghold of Lake Como's notorious pirate, Gian Giacomo de' Medici, nicknamed 'Il Medeghino', born during the Medici exile from Florence in 1498. He gained the castle from Francesco II, Duke of Milan, for helping to remove the French from Milan and assassinating the duke's best friend; he made it the base for his fleet of armed ships that patrolled the lake and extorted levies from towns and traders. He ended his career as the Marquis of Marignano, working for Charles V and oppressing the burghers of Ghent. His brother became intriguing Pope Pius IV, while his nephew was St Charles Borromeo, the holy scourge of Milan.

Next on the lake, **Dongo, Gravedona**, and **Sorico** once formed the independent republic of the Three Parishes that endured until the arrival of the Spaniards. In the Middle Ages the little republic was plagued by the attentions of the inquisitor Peter of Verona, who sent scores of citizens to the stake for doubting that the pope was Christ's representative on earth. Peter got a hatchet in his head for his trouble—and a quick canonization from the pope as St Peter Martyr. Gravedona was and still is the most important town of the three; it has a fine 12th-century church, the small **Santa Maria del Tiglio**, believed to have been originally a baptistry, with frescoes of St John the Baptist; it has some fine carvings (the centaur pursuing a deer is the Early Christian symbolism for the persecution of the Church), and an unusual tower. Nearby is another ancient church, **San Vicenzo**, with a 5th-century crypt.

Back on the east shore, **Cólico**, near the mouth of the Adda, is the gateway to the Valtellina (see below). At nearby Fuentes Montecchio you can still trace the perimeters of the massive fort built by the Spanish Governor of Milan in 1603 to guard the strategic entrance to the Valtellina. It gave its name to the alluvial and vaguely eerie **Pian di Spagna**. South of Cólico the road passes the peculiar green waters of the Lago di Piona, a basin formed of fossils and garnet notched into the side of Como. On the lick of land enclosing the basin stands the Romanesque **Abbazia di Piona**, with the ruined apse of a 7th-century church, a 'new' church consecrated in 1138, and a very pretty cloister of 1257. The Casamari Cistercians of the abbey distil and sell a potent herb liquor called *gocce imperiali*, for fire-safety reasons, best taken in very small doses.

WHERE TO STAY AND EATING OUT

This part of the lake is the place to look for the lake's most popular fish, twaite shad, which looks like a chubby herring and is served either dried, pressed in wooden barrels and barbecued, or marinated with laurel leaves.

Menaggio: The ******Grand Hotel Victoria**, Via Benedetto Castelli 7, tel (0344) 32 003, was built in 1806 next to the lake and during its renovation its original decor was carefully preserved, while it was fitted out with creature comforts like designer bathrooms, TVs, and frigo-bars. The public rooms are quite elegant, and there's a pool in the garden (open all year, L170 000). Another pleasant choice right on the lake, the *****Bellavista**, Via 4 Novembre 21, tel (0344) 32 136, has nice rooms for L85 000; open April–15 Oct. Menaggio also has a very fine youth hostel (tel 323 56).

Bellagio: One of the most romantic places to stay on the lake, Bellagio has several fine hotels, including the premier *******Grand Hotel Villa Serbelloni**, Via Roma 1, tel (031) 950 216, in a magnificent ornate villa in a magnificent flower-filled garden, enjoying some of Como's finest views. The frescoed public rooms are glittering and palatial, and there's a heated pool and private beach, tennis, boating and water-skiing, and dancing in the evening to the hotel orchestra. The rooms, all with bath, range from palatial suites to some that are a bit faded. Open 15 April–15 Oct; L320–350 000, depending on room and view. Open during the same period, the genial 16th-century *****Hotel Du Lac**, Piazza Mazzini 32, tel (031) 950 320, is near the centre, located on a terrace next to the lake. The rooftop garden has a fine view over the lake, and the comfortable rooms all have bath; open 17 April–17 Oct; L95 000. Located in a 19th-century villa, the *****Florence**, tel (031) 950 342, is right next to Bellagio's port. The terraces and many of the rooms have lake views, and the lobby is cosy with heavy beams and a Florentine fireplace. The rooms are good and unpretentious. Open mid-April to mid-Oct, rooms with bath are L90–100 000. Simple lodging, open all year: ***La Spiaggia**, tel (031) 950 313, is near the lake; rooms without bath L45 000.

Varenna: The ******Hotel Royal Victoria**, Piazza S. Giorgio 5, tel (0341) 830 102, is a fine old hotel, completely renovated in 1981. Right on the lake, in the midst of a 19th-century Italian garden, it has 45 very comfortable rooms, all with private bath, TV and frigo-bar. Open all year; L150 000.

Lecco and Its Lake

The Lago di Lecco, the less touristy leg of Lake Como, resembles a brooding fjord, its granite mountains plunging down steeply into the water, entwined in rushing streams and waterfalls, and carved with shadowy abysses—a landscape that so enchanted Leonardo da Vinci as he planned canals and water schemes for Lodovico Sforza that he used it in two of his most celebrated works, the *Virgin of the Rocks* and *The Virgin and St Anne*. The mountains of the east shore—Resegone and the Grigna range—are wild and pointed sharp dolomitic peaks of limestone shot through with fossils from a primordial sea.

GETTING AROUND
Lecco is connected by rail with Milan, Como, and Bergamo; from Lecco the line up to the Valtellina follows the eastern shore up to Còlico, then continues up to Chiavenna, with a branch line going east to Sondrio.

TOURIST INFORMATION
Lecco: Via Nazario Sauro 6, tel (0341) 362 360

Lecco

An industrial and sombre city, magnificently positioned at the foot of jagged Mount Resegone, Lecco grew up where the River Adda leaves Lake Como to continue its journey south (a typical hearsay entry in Pliny's *Natural History* records how the Adda passes through the entire lake without mingling its waters). In 1336, the river was spanned by the 11-arch **Ponte Azzone Visconti**, built as part of Azzone's defensive line from Lecco to Milan, though now shorn of its towers and most of its character. Another Visconti souvenir, the **Torre Visconti** stands in the pretty Piazza XX Settembre, where a market has been held every Wednesday and Saturday since 1149. **San Nicolò**, by the lake under the city's tallest campanile, has a chapel frescoed by a follower of Giotto.

Most Italians, however, come in search of Manzoniana. For Lecco was the childhood home and inspiration of Alessandro Manzoni (born in Milan in 1785, died 1873) and the setting of his *I Promessi Sposi* (The Betrothed), Italy's 19th-century fictional classic—one that looked at history through the eyes of the common man, and sparked pro-unification sentiments in the breast of every Italian who read it. In its day the *Sposi* was also a sensation for its language—a new, popular, national Italian that everyone could understand—no small achievement in a country of a hundred dialects, where the literary language had remained unchanged practically since Dante. Even now the *Sposi* remains required reading for every Italian school-child, a sacred cow breathlessly milked by every denizen of Italian culture.

The principal literary pilgrimage goal is the museum in Manzoni's boyhood home, the **Villa Manzoni**, now lost amid the urban sprawl on Via Amendola (open 9–2, closed Mon; adm free); on display are Manzoni's cradle, tobacco boxes, and nightcap, though it is the house itself, little changed since the 18th century, that forms the main attraction. A gallery of 18th-century Lombard art is being arranged upstairs. In Piazza Manzoni, there's a large **Monument to Manzoni**, the author sitting pensively over a base adorned with scenes in bas-relief from the novel (the Abduction of Lucia, the death of Don Rodrigo, and the marriage of the Betrothed). If it whets your appetite, ask the tourist office for its special Manzoni brochure that points out the various scenes and buildings from the novel, most of which (Lucia's house, Don Rodrigo's castle, the marriage church) are in **Olate**, a village above Lecco, to the east. At **Pescarenico**, an old fishing village just south of the Ponte Visconti, another scene from the novel took place at Padre Cristoforo's convent, now ruined; the village's quirky, triangular campanile, erected in the 1700s, survives in better condition and has been listed as a national monument. Pescarenico is one of the last true fishing villages on the lake, where the fishermen still use their traditional narrow, thin-bowed boats and nets.

Just east of Lecco towers **Monte Resegone**, a jaggedy, bumpetty Dolomite that got away; on weekends it becomes a major Milanese escape route, especially for rock-climbers. Those not up to grappling on crusty cliffs can take the funicular from Lecco to the **Piani d'Erna**, but mind that it's a clear day, when the view is extraordinary.

Villages up the east shore of the Lago di Lecco include the old silk town of **Abbadia Lariana**, where you can visit and watch live demonstrations at the **Silk Industry**

Museum in the 1917 Monti throwing-mill, with an impressive round throwing-machine of 432 spools from the 1850s. Just to the north, on a small spur, you can make believe you're walking into an illuminated book in the fresco-covered 15th-century church of **San Giorgio**. Next along the shore, **Mandello del Lario**, rolls on a different kind of wheels—those of Guzzi motorcycles, manufactured here since 1921; the plant, at Tonzànico, has a **Motorcycle museum**, open upon request.

The Grigna Range and its Val Varrone and Valsassina

All the towns on the east shore are overshadowed by the magnificent 'white towers' of the **Grigna Mountains**: **Grigna Meridionale** (2177 m), the southern group, may be approached by footpath from Mandello di Lario, or from **Ballabio Inferiore**, with its long and winding road up to the green saddle of **Piani Resinelli** and its Rifugio Porta, from where you can begin a remarkable trail called the **Direttissima** up to Rifugio Rosalba and the awesome, fantastical pinnacles rising over the Val Tesa.

The more massive and taller northern group, **Grigna Settentrionale** (2409 m), is bounded on the west by Lake Como and on the east by the **Valsassina**, which begins to the north of Ballabio Inferiore. The road cuts through a gloomy gorge to **Colle di Balisio**, another green saddle, with the crossroads for the popular ski resorts of **Barzio**, **Cremeno**, and little **Maggio**, while the main Valsassina road continues up to **Pasturo**, famous for its soft cheeses and the major market town of the Valsassina. Further up the road, around **Introbio** and its stalwart medieval **Arrigoni Tower**, is a land of abandoned silver, lead, and iron mines. To the east the town is dominated by the **Pizzo dei Tre Signori** (2554 m), so named because it once stood at the border of the Dukedom of Milan, the Republic of Venice, and Switzerland, while up the road towards Vimogno is the lovely waterfall, the **Cascata del Troggia**.

Primaluna, the next town, was the cradle of the Della Torre family, who ruled Milan from 1240 to the advent of the Visconti. Their coat-of-arms still emblazons some of the small palace-fortresses in town; the parish church, **S. Pietro** has paintings in the manner of Titian and the beautiful golden 15th-century **Torriani Cross**; neighbouring **Cortabbio**, scholars believe, was the first feudal court of the archbishop of Milan, where the earliest Christian tombstone in Lombardy was discovered (425 AD). At **Cortenova** the road forks again, and a hard choice it is because both routes take in spectacular mountain scenery. To explore Grigna Settentrionale, take the road towards Varenna by way of the little resort of **Esino Lario** and the road to **Cainallo** and Vó di Moncòdeno, an ice-filled gorge that appears in Leonardo's notes. The trail from here, while not stupendously difficult (in parts you'll have to hold tight to some chains), has enough sheer abysses and infernal pits to make it sufficiently exciting to most. The not-so-daring can take the road from Esino to the plateau of **Ortanella**, a natural balcony over the lake and site of the 1000-year-old church of S. Pietro, or take in Esino's **Grigna Mountain Museum**, housing local Gallic and Roman finds, minerals and fossils.

The right fork from Cortenova winds its way to Premana, the Val Varrone, and down to the lake at Dervio. Among the sights here is a waterfall in a 30-metre abyss called the **Tomba di Taìno**, located by Cosmasìra, near Vendrogno; the old hamlet of **Torre**, near Premana, an ancient Milanese stronghold where the older women still wear their traditional costumes; **Premana** itself, an iron town that specializes in scissors and, long ago, in the iron beaks of gondolas, some of which may be seen in the local ethnographic museum. From Premana the road to Dervio follows the **Val Varrone**, dotted with old settlements like **Treménico**, and an interesting church of 1583, **San Martino** at Introzzo, with a pulpit carved by Rococo master Antonio Fantoni and a campanile with an excellently preserved clock of 1707.

La Brianza

South of the Triangolo Lariano, between Como and Lecco, is La Brianza, a region of seven little lakes that span the legs of Lake Como like footprints or fragments of sky that *did* fall on Chicken Little. Milanese nobles erected summer villas on their shores in the 18th and 19th centuries, though the two lakes just south of Lecco, especially **Garlate**, are most closely associated with the silk industry; since 1950 the Abegg silk mill on the lake shore has been a **Silk Museum**, where you can find out more about one of the nicest things ever made by worms; exhibits include some 500 tools and machines, most impressive of which are the 19th-century throwing-machines, capable of 10,000 revolutions a minute (open the afternoon of the first Sunday of each month, or by request at Garlate's *municipio*). La Brianza is also known for its furniture and wine, and for a fine 10th-century church in **Carate Brianza**, on the road back to Milan.

Stendhal came to the banks of **Lake Annone** (the next little lake to the west, and the most interesting to visit) when Milan, as much as he loved it, got on his nerves; his farm, the 'Fattorie Stendhal' is now a hotel and restaurant. **Oggiono**, on the south shore of the lake, was the home of one of Leonardo's pupils, Marco d'Oggiono, who left a fine polyptych in **S. Eufemia church**, which still retains its Romanesque bell tower and an octagonal, 11th-century baptistry. South of Lake Annone, on jagged Monte Brianza, are the romantic ruins of the **Campanone della Brianza**, built by Queen Theodolinda of the Lombards; south of Campanone, the regional **Park of the Curone** (near Missaglia and Montevecchia) offers pretty walks through chestnut and birch woods and some fine rural countryside.

Another Dark Age relic, on the north shore of Annone at **Civate**, is the famous abbey of **San Calocero**, founded in 705 by two reform-minded French Benedictines. In the 1080s it led the post-Patariane reformation in Lombardy, and in the 1590s, after one of its monks became Pope Gregory XIV, it became an Olivetan monastery until its suppression in 1803. In the monastery's basilica, currently undergoing restoration, some unusual 11th-century frescoes were discovered behind the 17th-century vaulting, and in the Romanesque crypt; also to be seen are nothing less than the keys of St Peter, given him by Christ, as well as marble and silver caskets of the 6th and 7th centuries. Best of all, make the pretty hour's walk up from Civate to **Cornizzolo** for the round 10th-century church of **San Pietro al Monte**, reached by way of a long flight of steps and a door that was borrowed from a giant's oven (before setting out, ask at San Calocero to see if it's open). Inside its twin apses are remarkable 11th-century frescoes and stuccoes inspired by the Apocalypse, especially of the four rivers of the New Jerusalem, St Michael slaying the dragon, and the Christ of the Second Coming liberating the Lady Church; there's a rare *baldacchino* from the 1050s, decorated with reliefs, and the ancient crypt, unusually enough, also has frescoes and stuccoes. The adjacent, centrally planned **Oratorio di San Benedetto** has an unusual 12th-century painted altar.

WHERE TO STAY AND EATING OUT

Lecco (tel prefix 0341): The **Croce di Malta**, Via Roma 41, tel 363 134, is in the centre of town and has recently been remodelled. It's not far from the lake; rooms without bath L50 000, with L70 000. The tiny *Alberi, Lungolago Isonzo 4, tel 363 440, has the advantage of being right on the lake; also open all year, rooms without bath L40 000. Just over a kilometre outside Lecco, at Malgrate, ****Il Griso, Via Statale 29, tel 283 217 is a moderate-sized but elegant hotel with fine views of the lake from its wide terrace. There's a pool in the garden and one of the region's best gourmet restaurants, for which you should book in advance (rooms, all with bath, L160 000; meals, L75 000). Lecco has a fine restaurant in **Les Paysans**, Lungo Lario Piave 14, tel 369 233, a recently opened and elegant little place, with lake fish and seafood specialities, and good wine list (L55–65 000; closed Mon; 2 weeks in May and Oct).

Brianza: If you're touring in the Brianza, the little village of Viganà Brianza, half-way between Como and Milan, is worth a special trip for its restaurant **Pierino**, Via XXIV Maggio 26, tel (039) 956 020. Delicious regional specialities complement the chef's own innovations. Excellent wines and meals for around L60 000 (closed Aug, Mon, and Sun evenings).

In Erba, halfway between Como and Lecco, a 12th-century castle has been converted into the lovely *****Castello di Pomerio, Via Como 5, tel (031) 627 516. The interior has been meticulously restored, down to the frescoes. Many rooms have fireplaces, massive wooden beds (but modern bathrooms); the public rooms are furnished with beautiful antiques. Indoor and outdoor pools and tennis courts (L250 000).

Beyond Como: the Valleys of Sondrio

North and east of Lake Como lies the mountainous and little-known province of Sondrio, sandwiched between the Orobie Alps and Switzerland, along the upper valley of the glacier-fed river Adda. Its waters flow into Como and the Mediterranean; other rivers born in this alpine Lost Horizon end up in the Danube and Black Sea, while others trickle into the Rhine and the North Sea. Only four roads link Sondrio's two main valleys, the Valchiavenna and the Valtellina, with the rest of Italy. The province is among the least-exploited Alpine regions, offering plenty of opportunities to see more of the mountains and fewer of your fellow creatures, especially in the western reaches.

When the Spanish Habsburgs took Milan, the Valtellina, with its many Protestants, joined the Swiss Confederation. Yet even though they didn't possess it, it was of prime importance to the Spaniards during the Counter-Reformation, assuring their trouble-making troops the link between Milan, Austria, and the Netherlands. In 1620, the Spanish in Milan instigated the 'Holy Butchery' of 400 Protestants in the valley by their Catholic neighbours. The valley rejoined Italy only in the Napoleonic partition of 1797.

Those interested in a trekking holiday through the region's most spectacular scenery should request the Sondrio tourist office's booklet *L'Avventura in Lombardia* which, though in Italian, details a fine 20-day trail from Novate Mezzola through Stelvio National Park down to Capo di Ponte; another booklet from the tourist office has a complete listing of the area's alpine refuges.

Like the Valle d'Aosta, the Valtellina may seem an unlikely spot for wine, but that doesn't keep the locals from stubbornly tending their knotty vines, hung high above the valley on narrow terraces laboriously cut into the sunny, but steep and stony slopes of the mountains. To create these tiny vineyards, generations of Valtellinians have carried up baskets of soil on their backs; of necessity everything is done by hand. The Valtellina's four DOC red wines, all aged for two years in oak casks, are *Sassella*, *Grumello*, *Valgello*, and the diabolical-sounding *Inferno*, which gets its name from the extra heat and sun the vines receive just east of Sondrio.

GETTING AROUND
From Cólico the railway from Milan and Lecco forks, one branch heading north as far as Chiavenna, the other heading east as far as Tirano before veering north towards St Moritz. Sondrio is served with an efficent network of buses. Several lines go into Switzerland from Sondrio, Tirano, and Chiavenna; and there are direct coach connections with Milan.

TOURIST INFORMATION
Chiavenna: tel (0343) 33 442
Madesimo: Via Carducci, Via Carducci 27, tel (0343) 53 015

Valchiavenna

In Roman times Lake Como extended as far north as **Samolaco**; between here and Cólico lies the marshy Pian di Spagna and the shallow **Lake Mezzola**, an important breeding ground for swans. On the west shore of the lake stands the 10th-century Romanesque chapel of **San Fedelino**; on the east **Novate Mezzola** is the base for walks in the enchanting and unspoiled **Val Codera**, inaccessible to cars. The track up begins at Mezzolpiano (where you can park), and passes a granite quarry lost in the woods, as well as two tiny granite hamlets, **San Giorgio di Cola** and, beyond the chasm of the Gola della Val Ladrongo, **Codera**, with two tiny inns and a bar.

Chiavenna, the chief town in the district, is delightfully situated among the boulders of an ancient landslide in a lush valley. Amidst the rocks are natural cellars, the **crotti**, which maintain a steady, year-round temperature and have long been used for ripening local cheeses, hams and wine; some have been converted into popular wine cellars, celebrated in mid-September at the annual '*Sagra dei Crotti*'. The most important church in town, **San Lorenzo**, was begun in the 11th century and contains an interesting treasure, including a 12th-century golden 'Pax' cover for the Gospels; also note the carved octagonal font (1156) in the Romanesque baptistry. Above the Palazzo Baliani you can walk up to **Paradiso**, the town's botanical park, with a small archaeological museum (open 2–5, closed Mon; adm); another park, the **Marmitte dei Giganti**, 'the giants' kettles', actually contains remarkable round glacial potholes. The path up to the park passes *crotti* under the horsechestnuts and charming meadows; beyond the potholes a sign directs the way to the '*incisioni rupestri*'—etchings in the boulders left by the area's prehistoric inhabitants.

East of Chiavenna, in the Val Bregaglia, the road towards Switzerland passes the **Acqua Fraggia**, a waterfall near Borgonuovo; a seemingly endless stair leads to the ancient hamlet of Savogno atop the cascade. In 1618, a huge landslide buried the town of

Piuto, further up the valley; the excavations of this humble, 17th-century Pompeii, which you can visit, have revealed a number of finds now in the museum of the church of San Abbondio in **Borgonuovo**. In another nearby village, **Aurogo**, the 12th-century church of **San Martino** contains contemporary frescoes.

North of Chiavenna, the **San Giacomo valley** becomes increasingly rugged and steep, with dramatic landslides, glaciers, and waterfalls. There are two summer/winter resorts on the road—**Campodolcino** and the more developed **Madesimo**—before reaching the **Splugen Pass** (2118 m), generally closed six months of the year.

WHERE TO STAY AND EATING OUT   (tel prefix 0343)
Prices in Sondrio's resorts are a relief compared with those in the more fashionable Val d'Aosta and the Dolomites. The cuisine is also less influenced by international tastes. Buckwheat is the staff of life, in the Valtellina's grey *polenta taragna* and the narcotic noodles, *pizzoccheri*; there are delicious cheeses like *bitto* and the low-fat *matûsh*, chestnut-fed pork and salami, a delicious *bresaola* (cured beef) and fresh whipped cream on raspberries for dessert.

In the Valchiavenna, Madesimo is the best equipped with hotels, with the large ****Cascata et Cristallo**, Via Carducci 2, tel 53 108, with its pool and health centre at the top of the list, open all year; L90–130 000, depending on season. The more traditional **Alla Gran Baita**, Via Emet 19, tel 53 232, has long been popular among alpinists; also open all year; L46 000 without bath, L60 000 with. For *pizzoccheri* and other local treats, the **Osteria Vegia**, Via Emet 7, tel 54 082, has been the place to go for 280 years (L30 000).

The Lower Valtellina

TOURIST INFORMATION
Sondrio: Via C. Battisti 12, tel (0342) 512 500
Chiesa Valmalenco: Piazza SS. Giacomo e Filippo 1, tel (0342) 451 150

East of Cólico the road enters the Valtellina, the valley of the River Adda. The old, vine-wrapped villages and numerous churches along the lower valley are part of the **Costiera dei Cèch**, referring to its inhabitants, the Cèch, whose origin is as mysterious as the name. Their main town is **Morbegno**; from here buses make excursions towards the south, into the two scenic valleys, the **Valle del Bitto**, with iron-ore deposits that made them a prize of the Venetians for two centuries, and the rural **Val Tartano**, a 'lost paradise', dotted with alpine cottages, woods, and pastures, its declining population still farming as their ancestors did centuries ago. The road through the valley was finished only in 1971, though many hamlets in the valley even today are accessible only on foot or mule. A third valley running to the north, the wild granite **Val Masino**, is traversed by the magnificent 'Sentiero Roma', and also serves as the base for the ascent of Monte Disgrazia (3680 m) one of the highest peaks in the region. According to legend, it is haunted by the huge and hairy '*Gigiat*', a kind of monster goat—the Yeti of the Valtellina, seen by only a few intrepid alpinists. The six-day Sentiero Roma, laid out in the 1920s, begins at the little spa of Bagni di Masino, though there are other striking mountain paths from Bagni that can be walked in a single day, especially up to the meadows and torrents of the Piano Porcellizzo. **Val di Mello**, a little branch valley to the east, above San Martino, is equally tempting for its granite bulwarks and crystal streams and waterfalls. Near the village of Cataéggio, the landmark is an awesome granite boulder, the **Sasso Remenno**.

Sondrio

The provincial capital **Sondrio** is a modern town, dotted with a few old palaces and dominated by its oft-remodelled **Castello Masegra**, dating from 1041. Here, too, in the Palazzo Quadrio, you can visit the ethnographic **Museo Valtellinese**, with archaeological and art sections (9–12 and 2:30–5, closed weekends), or taste the upper Valtellina's famous red wines—*Sassella*, *Grumello* and the unusual *Inferno*. Rock hunters should not miss the valley north of Sondrio, the **Val Malenco**, mineralogically the richest valley in the Alps with 150 different kinds of minerals, including the commercially mined serpentine, or green marble, locally known as *pietra ollare*, for it was traditionally carved into local cooking pots, called '*laveggi*'. **Chiesa in Valmalenco** and **Caspoggio** are the main towns and ski resorts in the valley; in the summer Caspoggio has stables for riding tours of the region. The High Road (*alta via*) of the Val Malenco offers a seven-day trekking excursion around the rim of the valley, beginning at Torre di S. Maria, south of Chiesa; alternatively, the less ambitious can practically drive (or take a 2-hour walk) from San Giuseppe (on the road north of Chiesa, towards Chiareggio) up to the Rifugio Scarscen-Entova, for one of the most spectular mountain views in the area. Another fine (and easy) excursion is up to the rugged lakes of **Campo Moro**, on the east branch of the valley; a white road will take you as far as the Rifugio Zóia; from here it's an easy three-hour hike up to the glacier-blasted peaks around the Rifugio Marinelli.

South of Teglio, the main route 38 heads north to Tirano, while N. 39 tries its best to continue east through the Val Corteno towards Edolo (at the head of the Val Camonica). **Aprica** is the principal resort, but you can escape the crowds by continuing east to **Corteno Golgi**, near the head of two remote valleys, the **Val Brandet** and **Val Campovecchio**, both part of a little-known natural park of firs, rhododendrons, tiny lakes, wooden bridges, and old stone alpine huts. At Corteno you can hire a horse, or drive as far south as Sant' Antonio, where the two valleys fork.

WHERE TO STAY AND EATING OUT   (tel prefix 0342)
In Morbegno, the charmer is the fine old ***Margna**, Via Margna 24, tel 610 377, open all year, with a fine restaurant featuring local cuisine; all rooms have bath, L65 000. In Tartano, the main village of the serene Valtartano, ***La Gran Baita**, tel 645 043, is open all year and offers comfortable rooms with bath for L45–50 000.

Explorers in the Val Masino will find a warm welcome at one of the six little hotels in San Martino, all open throughout the year, like the *Tarca, tel 640 813, open from May to November (L36 000, none with bath) or the *Genzianella, in Via S. Martino, tel 640 831 (L42 000, all with bath). There are a few peaceful rooms as well as meals at the **Osteria Gatto Rosso**, in the Val di Mello (no phone). For more in the way of creature comforts, ***Terme Bagni Masino**, in Bagni del Masino, tel 640 803, will set you up, at least during the spa season (17 June–30 Sep, L48–56 000 without bath, L68–80 000 with).

In Chiesa in Valmalenco, ***Chalet Rezia, Via Marconi 27, tel 451 271 is a lovely little chalet in a peaceful setting, with a covered pool; open all year, all rooms have bath; L58–68 000. More basic choices in the area include **Miravalle, Via Rusca 50, tel 451 481 (L50 000, all with bath) or the **Baita dei Pini, a simple chalet way up at Chiareggio, tel 451 006 (open all year, L52 000 with bath).

The Upper Valtellina

TOURIST INFORMATION
Aprica: Corso Roma 156, tel (0342) 746 113
Valdidentro: Isolaccia, tel (0342) 985 331
Livigno: Via Gesa 55, tel (0342) 996 379
Bormio: Via Stelvio 10, tel (0342) 903 300

Ponte in Valtellina to Sondolo

The highway relentlessly rises through the valley; but if you're driving, take the scenic 'Castel road' running north of the highway and river from Sondrio, via Tresivio and the melancholy ruins of Grumello castle, then on to the old patrician town of **Ponte in Valtellina**. Ponte was the birthplace of astronomer Giuseppe Piazzi (1746–1826), discoverer of the first asteroid, but is mostly visited for its parish church of **San Maurizio**, and its unusual bronze *cimborio* (1578), or lantern, and frescoes by Bernardino Luini.

Further east along the castle road or highway, charming **Teglio** was the most important town of the Valtellina in the Middle Ages. It takes special pride in a dish called *pizzoccheri*, described as 'narcotic grey noodles with butter and vegetables', served up to bewildered visitors at the annual autumn '*Sagra dei Pizzoccheri*'. Teglio has the finest palace in the whole region, the **Palazzo Besta** (1539), embellished with fine *chiaroscuro* frescoes in its Renaissance courtyard; and the **Antiquarium Tellinum**, housing a fine example of local prehistoric rock incisions, the Stele di Caven, among other examples of the valley's prehistoric art (open winter 9–2, summer 9–1 and 2:30–5:30; adm). **San Pietro** has a fine 12th-century campanile, while above Teglio the mighty stump of its old tower offers fine views of the valley. Among the old lanes, look for the house with blackened arcades, once residence of a particularly adept and sought-after executioner.

Tirano, the rail terminus, has a number of 16th- and 17th-century palaces and the Valtellina's Renaissance masterpiece, the **Sanctuary of the Madonna**, built in 1505 a kilometre from the centre; inside is an ornate, inlaid-wood organ. Between Tirano and Teglio a road pushes southeast to the winter and summer resort of Aprica, with its school of competitive skiing, and beyond to Edolo in the Val Camonica (see pp. 264–5). Another road from Tirano follows the railway north through the Bernina Pass to St Moritz.

The Stelvio road continues up to **Grosotto**; the organ in its Church of the Virgin is a masterpiece of the woodcarver's art. The large old village of **Grósio** has been important since prehistoric times, as witnessed by the engravings in its **Parco delle incisioni rupestri**, similar to those in the National Park in the Val Camonica. It's the last village in Lombardy where you can still see women wearing their traditional costumes; in the 16th century it was the birthplace of Cipriano Valorsa, nicknamed the 'Raphael of the Valtellina', who was responsible for most of the frescoes in the region's churches, including those in Grosotto's **San Giorgio** and the **Casa di Cipriano Valorsa**. The imposing if ruined castle and the finest *palazzo* in town belonged to the local lords, the Visconti-Venosta. **Sondolo**, the next town, has a modern sanatorium and some courtly 16th-century frescoes in the church of Santa Marta.

Bormio and Stelvio National Park

The seat of an ancient county, not unjustifiably called the *'Magnifica Terra'*, Bormio is a fine old town with many frescoed palaces, recalling the days of prosperity when Venice's Swiss trade passed through its streets. Splendidly situated in a mountain basin, it is a major ski centre (the 1985 World Alpine Ski Championships were held here), with numerous lifts and an indoor pool. The **Chiesa del Crocifisso** has fine 15th-century frescoes, and there's a spa in nearby **Bagni di Bormio**.

Bormio is the main entrance into the **Parco Nazionale Dello Stelvio**, Italy's largest national park, founded in 1935 and encompassing the grand alpine massif of Ortles-Cevedale. A tenth of the park's 134,620 hectares is covered with over 100 glaciers, including one of Europe's largest, the 2000-hectare *Ghiacciaio dei Forni*. The peaks offer many exciting climbs, on **Grand Zebrù** (3850 m), **Ortles** (3905 m) and **Cevedale** (3778 m) amongst others. It also includes over 50 lakes and Europe's second-highest pass, the **Passo di Stelvio**, through which you can continue into the Alto Adige and Bolzano between the months of June and October; the pass is also an important winter and summer ski centre.

Stelvio is administered by the provinces of Sondrio, Trentino, and Bolzano, all of which have park visitors' centres. Bormio's is at Via Monte Braulio 56, tel (0342) 901 582; they can tell you where to find the 1500 km of marked trails, and a score of alpine refuges, or the best place to watch for the park's chamois, the not very shy marmots, the eagles, and other wildlife, including the ibex, reintroduced from Paradiso National Park in 1968. Unfortunately, the insatiable Italian hunter shot the last bear in these mountains in 1908. Hunting is now illegal in the Lombard section of the park, but continues in the eastern sections, causing no end of controversy each autumn between the anti-hunting and hunters' factions. At the visitors' centre, the **Giardino Botanico Rezia** contains many of the 1800 species of flora that grow in the park. Among the easiest walks are through the Valle dello Zebrù and through the Valle di Cedec to the Rifugio Pizzini Frattola, from the Albergo dei Forni.

Some 14 km east of Bormio, in the confines of the park, is 'the skiers' last white paradise', perhaps better known **Santa Caterina Valfurva**, a typical alpine village and cradle of ski champions, surrounded by snowy slopes from early autumn to late spring.

From Bormio a white road winds up along the Valle di Fraele, towards the source of the river Adda, into a landscape known as Italy's little Tibet, as much for its quantity of snow as for its rugged mountains. Two towers, the **Torri di Fraele**, once guarded the rocky route into Switzerland, much frequented by smugglers; one route, diverging to the west is known as the *sentiero dei Contrabbandieri*. The steep gorge of the Adda survives, if not the river (diverted by a power-thirsty hydroelectric industry).

From Bormio, the N. 301 follows the **Valdidentro** west into another part of 'Little Tibet'—the **Valle di Livigno**, though before reaching **Livigno** town you must first pass through Customs—for this old paradise for smugglers is now Europe's highest duty-free duty-free zone, a favourite weekend destination for Bavarians who barrel down through the Drossa tunnel to replenish their stereo or hooch supplies. 'Long live the sun and snow' is Livigno's motto; besides alcohol it has excellent skiing, with snow most of the year; it also preserves many of its old wooden houses.

WHERE TO STAY AND EATING OUT   (tel prefix 0342)
Ponte in Valtellina has the region's best restaurant, **Cerere**, tel 482 284, housed in a 17th-century palace. Cerere has long set the standard of classic Valtellina cuisine and its wine list includes the valley's finest; closed most of July and on Wed; L40–50 000. Grosio has a fine old hotel and restaurant in its ***Sassella**, Via Roma 2, tel 845 140; the rooms are all fitted with private bath and TVs (L68 000) while the restaurant serves a refined version of local specialities like *bresaola condita* (local sausage served with olive oil, lemon and herbs), *crêpes* with mushrooms and local cheese, smoked trout, and Valtellina's wines (L25–35 000). Another good place to go a-wine tasting is Grosio's **Enoteca Valtellinese**, 'Al bun vin' near the centre.

In Bormio you can go up-market at the ****Palace**, Via Milano 52, tel 903 131, a modern establishment with tennis, pool, and very comfortable rooms all with bath and TV. Open 6 Dec–18 Sept; L180–300 000. The ***Baita dei Pini**, Via Peccedi 15, tel 904 346, is a pleasant place, with very good rooms, all with bath; open Dec–April and 15 June–Sept; L90 000. Another luxury option, open all year, the ****Rezia**, Via Milano 9, tel 904 721, is near the centre with good, traditional rooms (all with bath; L170 000) and a good, traditional restaurant to match. On the menu are salami, *bresaola*, tagliatelle with *porcini* mushrooms, polenta and game (L45 0000 and up). A less expensive alternative, the **Everest**, Via S. Barbara 11, tel 901 291, has a garden and pleasant rooms; closed in Oct and Nov (60 000 all with bath). **Kuerc**, in the heart of old Bormio on Piazza Cavour 8, tel 904 738, was named after the ancient town council of Bormio, and is a good place to try local dishes in an attractive setting (L32 000; closed Wed, Nov, and May).

In duty-free-ville Livigno, the best place to sleep and eat is the grand old ***Alpina**, Via Bondi 3, tel 996 007. Decorated with wooden carvings and giant antlers, the Alpina specializes in venison dishes as well as the inevitable *pizzoccheri*; try the cheeses made in the local valleys. (L45 000, often very busy at weekends; rooms with bath L70 000).

Bergamo

At the end of *A Midsummer Night's Dream* everyone dances a 'Bergamasque' to celebrate the happy ending. Bergamo itself is happy and charming in the same spirit as its great peasant dance, a city that has given the world not only a dance but also the maestro of *bel canto* in the composer Gaetano Donizetti, the Venetian painters Palma Vecchio and Lorenzo Lotto, and the great master of portrait painting, Gian Battista Moroni.

Built on a hill on the edge of the Alps, the city owes much of its grace to the long rule of Venice (1428–1797); but it wasn't a one-way deal. Not only did Bergamo contribute two of Venice's most important late Renaissance artists, but the city's most brilliant and honourable *condottiere*, the 15th-century Bartolomeo Colleoni. Colleoni was so trusted by the Great Council that he was given complete control of Venice's armed forces; he also received the unique honour of an equestrian statue in Venice, a city that as a rule never erected personal monuments to anybody—though it helped that Colleoni left the Republic a fortune in his will in exchange for the statue. Somehow there was enough cash left over to build Colleoni a dashing tomb in his home town as well, one of the jewels of the old Città Alta. Bergamo also contributed so many men to Garibaldi in its enthusiasm for the Risorgimento that it received the proud title, 'City of the Thousand'.

GETTING AROUND

Bergamo is an hour's train ride from Milan and has frequent connections to Brescia as well, but only a few trains a day to Cremona and Lecco; for information, tel (035) 247 624. Buses go to Lake Iseo, as well as to Como, Edolo, and the Bergamask valleys. Both train and bus stations are located near each other at the end of Viale Giovanni XXIII; bus 1 from the station will take you to the funicular (if it's been repaired) to the historic upper city, or if not, will take you there itself. The airport has flights to Rome or Ancona.

TOURIST INFORMATION

Via Paleocapa 2, tel (035) 213 185 (in Città Bassa); Vicolo Aquila Nera 4, tel 232 730 (in Città Alta).

Up to the Piazza Vecchia

There are two Bergamos: the Città Alta, the medieval and Renaissance centre up on the hill, and the Città Bassa, pleasant, newer and spacious on the plain below, its streets laid out in the 1910s. The centre is the large, oblong **Piazza Matteotti** (from the station, walk up Viale Giovanni XXIII) with the grand 18th-century **Teatro Donizetti** and, on the right, the **Church of San Bartolomeo**, containing a fine 1516 altarpiece of the *Madonna col Bambino* by Lotto. Further up Viale Vittorio Emanuele II is the funicular up to the Città Alta; from the upper station Via Gombito leads in a few blocks to the beautiful **Piazza Vecchia**.

Architects as diverse as Frank Lloyd Wright and Le Corbusier have praised this square as one of Italy's finest, for its magnificent ensemble of Medieval and Renaissance buildings, all overlooking a low, dignified lion fountain. At the lower end stands the **Biblioteca Civica** (1594), designed after Sansovino's famous library in Venice. Directly across, an ancient covered stair leads up to the 12th-century **Torre Civica**, with a 15th-century clock and curfew bell that still warns the Bergamasks to bed at 10 pm; a lift takes visitors up for the fine views over Bergamo (daily except Mon, closed afternoons). Next to the stair, set up on its large rounded arches, is the 12th-century **Palazzo della Ragione**, with a Lion of St Mark added recently to commemorate the city's golden days under Venice, which seemed blessedly benign compared to some of the alternatives.

One of the best features of the Piazza Vecchia is that, through the dark, tunnel-like arches of the Palazzo della Ragione, are glimpses of a second square hinting more of a jewel-box than an edifice. This is the Piazza del Duomo, and the jewel-box reveals itself as the sumptuous, colourful façade of the 1476 **Colleoni Chapel**, designed for the old *condottiere* by Giovanni Antonio Amadeo while he was working on the Charterhouse at Pavia. The Colleoni Chapel is even more ornate and out of temper with the times, an almost-medieval tapestry that disregards the fine proportions and serenity of the Tuscans for a typically Venetian love of flourish. Amadeo also sculpted the fine tombs within, of Colleoni and his daughter Medea (Colleoni's, however, is empty—his remains were misplaced after a couple of temporary burials in the chapel before the tomb was finished). For some unknown reason, his empty tomb is double-decked, one beautifully carved sarcophagus under another, all under a fine equestrian statue. Young Medea's tomb is much calmer and was brought here in the 19th century from another church. The ornate ceiling is by Tiepolo, and there's a painting of the Holy Family by Goethe's constant companion in Rome, the Swiss Angelica Kauffmann.

Flanking and complementing the chapel are two works by Giovanni, a 14th-century master of Campione: the octagonal **Baptistry** and the colourful porch of the **Basilica Santa Maria Maggiore**, crowned by an equestrian statue of St Alexander. The church itself was begun around 1137 and is austerely Romanesque behind Giovanni da Campione's window-dressing. He also designed the attractive door with a scene of the Nativity of Mary. The Baroque interior, however, hits you like a gust of lilac perfume. Poor lyrical Donizetti deserved better than his tomb near the back of the church; the best art is up along the balustrade of the altar, with four wonderful wood-inlaid scenes designed by Lorenzo Lotto and executed by Capodiferro ('Ironhead') di Lovere, who managed to find an amazing selection of colours and shades of natural wood to work into the vivid scenes. The third building on the square is an insipid neoclassical **Cathedral**.

Although lacking in famous monuments, the rest of the Alta Città deserves a stroll; walk along the main artery, the Via Colleoni (the *condottiere* lived at Nos. 9–11) to the **Cittadella** with the city's natural history museum (9–12 and 2–4, closed Tues) and the bus stop for **San Virgilio**, with a panoramic viewpoint. From the Cittadella the quiet, medieval Via Arena leads around to the back of the cathedral, passing by way of the **Donizetti Museum** (open Mon–Fri 9–12 and 4–5). Another good place to aim for is the ruined 14th-century **Rocca**, the castle of the Visconti, whose unpleasant rule preceded that of the Venetians.

The Carrara Academy

Bergamo's great art museum lies half way between the upper and lower cities. To get there from the Città Alta's funicular station, walk along the mighty Venetian walls (the Via Delle Mura) and exit through the Porta Sant' Agostino. The first left is the pedestrian-only Via della Noca, which descends to the **Galleria dell'Accademia Carrara**, founded in 1780 and housing one of Italy's great provincial collections (open 9:30–12:30 and 2:30–5:30, closed Tues; adm). It boasts especially fine portraits—Botticelli's haughty *Giuliano de' Medici*, Pisanello's *Lionello d'Este*, Gentile Bellini's *Portrait of a Man*, Lotto's *Portrait of Lucina Brembati* with a vicious weasel under her arm and a sickly moon overhead, and another strange painting of uncertain origin, believed to be of Cesare Borgia, with an uncanny desolate background. There are fine portraits by Bergamo's master of the genre, Moroni, to whom Titian directed the Rectors of Venice, with the advice that only Moroni could 'make their portraits natural'. There are some excellent *Madonne con Bambini* by the Venetian masters, Giovanni Bellini, Mantegna (who couldn't do children), Crivelli (with his cucumber signature), as well as by the Sienese Landi. The plague saint San Sebastiano is portrayed by three contemporaries in remarkably different aspects—typically naked and pierced with arrows before a silent city, by Giovanni Bellini; well-dressed and rather sweetly contemplating an arrow, by Raphael; and sitting at a table, clad in a fur-trimmed coat, by Dürer. An eerie, black and silver *Calvary* is an unusual work by the same artist, and there is much, much more, by Italian and foreign artists as well.

From the Cararra, Via San Tommaso, Via Pignolo, and Via Torquato Tasso lead back down to the central Piazza Matteotti. There are fine altarpieces by Lorenzo Lotto along the way, in **San Bernardino** and **Santo Spirito**.

Around Bergamo

The year after Bartolomeo Colleoni was appointed Captain General of Venice he purchased a ruined castle at **Malpaga** (on the Cremona road), which he had restored; his heirs in the Cinquecento added a fine series of frescoes commemorating a visit to the castle of King Christian I of Denmark in 1474, portraying Colleoni hosting the de rigeur splendid banquets, jousts, hunts and pageants of Renaissance hospitality. It's open for visits if you ring in advance, tel (035) 840 003.

Southwest of Bergamo, **Caravaggio** was the birthplace of Michelangelo Merisi da Caravaggio and site of a popular pilgrimage sanctuary designed in a cool Renaissance style by Pellegrino Tibaldi. **Treviglio**, a large, rather dull town nearby, has an exquisite 15th-century polyptych in the Gothic church of San Martino; to the south **Rivolta d'Adda** boasts the **Zoo di Preistoria**, with lifesize replicas of the denizens of the Mesozoic era (closed Tues; adm). An even more mind-boggling roadside attraction beckons in **Capriate San Gervasio**, off the autostrada towards Milan, where **Il Parco Minitalia** cuts Italy down to size—400 metres from tip to toe, with mountains, seas, cities, and monuments all arranged in their proper place. Even a miniature train is on hand to take visitors up and down the boot (open every day). Due east of Bergamo, **Sotto del Monte** was the birthplace of beloved Pope Giovanni XXIII and an increasingly popular pilgrimage destination.

WHERE TO STAY   (tel prefix 035)
Most of Bergamo's hotels are in the Città Bassa, but one of the most atmospheric, the ****Agnello d'Oro**, Via Gombito 22, tel 249 883, is up in the medieval centre. It's a fine old 17th-century inn with cosy rooms, all with bath, for L62 000; the restaurant is also quite good. Another one, on the corner of the Piazza Vecchia, the ****Sole**, Via B. Colleoni 1, tel 218 238, isn't quite as nice and a shade noisier, but homey, with baths in every room (L55 000). The city's finest hotel, the ******Excelsior San Marco**, Piazzale Repubblica 6, tel 232 132, is well-located between the upper and lower towns, and offers air-conditioned, modern rooms, all with TV and bath, as well as one of Bergamo's best restaurants in its very modern and imaginative **Ristorante di Tino Fontana**, where a full meal of local and international specialities will set you back around L60 000; rooms are L250 000. *****Capello d'Oro e del Moro**, Viale Papa Giovanni XXIII 12, tel 242 606, is a plain but forthright establishment near the station, with optional air-conditioning. All rooms with bath, L95 000. A much cheaper option near the station, the ***Leon d'Oro**, Via P. Paleocapa 6 (third left off of Viale Papa Giovanni XXIII), tel 218 151; good rooms, though none with bath, L35 000.

EATING OUT
Bergamo prides itself on its cooking, and the city is well endowed with excellent restaurants. Many, surprisingly, feature seafood—Bergamo is a major inland fish market. The classic for

fish, **Da Vittorio**, Viale Papa Giovanni XXIII 21, tel 218 060, specializes in seafood prepared in a number of exquisite ways, as well as a wide variety of meat dishes, polenta, risotto, and pasta, and a superb bouillabaisse. Closed three weeks in Aug and Wed (L90–100 000). On Piazza Vecchia there are two excellent choices, **La Fontana**, tel 220 648, with a constantly changing menu that also features many seafood dishes, as well as duck, kid, venison or other meat dishes prepared by the young gourmet chef (L50–65 000). The other, **Taverna Colleoni**, tel 232 596, has more classical Italian cuisine and a speciality called *Tournedos Donizetti*, with green peppercorns and mustard (L50–65 000; closed Sun & Mon). For good pizza by the slice and bread shaped like *Commedia dell'Arte* figures, try **Il Fornaio**, Via V. Colleoni near Piazza Vecchia.

The Bergamask Valleys

North of Bergamo the scenery improves along the Bergamask valleys, as they plunge into the stony heart of the **Orobie Alps**, the mighty wall of mountains that isolates the Valtellina further north. Pick up the tourist office's booklets, *Orobie Inverno* (winter) or *Orobie Estate* (summer), which, though in Italian, have lists of all hotels, refuges, winter sports, and trails.

Val Brembana

There are two main Bergamask valleys: the western one, the Val Brembana, follows the course of the Bremba and was extremely important in the Middle Ages as the main route for caravans transporting minerals from the Orobies and Valtellina to Bergamo and Venice.

Just off the main road, in **Almenno San Bartolomeo**, the tiny, round 12th-century **Church of San Tomè** is a jewel of Lombard Romanesque, composed of three cylinders, one atop the other, prettily illuminated at night; its isolation makes it especially impressive. **Zogno**, further up the valley, is an important town and site of the **Museo della Valle Brembana**, with artefacts relating to the district's life and history (closed Mon and afternoons). Zogno is also the base for visiting **La Grotta delle Meraviglie**, with a long gallery of stalactites and stalagmites. **San Pellegrino Terme**, next up the valley, means mineral water to millions of Italians; once it was Lombardy's most fashionable spa, developed at the turn of the century around two Baroque/Liberty-style confections, the Grand Hotel and Casino. Excursions include a ride up the funicular for the view, and a visit to the 'Dream Cave', the **Grotto del Sogno**.

According to legend, the **Casa dell'Arlecchino** at Oneta (a village in the hills above **San Giovanni Bianco**) was the birthplace of the *Commedia dell'Arte* clown Harlequin; one story says the role was invented by a *Commedia dell'Arte* actor who lived there, named Ganassa, though more likely it is just a reminder of the many men and women of the Val Brembana who, like Harlequin, chose to forsake their poor hills to become servants in Venice or Bergamo. The humorous fresco on the façade is typical of the outdoor art you'll see everywhere in this region. There are any number of lovely, forgotten hamlets like Oneta in these mountains; many of them lie in a mini-region called the Val Taleggio, on the other side of the spectacular gorge of the **Torrente**

261

Enna. The road through it, beginning at San Giovanni Bianco, was completed only recently.

The next town, medieval **Cornello dei Tasso**, may be down to only 30 inhabitants, but it preserves its appearance as a relay station on the merchants' road, with an arcaded lane to protect the caravans of mules. In the 13th century, much of the business of expediting merchandise here was in the hands of the Tasso family, whose destiny, however, was far bigger than Cornello. One branch went on to run the post between Venice and Rome, while another moved to Germany in the 1500s organizing for Emperors Maximilian I and Charles V the first European postal service. Their extensive network of postal relay stations was in use into the 19th century, while the German spelling of their name, Taxis, went on to signify their privately licensed vehicles and from that, our modern taxis. One member of the family operating out of Sorrento was the father of the loony Renaissance poet Torquato Tasso. Besides the muleteers' arcades, you can see the ruins of the Tasso ancestral home, and a number of fine medieval buildings.

Beyond **Piazza Brembana** the road branches out into several mountain valleys. The most important and developed resort is **Foppolo**; besides winter sports it offers an easy ascent up the **Corno Stella**, with marvellous views to the north and east. Other good ski resorts include **Piazzatorre** and **San Simone** near Branzi; **Carona** is a good base for summer excursions into the mountains and alpine lakes. East of Piazza Brembana, a lovely road rises to **Roncobello**; from here your car can continue as far as the Baite di Mezzeno, the base for a bracing three-hour walk up to the **Laghi Gemelli**. From here experienced mountaineers can pick up the impressive *Sentiero delle Orobie*, a six-day trail that officially begins at Valcanale, to the east in the Valle Seriana and ends in the Passo della Presolana.

Another important village on the merchants' road, the prettily situated **Averara**, was the first station after the Passo San Marco, through which the road entered from the Valtellina. Besides the covered arcade for the caravans, there are a number of 16th-century exterior frescoes.

Valle Seriana and Clusone

The eastern valley, the **Valle Seriana**, is industrial in its lower half and ruggedly Alpine in the north. At the bottom of the valley, some 8 km from Bergamo, **Alzano Lombardo** (or Maggiore) is worth a brief stop for one of Italy's most striking Rococo pulpits, sculpted by Antonio Fantoni, completely covered with reliefs, statues, and soaring cherubs, who all manage to fit into the **Basilica di San Martino**, along with some fine 17th-century inlaid and intarsia work.

Fine old **Gandino** is another town to aim for, just off the main valley road; in the Middle Ages it was the chief producer of a heavy, inexpensive cloth called bergamask. The finest structure in town is the **Basilica**, a 17th-century garlic-domed church, with more fine works by Fantoni and a museum housing religious art and relics of the city's medieval textile industry. **Clusone**, further up, is capital and prettiest town of the Valle Seriana, with many frescoes and a beautiful 16th-century astronomical clock on the **town hall** in Piazza dell'Orologio—the most joyfully decorated building in Lombardy.

Near it, the **Oratorio del Disciplini** is adorned with an eerie 1485 fresco of the *Danse Macabre* and the Triumph of Death, where one skeleton mows the nobility and clergy down with arrows, while another fires a blunderbuss. There are more frescoes inside, and a *Deposition* by Fantoni. In the 1980s, more colourful paintings have been discovered and reclaimed from under the grimy stucco. Most are within a block or two of Piazza del Orologio, including one glorious, grinning Venetian lion.

Winter and summer resorts further north include the lovely **Passo della Presolana** and **Schilpàrio**, both located near dramatic Dolomite-like mountain walls.

Lake Iseo and the Val Camonica

The least visited of the larger lakes, Iseo (the Roman *Lacus Sebinus*) is fifth in size and a charming alternative to the glittering hordes that blacken the more celebrated shores. Even back in the 1750s it was the preferred resort of such eccentric Italophiles as Lady Mary Wortley Montagu, who disdained the English who 'herd together' by the larger lakes. Besides its wooded shores and backdrop of mighty mountains, Iseo bears triplet islands in its bosom, among them Monte Isola, the largest island in any European lake. Along the river Oglio, the main source of Iseo, runs the Val Camonica, a broad Alpine valley with nothing less than one of the world's greatest collections of prehistoric art.

GETTING AROUND
While buses from Bergamo run frequently to the lake towns of Tavernola and Lovere (there's also a direct bus from Milan to Lovere), Iseo is best approached from the southeast; trains run up to Iseo town and along the entire east shore of the lake from Brescia (or the rail junction at Rovato between Bergamo and Brescia). Steamers ply the lake between Lovere and Sarnico, calling at 15 ports; ask for a schedule at the Iseo tourist office, as the routes are complex and change seasonally—including dinner cruises for L 22 000 per person, on Saturday evenings in August.

There are also regular ferries (no cars) to Monte Isola from Sulzano, Lovere and Sale Marasino. From Pisogne several trains a day continue up the Val Camonica as far as Edolo.

TOURIST INFORMATION
Iseo: Lungolago Marconi 2, tel (030) 980 209
Darfo-Boario Terme: Piazza Einaudi 2, tel (0364) 531 609
Capo di Ponte: Via Briscioli, tel (0364) 42 080
Edolo: Piazza Martiri Libertà 2, tel (0364) 71 065
Ponte di Legno: Corso Milano 41, tel (0364) 91 122

Franciacorta and Lake Iseo

Between Brescia and Iseo lies the sleepy wine-growing region known as **Franciacorta**, the 'free court'—owing to its poverty—which was exempted from taxes, a fact that endeared it to the villa-building patricians of Lombardy. Today their mellowing old estates are surrounded by vineyards producing a fine DOC red and *Pinot Bianca*. While the countryside as a whole is the main attraction, the **Villa Lana** (now Ragnoli) in Colombaro is worth a stop for Italy's oldest cedar of Lebanon in its garden. Two other villages closer to Brescia have ancient churches—the Romanesque Olivetan abbey church at Rodengo, with three cloisters and frescoes by Romanino and Moretto, and **San Pietro in Lamosa**, founded by monks from Cluny in 1083, located in **Provaglio**. San Pietro overlooks an emerald peat-moss called **Le Torbiere**, which blossoms into an aquatic garden of pink and white waterlilies in late spring; the tourist office in Iseo rents out rowing boats to enable you to paddle through.

Iseo, between the lake and Le Torbiere, is one of the main shore resorts with its beaches and a venerable 12th-century church, **Pieve di Sant' Andrea**, on one of its shady streets. Steamers link it with **Sarnico**, a smaller resort to the west, sprinkled with Liberty-style villas, and with the real attraction of this lake, arcadian, car-less **Monte Isola**. This steep rock, a fair-sized copy of Gibraltar soaking in its own bathtub, has occasionally been a resort of painters and poets; the lack of cars is not progressive planning—there simply aren't any roads to drive them on.

Several genteelly decaying fishing villages dot the island's shore, connected to the mainland by tiny ferries (see above). Recreation is limited to walks through the olive and chestnut groves, perhaps as far as the sanctuary chapel on the top of the island—over a thousand feet above the lake. Monte Isola's people still catch fish in the lake, but their talent for making fine nets has led to a new business opportunity. Now they make the tennis nets for all the Italian championship tournaments.

Sale Marasino, one of the ferry ports to Monte Isola, is one of the prettier spots on the lake with its mountain terraces. From the nearby village of **Marone** you can hike up to the panoramic viewpoint of **Monte Guglielmo** (1949 m, with an alpine refuge), passing by way of **Cislano**, near Zone, with its spiky 'erosion pyramids', similar to the pyramids of the Dolomites. A few have large boulders neatly balanced on top. On Cislano's little parish church, there is an exterior fresco of St George and the dragon. Next along the shore, the old village of **Pisogne** has the last train station (with bus connections to Lovere); its church of **Santa Maria delle Neve** is covered with excellent frescoes by Romanino, who spent two years on the project.

Lovere, the oldest resort on Lake Iseo, has a fine church in its 15th-century frescoed **Santa Maria in Valvendra**, and a handful of good paintings in its **Galleria dell'Accademia Tadini** (especially a Madonna by Jacopo Bellini). Open afternoons, May–Sept. The highlight of Iseo's west shore is **Riva di Solto** (a steamer port), with its odd little bays and views across the water of the formidable Adamello mountains. **Tavernola Bergamasca** has a local steamer to Sarnico.

Val Camonica

From Pisogne the road and trains continue northeast into the Val Camonica, one of the most fertile of Alpine valleys. Its name is derived from a Rhaetian tribe, the Camuni, whose artistic ancestors used the smooth, glacier-seared Permian sandstone of their valley as tablets to engrave solar discs and labyrinths, mysterious figures and geometric designs, animals, weapons, and people. What is especially remarkable is the long, continuous period of the incisions: the oldest are from the Neolithic era (before 2200 BC) and the latest from the arrival of the Romans—a period spanning some 25 centuries, enabling scholars to trace intriguing prehistoric stylistic evolutions, from the random-scratched symbols of the late Stone Age to the finely drawn, realistic and narrative figures of the Bronze and Iron Ages. We can never really understand the significance these etchings had for their makers, but their magic must have been extraordinary: in the valley some 180,000 have so far been discovered. Some are beautiful, some ungainly and peculiar, some utterly mystifying, while a few are fuel for crackpot theories. Recently UNESCO has put the Val Camonica on its select list of sites to be protected as part of the artistic patrimony of humanity.

Some 12 km from Pisogne, some early incisions from the 3rd millennium BC may be seen in a lovely park at Luine, near the spa **Boario Terme**. Unfortunately the rock here has weathered more than further north at Capo di Ponte and the graffiti are often hard to decipher. Continuing up the road that brings you to Luine, route 294, will give you the opportunity for a scenic detour up the **Valle d'Angolo** and its wild and narrow **Dezzo Ravine**.

When the Romans conquered the valley their capital was **Cividate Camuno**, and it remembers their passing with mosaics and tombstones and local finds in its small **archaeological museum** (9–2, closed Mon). It also has a fine 12th-century tower, and churches with frescoes by the excellent quattrocento painter Da Cemmo in the environs, at **Esine** and **Bienno** (Santa Maria Annunziata). **Breno**, the modern capital of the valley, lies under an imposing medieval castle; its 14th-century church of **Sant' Antonio** contains frescoes by Romanino, and its **Museo Camuno** in the town hall has an interesting ethnographic collection from the valley. From here a mountain road winds up to the Passo di Croce Domini and Lake Idro (see below).

Capo di Ponte

Capo di Ponte is the centre for visiting the best of the prehistoric engravings, located in the **Parco Nazionale delle Incisioni Rupestri Preistòrichi** (open daily 9 until an hour before sunset; adm; guided visits may be arranged through the tourist office or the park itself, tel 42 140). The main attraction is the **Naquane rock**, etched with some 900 figures in the Iron Age. Across the Ogilio, in **Cemmo**, there are two other magnificent rocks, the first ones to be discovered, and a few kilometres south of Capo di Ponte, in the tiny medieval hamlet of **Foppe** (near **Nadro**) a second section of the park was opened after the discovery in 1975 of another great concentration of incisions, reached via a beaten path from the village. In Nadro, Capo di Ponte's **Centro Camuno di Studi Preistorici** has its museum, with plans of the Camuni culture's sites among other explanatory items. Besides prehistoric art, Capo di Ponte also has two picturesque 11th-century churches: **San Siro**, with its three tall apses built on a hill directly over the river, and the Cluniac monastery church of **San Salvatore**.

Further up the valley the scenery becomes grander as the Adamello group of the Brenta Dolomites looms up to the right. Beautiful excursions into the range are possible from **Cedegolo**, into the lovely **Valsaviore** with its mountain lakes Arno and Salarno and ascents up Mount Adamello (3555 m), and from **Malonno**, along the scenic road through the chestnut woods of the **Valle Malga,** with more pretty lakes and easy ascents (Corno delle Granate, 3111 m).

Surrounded by majestic mountains, **Edolo** stands at the crossroads of the valley and the road from Sondrio to the Passo di Tonale. It is a base for numerous mountain excursions, and for the ski resorts of the **Valle di Corteno, Ponte di Legno** (the most developed) and **Passo di Tonale.** From the Passo di Tonale you can continue east into Trentino's lovely Val di Sole, while a road from Ponte di Legno cuts through Stelvio National Park to Bormio.

WHERE TO STAY AND EATING OUT

In Iseo, the *****Moselli,** Via Fenice 17, in Pilzone, tel (030) 980 001, is a good choice near the beach, with a garden; all rooms have bath (L48–60 000). For a fine glass of wine (from Franciacorta and beyond) and a good plate of lake trout, among other local specialities, try **Il Volto,** Via Mirolte 33, tel (030) 811 462 (closed Wed, Thurs lunch, last 3 weeks in July; L30–40 000). In Rovato, on the edge of the Franciacorta, there's another excellent place to feast on the freshest of fish: **Tortuga,** Via A. Angelini 10, tel (030) 722 980, although these delights of the deep are brought in on the express train from the ports of the Marches. Specialities include wonderful crustacean and mollusc antipasti and delicate scampi as a recommended choice for seconds. There's a garden for outdoor dining as well (L70 000; closed Sun eve and Mon, 2 weeks in Jan, and lunch in Aug).

The newest and one of the most interesting places to stay and dine on Lake Iseo is the ******Cantiere** in Sarnico (Via Montegrappa 9, tel (035) 910 091), in an old building freshly remodelled by its new owners. The very comfortable rooms, all with bath, go for L150 000, while in the restaurant you can enjoy a great *menu degustazione* for L50 000, featuring dishes like risotto with oysters and prosciutto, veal cutlets with asparagus, wild mushroom soup, exquisite fish dishes and desserts that hit the spot. A pleasant, tranquil hotel, the *****Montisola Palace,** is in the village of Menzino on Monte Isola, tel (030) 982 5087, with a pool in addition to its beach, tennis courts, and fine rooms, all with private bath, L85 000; it also has self-catering flats available. A more economical choice on the island, the little ****Canogola,** Via Porto (loc. Siviano), tel (030) 982 5130, offers quiet seaside rooms, all with bath, for L64 000.

Most of the hotels in the Val Camonica are concentrated in Boario Terme or in the mountain resorts at the northern end. In Boario the plush ******Grand Hotel Boario e Delle Terme,** Via Manzoni 2, tel (0364) 531 061, is the duchess of valley lodgings, offering mineral water treatments in a lovely garden setting; there's an outdoor pool and tennis and rooms that really aren't too dear by Italian Grand Hotel standards. It's open from 15 May–10 Oct (L100 000, all with bath). If you're here overnight on the way to the rock engravings try the ****Primavera,** Via Manifattura 22, tel (0364) 531 453, a small but pleasant place, open all year, rooms without bath for L45 000, with L55 000. In Ponte di Legno the sleek and modern ******Mirella,** Via Roma 21, tel (0364) 91 661, is the top choice, with a pool and tennis among its facilities, L180 000. A less glamorous but adequate choice up at the Passo del Tonale—and open all year—is the ****Dolomiti,** Via Case Sparse Tonale, tel (0364) 91 344; rooms with bath L70 000. A good place to eat in Ponte di Legno, **Al Maniero,** Via Roma 54, tel (0364) 91 093, features hearty local cuisine in a cosy, happy atmosphere for around L35 000.

Brescia

The second city of Lombardy, Brescia may be busy and prosperous, but it's no one's preferred art town, even though it has a full day's supply of art, architecture, and delightful corners to visit. But it won't be your favourite. Perhaps it's the vaguely sinister aura of having been Italy's chief manufacturer of arms for the last 400 years. Perhaps it's because the local Fascists saw fit to punch out the heart of the old city and replace it with a soulless, chilling piazza designed on the principle that might is right. The Brescians seem to detest it, but it's hard to avoid; they would do well to raze it and the subliminal memories it evokes.

History

Brescia was originally a Gaulish settlement, an origin remembered only in its name Brixia, from the Celtic *brik* ('hill'). Brixia was an ally of Rome early on, and in 26 BC achieved the favoured status of a *Colonia Civica Augusta*, when it was embellished with splendid monuments. By the 8th century Brescia had recovered enough from the barbarian invasions to become the seat of a Lombard duchy under King Desiderius, whose daughter Ermengarda was sought in marriage by Charlemagne as the condition for the Emperor's crown. He later repudiated her, and the forlorn Ermengarda returned to Brescia to die in the Abbey of San Salvatore, founded by her mother.

In the 11th century Brescia joined the Lombard League against the tyranny of Frederick Barbarossa and produced the great Benedictine monk, Arnold of Brescia, who went to Rome to preach against the tyranny of possessions and a worldly, materialistic Church, only to be executed for his troubles by the pope. Brescia itself was too tempting a prize to be left in peace by the region's thugs. Power struggles began with the unspeakable Veronese Ezzelino da Romano in 1258 and ended with the detested Visconti in 1421, when the notables, weary of the game of musical chairs in their government, invited the Venetians to adopt the city. The Venetians were grateful to get it, for strategic reasons, and for the access it gave to the area's unusually pure iron deposits. By the 16th century Brescia had become Italy's major producer of firearms and so indispensable to Venice that the Republic imposed emigration restrictions on Brescia almost as severe as those placed on the glassmakers of Murano.

Venetian rule not only brought a great measure of peace and prosperity to Brescia, but initiated an artistic flowering as well. The Brescian Vincenzo Foppa (1485–1566) was a key figure in the Lombard Renaissance, whose monumental paintings were among the first to depict a single, coherent atmosphere. Towards the end of the century, Girolamo Romanino (1485–1566) synthesized Lombard and Venetian schools, while his contemporary Moretto da Brescia (1498–1554) was an ardent student of Titian and contributed the first Italian full-length portrait. His star pupil was Moroni of Bergamo. Recently, a forgotten painter, Giacomo Antonio Ceruti (1698–1767), has been the centre of interest for his realist, unromanticized genre paintings of Brescia's humble, demented, and down-and-out—a unique subject for the place and time.

GETTING AROUND

Brescia is the main transport hub for western Lombardy and Lake Garda, on the main Milan-Venice rail line, 75 minutes from Milan, and an hour from Verona, and less to

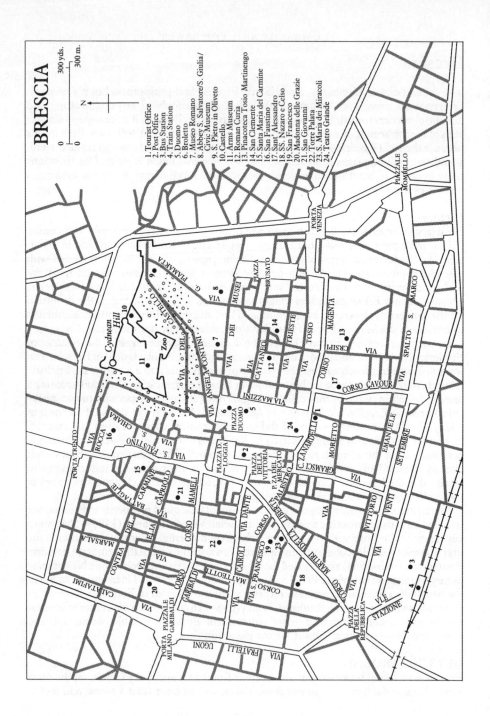

BRESCIA

0   300 yds.

0   300 m.

N

1. Tourist Office
2. Post Office
3. Bus Station
4. Train Station
5. Duomo
6. Broletto
7. Museo Romano
8. Abbey S. Salvatore/S. Giulia/
   Civic Museum
9. S. Pietro in Oliveto
10. Castello
11. Arms Museum
12. Roman Curia
13. Pinacoteca Tosio Martinengo
14. San Clemente
15. Santa Maria del Carmine
16. San Faustino
17. Sant' Alessandro
18. SS. Nazaro e Celso
19. San Francesco
20. Madonna delle Grazie
21. San Giovanni
22. Torre Palata
23. S. Maria dei Miracoli
24. Teatro Grande

Desenzano del Garda, the main station on Lake Garda. Another railway line wends its way north through the mountains to Edolo (2½ hours). Taking in the east shore of Lake Iseo, trains go to Bergamo (1 hour) and Lecco (2 hours); to Cremona (just over an hour); to Parma via Piadena (2 hours). For FS information, call 52 449.

There is an even more extensive coach network, with frequent links to the towns of Lakes Garda and Iseo and less frequently to Idro; also to Turin and Milan, Padua and the Euganean Hills, Marostica, Bassano del Grappa, and Belluno; to Trento via Riva and to the resorts of Pinzolo and Madonna di Campiglio in Trentino, as well as to all points in the province. For information, call 44 061.

The bus and railway stations are located next to each other just south of the city centre on Viale Stazione. Bus C connects them to the centre, or walk in 10 minutes up the Corso Martiri della Libertà.

TOURIST INFORMATION
Corso Zanardelli 34, tel (030) 43 418

The Central Squares
Hurry, like the Brescians do, through the deathly pale and grim 1930s **Piazza Vitto-riale**, duck behind its varicoloured post office, and enter into a far more benign display of power in Brescia's Venetian-style **Piazza Loggia**, the city's most elegant square. It has two fine loggias—one belonging to the Venetian Renaissance **Monte di Pietà Vecchia** (1489), and the other to the three-arched building known simply as the **Loggia**, an almost frilly confection designed in part by Sansovino and Palladio, the greatest Renais-sance architects of the Veneto. Another remainder of the Serenissima is the **Torre dell'Orologio**, a copy of the one in St Mark's Square, complete with two bell-ringing figures on top.

Looming up behind the clock tower is the third-highest dome in Italy, the pearl-white, green-lead-roofed crown of the **Duomo**, built in 1602 by Giambattista Lantana. From the **Piazza del Duomo** itself, however, the dome is hidden by a high, marble false front, its upper section as insubstantial as the wooden façades of a frontier town. Over the door a bust of Brescia's great Cardinal Querini 'winks mischievously, as if inviting the faithful to enter'. You should take him up on it, not so much for the few paintings by Romanino (by the bishop's throne) and Moretto that try to warm the cold interior, as to enter the connecting **Duomo Vecchio** (closed from New Year's Day to Easter). Built in the 11th century over the ruins of the ancient Basilica of San Filastrio and the ancient Roman baths, the singular cathedral may well be the only one in Italy designed in the shape of a top hat, low and rotund, with a massive cylindrical tower rising from its centre, supported by eight pillars. Inside, its simple form is broken only by a 15th-century raised choir. The altarpiece, an *Assumption* by Moretto, is one of his greatest works. The crypt of San Filastrio, the only part of the ancient church to survive, holds a grab-bag of Roman and early medieval columns and mosaics from the Roman baths. Several medieval bishops are entombed about the walls, most impressively Bishop Mernardo Maggi in his sarcophagus (1308); the cathedral treasure contains two precious 11th-century relics—the *Stauroteca*, a reliquary box containing a fragment of the True Cross, and the banner once borne on the *Carroccio* (sacred ox-cart) of the Brescian armies.

Just behind the new cathedral, on Via Mazzini 1, you can visit the **Biblioteca Queriniana**, containing the 18th-century collection of rare books and manuscripts compiled by Cardinal Querini, including the 6th-century 'Purple Evangeliary' and Eusebius' 11th-century Concordances of the Gospels; the cardinal is said to have snubbed the Vatican library in preference for his own (open 8:30–12 and 2:30–6, closed Sat afternoon). On the other side of the Duomo, the 12th-century **Broletto** was the civic centre prior to the construction of the Loggia; its formidable tower, the **Pegol** predates it by a century.

Roman Brixia

From behind the Broletto, turn right on the ancient *Decumanus Maximus*, now the **Via dei Musei**, leading to the heart of the old Roman city with the ruins of its forum in the **Piazza del Foro**. Looming above are the mighty columns of the **Capitoline Temple**, erected by the Emperor Vespasian in AD 73 and preserved for posterity by a medieval mud-slide that covered it until its discovery in 1823; in 1955, an earlier, Republican-era Capitoline temple was discovered beneath Vespasian's, with unusual mosaics of natural stone.

The Capitoline Temple is divided into three *cellae*, probably dedicated to the three principal Roman deities—Jupiter, Juno, and Minerva. They are filled with the inscriptions, tombstones, and mosaics of the **Civico Museo Romano**—a considerable collection thanks to the foresight of the 1485 municipal council, which forbade the sale or transport of antiquities outside Brescia. The museum's best treasures, however, are upstairs, and include a 2-m bronze Winged Victory, who, without the object she once held, seems to be snapping her fingers in a dance step. She, and six gilded bronze busts of emperors, were found during the excavations of the temple. There's a gilt bronze figurine of a prisoner, believed to be the great Gaulish chief Vercingetorix, a beautiful Greek amphora of the 6th century BC, and a facsimile of the fascinating, 7.5-m long Peutringer Map of Vienna, itself a 12th-century copy of a Roman road map (open Tues, Thurs, and Fri 9–12 and 2–5, Sat 2–5, and Sun 9–12).

Next to the temple is the unexcavated *cavea* of the **Roman Theatre**, while further down the Via dei Musei lies the most important complex of Lombard Brescia, the **Abbey of San Salvatore**, founded in the 8th century and disbanded at the end of the 18th. Its church of Santa Giulia, added in the 16th century, and the 8th-century Basilica of San Salvatore, have been restored to house **Brescia's Civic Museum**. San Salvatore is especially interesting for the fragments of its lovely stucco decoration, in the same style as Cividale del Fruili's 8th-century Tempietto Lombardo. The old nunnery contains a **Museum of Modern Art**, while Santa Giulia houses the **Museum of Christian Art**, a magnificent collection with two exceptional masterpieces: the 8th-century Lombard Cross of Desiderius, studded with 212 gems and cameos, including one from the 4th century of a Roman woman with her two children, all peering warily into the approaching Dark Ages; the Brescians like to believe it is the great *Galla Placidia* of Ravenna. The other treasure is a 4th-century ivory coffer called the *Lipsanoteca*, adorned with beautiful bas-reliefs of scriptural scenes. One of the lovely 5th-century ivory diptychs originally belonged to the father of the philosopher Boethius. Lombard jewellery, medieval art, and Renaissance medals round out the collection.

The Cydnean Hill

The lyric poet Catullus, who considered Brixia the mother of his native Verona, was the first to mention the Cydnean hill that rises up behind the Via dei Musei. This was the core of Gaulish and early Roman Brixia—if you take Via Piamarta from Santa Giulia you'll pass by the ruins of the city's one surviving **Roman gate** as well as the attractive 1510 **San Pietro in Oliveto**, named after the ancient silvery olive grove that surrounds the church. Up on top are the imposing walls of the medieval **Castello**, with its round 14th-century **Mirabella Tower**, built on a Roman foundation. There's a small children's zoo in the castle garden, a dull Risorgimento museum, and the recently remodelled **Luigi Marzoli Museum of Arms**, one of Italy's most extensive collections of Brescia's bread-and-butter industry (open Tues, Wed, and Fri 10–12 and 3–7, Sat 3–7, Sun 10–12; adm).

The Pinacoteca

From the Capitoline Temple Via F. Crispi descends to the Via Carlo Cattaneo; at No. 3, in the Piazza Labus near the intersection, you can make out the columns and lintels of the ancient Roman **Curia** imprinted like a fossil in the wall of a house. Further down, Via Crispi opens up into the Piazza Moretto, site of the **Galleria Tosio-Martinengo**, Brescia's main art repository (open 9–12 and 2–5, Sat 9–12 and Sun 2–5, closed Mon and Fri; adm.) This houses a fine collection of the local school, including paintings by Foppa, Moretto (his *Salome* is a portrait of the great Roman courtesan-poetess Tullia d'Aragona), Romanino, Moroni, and the later Ceruti, as well as a painting by Lorenzo Lotto and two early works by Raphael—a not altogether wholesome, beardless *Redeemer* and a lovely *Angel*.

From the gallery Via Moretto will take you back to the centre and the busy shops under the porticoes of Via Mazzini, and Corso Zanardelli.

The West Side

In the neighbourhoods west of the Piazza del Loggia and the Corso Martiri della Libertà there are a handful of monuments worth a look if you have an hour to spare. Just west of the Via S. Faustino (which leads north from the Piazza del Loggia) there are two unusual churches—**San Faustino in Riposo**, a cylindrical, steep-roofed drum of a church from the 12th century (near the intersection with Via dei Musei), and further up, the 14th-century **Santa Maria del Carmine**, crowned with a set of Mongol-like pinnacles; it contains frescoes by Foppa and a 15th-century terracotta Deposition group.

Just off the Corso G. Mameli (the western extension of Via dei Musei) **San Giovanni** is a Renaissance church with good works by Moretto and the Bolognese painter Francia. Further along the Corso stands the giant **Torre Palata**, a survivor from the rough-and-tumble 13th century, with a travesty of a 16th-century fountain like a bunion on its foot. From here Via della Pace heads south to the venerable 13th-century **San Francesco**, with 13th-century frescoes, and the nearby (at the intersection of Corso Martiri) **Santa Maria dei Miracoli** with a fine, ornate Renaissance façade. Further south, off the Corso Martiri on Via Bronzetti, the 18th-century **Santi Nazaro e Celso** houses a 1522 polyptych by Titian, portraying a Risen Christ in the central panel; as is often the case, Titian's care to produce the last word in emotional realism in his religious art goes overboard into a numbing vision of spiritual banality.

WHERE TO STAY (tel prefix 030)
Brescia's hotels cater mainly to business clients, and its best hotels are comfortable if not inspiring. Near the centre by the castle, the ****Master, Via L. Apollonio 72, tel 399 037, has the best rooms in town if the dumbest name; all have TV and bath (L170 000). A bit further out of the centre, the very modern ****Ambasciatori, Via Crocefissa di Rosa 92, tel 308 461, with a garage, is a good bet for motorists; it also has very good, air-conditioned rooms for L120 000, all with private bath and TV. Among the less expensive choices the **Nuovo Orologio, Via C. Beccaria 17, tel 54 057, is pleasant enough, with a bar but no restaurant (L50 000 without bath, L60 000 with). Or there's the *Regina e Due Leoni, near the art gallery on Corso Magenta 14, tel 59 276, housed in an older building but cosy just the same (L40 000 without bath, L50 000 with), or the convenient but totally nondescript *Stazione, near the bus and train stations on Vicolo Stazione 17, tel 52 128, with bathless rooms for L38 000.

EATING OUT
Brescians are not known for their cooking, and in fact are looked upon as rather stolid conservatives at the table. Kid is a popular item on the local menu, and the stews, meat on a skewer and polenta dishes the Brescians favour have been the vogue since the Renaissance. The city's most celebrated restaurant, La Sosta, Via San Martino della Battaglia 20, tel 295 603, is charmingly set in a 17th-century stable that has been stripped and made elegant, though a few horsey reminders may be seen in the pictures on the wall and the hitching rings on the pillars. The food, though good, is 'international' and a bit dull (L60 000; closed Mon & Aug). There's more imaginative dining but rather less atmosphere at Alla Stretta, Via Stretta 63, tel 200 2327, with good fish and traditional Brescian meat dishes (L50–60 000). For plain, hearty Brescian cooking at humane prices, Da Walter, on Via San Faustino 35 (north of Piazza Loggia) has full meals for L20 000.

The best restaurant in Brescia is actually 10 km away to the north, in Concesio, where the excellent Miramonti L'Altro, Via Crosette 34, tel 275 1063, features a menu that delights both the gourmet and traditionalist, with specialities that include raw and smoked salmon, mushrooms in season, breast of duck in ginger, kid cooked Brescian style. For afters, there's a fine array of mountain cheeses, or one of Miramonti's great desserts; closed Sun eve, Mon and Aug (L60–70 000).

Around Brescia

TOURIST INFORMATION
Idro: Via Trento 46, tel (0365) 83 224
Anfo: Via Roma 23, tel (0365) 809 022

Besides Lakes Garda and Iseo, there are a number of worthwhile excursions into the region's mountain valleys—as well as one to the south in the plain, to Montirone and the fine Villa Lechi, built in 1740 by Antonio Turbino and changed little since the day when Mozart slept there. It has frescoes by Carlo Carloni and period furnishings; the stables and park are equally well preserved.

To the north stretches the Valtrompia, a scenic agricultural valley. Its largest town,

Gardone Val Trompia, was one of the main producers of firearms for Venice and enjoyed the special protection of the Republic; it still makes hand-crafted sports rifles. North of Gardone the valley narrows as the road climbs to two fine summer resorts, **Bovegno** and **Collio**. The high mountains around the latter permit skiing in the winter. Beyond Collio a new road continues up to the scenic **Passo del Maniva** and over to the Passo di Croce Domini.

Lake Idro

Long, narrow, and winding **Lake Idro** (Roman *Eridio*), lies over the mountains from Collio, at the head of the Val Sabbia. Surrounded by rugged mountains and rural villages, it is the highest of the Lombard lakes and one of the best for trout fishing, windsurfing, and sailing. The lake is named after the small south-shore resort town of **Idro**, with low-key sandy beaches and family-oriented places. On the panoramic west shore, **Anfo**, Idro's main sailing centre, is marked by a Venetian stronghold. A turn-off north of Anfo leads to the prettiest town in the region, **Bagolino**, on the trout-filled River Caffaro, with its peaceful medieval streets and the 15th-century church of **San Rocco**, frescoed in the 1400s by Da Cemmo; modern residents produce fine, hand-knotted woollen carpets.From Lake Idro you can continue up the Chiese river into Trentino's Val Giudicarie towards Tione.

Lake Garda

The Italian lakes culminate in Garda, largest (48 km long and 16 km across at its widest point), bluest, and most dramatic, the fabled Riviera of the Dolomites. With the profile of a tall-hatted witch, its wild and romantic shores have enchanted the Romans, who knew it as *Lacus Benacus*. If the waters of Lake Como are mingled with memories of the two Plinys, Garda's shores recall two of Italy's greatest poets of pure passion: ancient Rome's tragic, love-lorn Catullus and that modern fire hazard, Gabriele D'Annunzio. For chilblained travellers from the north, its Mediterranean olives, vines, and lemon groves, its slender cypresses and exotic palm trees have long signalled the beginning of their own dream Italy. No tourist office could concoct a more scintillating Mediterranean oasis to stimulate what the Icelanders call 'a longing for figs', that urge to go south.

Perhaps it's because Lake Garda is more 'Italian' that it seems less infected by the maiden auntiness of its more northerly, Swissified sisters. Less stuffy and status-conscious, it is the most popular lake, attracting a wide range of visitors, from beach bums to package tourists, from garden lovers to sailors who come to test their mettle on Garda's unusual winds, first mentioned by Virgil: the *sover* which blows from the north from midnight through the morning, and the *ora*, which blows from the south in the afternoon and evening. Storms are not uncommon but, on the other hand, the breezes are delightfully cool in the summer. In the winter Garda enjoys a mild climate, less oppressed by clammy fogs and mists than the other lakes. Although services are at a minimum, winter is an ideal time to visit, when the jagged peaks that surround it shimmer with snow and you can better take in the voluptuous charms that brought visitors to its shores in the first place.

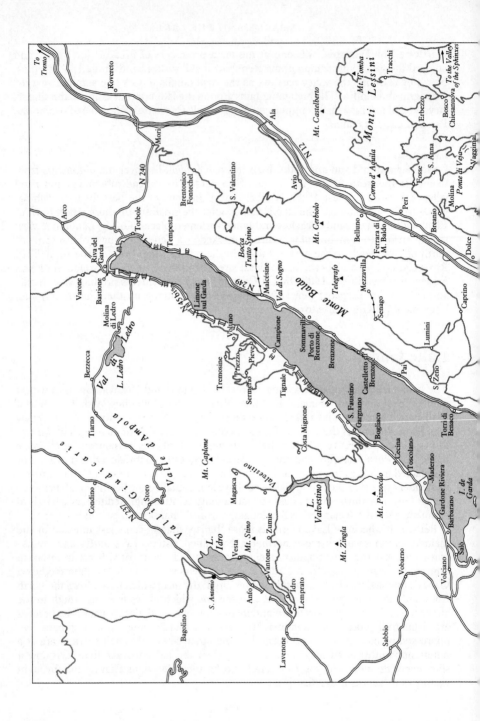

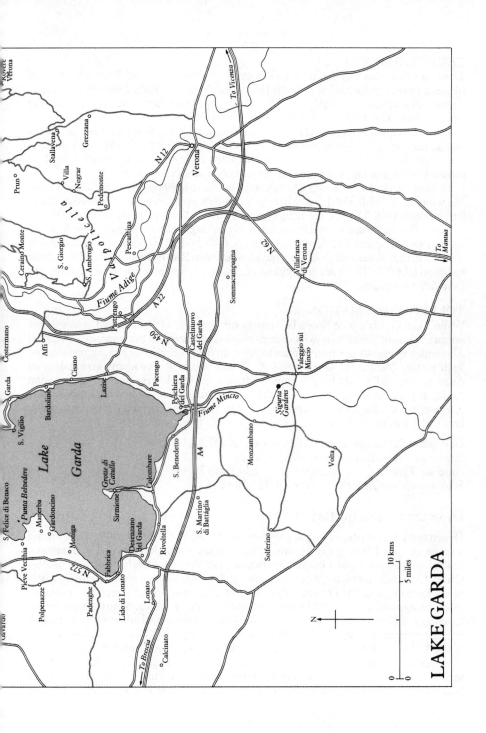

LAKE GARDA

GETTING AROUND

There are two train stations near Lake Garda, at Desenzano and Peschiera, both of which are landings for the lake's hydrofoils (*aliscafi*) and steamers. Buses from Brescia, Trento, and Verona go to their respective shores; for Desenzano, the principal starting point for Lake Garda, there are buses from Brescia, Verona and Mantua, and two exits from the Serenissima Autostrada. Other bus lines run up and down the road that winds around the lake shores—a marvel of Italian engineering, called La Gardesana, Occidentale on the west and Orientale on the east. In summer, however, their scenic splendour sometimes pales before the sheer volume of holiday traffic.

All boat services on the lake are operated by *Navigazione sul Lago di Garda*, Piazza Matteotti 2, tel (030) 914 1321, where you can pick up a timetable; the tourist offices have them as well. The one car ferry crosses from Maderno to Torri; between Desenzano and Riva there are several hydrofoils a day, calling at various ports (2 hours) as well as the more frequent and leisurely steamers (4¹/₂ hours). Services are considerably reduced in the off-season. Full fare from Desenzano to Riva by steamer is L9500, on the hydrofoil L14 000. There are also regular afternoon cruises from July to mid-September from different points.

TOURIST INFORMATION

While Lake Garda's west shore belongs to the province of Brescia in Lombardy, its northern tip is in Trentino and its eastern shore is in Venetia in the province of Verona. Although this results not from a plan to divvy up the tourist dollar among regions, but from history (readers of Goethe will recall how the poet was nearly arrested as an Austrian spy while sketching a ruined fortress on the Veneto shore), each region parochially fails to acknowledge that Lake Garda exists beyond its own boundaries; their maps often leave the opposite shores blank, if they draw them in at all. Be sure to watch area codes when telephoning.

Desenzano del Garda: Piazza Matteotti 27, tel (030) 914 1510
Sirmione: Viale Marconi 2, tel (030) 916 114
Gardone Riviera: Corso Repubblica 35, tel (0365) 20 347
Saló: Lungolago Zanardelli 39, tel (0365) 21 423

Desenzano and Solferino

Desenzano del Garda, on a wide gulf dotted with beaches, is the lake's largest town and its main gateway (if you arrive by train, a bus will take you to the centre). Life is centred around its port cafés and a dramatic statue of Sant' Angela, foundress of the Ursuline Order. Originally a settlement of pile dwellings, Desenzano was a popular holiday resort of the Romans, and one of their villas has been excavated on Via Crocifisso, revealing colourful mosaics from the 4th century and artefacts now in the small museum on the site (open 9–4, till 5 in summer, closed Mon; adm). In Desenzano's 16th-century cathedral, pride of place goes to an unusual 18th-century *Last Supper* by Gian Domenico Tiepolo. A small antiques market takes place around the first weekend of each month.

Besides Lake Garda, Desenzano is the base for visiting the low war-scarred 'Risorgimento' hills to the south. The two most important battles occurred on the same day, 24 June 1859, in which Napoleon III defeated Emperor Franz Joseph at **Solferino** and

King Vittorio Emanuele defeated the Austrian right wing at **San Martino della Battaglia**, 8 km away. It was the beginning of the end for the proud Habsburgs in Italy, but the Battle of Solferino had another consequence as well—the terrible suffering of the wounded so appalled the Swiss Henry Dunant that he formed the idea of founding the Red Cross. At San Martino you can climb the lofty **Torre Monumentale** erected 1893, containing paintings and mementos from the battle (open 8:30–1 and 2–5, closed Tues). Solferino is marked by an old tower of the Scaligers of Verona, the **Spia d'Italia**, with a collection of uniforms; there's a battle museum by the church of **San Piero**, containing 7000 graves, and a memorial to Dunant and the Red Cross, erected in 1959 (all same hours as the San Martino tower).

Perhaps even more important was the battle averted in these hills at the end of the Roman empire. Attila the Hun, having devasted northeast Italy, was on his way to Rome when he met Pope St Leo I here. The Pope, with Saints Peter and Paul as his translators, informed Attila that if he should continue to Rome he would be stricken by a fatal nosebleed, upon which the terrible Hun turned aside, sparing central Italy.

Sirmione

> Sweet Sirmio! thou, the very eye
> Of all peninsulas and isles,
> That in our lakes of silver lie,
> Or sleep enwreathed by Neptune's smiles

So wrote Catullus, Rome's greatest lyric poet, born in Verona in 84 BC, only to die some 30 years later in the fever of a broken heart. When he wasn't haunting the Palatine home of his fickle mistress 'Lesbia' , he is said to have visited the villa his family kept, like many well-to-do Romans, on the narrow 4-km-long peninsula of **Sirmione** that pierces Lake Garda like a pin. Just over 90 m across at its narrowest point, Sirmione is the most

Sirmione, Garda

277

visually striking town on Lake Garda, and the principal attraction are the lovely **Grotte di Catullo**, entwined with ancient olive trees on the tip of the rocky promontory— romantic ruins with a capital R, though not of Catullus' villa, but of a great Roman bath complex (Sirmione is famous even today for its thermal spa). The views across the lake to the mountains are magnificent; there's also a small antiquarium on the site with mosaics and frescoes (9 until sunset, closed Mon; adm).

The medieval centre of Sirmione is dominated by one of the most memorable of Italian castles, the fairytale **Castello Scaligera**, built by Mastino I della Scala of Verona in the 13th century and surrounded almost entirely by water. There's not much to see inside, but fine views from its swallow-tail battlements (open 9–1, 9–6 from April–Oct; adm expensive). Also worth a look is the ancient Romanesque **San Pietro in Mavino**, with 13th-century frescoes. Cars are not permitted over its bridge into the town, and the best swimming is off the rocks on the west side of the peninsula.

Saló

From Sirmione the steamer passes the lovely headlands of Manerba and Punta San Fermo and the **Island of Garda**, the lake's largest, where St Francis visited the former monastery; ruined, it formed the base of a monumental 19th-century Venetian-Gothic style palace, now owned by the Borghese princes, one of whom, Scipione, made the famous drive from Peking to Paris in the early days of the automobile. **Saló** (the Roman *Salodium*) enjoys one of the most privileged locations on the lake; it gave its name to Il Duce's last dismal stand, the puppet Republic of Saló of 1944, formed after the Nazis rescued him from his prison in an Abruzzo ski lodge. Saló has a number of fine buildings, including a late Gothic **Cathedral** with a Renaissance portal of 1509 and paintings within by Romanino, Moretto da Brescia, and a golden polyptych by Paolo Veneziano. **L'Ateneo**, in the Renaissance Palazzo Fantoni, contains a collection of 13th-century manuscripts and incunabula. North of Saló begins the **Brescia Riviera**, famous for its exceptional climate and exotic trees and flowers.

Gardone Riviera and D'Annunzio's Folly

Gardone Riviera, its shore marked by the tall, 1920s reconstruction of its **Torre di S. Marco**, has long been the most fashionable resort on the Brescia Riviera, if not on all of Lake Garda, ever since 1880 when a German scientist noted the almost uncanny consistency of its climate; profiting from its mildness is the loveliest sight in Gardone, **Giardino Botanico Hruska**, with imported tufa cliffs and artificial streams, and plants from Africa, the Alps, and the Mediterranean (open 8 am–7 pm, shorter hours in the winter; adm).

Above the garden it's a short walk to the equally uncanny **Il Vittoriale**, the last home of Gabriele D'Annunzio (1863–1938) (open from 9–12:30 and 2–5:30, except Mon; adm expensive. Try to arrive at 9 am to avoid the crowds and tour buses. There's an option of buying a ticket to the uninteresting museum and grounds only).

Gabriele D'Annunzio was a poor boy from the Abruzzo who became the greatest writer and poet of his generation, but not one who was convinced that the pen was mightier than the sword; a fervent right-wing nationalist, he was one of the chief warmongers urging Italy to intervene in World War I. Later he led his 'legionaries' in the famous unauthorized invasion of Fiume, which, though promised to Italy before its entrance into the First World War, was just being ceded to Yugoslavia. D'Annunzio instantly became a national hero, stirring up a diplomatic furore before coming home. For Mussolini the popular old jingoist was an acute embarrassment, and he decided to pension him off in 1925—in a luxurious Liberty-style villa designed by Gian Carlo Maroni, ostentatiously to give the debt-ridden poet a secure home in gratitude for his patriotism, but in reality to shut him up in a gilded cage. D'Annunzio dubbed the villa, formerly owned by a German family, 'Il Vittoriale' after Italy's victory over Austria in 1918 and proceeded to redecorate it and pull up its lovely garden to create an unrivalled arena of domestic kitsch.

Luigi Barzini describes D'Annunzio as 'perhaps more Italian than any other Italian' for his love of gesture, spectacle, and theatrical effect—what can you say about a man who would announce that he had once dined on roast baby? Yet for the Italians of his generation, no matter what their politics, he exerted a powerful influence in thought and fashion; he seemed a breath of fresh air, a new kind of 'superman', hard and passionate yet capable of writing exquisite, intoxicating verse; the spiritual father of the Futurists, ready to destroy the old bourgeois *Italia vile* of museum curators and parish priests and create in its stead a great modern power, the 'New Italy'. He lived a life of total exhibitionism, according to the old slogan of an American brewery, 'with all the gusto he could get'—extravagantly, decadently and beyond his means, the trend-setting aristocratic aesthete with his borzois, 'the Divine' Eleanora Duse and innumerable other loves (preferably duchesses). Apparently he thought the New Italians should all be as eccentric and clever, and he disdained the conformity and corporate state of the Fascists.

D'Annunzio made Il Vittoriale his personal monument and in his inexhaustible egotism knew that one day the gaping hordes would be tramping through, marvelling at his exquisite taste. Unfortunately the guides speak only Italian, so to fill in the gaps if you don't, the tour begins with what must be called a 'cool reception' room for guests D'Annunzio disliked, austere and formal compared to the comfy one for favourites. When Mussolini came to call he was entertained in the ice chamber; D'Annunzio, it is said, escorted Il Duce over to the mirror and made him read the inscription he had written above: 'Remember that you are of glass and I of steel'. Perhaps you can make it out if your eyes have had time to adjust to the gloom. Like Aubrey Beardsley and many of the characters played by Vincent Price, D'Annunzio hated the daylight and had the windows painted over, preferring low electric lamps.

The ornate organs in the music room and library were played by his young American wife, who gave up a promising musical career to play for his ears alone. His bathroom, with 2000 pieces of bric-à-brac, somehow manages to have space for the tub; the whole house is packed solid with a feather-duster's nightmare of art and junk. In his spare bedroom, adorned wth leopard-skins, you can see the cradle-coffin he liked to lie in to think cosmic thoughts about his mortality. He made the entrance to his study low so all would have to bow as they entered; here he kept a bust of La Duse, but covered, to keep her memory from distracting him. The dining room, with its bright movie-palace sheen, is one of the more delightful rooms. D'Annunzio didn't care much for it, and left his guests here to dine on their own with his pet tortoise, which he embalmed in bronze after the creature expired of indigestion, a subtle reminder of the dangers of overeating.

In the adjacent auditorium hangs the bi-plane D'Annunzio used to fly over Vienna in the war, while out in the garden the prow of the battleship *Puglia* from the Fiume adventure juts out, mast and all, in a copse of cypresses. Walk above this to the white travertine **Mausoleum** on its hill, baking and glaring in the bright sun like a kind of Stonehenge set up by an evil race from an alien galaxy. Within three concentric stone circles the sarcophagi of legionary captains respectfully pay court to the plain tomb of D'A himself, raised up on columns high above the others to be the closest to his dark star, all in jarring contrast to the mausoleum's enchanting views over the lake.

WHERE TO STAY AND EATING OUT
If you come to Garda in July or August without a reservation, it can mean big disappointment. For lower prices and more chance of a vacancy, try the small towns on the east shore; also check at the tourist offices for rooms in private homes. At least half-pension will be required in season at most hotels, and despite the mild climate most close after October or November until March.

Sirmione: For a total immersion in the peninsula's romance, the *******Villa Cortine**, Via Grotte 6, tel (030) 916 021, can't be surpassed, offering its guests perhaps the rarest amenity to be found in Sirmione—tranquillity. Its enchanting, century-old Italian garden occupies almost a third of the entire peninsula with its exotic flora, venerable trees, statues and fountains running down to the water's edge. The Neoclassical villa itself was built by an Austrian general, and was converted into a hotel in 1954, preserving its frescoed ceilings and elegant furnishings. The rooms are plush, the atmosphere perhaps a bit too exclusive but ideal for a break from the real world, with private beach and dock, pool and tennis. Open March–Oct, full-board obligatory—L310–325 000 per person in a double with bath. Down a notch but still very,very comfortable, the ******Hotel Eden**, Piazza Carducci 18, tel (030) 916 481, is housed in a medieval building in the centre of Sirmione, beautifully remodelled within with fine marbles and coordinated bedrooms with princely bathrooms, TV, and air conditioning; open March–Oct, no restaurant; L125 000 with breakfast. Although it's more attractive on the outside than in the rooms, the ****Hotel Grifone**, near the Scaliger castle on Via Bocchio 6, tel (030) 916 014, has a great location, and some rooms have lovely lake views; closed Nov–March (all rooms with bath, L55–60 000). It shares the weathered stone house with the more elegant **Ristorante Grifone de Luciano**, tel (030) 916 097, serving simple but delicious fish and more for around L50 000. Another fine place to dine with views that rival the food is the **Piccolo Castello**, Via Dante 9, tel (030) 916 138, facing the Scaliger castello, with fish and meat specialities from the grill (L35 000).

One of Italy's finest restaurants is near the peninsula at Lugana di Sirmione: the classy **Vecchia Lugana**, Via Lugana Vecchia, tel (030) 919 012, where the menu changes four times a year to adapt to the changing seasons and the food is exquisite, prepared with a light and wise touch—try the divine mousse of lake trout—L75 000, with wine (closed Mon eve, Tues, & Jan).

Saló: Although less glamorous than some of its neighbours, Saló has one of Lake Garda's loveliest hotels, the ******Laurin**, Viale Landi 9, tel (0365) 22 022, an enchanting Liberty-style villa converted into a hotel in the 1960s, maintaining its elegant décor. The charming grounds include a swimming-pool and beach access; all rooms have bath and TV; open Feb–mid-Dec; L165–190 000. For a good, reasonably priced and traditional meal, try the **Trattoria alla Campagnola**, Via Brunati 11, tel (0365) 22 153. Garden-fresh vegetables served with every dish, homemade pasta, and mushrooms in season (L40 000); closed Mon, Tues lunch, & Jan.

Gardone Riviera: Gardone Riviera and its suburb Fasano Riviera have competing de luxe Grand Hotels, both old pleasure domes. When Gardone's contender, the ****Grand Hotel, Via Zanardelli 72, tel (0365) 20 261, was built in 1881, its 180 rooms made it one of the largest resort hotels in Europe. It is still one of Garda's landmarks, and its countless chandeliers glitter as brightly as when Churchill stayed in 1948, still licking his wounds after taking a beating in the election. Almost all of the palatial air-conditioned rooms look on to the lake, where guests can luxuriate on the garden terraces, swim in the heated outdoor pool or off the private sandy beach. The dining room and delicious food match the quality of the rooms; closed mid-Oct to mid-April; L120–200 000. Fasano's ****Grand Hotel Fasano, Via Zanardelli 160, tel (0365) 21 051, was built in the mid 1800s as a Habsburg hunting palace and converted to a hotel at the turn of the century. Surrounded by a large park, the owners have furnished the hotel almost entirely with Belle Epoque furnishings; there are tennis courts, a heated pool, and private beach; the restaurant is one of Lake Garda's best. Open May–Sept, rooms are L110–200 000.

Another fine place to lodge in Fasano, the ****Villa del Sogno, Via Zanardelli 107, tel (0365) 20 228, was its creator's 'Dream Villa' of the 1920s—done in grand Renaissance style. Although not on the lake, it has a private beach five minutes' walk away and a pool in its flower-filled garden. Open March–Oct, rooms, all with bath, L120–190 000. Back in Gardone, the less expensive but lovely ***Villa Fiordaliso, Via Zanardelli 132, tel (0365) 20 158, is a fine turn-of-the-century hotel, where the historically minded can request the suite where Mussolini and his mistress Claretta Petacci spent the last weeks of their lives. Located in a serene park, with a private beach, all seven rooms have bath and TV; it also boasts an elegant restaurant, open to the public, featuring classic Lombard and Garda dishes; specialities *insalata di coniglio all'aceto balsamico* (rabbit salad in balsamic vinegar) and lots of pasta dishes with vegetable sauces. Closed Nov–Feb, rooms L95 000; meals L65 000 (closed Sun eve, Mon). The ***Bellevue, Via Zanardelli 81, tel (0365) 20 235, is above the main road overlooking the lake, with a pretty garden sheltering it from the traffic. Rooms are modern, and all have private bath. Open April–10 Oct, L80 000. *Pensione Hohl, Via dei Colli 4, tel (0365) 20 160, half-way up to Il Vittoriale, is another former villa in a pleasant garden. None of the rooms have baths but they're quiet and a steal in Gardone for L42 000.

Garda's West Shore: Gardone to Riva

TOURIST INFORMATION

Gargnano: Piazza Feltrinelli 2, tel (0365) 71 222
Toscolano-Maderno: Via Lungolago 18, tel (0365) 641 330
Limone: Via Comboni 15, tel (0365) 954 070
Riva: Giardini di Porta Orientale 8, tel (0464) 554 444
Arco: Viale delle Palme 1, tel (0464) 532 255

Toscolano-Maderno and Gargnano

The single *comune* of Toscolano-Maderno has one of the finest beaches on Lake Garda, a fine 9-hole golf course, the car ferry to Torri, and the distinction of having been the site of *Benacum*, the main Roman town on the lake. Toscolano had a famous printing press in the 15th century, and was the chief manufacturer of nails for Venice's galleys. Most of the Roman remains, however, have been incorporated into the fine 12th-century church of **Sant'Andrea** in Maderno, restored in the 16th century by St Charles Borromeo. **Gargnano** seems more of a regular town than a resort, though it was here, in a villa owned by the editor Feltrinelli (whose chain of bookstores are a blessing to the English-speaking traveller in Italy) that Mussolini ruled the Republic of Saló. The main sight in town is the 13th-century **Franciscan church and cloister**; in the latter the columns are adorned with carvings of citrus fruit, a reminder of the ancient tradition that the Franciscans were the first to cultivate citrus fruits in Europe.

North of Gargnano the lake narrows and the cliffs close into the shore; here *La Gardesana* road pierces tunnel after tunnel like a needle as it hems through some of the most striking scenery along the lake. An equally splendid detour is to turn off after Gargnano at **Campione**, a tiny hamlet huddled under the cliffs, along the old military road for **Tremosine**, atop a 300 m precipice that dives down sheer into the blue waters below; from the top there are views that take in the entire lake. The road from Tremosine rejoins the lake and *La Gardesana* at the next town along the lake, **Limone sul Garda**.

Although it seems obvious that Limone was named after its lemon groves, prominent in the neat rows of terraced white posts and trellises, scholars sullenly insist it was derived instead from the Latin *Limen*. Nor is it true that Limone was the first to grow lemons in Europe (the Arabs introduced them into Sicily and Spain), but none of that takes away from one of the liveliest resorts on the lake, with a beach over 3 km long.

Riva del Garda

After Limone the lake enters into the Trentino region and the charming town of Riva, snug under the amphitheatre of mountains. During the days of Austrian rule (1813–1918), Riva first blossomed as a resort, nicknamed the 'Southern Pearl on the Austro-Hungarian Riviera'. It is one of best bases for exploring both the lake and the Trentino mountains to the north.

The centre of town is the Piazza Tre Novembre with its plain, 13th-century **Torre Apponale**; just behind it, surrounded by a natural moat, stands the sombre grey bulk of the 12th-century castle, the **Rocca**, housing a civic museum with local archaeological finds from the prehistoric settlement at Lake Ledro and from Roman Riva (open 9–12 and 2:30–6; closed Mon). The early 17th-century church of the **Inviolata** was built by an unknown but imaginative Portuguese architect with a fine gilt and stucco Baroque interior. A funicular (or a steep path) makes the ascent to the Venetian watchtower, the 1508 **Bastione**.

There are a number of pleasant excursions from Riva, but one of the best is the closest, the **Cascata del Varone**, a lovely 87 m waterfall in a tight gorge only 3 km away, near the village of Varone. Another fine excursion is up over the exciting Ponale Road (N. 240) to green **Lake Ledro**, noted not only for its pretty setting, in wooded hills, but for the remains of a Bronze Age (1500 BC) settlement of *palafitte* lake dwellings, discovered in

1929; one has been reconstructed near the ancient piles around **Molina**, where there's also a museum, with pottery, axes, daggers, and amber jewellery recovered from the site. From here you can continue to Lake Idro, through the shadowy narrow gorge of the **Valle d'Ampola**. Another excursion is up to **Arco** (Roman *Arx*, 'stronghold'), a popular health resort in the days of the Austro-Hungarian Empire. Among the sights are a 16th-century palace, former property of the cultured Counts of Arco, who also built the castle crowning the town, set in clusters of cypresses—a half-hour's walk up, and worth it for the views. Arco has a fine collegiate church, **S. Maria Assunta**, designed by a follower of Palladio, and a botanical garden once owned by the Archduke.

WHERE TO STAY AND EATING OUT

Gargnano: In Gargnano's suburb, Villa di Gargano, *****Baia d'Oro**, Via Gamberera 13, tel (0365) 71 171, is a small but charming old hotel on the lakefront with an artistic inn-like atmosphere. It has a private beach, and picturesque terrace; all rooms have baths (open 20 March–Oct; L95 000). For a pure Victorian ambience, even if furnishings are replicas, reserve at the *****Hotel Giulia**, Viale Rimembranza tel (0365) 71 289; added attractions are its fine lake views, beach, and good food. (Open March–15 Oct, all rooms have bath; L82–95 000.) Eating out in Gargnano is a pleasure at the celebrated **La Tortuga**, Via XXIV Maggio 5 (near the harbour), tel (0365) 71 251, a gourmet haven on Lake Garda featuring delicate dishes based on seasonal ingredients and fish from the lake, perfectly prepared; delicious vegetable soufflés, innovative meat courses, mouth-watering desserts and fresh fruit sorbets, grand wine and liquor lists. Closed Mon eve and Tues; reservations a must (around L85 000).

Limone: Prices here are not as astronomical as other resorts. The finest, ******Le Palme**, Via Porto 36, tel (0365) 954 681, is housed in a pretty Venetian villa, preserving much of its original charm with modern up-to-date amenities. Located in the old centre of Limone, and named after its two ancient palm trees, it has a fine terrace and tennis courts, though no beach. Open end of March–Oct, all 28 rooms have private baths; L75–88 000. Many of the lakeside choices here are large and ungainly, if inexpensive by Garda standards, but *****Sogno del Benaco**, Lungolago Marconi 7, tel (0365) 954 026, is of a more reasonable size and is open all year (L48 000).

Riva: When German intellectuals like Nietzsche or Günter Grass need a little rest and relaxation in Italy, they check in at the ******Hotel du Lac et du Parc**, Viale Rovereto 44, tel (0464) 551 500. Set in a large lakeside garden, the hotel is spacious, airy and tranquil, and the rooms all have bath and TV; and there are indoor and outdoor pools, a beach, sailing school, gym, sauna, and tennis. Closed Nov–March; L210–250 000. Right on the port in Riva's main square, the *****Hotel Sole**, Piazza III Novembre, tel (0464) 552 686, has plenty of atmosphere and a beautiful terrace; most rooms, which vary widely in size and quality, look out over the lake; most have private bath. Open all year round, L60–85 000 without bath, L80–140 000 with. A fine economy choice is the ***Villa Minerva**, Viale Roma 40, tel (0464) 553 031, not far from the centre and very pleasant—and popular. Open all year, L32–37 000 without bath, L45–50 000 with. The best place to eat around Riva is **Vecchia Riva**, Via Bastione 3, tel (0464) 555 061, where you can dig your fork into a spicy antipasta made of goose, and pasta dishes like *pennette con le code di scampi* or *farfalline al radicchio*, swordfish, smoked trout, or a number of meat dishes; L55 000, closed Tues.

In Arco: *__Hotel Garden__, Via Caproni 25, tel (0464) 516 379, is a modern hotel under the mountain, with a small pool (15 Mar–30 Oct), showers in each room, L40 000.

Riva to Peschiera: the East Shore

TOURIST INFORMATION
Torbole: Lungolago Verona 19, tel (0464) 505 177
Malcésine: Via Capitanato 1, tel (045) 740 0555
Garda: Lungolago Regina Adelaide 25, tel (045) 725 5194
Torri del Benaco: Via Gardesana 37, tel (045) 722 5120
Bardolino: Piazza Matteotti 53, tel (045) 721 0078
Peschiera del Garda: Piazza Betteloni 5, tel (045) 755 0381
Lazise: Via Fontana 14, tel (045) 758 0114

Torbole

The northern part of the east shore is dominated by the long ridge of **Monte Baldo**, rising up over **Torbole** at the mouth of the Sacra, the main river flowing into Lake Garda. Torbole is a pleasant resort, where the winds especially favour sailing and wind-surfing, but it's also famous in the annals of naval history. In 1437, during a war with the Visconti, the Venetians were faced with the difficulty of getting supplies to Brescia because the Milanese controlled Peschiera and the southern reaches of Lake Garda. A Greek sailor came up with the following suggestion: that the Venetians sail a fleet of provision-packed warships up the Adige to its furthest navigable point, then transport the vessels over Monte Baldo into Lake Garda. Anyone who has seen Herzog's film *Fitzcarraldo* will appreciate the difficulties involved, and the amazing fact that, under the command of Venice's great *condotierre* Gattamelata and aided by 2000 oxen, the 26 ships were launched at Torbole only 15 days after leaving the Adige. Yet after all that trouble the supplies never reached Brescia. The same trick, however, perhaps even suggested by the same Greek, enabled Mohammed II to bring his fleet into the upper harbour of Constantinople the following year, leading to the capture of the city.

Malcésine

South of Torbole and the forbidding sheer cliffs of the Monte de Nago hanging perilously over the lake (which nevertheless attract their share of human flies), the *Gardesana Orientale* passes into the Veneto at **Malcésine**, the loveliest town on the east shore. The Veronese, and later Venetians, have always taken care to protect this part of the coast, or the '*Riviera degli Olivi*' as they've dubbed it, and the town is graced by the magnificent 13th-century **Scaliger castle**, rising up on a sheer rock over the water. The castle houses a small museum, but is especially worth visiting for the views from its tower (open April–Oct 9–8 pm; otherwise weekends and holidays only, 9–5, adm). It was while sketching this castle that Goethe was suspected of spying; Malcésine has since made up by erecting a bronze bust of the poet in a broad-rimmed hat.

Besides the Scaliger castle, there's the 16th-century **Palace of the Venetian Captains of the Lake** now the Municipio, in the centre of Malcésine's web of medieval streets. A cableway runs up to **Bocca Tratto Spino**, just below the highest peak of Monte Baldo, the Punta del Telegrafo (2201 m); its ski slopes are very popular with the Veronese, and its views are ravishing.

Torri del Benaco and Garda

Further south, past a stretch of shore silvery with olives, there are two pretty resort towns on either side of the promontory of San Vigilio. The first, **Torri del Benaco** (Roman *Castrum Turrium*) is defended by a 1383 **Scaliger castle**; in the church of **Santa Trinità** there are 14th-century Giottoesque frescoes. The ferry boat crosses over from here for Maderno; the steamer continues around the lovely, cypress-tipped **Punta di San Vigilio** with its Renaissance **Villa Guarienti** by the great Venetian architect Sammicheli, the old church of San Vigilio, and a 16th-century tavern.

Between Punta di San Vigilio and the distinct soufflé-shaped headland called the Rocca lies **Garda**, which gave the lake its modern name. Although Garda was founded before the Romans (prehistoric graffiti and a necropolis have been found in its outskirts), it adopted the name the Lombards gave it, *Warthe*, 'the watch'. After Charlemagne defeated the Lombards Garda became a county, and in an ancient castle on the Rocca, of which only a few stones remain, the wicked Count Berenguer secretly held Queen Adelaide of Italy in 960, after he murdered her husband Lotario and she refused to wed his son. After a year she was discovered by a monk, who spent another year plotting her escape. She then received the protection of King Otto I of Germany, who defeated Berenguer, married the widowed queen, and thus became Holy Roman Emperor. Garda has many fine old palaces, villas, and narrow medieval lanes, and is the last really scenic spot on the lake.

East from Garda, the road climbs to **Caprino Veronese**, the capital of Monte Baldo, where you can visit **Palazzo Carlotti**, with a remarkable ceiling painted with grotesques. A winding road from here runs north along the entire eastern flank of Baldo, past **Ferrara di Monte Baldo**, set in a pretty green saddle of pasturelands, with the Monte Baldo botanical garden. The road carries on all the way north to Mori and the N. 240 to Torbole, without any little roads daring to cross the mighty mountain down to Garda's shore.

Bardolino and Peschiera

Bardolino's most important crop is familiar to any modern Bacchus, and more than a few Austrians and Germans pour into town from 15 Sept–15 Oct for a 'grape cure'. Between the vineyards rises a fine collection of 19th-century villas. It has two important churches: the 8th-century **San Zeno** and the 12th-century **San Severo** with frescoes. The next town, **Lazise**, was the main Venetian port, and by its harbour retains an ensemble of Venetian buildings as well as another fine Scaliger castle. Just east of here, in **Pastrengo**, there's the **Dinosaur Park** and **Garda Safari** for addicts of concrete brontosauri, with a zoo and reptilarium all rolled up in one, and an autosafari replete with Tibetan oxen, jaguars, tigers, and hippos, in a tropical garden setting.

Peschiera del Garda is an old military town on the railway from Verona, near the mouth of the River Mincio that drains Lake Garda. Its strategic position has caused it to be fortified since Roman times, though the imposing walls that you see today are

16th-century Venetian, reinforced by the Austrians when Peschiera was one of the corners of the Empire's 'Quadrilateral'. Today, like Desenzano, Peschiera is mainly a transit point to the lake, but its purifying plant still helps it to fulfil its ancient role as a defender, this time of the lake's ecology and fish population. Here, too, you can treat the children at **Gardaland**, Italy's largest and most popular amusement park (to the tune of 2 million visitors a year) with its Magic Mountain, Colorado boat ride, reproduction of the Valley of the Kings, the Amazon, electronic robots etc. etc. etc. for a perfect day of packaged fun.

The region south of Peschiera is known for its white wine *Custoza*, and for the pretty gardens and groves that line the Mincio River between Peschiera and the swampy lakes of Mantua. The greatest of these, the **Sigurtà Gardens** , were the 40-year project of 'Italy's Capability Brown'—500,000 square metres, containing 20 different Anglo-Italian gardens of flowering plants and trees, along 7 km of porphyry paths. The Sigurtà Gardens are near **Valeggio**, an attractive town in its own right, with a castle and bridge built by the Visconti.

WHERE TO STAY AND EATING OUT (tel prefix 045)
The east shore of Garda is more family oriented, slower paced, and less expensive.

In Malcésine: Next to the lake and not far from the centre, the ***Excelsior Bay**, Lungolago, tel 740 0380, is a fine resort hotel with a pool and garden, and splendid views from the balconies of its rooms. Open end of March–end of Oct; L40–50 000 without bath, L55–87 000 with. Another good choice is the ***Malcésine**, Piazza Pallone 2, tel 740 0173, pleasantly situated in its garden with swimming terrace; nice rooms all with bath. Open 22 March–15 Oct; L45–65 000. **Hotel Panorama**, up in Val di Monte 9, tel 740 0171, has fine views over the lake, and a tennis court and swimming-pools besides (L48–65 000, all with bath; open May–Sept).

In Torri del Benaco: The ***Gardesana**, Piazza Calderini 20, tel 722 5411, is the most comfortable hotel, right on the harbour with splendid views of lake and castle. Breakfast and meals are served on the harbour patio when the weather is good. All rooms have bath; L65–100 000.

Garda: ****Eurotel**, Via Gardesana, tel 725 5279, is large, modern, and luxurious and again, good value compared with the west-shore hotels. It has a fine garden and pool, and is open from 9 April–Oct; L56–94 000, according to season, all rooms with bath. The very stylish ****Regina Adelaide**, Via XX Settembre, tel 725 5013 has a golf course, frigo-bars and TVs in each room (L60–110 000, all with bath). The ***Hotel du Parc**, Via Marconi 3, tel 725 5343, is a pleasant lakeside villa, open all year; all rooms with bath, L50–100 000.

Bardolino: One of the nicest lakeside hotels is the hot Italian pink **Riviera**, Via Lungolago Lenotti 12, tel 721 0023, with a beach and little garden of palm trees. There are cheaper, but not as attractive rooms in the annexe (L39–46 000 without bath, L30–60 000 with; open April–mid-Oct). You can dine well at **Aurora**, Via San Severo 18, tel 721 0038, near Bardolino's pretty Romanesque landmark. Specialities include the denizens of the lake, especially trout prepared in a variety of styles (L40–50 000; closed Mon & Nov).

ARCHITECTURAL, ARTISTIC
AND HISTORICAL TERMS

Ambones: twin pulpits in some southern churches (singular: *ambo*), often elaborately decorated.

Atrium: entrance court of a Roman house or early church.

Badia: *abbazia*, an abbey or abbey church.

Baldacchino: baldachin, a columned stone canopy above the altar of a church.

Basilica: a rectangular building, usually divided into three aisles by rows of columns. In Rome this was the common form for lawcourts and other public buildings, and Roman Christians adapted it for their early churches.

Broletto: a medieval town hall.

Calvary chapels: a series of outdoor chapels, usually on a hillside, that commemorate the stages of the Passion of Christ.

Campanile: a bell-tower.

Campanilismo: local patriotism; the Italians' own word for their historic tendency to be more faithful to their home towns than to the abstract idea of 'Italy'.

Cardo: transverse street of a Roman *castrum*-shaped city.

Carroccio: a wagon carrying the banners of a medieval city and an altar; it served as the rallying point in battles.

Cartoon: the preliminary sketch for a fresco or tapestry.

Caryatid: supporting pillar or column carved into a standing female form; male versions are called *telamons*.

Castrum: a Roman military camp, always neatly rectangular, with straight streets and gates at the cardinal points. Later the Romans founded or refounded cities in this form, hundreds of which survive today (Aosta, Pavia, Como, and Brescia are clear examples).

Cavea: the semicircle of seats in a classical theatre.

Cenacolo: fresco of the Last Supper, often on the wall of a monastery refectory.

Ciborium: a tabernacle; the word is often used for large, freestanding tabernacles, or in the sense of a baldacchino.

Comune: commune, or commonwealth, referring to the governments of the free cities of the Middle Ages. Today it denotes any local government, from the Comune di Roma down to the smallest village.

Condottiere: the leader of a band of mercenaries in late medieval and Renaissance times.

Confraternity: a religious lay brotherhood, often serving as a neighbourhood mutual-aid and burial society, or following some specific charitable work (Michelangelo, for example, belonged to one that cared for condemned prisoners in Rome).

Cupola: a dome.

Cyclopean walls: fortifications built of enormous, irregularly-shaped polygonal blocks, as in the pre-Roman cities of Latium.

Decumanus: street of a Roman *castrum*-shaped city parallel to the longer axis, the central, main avenue called the Decumanus Major.

Duomo: cathedral.

Forum: the central square of a Roman town, with its most important temples and public buildings. The word means 'outside', as the original Roman Forum was outside the first city walls.

Fresco: wall painting, the most important Italian medium of art since Etruscan times. It isn't easy; first the artist draws the *sinopia* (q.v.) on the wall. This is covered with plaster, but only a little at a time, as the paint must be on the plaster before it dries. Leonardo da Vinci's endless attempts to find clever shortcuts ensured that little of his work would survive.

Ghibellines: one of the two great medieval parties, the supporters of the Holy Roman Emperors.

Gonfalon: the banner of a medieval free city; the *gonfaloniere*, or flag-bearer was often the most important public official.

Grotesques: carved or painted faces used in Etruscan and later Roman decoration; Raphael and other artists rediscovered them in the 'grotto' of Nero's Golden House in Rome.

Guelphs: (see *Ghibellines*). The other great political faction of medieval Italy, supporters of the Pope.

Intarsia: work in inlaid wood or marble.

Lozenge: the diamond shape—along with stripes, one of the trademarks of Pisan architecture.

Narthex: the enclosed porch of a church.

Palazzo: not just a palace, but any large, important building (though the word comes from the Imperial *palatium* on Rome's Palatine Hill).

Palio: a banner, and the horse race in which city neighbourhoods contend for it in their annual festivals.

Pantocrator: Christ 'ruler of all', a common subject for apse paintings and mosaics in areas influenced by Byzantine art.

Pieve: a parish church, especially in the north.

Polyptych: an altarpiece composed of more than three panels.

Predella: smaller paintings on panels below the main subject of a painted altarpiece.

Presepio: a Christmas crib.

Pulvin: stone, often trapezoidal, that supports or replaces the capital of a column; decoratively carved examples can be seen in many medieval cloisters.

Putti: flocks of plaster cherubs with rosy cheeks and bums that infested much of Italy in the Baroque era.

Quadriga: chariot pulled by four horses.

Quattrocento: the 1400s—the Italian way of referring to centuries (*duecento, trecento, quattrocento, cinquecento*, etc.).

Rocca: a citadel.

Sacro Monte: in Piedmont, a series of outdoor chapels decorated with frescoes and sculptures symbolizing the New Jerusalem.

Sinopia: the layout of a fresco (q.v.), etched by the artist on the wall before the plaster is applied. Often these are works of art in their own right.

Stigmata: a miraculous simulation of the bleeding wounds of Christ, appearing in holy men like St Francis in the 12th century.

Telamon: see *caryatid*.

Thermae: Roman baths.

Tondo: round relief, painting or terracotta.

Transenna: marble screen separating the altar area from the rest of an early Christian church.

Triclinium: the main hall of a Roman house, used for dining and entertaining.

Triptych: a painting, especially an altarpiece, in three sections.

Trompe l'oeil: art that uses perspective effects to deceive the eye—for example, to create the illusion of depth on a flat surface, or to make columns and arches painted on a wall seem real.

Tympanum: the semicircular space, often bearing a painting or relief, above the portal of a church.

CHRONOLOGY

BC

80,000	Give or take 10,000 years: Palaeolithic settlements along the Riviera
8000	First rock incisions in the Val Camonica
c. 1800	Celto-Ligurians begin to occupy north
500s	Greeks and Phoenicians establish trading post with native Ligurians at Genoa
236–222	Romans conquer Po Valley from Gauls
222	Celtic Mediolanum (Milan) comes under Roman rule; Roman colony of Ticinum (Pavia) founded
219	Hannibal and his elephants cross the Alps
205	Genoa sides with Rome and is destroyed by Carthaginians; is rebuilt by Roman praetor Spurius Cassius
177	Romans found colony at Luni
87	Catullus born at Sirmione
70	Virgil born at Mantua
24	Terentius Varro captures capital of Salassian Gauls, and renames it Augusta Praetoria (Aosta)

AD

23–79	Pliny the Elder, of Como
62–120	Pliny the Younger, of Como
284–305	Diocletian divides Roman Empire in two; Milan becomes most important city in West, pop. 100,000
313	Edict of Milan—Constantine makes Christianity the religion of the empire
374–397	St Ambrose, bishop of Milan
387	St Ambrose converts and baptizes St Augustine in Milan
539	Goths slaughter most of male Milanese
567	Lombards overrun most of Italy, and make Pavia their capital
590s	Pope Gregory the Great converts Queen Theodolinda and the Lombards to orthodox Christianity
c. 730	Desiderius, King of the Lombards, born near Brescia
778	Charlemagne defeats last Lombard king, Desiderius, and repudiates his wife, Desiderius' daughter, and is crowned King of Italy in Pavia.
888	Berenguer crowned king of Italy at Pavia
1033–1109	St Anselm, Archbishop of Canterbury, born at Aosta
1045	Adelaide of Susa weds Oddo, son of Umberto the White Handed of Savoy, establishing Savoy rule on both sides of the Alps in Savoy-Piedmont

290

1109–1155	Arnold of Brescia, monk and preacher against worldly Church, only to be hanged by Pope
1127	Como destroyed by Milanese, rebuilt by Barbarossa
1142	Founding of the Marquisate of Saluzzo
1154	Milan sacked by Barbarossa
1155	Barbarossa crowned king of Italy at Pavia
1156	Barbarossa sacks Milan again
1158	Milan obliterates rival Lodi; Lodi rebuilt by Barbarossa
1161	Barbarossa destroys Milan
1168	Castellans of Monferrato rebel against Barbarossa and found Alessandria
1170s	Peter Waldo in the south of France founds the Waldenses sect; persecuted as heretics, many settle in the remote Vaudois valleys of Piedmont
1176	Lombard League defeats Barbarossa at Legnano
1183	Treaty of Constance recognizes independence of Lombard cities
1252	Inquisitor St Peter Martyr axed in the head at Lake Como
1275	Asti, warring with Alba, holds first Palio; Alba does the same with donkeys
1277	The Visconti overthrow the Torriani to become *signori* of Milan
1282	Battle of Meloria; Genoa replaces Pisa as Tyrrhenian maritime power, with trading colonies as far as the Crimea
1311–13	Emperor Henry VII rules Genoa
1318–35	Robert of Anjou, King of Naples, rules Genoa
1319	Princes of the Paleologo family establish Duchy of Monferrato
1334	Azzone Visconti captures Cremona
1335	Como becomes fief of Milan
1339	Genoa excludes nobles from government and establishes popular dogeship, electing Simone Boccanegra
1348–9	The Black Death wipes out a third of the Italians
1379	Venice defeats Genoa at Chioggia and becomes main power in the east
1382	Genoa, unable to govern itself, lets Savoy do it
1386	Gian Galeazzo Visconti begins Milan cathedral
1390–92	Genoa surrenders power to Savoy again
1396–1409	Genoa ruled by Charles VI of France; Gian Galeazzo Visconti founds the Certosa of Pavia
1402	Gian Galeazzo Visconti, conqueror of northern Italy, plans to capture Florence but dies of plague
1407	Genoa conquers Corsica
1409–13	Monferrato's turn to run Genoa
1421–35	Genoa under Filippo Maria Visconti; the Genoese fleet crushes Aragon
1428–1797	Bergamo and Brescia ruled by Venice
1441	Bianca Visconti weds Francesco Sforza, with Cremona as her dowry
1447–1450	Ambrosian republic—Milan's attempt at democracy

1447–1506	Christopher Columbus of Genoa
1450	Francesco Sforza made Duke of Milan
1466–99	Sforza rule of Genoa
1466–1560	Andrea Doria, Admiral of Genoa
1492	The Genoese captain Columbus sails the ocean blue
1494	Wars of Italy begin with French invasion of Charles VIII
1495	Battle of Fornovo; Leonardo begins *Last Supper*
1497	Company of Divine Love founded at Genoa, a charitable institution soon to become an important voice of Church reform, but unheeded by Popes
1499–1512	Louis XII of France rules Genoa
1500	Duke of Milan, Lodovico il Moro, captured by French at Novara
1509	Defeat of Venice at Agnadello by Louis XII of France, Pope Julius II, Emperor Maximilian, and the League of Cambrai; Venice loses new acquisition of Cremona, but soon regains Brescia and Bergamo and other *terra firma* real estate
1522	Spanish troops sack Genoa
1525	Battle of Pavia; Spaniards capture French King Francis I
1527–93	Giuseppe Arcimboldi, first surrealist, of Milan
1528	Andrea Doria, backed by Spain, chases French out of Genoa
1532	Waldensians in Piedmont join Swiss Reformation
1533	Federico Gonzaga of Mantua picks up Monferrato by marriage
1538–84	St Charles Borromeo, Archbishop of Milan
1557	Duke Emanuele Filiberto defeats the French at St Quentin
1559	Treaty of Cateau-Cambresis confirms Spanish control of Italy and returns Turin to the House of Savoy
1567–1643	Claudio Monteverdi, opera composer, of Cremona
1573–1610	Michelangelo da Caravaggio
1578	Emanuele Filiberto brings Holy Shroud to Turin
1596–1684	Nicolò Amati, violin maker, of Cremona
1620	Spanish governor of Milan orders 'Day of Holy Butchery' in the Valtellina; Catholics massacre Protestants, initiating 20 years of war
1630	Plague in Milan (described by Manzoni in *The Betrothed*)
1644–1737	Stradivarius, violin maker, of Cremona
1657	Plague in Genoa
1665	Carlo Emanuele II, with help from Louis XIV persecutes Waldensians in Piedmont; Cromwell and Milton protest
1668–78	French keep the 'Man in the Iron Mask' at Pinerolo prison
1683–1745	Giuseppe Guarneri, violin maker, of Cremona
1684	Louis XIV conquers Genoa
1694–1775	St Paul of the Cross, founder of the Passionist Order, of Ovada (near Acqui Terme in Piedmont)
1698	Henri Arnaud reconquers Vaudois for Waldensians; Vittorio Amedeo recognizes them as subjects of Savoy
1700–13	War of the Spanish Succession

1713	Austrians pick up Milan
1720	Piedmont becomes the Kingdom of Piedmont-Sardinia
1734–46	Austrians rule Genoa
1745	Alessandro Volta, the physicist, born in Como
1755	Genoa sells Corsica to France
1778	La Scala inaugurated
1785	Alessandro Manzoni, author of *I Promessi Sposi* born in Milan
1784–1840	Nicolò Paganini, of Genoa
1790	Wordsworth lives by Lake Como
1796	Napoleon first enters Italy, defeats Austrians at Lodi, and makes Milan capital of his Cisalpine Republic
1798–1848	Gaetano Donizetti, of Bergamo
1800	Napoleon defeats the Austrians at Marengo
1805	Napoleon crowns himself with the Iron Crown of Italy in Milan Cathedral
1805–72	Giuseppe Mazzini, ideologist of Risorgimento, of Genoa
1809–12	Napoleon interns Pope Pius VII at Savona
1810–61	Count Camillo Cavour, Prime Minister of Vittorio Emanuele II
1813	Rossini composes *Tancredi* on shores of Lake Como
1814	Overthrow of French rule
1815	Treaty of Vienna annexes Liguria to Piedmont
1815–88	St John Bosco
1816–17	Queen Caroline of England at Lake Como
1820	Constitutionalist revolts in Piedmont
1822	Shelley settles in villa near Lerici, but drowns on his way home from Livorno
1831	Mazzini founds *Giovane Italia*; Bellini composes *Norma* on the shores of Lake Como
1842–1928	Giovanni Giolitti, five times prime minister of Italy, born at Mondovì
1844	Dickens in Genoa
1848	Revolutions across Italy; Austrians defeat Piedmont at war
1849	Restoration of autocratic rule
1852	Cavour becomes Prime Minister of Piedmont
1853	Verdi composes *La Traviata* in a villa on Lake Como
1854	Piedmont enters Crimean War
1859–60	Piedmont, with the help of Napoleon III, annexes Lombardy at battle of Solferino; in return gives France Nice and Savoy while Garibaldi's 'Thousand' conquer Sicily and Naples
1860–65	Turin is capital of Italy; in 1865 capital moved to Florence
1870	Italian troops enter Rome; unification completed and Rome becomes capital
1871	Mont Cenis (Fréjus) railway Tunnel, first great transalpine tunnel, opened between France and Italy
1874	Maria Alexandrovna, Empress of Russia, retires at San Remo
1878	Tchaikovsky at San Remo; completes Fourth Symphony and *Eugene Onegin*

1879	Queen Victoria takes a holiday by Lake Maggiore
1880s	Edward Lear spends the last years of his life at San Remo
1881	Angelo Roncalli (Pope John XXIII) born at Sotto il Monte, near Bergamo
1896	Alfred Nobel dies at San Remo
1899	First Fiats made in Turin
1900	King Umberto I assassinated by anarchist
1901	Verdi dies in his hotel room in Milan
1902–7	Period of industrial strikes
1904	Elgar composes 'In the South' overture in Alassio
1905	Completion of the Simplon Tunnel, the longest rail tunnel in the world
1908	Olivetti founded in Ivrea
1910	Peruvian Georges Chavez makes the first flight over the Alps, only to be killed in a crash near Domodossola
1915	Italy enters World War I
1925	Mussolini makes Italy a fascist dictatorship
1925–27	D. H. Lawrence at Lake Como
1938	Gabriele D'Annunzio dies at Il Vittoriale, by Lake Garda
1940	Italy enters World War II
1943	Mussolini deposed; rescued by Germans to found puppet government of Salò in north; Milan burns for days in air raids
1944	Vittorio Emanuele III abdicates
1945	National referendum makes Italy a republic; King Umberto II exiled in Switzerland; new Italian constitution grants the Valle d'Aosta regional and cultural autonomy
1947	After a plebiscite, Tenda and Briga in the Maritime Alps vote to be French
1956	Italy becomes a charter member in the Common Market
1950s–60s	Continuing 'economic miracle', led by Lombardy and Piedmont, brings Italy into line with the rest of Europe
1965	Completion of Mont Blanc motorway tunnel
1980	Completion of Mont Cenis (Fréjus) motorway Tunnel
1983	Major landslides wreak havoc in the Valtellina
1988	More landslides and floods in the Valtellina
1992	Genoa's Columbus Exhibition

LANGUAGE

The fathers of modern Italian were Dante, Manzoni, and television. Each did his part in creating a national language from an infinity of regional and local dialects; the Florentine Dante, the first 'immortal' to write in the vernacular, did much to put the Tuscan dialect in the foreground of Italian literature. Manzoni's revolutionary novel, *I promessi sposi* (The Betrothed), heightened national consciousness by using an everyday language all could understand in the 19th century. Television in the last few decades is performing an even more spectacular linguistic unification; although the majority of Italians still speak a dialect at home, school, and work, their TV idols insist on proper Italian.

Perhaps because they are so busy learning their own beautiful but grammatically complex language, Italians are not especially apt at learning others. English lessons, however, have been the rage for years, and at most hotels and restaurants there will be someone who speaks some English. In small towns and out-of-the-way places, finding an Anglophone may prove more difficult. The words and phrases below should help you out in most situations, but the ideal way to come to Italy is with some Italian under your belt; your visit will be richer, and you're much more likely to make some Italian friends.

Italian words are pronounced phonetically. Every vowel and consonant (except 'h') is sounded. Consonants are the same as in English, except the *c* which, when followed by an 'e' or 'i', is pronounced like the English 'ch' (*cinque* thus becomes cheenquay). Italian *g* is also soft before 'i' or 'e' as in *gira*, pronounced jee-ra. *H* is never sounded; *z* is pronounced like 'ts'. The consonants *sc* before the vowels 'i' or 'e' become like the English 'sh' as in *sci*, pronounced shee; *ch* is pronouced like a 'k' as in *Chianti*, kee-an-tee; *gn* as 'ny' in English (*bagno*, pronounced ban-yo; while *gli* is pronounced like the middle of the word million (*Castiglione*, pronounced Ca-steely-oh-nay).

Vowel pronunciation is: *a* as in English father; *e* when unstressed is pronounced like 'a' in fate as in *mele*, when stressed can be the same or like the 'e' in pet (*bello*); *i* is like the i in machine; *o* like 'e', has two sounds, 'o' as in hope when unstressed (*tacchino*), and usually 'o' as in rock when stressed (*morte*); *u* is pronounced like the 'u' in June.

The accent usually (but not always!) falls on the penultimate syllable. Also note that in the big northern cities, the informal way of addressing someone as you, *tu*, is widely used; the more formal *lei* or *voi* is commonly used in provincial districts.

Useful Words and Phrases

yes/no/maybe	*si/no/forse*
I don't know	*Non lo so*
I don't understand (Italian).	*Non capisco (italiano).*
Does someone here	*C'è qualcuno qui*
speak English?	*chi parla inglese?*
Speak slowly	*Parla lentamente*
Could you assist me?	*Potrebbe aiutarmi?*

Help!	*Aiuto!*
Please	*Per favore*
Thank you (very much)	*(Molto) grazie*
You're welcome	*Prego*
It doesn't matter	*Non importa*
All right	*Va bene*
Excuse me	*Scusi*
Be careful!	*Attenzione!*
Nothing	*Niente*
It is urgent!	*E urgente!*
How are you?	*Come sta?*
Well, and you?	*Bene, e lei?*
What is your name?	*Come si chiama?*
Hello	*Salve* or *ciao* (both informal)
Good morning	*Buongiorno* (formal hello)
Good afternoon, evening	*Buona sera* (also formal hello)
Good night	*Buona notte*
Goodbye	*Arrivederla* (formal), *arrivederci, ciao* (informal)
What do you call this in Italian	*Come si chiama questo in Italiano?*
What	*Che*
Who	*Chi*
Where	*Dove*
When	*Quando*
Why	*Perchè*
How	*Come*
How much	*Quanto*
I am lost	*Mi sono smarrito*
I am hungry	*Ho fame*
I am thirsty	*Ho sede*
I am sorry	*Mi dispiace*
I am tired	*Sono stanco*
I am sleepy	*Ho sonno*
I am ill	*Mi sento male*
Leave me alone	*Lasciami in pace*
good	*buono/bravo*
bad	*male/cattivo*
It's all the same	*Fa lo stesso*
slow	*piano*
fast	*rapido*
big	*grande*
small	*piccolo*
hot	*caldo*
cold	*freddo*
up	*su*

296

down	*giù*
here	*qui*
there	*lì*

Shopping, Service, Sightseeing

I would like...	*Vorrei...*
Where is/are...	*Dov'è/Dove sono...*
How much is it?	*Quanto viene questo?/Quante'è/Quanto costa questo?*
open	*aperto*
closed	*chiuso*
cheap/expensive	*a buon prezzo/caro*
bank	*banca*
beach	*spiaggia*
bed	*letto*
church	*chiesa*
entrance	*entrata*
exit	*uscita*
hospital	*ospedale*
money	*soldi*
museum	*museo*
newspaper (foreign)	*giornale (straniero)*
pharmacy	*farmacia*
police station	*commissariato*
policeman	*poliziotto*
post office	*ufficio postale*
sea	*mare*
shop	*negozio*
room	*camera*
telephone	*telefono*
tobacco shop	*tabaccaio*
toilet	*toilette/bagno*
Men	*Signori/Uomini*
Women	*Signore/Donne*

TIME	
What time is it?	*Che ore sono?*
month	*mese*
week	*settimana*
day	*giorno*
morning	*mattina*
afternoon	*pomeriggio*
evening	*sera*
today	*oggi*
yesterday	*ieri*
tomorrow	*domani*

soon	*presto*
later	*dopo/più tarde*
It is too early	*E troppo presto*
It is too late	*E troppo tarde*

DAYS

Monday	*lunedì*
Tuesday	*martedì*
Wednesday	*mercoledì*
Thursday	*giovedì*
Friday	*venerdì*
Saturday	*sabato*
Sunday	*domenica*

NUMBERS

one	*uno/una*
two	*due*
three	*tre*
four	*quattro*
five	*cinque*
six	*sei*
seven	*sette*
eight	*otto*
nine	*nove*
ten	*dieci*
eleven	*undici*
twelve	*dodici*
thirteen	*tredici*
fourteen	*quattordici*
fifteen	*quindici*
sixteen	*sedici*
seventeen	*diciassette*
eighteen	*diciotto*
nineteen	*diciannove*
twenty	*venti*
twenty-one	*ventuno*
twenty-two	*ventidue*
thirty	*trenta*
thirty-one	*trentuno*
forty	*quaranta*
fifty	*cinquanta*
sixty	*sessanta*
seventy	*settanta*
eighty	*ottanta*
ninety	*novanta*

hundred	*cento*
one hundred and one	*cento uno*
two hundred	*duecento*
thousand	*mille*
two thousand	*due mila*
million	*milione*
a thousand million	*miliardo*

TRANSPORT

airport	*aeroporto*
bus stop	*fermata*
bus/coach	*auto/pulmino*
railway station	*stazione ferroviaria*
train	*treno*
platform	*binario*
port	*porto*
port station	*stazione marittima*
ship	*nave*
automobile	*macchina*
taxi	*tassi*
ticket	*biglietto*
customs	*dogana*
seat (reserved)	*posto (prenotato)*

TRAVEL DIRECTIONS

I want to go to...	*Desidero andare a...*
How can I get to...?	*Come posso andare a...?*
Do you stop at...?	*Ferma a...?*
Where is...?	*Dov'è...?*
How far is it to...?	*Quanto siamo lontani da...?*
When does the... leave?	*A che ora parte...?*
What is the name of this station?	*Come si chiama questa stazione?*
When does the next... leave?	*Quando parte il prossimo...?*
From where does it leave?	*Da dove parte?*
How long does the trip take...?	*Quanto tempo dura il viaggio?*
How much is the fare?	*Quant'è il biglietto?*
Have a good trip!	*Buon viaggio!*
near	*vicino*
far	*lontano*
left	*sinistra*
right	*destra*
straight ahead	*sempre diritto*
forward	*avanti*
backward	*in dietro*
north	*nord/settentrionale*
south	*sud/mezzogiorno*

east	*est/oriente*
west	*ovest/occidente*
around the corner	*dietro l'angolo*
crossroads	*bivio*
street/road	*strada*
square	*piazza*

DRIVING
car hire	*noleggio macchina*
motorbike/scooter	*motocicletta/Vespa*
bicycle	*bicicletta*
petrol/diesel	*benzina/gasolio*
garage	*garage*
This doesn't work	*Questo non funziona*
mechanic	*meccanico*
map/town plan	*carta/pianta*
Where is the road to...?	*Dov'è la strada per...?*
breakdown	*guasto* or *panna*
driving licence	*patente di guida*
driver	*guidatore*
speed	*velocità*
danger	*pericolo*
parking	*parcheggio*
no parking	*sosta vietato*
narrow	*stretto*
bridge	*ponte*
toll	*pedaggio*
slow down	*rallentare*

Italian Menu Vocabulary

Antipasti
These before-meal treats can include almost anything; among the most common are:

Antipasto misto	mixed antipasto
Bruschetto	garlic toast
Carciofi (sott'olio)	artichokes (in oil)
Crostini	liver pâté on toast
Frutta di mare	seafood
Funghi (trifolati)	mushrooms (with anchovies, garlic, and lemon)
Gamberi al fagioli	prawns (shrimps) with white beans
Mozzarella (in carrozza)	buffalo cheese (fried with bread in batter)
Olive	olives
Prosciutto (con melone)	raw ham (with melon)
Salame	cured pork
Salsicce	dry sausage

Minestre e Pasta

These dishes are the principal typical first courses (*primo*) served throughout Italy.

Agnolotti	ravioli with meat
Cacciucco	spiced fish soup
Cannelloni	meat and cheese rolled in pasta tubes
Cappelletti	small ravioli, often in broth
Crespelle	crepes
Fettuccine	long strips of pasta
Frittata	omelette
Gnocchi	potato dumplings
Lasagne	sheets of pasta baked with meat and cheese sauce
Minestra di verdura	thick vegetable soup
Minestrone	soup with meat, vegetables, and pasta
Orecchiette	ear-shaped pasta, usually served with turnip greens
Panzerotti	ravioli filled with mozzarella, anchovies, and egg
Pappardelle alla lepre	pasta with hare sauce
Pasta e fagioli	soup with beans, bacon, and tomatoes
Pastina in brodo	tiny pasta in broth
Penne all'arrabbiata	quill shaped pasta in hot spicy sauce
Polenta	cake or pudding of corn semolina, prepared with meat or tomato sauce
Risotto (alla Milanese)	Italian rice (with saffron and wine)
Spaghetti all'Amatriciana	with spicy sauce of salt pork, tomatoes, onions, and chilli pepper
Spaghetti alla Bolognese	with ground meat, ham, mushrooms, etc.
Spaghetti alla carbonara	with bacon, eggs, and black pepper
Spaghetti al pomodoro	with tomato sauce
Spaghetti al sugo/ragu	with meat sauce
Spaghetti alle vongole	with clam sauce
Stracciatella	broth with eggs and cheese
Tagliatelle	flat egg noodles
Tortellini al pomodoro/panna/in brodo	pasta caps filled with meat and cheese, served with tomato sauce/with cream/in broth
Vermicelli	very thin spaghetti

Second Courses

Carne — **Meat**

Abbacchio	milk-fed lamb
Agnello	lamb
Animelle	sweetbreads
Anatra	duck
Arista	pork loin
Arrosto misto	mixed roast meats
Bistecca alla fiorentina	Florentine beef steak

301

Bocconcini	veal mixed with ham and cheese and fried
Bollito misto	stew of boiled meats
Braciola	pork chop
Brasato di manzo	braised meat with vegetables
Bresaola	dried raw meat similar to ham
Capretto	kid
Capriolo	roe deer
Carne di castrato/suino	mutton/pork
Carpaccio	thin slices of raw beef in piquant sauce
Cassoeula	winter stew with pork and cabbage
Cervello (al burro nero)	brains (in black butter sauce)
Cervo	venison
Cinghiale	boar
Coniglio	rabbit
Cotoletta (alla Milanese/alla Bolognese)	veal cutlet (fried in breadcrumbs/with ham and cheese)
Fagiano	pheasant
Faraono (alla creta)	guinea fowl (in earthenware pot)
Fegato alla veneziana	liver and onions
Involtini	rolls (usually of veal) with filling
Lepre (in salmi)	hare (marinated in wine)
Lombo di maiale	pork loin
Lumache	snails
Maiale (al latte)	pork (cooked in milk)
Manzo	beef
Osso buco	braised veal knuckle with herbs
Pancetta	rolled pork
Pernice	partridge
Petto di pollo (alla fiorentina/bolognese/sorpresa)	boned chicken breast (fried in butter/with ham and cheese/stuffed and deep fried)
Piccione	pigeon
Pizzaiola	beef steak with tomato and oregano sauce
Pollo (alla cacciatora/alla diavola/alla Marengo)	chicken (with tomatoes and mushrooms cooked in wine/grilled/fried with tomatoes, garlic and wine)
Polpette	meatballs
Quaglie	quails
Rane	frogs
Rognoni	kidneys
Saltimbocca	veal scallop with prosciutto and sage, cooked in wine and butter
Scaloppine	thin slices of veal sautéed in butter
Spezzatino	pieces of beef or veal, usually stewed
Spiedino	meat on a skewer or stick
Stufato	beef braised in white wine with vegetables

Tacchino	turkey
Trippa	tripe
Uccelletti	small birds on a skewer
Vitello	veal

Pesce	**Fish**
Acciughe or Alici	anchovies
Anguilla	eel
Aragosta	lobster
Aringa	herring
Baccalà	dried cod
Bonito	small tuna
Branzino	sea bass
Calamari	squid
Cappe sante	scallops
Cefalo	grey mullet
Coda di rospo	angler fish
Cozze	mussels
Datteri di mare	razor (or date) mussels
Dentice	dentex (perch-like fish)
Dorato	gilt head
Fritto misto	mixed fried delicacies, usually fish
Gamberetto	shrimp
Gamberi (di fiume)	prawns (crayfish)
Granchio	crab
Insalata di mare	seafood salad
Lampreda	lamprey
Merluzzo	cod
Nasello	hake
Orata	bream
Ostriche	oysters
Pesce spada	swordfish
Polipi/polpi	octopus
Pesce azzurro	various types of small fish
Pesce di San Pietro	John Dory
Rombo	turbot
Sarde	sardines
Seppie	cuttlefish
Sgombro	mackerel
Sogliola	sole
Squadro	monkfish
Tonno	tuna
Triglia	red mullet (rouget)
Trota	trout
Trota salmonata	salmon trout
Vongole	small clams
Zuppa di pesce	mixed fish in sauce or stew

Contorni	**Side dishes, vegetables**
Asparagi (alla fiorentina)	asparagus (with fried eggs)
Broccoli (calabrese, romana)	broccoli (green, spiral)
Carciofi (alla giudia)	artichokes (deep fried)
Cardi	cardoons, thistles
Carote	carrots
Cavolfiore	cauliflower
Cavolo	cabbage
Ceci	chickpeas
Cetriolo	cucumber
Cipolla	onion
Fagioli	white beans
Fagiolini	French (green) beans
Fave	broad beans
Finocchio	fennel
Funghi (porcini)	mushroom (boletus)
Insalata (mista, verde)	salad (mixed, green)
Lattuga	lettuce
Lenticchie	lentils
Melanzana (al forno)	aubergine/eggplant (filled and baked)
Mirtilli	bilberries
Patate (fritte)	potatoes (fried)
Peperoni	sweet peppers
Peperonata	stewed peppers, onions, etc. similar to ratatouille
Piselli (al prosciutto)	peas (with ham)
Pomodoro	tomato(es)
Porri	leeks
Radicchio	red chicory
Radice	radishes
Rapa	turnip
Sedano	celery
Spinaci	spinach
Verdure	greens
Zucca	pumpkin
Zucchini	zucchini (courgettes)

Formaggio	**Cheese**
Bel Paese	a soft white cow's cheese
Cascio/Casciocavallo	pale yellow, often sharp cheese
Fontina	rich cow's milk cheese
Groviera	mild cheese (gruyère)
Gorgonzola	soft blue cheese
Parmigiano	Parmesan cheese
Pecorino	sharp sheep's cheese
Provalone	sharp, tangy cheese; dolce is more mild
Stracchino	soft white cheese

Frutta	**Fruit, nuts**
Albicocche	apricots
Ananas	pineapple
Arance	oranges
Banane	banana
Cachi	persimmon
Ciliege	cherries
Cocomero	watermelon
Composta di frutta	stewed fruit
Dattero	date
Fichi	figs
Fragole (con panna)	strawberries (with cream)
Frutta di stagione	fruit in season
Lamponi	raspberries
Macedonia di frutta	fruit salad
Mandarino	tangerine
Melagrana	pomegranate
Mele	apples
Melone	melon
More	blackberries
Nespola	medlar fruit
Pera	pear
Pesca	peach
Pesca noce	nectarine
Pompelmo	grapefruit
Prugna/susina	plum
Uve	grapes

Dolci	**Desserts**
Amaretti	macaroons
Cannoli	crisp pastry tubes filled with ricotta, cream, chocolate or fruit
Coppa gelato	assorted ice cream
Crema caramella	caramel topped custard
Crostata	fruit flan
Gelato (produzione propria)	ice cream (homemade)
Granita	flavoured ice, usually lemon or coffee
Monte Bianco	chestnut pudding with whipped cream
Panettone	sponge cake with candied fruit and raisins
Panforte	dense cake of chocolate, almonds, and preserved fruit
Saint Honoré	meringue cake
Semifreddo	refrigerated cake
Sorbetto	sorbet/sherbet
Spumone	a soft ice cream
Tiramisù	cream, coffee, and chocolate dessert

Torrone	nougat
Torta	cake, tart
Torta millefoglie	layered pastry with custard cream
Zabaglione	whipped eggs and Marsala wine, served hot
Zuppa inglese	trifle

Bevande / Beverages

Acqua minerale con/senza gas	mineral water with/without fizz
Aranciata	orange soda
Birra (alla spina)	beer (draught)
Caffè (freddo)	coffee (iced)
Cioccolata (con panna)	chocolate (with cream)
Gassosa	lemon flavoured soda
Latte	milk
Limonata	lemon soda
Succo di frutta	fruit juice
Tè	tea
Vino (red, white, rosé)	wine (rosso, bianco, rosato)

Cooking Terms / Miscellaneous

Aceto (balsamico)	vinegar (balsamic)
Affumicato	smoked
Aglio	garlic
Alla brace	on embers
Bicchiere	glass
Burro	butter
Caccia	game
Conto	bill
Costoletta/Cotoletta	chop
Coltello	knife
Cotto adagio	braised
Cucchiaio	spoon
Filetto	fillet
Forchetta	fork
Forno	oven
Fritto	fried
Ghiaccio	ice
Griglia	grill
Limone	lemon
Magro	lean meat/or pasta without meat
Mandorle	almonds
Marmellata	jam
Menta	mint
Miele	honey
Mostarda	candied mustard sauce
Nocciole	hazelnuts

Noce	walnut
Olio	oil
Pane (tostato)	bread (toasted)
Panini	sandwiches
Panna	fresh cream
Pepe	pepper
Peperoncini	hot chilli peppers
Piatto	plate
Pignoli/pinoli	pine nuts
Prezzemolo	parsley
Ripieno	stuffed
Rosmarino	rosemary
Sale	salt
Salmi	wine marinade
Salsa	sauce
Salvia	sage
Senape	mustard
Tartufi	truffles
Tazza	cup
Tavola	table
Tovagliolo	napkin
Tramezzini	finger sandwiches
Umido	cooked in sauce
Uovo	egg
Zucchero	sugar

Useful Hotel Vocabulary

Vorrei una camera doppia, per favore	I'd like a double room please
Vorrei una camera singola, per favore	I'd like a single room please
con bagno, senza bagno	with bath, without bath
per due notti	for 2 nights
Partiamo domani mattina	We are leaving tomorrow morning
C'è una camera con balcone?	Is there a room with a balcony?
Mancano acqua calda, sapone, luce, carta igienica, asciugamani, coperte, cuscini, attaccapanni	There isn't (aren't) any hot water, soap, light, toilet paper, towels, blankets, pillows, coathangers
Posso pagare con carta di credito?	May I pay by credit card?
Per favore potrei vedere un'altra camera?	May I see another room please?
Si, va bene, grazie	Yes, that's fine, thank you
E' compresa la prima colazione?	Is breakfast included?
Come posso raggiungere il centro città?	How do I get to the town centre?

FURTHER READING

General and Travel

Barzini, Luigi, *The Italians* (Hamish Hamilton, 1964). A perhaps too clever account of the Italians by an Italian jounalist living in London, but one of the classics.

Goethe, J. W., *Italian Journey* (Penguin Classics, 1982). An excellent example of a genius turned to mush by Italy; brilliant insights and big, big mistakes.

Haycraft, John, *Italian Labyrinth* (Penguin, 1987). One of the latest attempts to unravel the Italian mess.

Morton, H. V., *A Traveller in Italy* (Methuen, 1957). Among the most readable and delightful accounts of Italy in print. Morton is a sincere scholar, and a true gentleman. Also a good friend to cats.

Nichols, Peter, *Italia, Italia* (Macmillan, 1973). An account of modern Italy by an old Italy hand.

History

Burckhardt, Jacob, *The Civilization of the Renaissance in Italy* (Harper & Row, 1975). The classic on the subject (first published 1860), the mark against which scholars still level their poison arrows of revisionism.

Clark, Martin, *Modern Italy: 1871 to the Present Day* (Longman 1983).

Hale, J. R., editor, *A Concise Encyclopaedia of the Italian Renaissance* (Thames and Hudson, 1981). An excellent reference guide, with many concise, well-written essays.

Herder, Harry, *Italy in the Age of the Risorgimento 1790–1870* (Longman, 1983). Light shed on a very confusing period, where most of the action happens in the northwest.

Hibbert, Christopher, *Benito Mussolini* (Penguin, 1965, 1979).

Joll, James, *Gramsci* (Fontana, 1977). A look at the father of modern Italian Communism, someone we all should get to know better.

Mack-Smith, Dennis, *A History of Italy*.

Procacci, Giuliano, *History of the Italian People* (Penguin, 1973). An in-depth view from the year 1000 to the present—also an introduction to the wit and subtlety of the best Italian scholarship.

Rand, Edward Kennard, *Founders of the Middle Ages* (Dover reprint, New York), a little-known, but incandescently brilliant work that can explain Jerome, Augustine, Boethius and other intellectual currents of the decaying classical world.

Art and Literature

Boccaccio, Giovanni, *The Decameron* (Penguin, 1972). The ever-young classic by one of the fathers of Italian literature. Its irreverent worldliness still provides a salutary antidote to whatever dubious ideas persist in your mental baggage.

Calvino, Italo, *Invisible Cities, If Upon a Winter's Night a Traveller* (Picador). Provocative fantasies that could only have been written by an Italian. Something even better is his recent compilation of *Italian Folktales*, a little bit Brothers Grimm and a little bit Fellini.

Cellini, *Autobiography of Benvenuto Cellini* (Penguin, trans. by George Bull). Fun reading by a swashbuckling braggart and world-class liar.

Clark, Kenneth, *Leonardo da Vinci* (Penguin, 1990).

Dante Aligheri, *The Divine Comedy* (plenty of equally good translations). Few poems have ever had such a mythical significance for a nation. Anyone serious about understanding Italy and the Italian world view will need more than a passing acquaintance with Dante.

Gadda, Carlo Emilio, *That Awful Mess on Via Merulana* (Quartet Books, 1980). Italy during the Fascist era.

Gilbert/Linscott, *Complete Poems and Selected Letters of Michelangelo* (Princeton Press, 1984).

Leonardo da Vinci, *Notebook* (Oxford, 1983).

Levi, Carlo, *Christ Stopped at Eboli* (Penguin, 1982). Disturbing post-war realism.

Levy, Michael, *Early Renaissance* (1967) and *High Renaissance* (1975), both by Penguin. Old-fashioned accounts of the period, with a breathless reverence for the 1500s—but still full of intriguing interpretations.

Murray, Linda, *The High Renaissance* and *The Late Renaissance and Mannerism* (Thames and Hudson, 1977). Excellent introduction to the period; also Peter and Linda Murray, *The Art of the Renaissance* (Thames and Hudson, 1963).

Pavese, Cesare, *The Moon and the Bonfire* (Quartet, 1979). Postwar classic.

Petrarch, Franceso *Canzionere and Other Works* (Oxford, 1985). The most famous poems by 'the First Modern Man'.

Vasari, Giorgio, *Lives of the Artists* (Penguin, 1985). Readable, anecdotal accounts of the Renaissance greats by the father of art history, also the first professional Philistine.

Wittkower, Rudolf, *Art and Architecture in Italy 1600–1750* (Pelican, 1986). The classic on Italian Baroque, with special sections on Piedmont.

GENERAL INDEX

Note: Page references in *italics* indicate illustrations; references
in **bold** indicate maps.

INDEX OF ARTISTS AND CRAFTSMEN

318

Please use these forms to tell us about the hotels or restaurants you consider to be special and worthy of inclusion in our next edition, as well as to give any general comments on existing entries.

Hotels

Name ....

Address ....

Tel... Price of double room ....

Description/Comments ....

....

....

Name ....

Address ....

Tel... Price of double room ....

Description/Comments ....

....

....

Name ....

Address ....

Tel... Price of double room ....

Description/Comments ....

....

....

Name ....

Address ....

Tel... Price of double room ....

Description/Comments ....

....

....

Restaurants

Name ....

Address ....

Tel.. Price per person ....

Description/Comments ....

....

....

Name ....

Address ....

Tel.. Price per person ....

Description/Comments ....

....

....

Name ....

Address ....

Tel.. Price per person ....

Description/Comments ....

....

....

Name ....

Address ....

Tel.. Price per person ....

Description/Comments ....

....

....